European Group 1 Winners of 2018

SIEGLINDE McGEE

Set in 10.5 pt Garamond

ISBN 9781791335304

Cover: Roaring Lion and Saxon Warrior fight out the finish of the Group 1 Qipco Irish Champion Stakes at Leopardstown. Photo: Caroline Norris

Disclaimer
Every effort has been made to ensure that the information in this book is accurate and up to date. The author accepts no liability or responsibility for any loss or damage caused, or thought to be caused, by anything contained within the book.

ABOUT THE AUTHOR

Sieglinde discovered horse racing by chance on Grand National day 1982 and was instantly hooked, reading and watching everything she could about it. She started writing on the subject in the summer of 1983, began keeping personal databases on racing and pedigrees the following year, and got her first job in racing five years after that – doing course wires (tipping) and bloodstock sales reports for *The Sporting Life*, maintaining a small pedigree database, and producing press releases for a major stud.

She has been widely published on racing and pedigrees over the past three decades, wrote and produced her own non-published 'Timeform Annual-style' books for several years in the 1990s, has been writing for *The Irish Field* since the spring of 2000, and on her own website (www.sieglindemcgee.com) for the past two and a half years.

In 2005, she was conferred with a doctorate from Trinity College Dublin for a thesis titled *Behavioural Reactivity and Ensuing Temperamental Traits in Young Thoroughbred Racehorses (Equus caballus)* – the culmination of four years of postgraduate research. She is also a graduate of Dublin City University and of the world-famous Thoroughbred Breeding course at the Irish National Stud. She taught in Trinity College Dublin and for Oscail (now DCU Connected) for several years, and is the author of *Key Research & Study Skills in Psychology*, which was published by SAGE in 2010.

CONTENTS

INTRODUCTION

The 2018 flat racing year was a good one. Alpha Centauri, Laurens, and Roaring Lion won four Group 1 races apiece, the latter earning the Cartier Award as Horse of the Year. There were some surprises – Billesdon Brook's 66/1 victory in the 1000 Guineas being a notable one – some moments of brilliance – such as Cracksman's repeat runaway Champion Stakes performance – and some major wins for the less high-profile stables. The latter include Romanised winning the Irish 2000 Guineas for trainer Ken Condon, Mabs Cross taking the Prix de l'Abbaye de Longchamp for the Michael Dods team, and Skitter Scatter's victory in the Moyglare Stud Stakes, trained by Patrick Prendergast. This was also the year in which Luca Cumani retired and it was fitting that he got one more Group 1 winner, his 50th, with God Given's success in Italy in November.

Aidan O'Brien sent out 13 individual top-level winners, Charlie Appleby struck gold with 10 different horses, but the six saddled by John Gosden included Roaring Lion, Cracksman, champion stayer Stradivarius, brilliant two-year-old Too Darn Hot and, of course, the great Enable who won a second Prix de l'Arc de Triomphe, despite missing most of the year due to a setback, and then followed that with an historic victory in the Breeders' Cup Turf.

We saw some exciting prospects for 2019's classics, and potential Commonwealth Cup horses, including Too Darn Hot, Quorto and Ten Sovereigns who finished their first year as undefeated Group 1 stars, each having shown a touch of brilliance. The middle-distance division, however, could be the highlight of the year if the major players are back in training and in form. Just imagine Enable, Sea Of Class, and Magical, plus the Japanese champion Almond Eye taking each other on in the Arc, along with whatever stars emerge between now and then. Fillies and mares filled the first four places in the Arc in 1983. It could happen again.

Stradivarius went through his campaign undefeated in five starts, including the Gold Cup and Goodwood Cup, and he collected the £1 million Weatherbys Hamilton Stayers' Million bonus – the first year that this challenge was offered. Can he repeat the sequence again in 2019? The Freddy Head-trained gelding Call The Wind emerged as a potential rival late in the season, as did Melbourne Cup hero Cross Counter. That Charlie Appleby-trained rising star stays two miles well, although his pedigree casts a slight doubt over his prospects over the extra half-mile.

It was surprising that of all the Group 1 classics, only Alpha Centauri (Irish 1000 Guineas), Sea Of Class (Irish Oaks) and Laurens (Prix de Diane) won another race after that big one. The latter pair are due to remain in training.

There are, of course, quite a few of the Group 1 stars of 2018 who won't be back in action next season. The injury that Alpha Centauri sustained at Leopardstown in mid-September ended her track career, but she represents one of the most famous families in the stud book and could develop as notable a profile as a broodmare as she did as a racehorse.

Of the colts, Cracksman (Dalham Hall Stud), Expert Eye (Banstead Manor Stud), Havana Grey (Whitsbury Manor Stud), Hawkbill (Dalham Hall Stud), Iquitos (Gestut Ammerland), Jungle Cat (Kildangan Stud), Lancaster Bomber (National Stud), Lightning Spear (Tweenhills Farm & Stud), Merchant Navy (Coolmore Stud), Poet's Word (Nunnery Stud), Recoletos (Haras Du Quesnay), Roaring Lion (Tweenhills Farm & Stud), Saxon Warrior (Coolmore Stud), and U S Navy Flag (Coolmore Stud) are all about to embark on stallion careers.

On the pedigree front, two mares were represented by two Group 1 winners of 2018: Halfway To Heaven (Magical, Rhododendron) and In Clover (Call The Wind, With You). Galileo, with seven, and Dubawi, with five, led the way among the sires, but it was Pivotal who dominated as a broodmare sire, with eight top-level winners representing his daughters. Many distinct branches of the Northern Dancer male line have developed over the years, but it catches the eyes that all but 11 of the horses reviewed here represent some branch of what was his dynasty.

In all, a total of 66 horses won a Group 1 race in Europe in 2018 and a further 11 European-trained horses won at the highest level on another continent. Each is reviewed here, with a recap of their racing record and an examination of their pedigree and future prospects. The book also presents listings of these Group/Grade 1 winners by their sire, grandsire, great-grandsire, dam, broodmare sire, breeders, owners, and trainer (by country), along with details of every Group 1 race run in Europe during the year, and of those major races won elsewhere by European-trained horses. The index at the back includes every Group/Grade 1 winner and stallion mentioned in the book.

Readers may notice that some horses have not been given a suffix with their names, in pedigree charts or the various indexes. This is not an error or an omission. The suffix indicates the country in which the horse was born, but those who were born in Ireland or the UK did not get suffixes until 1988. Therefore, horses born in those countries before that year do not have one.

Roll on 2019!

Sieglinde McGee
9th December 2018

ACCIDENTAL AGENT (GB)

The great stallion Danzig (by Northern Dancer) had a profound impact on global racing and breeding. There are two major branches of his line: those formed by Danehill and by Green Desert. This year's shock winner of the Group 1 Queen Anne Stakes at Ascot represents the first of those branches as he comes from the first crop of the late classic-placed, Group 2 Duke of York Stakes winner Delegator (by Dansili), who spent four seasons at Overbury Stud in Gloucestershire.

Delegator's initial crop also includes the talented filly Delectation, who won a Group 3 contest over six furlongs at Ayr as a juvenile before going on to further pattern success in the Group 3 Schwarzgold Rennen and Group 3 Grosse Europa Meile – that treble being scored by an accumulated margin of eight and a quarter lengths. Accidental Agent, on the other hand, was notching up his first blacktype success when beating old rival Lord Glitters by half a length over the straight mile at Ascot. He had put up an eye-catching performance when sixth behind Rhododendron in the Group 1 Lockinge Stakes a month before, was third to Century Dream in a mile listed contest at Ascot on his seasonal reappearance and was a high-class handicapper in 2017, rated 120 by Timeform.

Now that he has won at the highest level he has set up the prospect of a stallion career in his future. Hitting a peak as a four-year-old may suggest that he was a late maturer, but this colt won two of his four starts as a juvenile, one over seven furlongs at Chepstow in late July and the other a valuable six-furlong sales race over six at Newmarket two months later.

Accidental Agent is owned and bred by Gaie Johnson Houghton, who has had the family for several generations. He was bought back for just 8,000gns from Book 2 of the Tattersalls October Yearling Sale, and he is trained by the owner's daughter, Eve Johnson Houghton.

He is the first foal out of Roodle (by Xaar), who won over five and seven furlongs, and his dam's string of successful siblings feature Prize Exhibit (by Showcasing) and Mohaather (by Showcasing). The first-named finished third in the Group 3 Oh So Sharp Stakes and fourth (no blacktype) in the Grade 1 Breeders' Cup Juvenile Fillies Turf at two but went on to become a prolific blacktype performer in the USA. The best of her seven wins came in the Grade 2 San Clemente Handicap at Del Mar, plus the Grade 2 Monrovia Stakes, Grade 3 Senorita Stakes and Grade 3 Megahertz Stakes all at Santa Anita, and the races in which she was placed included the Grade 1 Del Mar Oaks and Grade 2 Yellow Ribbon Invitational Handicap. Mohaather, on the other hand, is the Marcus Tregoning-trained juvenile who sprang a surprise in the Group 3 Molson Coors Stakes (registered as the Horris Hill Stakes) over seven furlongs at Newbury in October, taking his record to two wins from three starts.

They are out of Roodeye (by Inchinor), who earned her blacktype when third in the Listed Dick Poole Stakes at Salisbury as a juvenile, and that mare is one of five blacktype earners out of Listed Firth of Clyde Stakes runner-up Roo (by Rudimentary). Three of those have been listed placed – including New Day Dawn (by Dawn Approach), who was runner-up in a mile listed contest at Haydock in August and then sold for 260,000gns in Newmarket in December as a prospective broodmare – but Gallagher (by Bahamian Bounty) was second in each of the Group 1 Prix Morny, Group 2 Mill Reef Stakes and Group 2 Richmond Stakes – all over six furlongs.

It was over that trip that Roo's star sibling and relations got their best wins. Half-brother Bannister (by Inchinor) won the Group 2 Gimcrack Stakes at York, 'nephew' Astaire (by Intense Focus) – who is out of the unraced Runway Dancer (by Dansili) – took the Group 1 Middle Park Stakes, and Dead Certain (by Absalom), who is a half-sister to Roo's dam Shall We Run (by Hotfoot), was the Group 1 Cheveley Park Stakes heroine of 1989. That star filly also won the Group 2 Lowther Stakes and Group 3 Queen Mary Stakes that year, she went on to add the Group 2 Prix Maurice de Gheest and take second in the Group 3 Cork and Orrery Stakes at Royal Ascot, and her descendants include several stakes winners.

Pounelta (by Tachypous), a winning half-sister to Dead Certain, also deserves a mention as she was the dam of 1999's Group 3 Jersey Stakes winner Lots Of Magic (by Magic Ring), a grandson of Green Desert (by Danzig).

Accidental Agent's emergence as a Group 1 winner is something of a surprise, despite his 120 Timeform figure from last year, and so far it has remained a career highlight for him. After Ascot, he finished well down the field behind Alpha Centauri in the Group 1 Prix Jacques le Marois at Deauville and was then last of five in the Group 2 Shadwell Joel Stakes at Newmarket, also over a mile. He was very slowly away in the latter, but although making up the lost ground, he was beaten sufficiently far from home to suggest that this was just not a good day for him. He is, however, a highly talented horse at his best and it will be interesting to see what's next for him.

SUMMARY DETAILS

Bred: Mrs R F Johnson Houghton
Owned: Mrs R F Johnson Houghton
Trained: Eve Johnson Houghton
Country: England
Race record: 0121-0012140-30100-
Career highlights: 5 wins inc Queen Anne Stakes (Gr1), 2nd Dubai Duty Free Tennis Championships Cup Stakes (L), 3rd Celebrating The Commonwealth Paradise Stakes (L)

ACCIDENTAL AGENT (GB) - 2014 bay colt

Delegator (GB)	Dansili (GB)	Danehill (USA)
		Hasili (IRE)
	Indian Love Bird (GB)	Efisio
		Indian Love Song
Roodle (GB)	Xaar (GB)	Zafonic (USA)
		Monroe (USA)
	Roodeye (GB)	Inchinor (GB)
		Roo (GB)

ADVERTISE (GB)

This has been a really good year for two-year-old colts and if the brightest stars among them fulfil their promise in 2019 then it could be a vintage year for the classics and Commonwealth Cup horses. As is often the case, it was the Group 2 Coventry Stakes that gave us the first cause for enthusiasm about the crop, with an impressive victory for Calyx overshadowing excellent efforts by the second and third: Advertise and Sergei Prokofiev. The winner met with a setback and was not seen out again, and the third went on an eye-catching pattern success at Newmarket in October, whereas Advertise took the honours as the first juvenile Group 1 scorer of the year.

The Martyn Meade-trained colt had looked a bright prospect when winning a six-furlong Newbury maiden on his debut in mid-May. Ascot was his second start, and then he put up a stylish performance in the Group 2 Arqana July Stakes at Newmarket, beating Konchek by two lengths. He followed that with a half-length defeat of So Perfect in the Group 1 Keeneland Phoenix Stakes at the Curragh, looking every inch a leading sprint prospect for 2019. The Group 1 Juddmonte Middle Park Stakes may have seemed an obvious next step, but he bypassed that potential clash with Ten Sovereigns to take on Too Darn Hot in the Group 1 Darley Dewhurst Stakes at Newmarket. Chasing home that now Timeform 127p-rated rising star confirmed his position among the best of his age group. His Timeform rating is 119, placing him fifth on their roll of honour.

Advertise, who was bred by Cheveley Park Stud and sold for £60,000 at the Goffs UK Doncaster Premier Yearling Sale, may try to give his young sire a second Group 1 Commonwealth Cup star, but his Dewhurst run plus his entry in the Group 1 Tattersalls Irish 2000 Guineas suggest that a classic bid may be on the cards first.

With Quiet Reflection, Tasleet and Soldier's Call among his offspring, some may immediately think of Whitsbury Manor Stud stallion Showcasing (by Oasis Dream) as being a sprint sire, but he has also got several high-class performers at around a mile, including US Grade 2 scorers Prize Exhibit and Projected, New Zealand-bred Group 2 winner Xpression, and this year's French pattern winner Dice Roll, who finished third in the Group 1 Poule d'Essai des Poulains (French 2000 Guineas). It would be no surprise to see him get a Group 1 classic star some day, a feat that his half-brother Camacho (by Danehill) achieved this year.

Advertise is the third foal and second winner out of Furbelow (by Pivotal), a Cheveley Park-bred mare who won easily over six furlongs on Polytrack on her second of three starts, all as a three-year-old. Her siblings have won in sprints and over middle-distances, they include US listed scorer Red Diadem (by Pivotal) and also Adorn (by Kyllachy), the dam of Group 2 Richmond Stakes winner Saayerr (by Acclamation).

Her dam, Red Tiara (by Mr Prospector), is an unplaced daughter of the talented Heart Of Joy (by Lypheor). Also a Cheveley Park homebred, that filly won the Group 3 Nell Gwyn Stakes shortly before chasing home Salsabil in the Group 1 1000 Guineas at Newmarket. She was then runner-up to In The Groove in the Group 1 Irish 1000 Guineas, third to Chimes Of Freedom in the Group 1 Coronation Stakes at Ascot, and later a Grade 1-placed Grade 2 scorer in the USA before going on to produce the leading Japanese sprinter Meiner Love (by Seeking The Gold).

If you go back farther on the page then you will find that the fourth dam of Advertise is Mythographer (by Secretariat), a placed daughter of Arachne (by Intentionally) – a blacktype scorer and 10-time winner in the USA – and so a half-sister to Grade 1 United Nations Handicap, Grade 2 Manhattan Handicap and Grade 2 Lexington Stakes star Acaroid (by Big Spruce), and to the prolific Arachnoid (by Dr Fager), a stakes winner who was a track record-setter over eight and a half furlongs. Those horses are, of course, distantly connected to the colt, but they add to the evidence that this is family with a long-established history of producing horses who can do well at a mile.

SUMMARY DETAILS

Bred: Cheveley Park Stud Ltd
Owned: Phoenix Thoroughbreds Limited 1
Trained: Martyn Meade
Country: England
Race record: 12112-
Career highlights: 3 wins inc Keeneland Phoenix Stakes (Gr1), Arqana July Stakes (Gr2), 2nd Darley Dewhurst Stakes (Gr1), Coventry Stakes (Gr2)

ADVERTISE (GB) - 2016 bay colt

Showcasing (GB)	Oasis Dream (GB)	Green Desert (USA)
		Hope (IRE)
	Arabesque (GB)	Zafonic (USA)
		Prophecy (IRE)
Furbelow (GB)	Pivotal (GB)	Polar Falcon (USA)
		Fearless Revival
	Red Tiara (USA)	Mr Prospector (USA)
		Heart Of Joy (USA)

ALPHA CENTAURI (IRE)

We have seen some outstanding fillies and mares in action in recent decades and the Niarchos family's Miesque (by Nureyev) is among them. A star at two, three and four – with Timeform ratings of 124, 131 and 134 respectively – the François Boutin-trained bay won 10 times at the highest level including the 1000 Guineas, Poule d'Essai des Pouliches (French 1000 Guineas), two editions of the Prix Jacques le Marois, and back-to-back runnings of the Breeders' Cup Mile.

Many champion racemares have disappointed at stud, but not her. She went on to have a considerable influence on the global racing and bloodstock scene, and that impact is not only still strong but may be strengthening. In 2018, for example, she is the direct female ancestor of two European Group 1 classic winners and, like her, one of those is a miler who generated plenty of excitement and fans.

Miesque's grandson Study Of Man (by Deep Impact) won the Group 1 Prix du Jockey Club (French Derby) at Chantilly shortly her great-granddaughter Alpha Centauri (by Mastercraftsman) gave trainer Jessica Harrington a first classic success at the Curragh. That Group 1 Irish 1000 Guineas heroine then put up one of the most impressive performances of the week at Royal Ascot, smashing the track record while thrashing her rivals by six lengths and more in the Group 1 Coronation Stakes. Threading was the one who chased her home, the subsequent pattern scorer Veracious was another length and three-quarters back in third, and it the same margin again back to the fourth, Group 1 1000 Guineas heroine Billesdon Brook, a filly bred to stay farther.

Timeform rated her 127 for this win (she finished the year 1lb higher), placing her equal at that time with Mendelssohn at the top of the three-year-old division, but although that colt did not make the forward progression hoped for (and he was dropped to 123), the filly did. She followed up with a four-and-a-half-length defeat of Altyn Orda in the Group 1

Tattersalls Falmouth Stakes at Newmarket and then put up the best performance of her career, thrashing four-year-old and leading French colt Recoletos by two and a half lengths in the Group 1 Prix du Haras de Fresney-le-Buffard Jacques le Marois at Deauville, on ground described as good-to-soft. With You was another three and a half lengths behind in third, with Noor Al Hawa fourth and the Group 1-winning colts Romanised and Intellogent filling the next two placings.

Her Group 1 four-timer had been completed by an aggregate margin of almost 15 lengths and it was expected that she would extend her sequence in the Group 1 Coolmore Fastnet Rock Matron Stakes at Leopardstown on Irish Champions Weekend in mid-September. Despite facing fellow four-time Group 1 star Laurens, she was sent off a short odds-on favourite, but having come with her challenge, it all went wrong in the final furlong. She gave her all, but having changed lead twice in quick succession it was clear that something was amiss, and she could not peg back her English-trained rival, who took the prize by three-parts of a length. Last year's juvenile filly champion Clemmie was another length-and-a-quarter back in third. Before the race, there had been talk of a potential Grade 1 Breeders' Cup Mile challenge, and a possible four-year-old campaign for the brilliant grey, but a veterinary assessment found that she had chipped her off fore fetlock. Her career on the track was over.

A sound surface suited Alpha Centauri well – it was fast at Ascot and had heavy in the description on both occasions that she was out of the frame – and although she had been entered for the Group 1 Darley Irish Oaks, it was no surprise to see her bypass that classic in favour of staying at the mile. Some in her family have stayed 12 furlongs well, but the overall tendency has been for talent at up to 10 and a half furlongs, with some proving best at up to the mile.

Her Coolmore Stud-based sire, Mastercraftsman (by Danehill Dancer), excelled that distance, and over 10 furlongs and she is one of 11 top-level scorers for him among 56 stakes winners, a tally that includes this year's US Grade 1 heroine A Raving Beauty and December's New Zealand mile Group 1 scorer Danzdanzdance, plus his first-crop European Group 1 stars Amazing Maria, Kingston Hill, and The Grey Gatsby.

Her grandam is East Of The Moon (by Private Account), who won the Group 1 Poule d'Essai des Pouliches, Group 1 Prix Jacques le Marois and Group 1 Prix de Diane (by French Oaks). That dual classic heroine is, of course, a half-sister to triple mile Group 1 star and leading international sire Kingmambo (by Mr Prospector), to pattern scorer and Group 1 sire Miesque's Son (by Mr Prospector), and to broodmares of note, including Second Happiness (by Storm Cat), dam of the aforementioned Study Of Man.

Another is Monevassia (by Mr Prospector), a non-winner on the track. Her daughter Rumplestiltskin (by Danehill) was a champion at two when she won the Group 1 Moyglare Stud Stakes and Group 1 Prix Marcel Boussac, and that star's offspring include Group 1 Yorkshire Oaks heroine and Group 1 Irish Oaks runner-up Tapestry (by Galileo). Monevassia is also the dam of Group 3 Grangecon Stud Balanchine Stakes winner I Am Beautiful (by Rip Van Winkle), and those produced by her other daughters include Japanese ace Real Steel (by Deep Impact), a dual classic-placed winner of the Group 1 Dubai Turf at Meydan. He will begin his stallion career at the famous Shadai Stallion Station in Japan in 2019.

Miesque's stakes-placed daughter Moon Is Up (by Woodman) is another of note as she is the dam of South African mile Grade 1 winner Amanee (by Pivotal) and grandam of Group 1 Poule d'Essai des Poulains (French 2000 Guineas) and Grade 1 Breeders' Cup Mile scorer Karakontie (by Bernstein). He stands at Gainesway Farm in Kentucky, will be a freshman sire of 2019, and his first yearlings made up to $220,000 in the auction ring.

Massaraat, a stakes-winning full-sister to Miesque, also deserves mention as her descendants include 2018's Group 2 King Edward VII Stakes and Group 2 Great Voltigeur Stakes winner Old Persian (by Dubawi), who is out of a full-sister to 2007's Group 2 Ribblesdale Stakes heroine Silkwood (by Singspiel).

Alpha Centauri is the sixth foal out of East Of The Moon's unraced daughter Alpha Lupi (by Rahy), and that makes her a half-sister to former Ballydoyle team member Tenth Star (by Dansili) who showed his best form as a two-year-old. He took the seven-furlong Listed Golden Fleece Stakes by four lengths, was odds-on when only third to Remember Alexander in the Group 3 Tyros Stakes a few weeks later, but then put up a better performance to chase home stablemate Daddy Long Legs in the Group 2 Royal Lodge Stakes over a mile at Newmarket.

Alpha Lupi's current two-year-old, Etoile Filante, is a daughter of international Group 1 star So You Think (by High Chaparral) – whose offspring have so far done much better in the southern hemisphere than here – and her yearling is a second-crop daughter of runaway Group 1 Deutsches Derby hero and Lanwades Stud stallion Sea The Moon (by Sea The Stars), a leading freshman sire of 2018. The mare's siblings include Group 3 Prix d'Arenberg scorer Moon Driver (by Mr Prospector), and the stakes-placed trio Helike (by Rahy), Mojave Moon (by Mr Prospector) and Canda (by Storm Cat), with the latter being of particular note because of what she achieved at stud. The Jonathan Pease-trained bay was runner-up in both the Listed Prix Yacowlef and Listed Criterium de Vitesse at two, and her second foal was blacktype sire Evasive (by Elusive Quality), who won the Group 3 Horris Hill Stakes at two and finished fourth to Mastercraftsman in the Group 1 St James's Palace Stakes at Ascot the following summer. In 2017, Canda's son Autocratic (by Dubawi), a Cheveley Park Stud homebred trained by Sir Michael Stoute, won the Group 3 Brigadier Gerard Stakes at Sandown.

Four-time Group 1 star Alpha Centauri – who was crowned Champion Three-Year-Old Filly at the Cartier Awards in November – was a high-class juvenile who trounced Actress in a listed contest at Naas before failing narrowly against Different League in the Group 3 Albany Stakes at Ascot, both over six furlongs, and that smart early form boosts the prospects that at least some of her future offspring who race may show talent at two. But everything about her overall racing record and pedigree suggests that her progeny will likely also be seen to best effect as three-year-olds and, possibly at four. It is disappointing that her track career ended as it did, but it is unlikely that we have heard the end of her.

SUMMARY DETAILS

Bred: Niarchos Family
Owned: Niarchos Family
Trained: Jessica Harrington
Country: Ireland
Race record: 1120-011112-
Career highlights: 6 wins inc Tattersalls Irish 1000 Guineas (Gr1), Coronation Stakes (Gr1), Tattersalls Falmouth Stakes (Gr1), Prix du Haras de Fresney-le-Buffard Jacques le Marois (Gr1), Coolmore Stud Irish EBF Fillies' Sprint Stakes (L), 2nd Coolmore Fastnet Rock Matron Stakes (Gr1), Albany Stakes (Gr3)

ALPHA CENTAURI (IRE) - 2015 grey filly

Mastercraftsman (IRE)	Danehill Dancer (IRE)	Danehill (USA)
		Mira Adonde (USA)
	Starlight Dreams (USA)	Black Tie Affair
		Reves Celestes (USA)
Alpha Lupi (IRE)	Rahy (USA)	Blushing Groom (FR)
		Glorious Song (CAN)
	East Of The Moon (USA)	Private Account (USA)
		Miesque (USA)

ALPHA DELPHINI (GB)

Alpha Delphini has been a consistently capable sprinter for much of his career but, as some horses manage, his record also shows a performance-of-a-lifetime effort. A top-notch handicapper whom Timeform rated 116 at four and five years of age, he finished third to Mabs Cross in the Group 3 Palace House Stakes on his second start of 2018, was short-headed by Muthmir in the Listed Betway Achilles Stakes at Haydock, lost out by a head to Mr Lupton in the Listed John Smith's City Walls Stakes at York, and then sprang a 40/1 shock to beat an improved Mabs Cross by a nose in the Group 1 Coolmore Nunthorpe Stakes over that same course and distance. The pair met again in the Group 1 Qatar Prix de l'Abbaye de Longchamp in October, which the filly won while the gelding finished unplaced.

A 20,000gns graduate of Book 2 of the Tattersalls October Yearling Sale, he is a first-crop son of Mickley Stud stallion Captain Gerrard (by Oasis Dream) and, so far, is his only stakes winner. That horse won the Group 3 Cornwallis Stakes and two listed races as a juvenile, added the Group 3 Palace House Stakes at three, and he gets plenty of multiple winning offspring including handicappers in the 85-105 range.

Alpha Delphini is out of an unraced full-sister to a stayer, but that mare has been producing sprinters. Her name is Easy To Imagine (by Cozzene), her first foal is the prolific handicapper Masai Moon (by Lujain) and her second-born is Tangerine Trees (by Mind Games). That 15-time scorer won a listed sprint at the age of five but excelled at six, taking the Group 3 Palace House Stakes, Listed Beverley Bullet Sprint Stakes and then the Group 1 Prix de l'Abbaye de Longchamp.

The mare's three-year-old, Fairy Falcon (by Sepoy), is also trained by Smart, and having won a five-furlong Thirsk novice event by three lengths in early August – her second start – she was not disgraced when fifth to Intense Romance in a listed contest over a half-furlong farther on heavy ground at Ayr a few weeks later. The year-younger Kurious (by Kuroshio) made a winning debut for Henry Candy stable at Sandown in early Junem and she was only beaten by about two and a half lengths when ninth of 22 in the Group 2 Queen Mary Stakes at Royal Ascot.

Easy To Imagine, a half-sister to a Grade 3-placed sprinter in the USA, is out of Zarani Sidi Anna (by Danzig), a talented filly who was placed in both the Group 1 Coronation Stakes and Grade 1 Milady Handicap yet never won a stakes race. The mare's siblings include the dam of US Grade 2 scorer Striking Dancer (by Smart Strike) and of this year's Group 2 Gran Premio del Jockey Club Italiano winner Raymond Tusk (by High Chaparral), as well as the grandam of Group 3 Bahrain Trophy winner and Group 2 King Edward VII Stakes runner-up Mr Singh (by High Chaparral).

Ability over a mile and upwards is also evident in the next generation of the pedigree as Emmaline (by Affirmed), the stakes-winning third dam, was a half-sister to several blacktype horses, notably multiple US Grade 1 star Bates Motel (by Sir Ivor) – whose top-level wins included the Santa Anita Handicap – and his Grade 1-winning half-brother Hatim (by Exclusive Native), who spent some time at stud in Ireland without making an impact.

All of this suggests that the bulk of the speed shown by Alpha Delphini must be due to his sire, and it will be interesting to see if Captain Gerrard can come up with others who are at least as talented.

SUMMARY DETAILS

Bred: Mrs B A Matthews
Owned: The Alpha Delphini Partnership
Trained: Bryan Smart
Country: England
Race record: 0-2010-1031112-030020011-232210-
Career highlights: 8 wins inc Coolmore Nunthorpe Stakes (Gr1), totescoop6 Beverley Bullet Sprint Stakes (L), 2nd Dubai International Airport World Trophy Stakes (Gr3), John Smith's City Walls Stakes (L), Betway Achilles Stakes (L), 3rd

Armstrong Aggregates Temple Stakes (Gr2), Longholes Palace House Stakes (Gr3)

ALPHA DELPHINI (GB) - 2011 bay gelding

Captain Gerrard (IRE)	Oasis Dream (GB)	Green Desert (USA)
		Hope (IRE)
	Delphinus (GB)	Soviet Star (USA)
		Scimitarra
Easy To Imagine (USA)	Cozzene (USA)	Caro
		Ride The Trails (USA)
	Zarani Sidi Anna (USA)	Danzig (USA)
		Emmaline (USA)

ATHENA (IRE)

It can be disappointing and something of an anticlimax when a longshot takes a championship race, especially if it proves to be a one-off, their performance-of-a-lifetime effort. A Group 1-placed Group 2 winner produced such a display at Longchamp in 1993 when beating White Muzzle, Opera House, Intrepidity and Only Royale in the Group 1 Prix de l'Arc de Triomphe, with big-race favourite Hernando and fellow classic stars Wemyss Bight, User Friendly and Shemaka finishing out the back. Timeform awarded the winner an end-of-year rating of 126. A Group 2 success and a single Group 1 placing from four subsequent starts was all the horse managed in the remainder of its career, and it seemed that this would go down as one of the less memorable winners of the great race.

It is now 25 years on, and that Arc winner is one of the most famous in the race's history, almost a household name, and it is because of what she and her descendants have achieved at stud. Urban Sea (by Miswaki) was an ordinary Arc winner – if we can call a horse such – but she is one of the greatest and most influential broodmares of all time. The list of major winners who have descended from her and her sons and daughters, is much too long to post here, although this year's Prix de l'Arc de Triomphe paints a picture of her legacy as each of the first eight home – Enable, Sea Of Class, Cloth Of Stars, Waldgeist, Capri, Salouen, Kew Gardens, and Nelson – has her somewhere in the first few generations of their pedigree chart.

The usual way to talk about descent from a mare is through her direct female line only, rather than through male lines, and in 2018 her distaff line struck again at the highest level when Masar (by New Approach) won the Group 1 Investec Derby at Epsom and when Athena won the Grade 1 Belmont Oaks Invitational Stakes in New York. The latter, an Aidan O'Brien-trained three-year-old, took the 10-furlong turf contest by two and a half lengths just six days after finishing third to Urban

Fox in the Group 1 Juddmonte Pretty Polly Stakes over the same trip at the Curragh.

That is admirable toughness, and although she failed to make the frame in four subsequent outings, and had taken seven starts before winning a maiden, the combination of that strength with her pedigree could make her a future broodmare of note.

The race that preceded her maiden success was a two-length second to Sea Of Class in a 10-furlong listed contest on fast ground at Newbury in May, the one immediately after her maiden was an eight-length fourth to Magic Wand in the Group 2 Ribblesdale Stakes at Ascot, and two months after her US victory she finished fourth to Roaring Lion in the Group 1 Qipco Irish Champion Stakes. It was her only time wearing a hood and she was only beaten by a total of four and a quarter lengths, which was at least as good as the form of her best win.

With so many races behind her at this point, plus that all-important top-level win on her record, it seems likely that Athena will be going to stud in 2019 rather than staying in training. She has an official handicap mark of 113 and further improvement does not look likely.

She represents the first crop of 2000 Guineas and dual Derby hero Camelot (by Montjeu) and that young Coolmore stallion has made a highly promising start to his stud career as that initial batch of foals also includes Group 1 Irish Derby winner Latrobe, Grade 1-placed pattern winner Hunting Horn, three other pattern race scorers and five listed winners. His second crop features Group 1 Criterium de Saint-Cloud heroine Wonderment and pattern-placed stakes winner Arthur Kitt. Being a great-granddaughter of prolific champion sire Sadler's Wells (by Northern Dancer) also makes her somewhat closely related to Urban Sea's most celebrated son.

Galileo (by Sadler's Wells), her third stakes winner from her first three foals, was a Timeform 134-rated King George and dual Derby hero before going on to become a stallion of rare dominance and influence. In October 2018 he moved into second place on the all-time list of sires of Group/Grade 1 winners, then added another one to his tally. His 75 top-level winners among 288 stakes winners inched him ahead of his own great sire – who got 73 Group/Grade 1 winners among 294 stakes winners – and to break the all-time records he must surpass the figures of 83 from 348 set by another great and late Coolmore stallion, Danehill (by Danzig). Galileo already has 14 sons who have got at least one top-level winner somewhere among the world's Category I-listed countries – notably classic sires Frankel, New Approach and Teofilo – and the Group 1 stars produced from his daughters include, in 2018, Saxon Warrior (by Deep Impact), U S Navy Flag (by War Front), and Magna Grecia (by Invincible Spirit).

His full-brother Black Sam Bellamy (sire of triple Group 1 winner Earl Of Tinsdal) won twice at the highest level, and full-sister All Too Beautiful was an Oaks-placed Group 3 winner. His half-brothers include Group 3 scorer Urban Ocean (by Bering) and classic-placed stakes winner Born To Sea (by Invincible Spirit), his half-sisters include US Grade 1 scorer My Typhoon (by Giant's Causeway) and classic-placed stakes winner Melikah (by Lammtarra), and the latter is, of course, the third dam of Masar.

The most famous of his brothers, of course, is Timeform 140-rated champion Sea The Stars (by Cape Cross), the Arc, Derby, Guineas, Eclipse, Juddmonte International and Irish Champion Stakes winner who has followed in Galileo's hoofprints by becoming one of Europe's leading sires. The Gilltown Stud stallion's long list of blacktype scorers of 2018 includes Group 1 Gold Cup-winning champion Stradivarius and Arc-placed classic heroine Sea Of Class, and his prior top-level winners – among a total of nine, and counting – include Taghrooda, dual Derby hero Harzand (first foals in 2018) and runaway Deutsches Derby star Sea The Moon, a Lanwades Stud-based freshman sire of two pattern winners this year.

That briefly covers the eight winning offspring of Urban Sea, but it is her non-winning daughter Cherry Hinton (by Green Desert) who has given us Athena. She was highly tried, was runner-up in the Group 3 Blue Wind Stakes over 10 furlongs at Naas on her second start, finished third in a nine-furlong Curragh listed race on the last of five outings, and was outclassed in both the Group 1 Oaks at Epsom and Group 1 Coronation Stakes at Ascot in between those efforts.

Cherry Hinton's first foal, Wading (by Montjeu), won the Group 2 Rockfel Stakes on the last of just three starts and is off to a good start at stud her first three foals include Group 3-placed sprinter Lost Treasure (by War Front) – who was a one-length fifth in the Group 1 Prix de l'Abbaye de Longchamp – and also Just Wonderful (by Dansili), who won the Group 3 Flame Of Tara Stakes and Group 2 Rockfel Stakes before finishing fourth to exciting US filly Newspaperofrecord in the Grade 1 Breeders' Cup Juvenile Fillies Turf at Churchill Downs in early November.

Bracelet (by Montjeu) arrived two years after Wading was born, and although also lightly raced, her four wins from six starts featured victory in the Group 1 Darley Irish Oaks – by a neck from Tapestry – the Group 2 Ribblesdale Stakes, and the Group 3 Leopardstown 1000 Guineas Trial Stakes. Next came Simply A Star (by Giant's Causeway), who was twice listed-placed over five furlongs in Ireland, and Cherry Hinton's two youngest of racing age are Athena and Goddess. The latter is a full-sister to the Grade 1 star, and although unplaced in a seven-furlong Curragh maiden on her debut in late June, her 10-length victory over the same trip at Leopardstown two weeks later earned rave reviews. She was a big disappointment in the Group 3 Jockey Club of Turkey Silver Flash Stakes on her final start, but that was at a time when there was a health cloud over some of the Ballydoyle runners, and this dual classic-entered bay remains an exciting prospect for 2019.

Athena, as noted, has unlimited potential as a future broodmare prospect, and yet all of the above represents just the first two generations of her pedigree. Those are, of course, the most influential and, mathematically speaking, make the largest contribution to her genetic make-up, but it would be quite an omission not to comment on the third and fourth generations of her family.

Her third dam is the Group 3 Oaks Trial Stakes third Allegretta (by Lombard) and, in addition to Urban Sea, she gave us Timeform 132-rated Group 1 2000 Guineas winner King's Best (by Kingmambo; sire of Timeform 133-rated Derby and Arc hero Workforce) and Group 3 Prix de Flore scorer Allez Les Trois (by Riverman), and her many blacktype descendants include Group 1 winners Anabaa Blue (by Anabaa; sire of a US Grade 1 winner) Tamayuz (by Nayef; sire of Group 1 winners) and Anzillero (by Law Society), Group 1-placed pattern winners Mustajeeb (by Nayef; freshman sire of 2019) and Armande (by Sea The Stars), and multiple pattern scorer Tertullian (by Miswaki) who has been champion sire in Germany.

Allegretta – a daughter of stakes-placed, four-time winner Anatevka (by Espresso) – was a full-sister to German champion and dual Group 2 scorer Anno and a half-sister to Group 1-placed Group 2 winner Anatas (by Priamos), but the identity of three of her sisters is more notable. Stakes-placed half-sister Anna Charlotta (by Charlottown) is the fifth dam of this year's Breeders' Cup-placed multiple US Grade 1 star A Raving Beauty (by Mastercraftsman), whereas non-winner Amethysta (by Gulf Pearl) was the dam of classic-placed Group 2 winner Apollonios (by Lombard) and grandam of Australian Group 1 1000 Guineas scorer Azzurro (by Bluebird).

The third one is her full-sister Alya who earned her blacktype when runner-up in the Group 2 Preis der Diana (German Oaks). None of her offspring was a stakes winner, but her grandson Adlerflug (by In The Wings) was a Deutsches Derby hero and three-year-old champion before going on to become a leading sire in Germany, and her descendants also include Group 2 scorers Auvray (by Le Havre), Knife Edge (by Zoffany), and Arrigo (by Shirocco).

Athena is, without doubt, one of the most valuable young broodmare prospects around and it will be fascinating to see what can come up with at stud.

SUMMARY DETAILS

Bred: Roncon & Chelston
Owned: Derrick Smith, Mrs John Magnier & Michael Tabor

Trained: Aidan O'Brien
Country: Ireland
Race record: 00-402214310400-
Career highlights: 2 wins inc Belmont Oaks Invitational
Stakes (Gr1), 2nd Haras de Bouquetot Fillies' Trial Stakes (L),
3rd Juddmonte Pretty Polly Stakes (Gr1)

ATHENA (IRE) - 2015 bay filly

Camelot (GB)	Montjeu (IRE)	Sadler's Wells (USA)
		Floripedes (FR)
	Tarfah (USA)	Kingmambo (USA)
		Fickle (GB)
Cherry Hinton (GB)	Green Desert (USA)	Danzig (USA)
		Foreign Courier (USA)
	Urban Sea (USA)	Miswaki (USA)
		Allegretta

BENBATL (GB)

One of 2017's prominent European three-year-olds, Benbatl was back in action very early in 2018 and made a perfect to the campaign, signalling that he could be set to make an impact in Europe upon his return to Newmarket. He kicked off with a two-and-a-quarter-length defeat of Emotionless in the Group 3 Singspiel Stakes over nine furlongs on turf at Meydan in January – his first outing for four months – and then followed-up with victory in the Group 2 Al Rashidiya over the same course and distance, beating Bay Of Poets by three and three-quarter lengths.

These performances demonstrated his wellbeing and indicated that he was at least as good at four as he was the year before, but he still had some progress to make if he was to be up to winning at the highest level in Europe. He did both, but first came a pair of Group 1 performances in Dubai – a three-quarter-length second to Blair House in the Jebel Hatta followed by an eye-catching defeat of a trio of top-class Japanese horses in the Dubai Turf, both over nine furlongs. He beat the mare Vivlos by three and a quarter lengths, four-year-old Deirdre and six-year-old Real Steel were a neck back in a dead-heat for third.

Benbatl was sent off favourite for the Group 1 Queen Anne Stakes over the mile at Ascot in mid-June but, like some who do well in Dubai, his European return was disappointing. He finished only tenth, albeit beaten by just five and a quarter lengths by the winner, Accidental Agent. From there he went to Munich, where he beat Stormy Antarctic by two and three-quarter lengths to take the Group 1 Grosser Dallmayr-Preis Bayerisches Zuchtrennen over 10 furlongs, then to York when he was a somewhat disappointing fifth behind Roaring Lion in the Group 1 Juddmonte International Stakes.

This brought his European season to an end as he returned to the southern hemisphere, this time to Australia where, on his first outing, he short-headed old rival Blair House in the

10-furlong Group 1 Ladbrokes Stakes at Caulfield. A fortnight later, he chased home Winx as the great mare took her fourth edition of the Group 1 Ladbrokes Cox Plate in style over 10 furlongs at Moonee Valley. The margin of defeat was two lengths, although the winner was eased close to home, and Benbatl finished two and three-quarter lengths clear of the third, Humidor.

Benbatl did not make his racecourse debut until April of his three-year-old season, and that seven-length score over seven furlongs at Doncaster was followed by three good efforts in defeat. He was a two-length third to Eminent in the Group 3 Craven Stakes at Newmarket, chased home three-quarter-length winner Permian in the Group 2 Dante Stakes at York and then finished fifth to Wings Of Eagles in the Group 1 Investec Derby at Epsom, beaten by just three and a half lengths. Less than three weeks later he picked up his first pattern success with a half-length score in the Group 3 Hampton Court Stakes over 10 furlongs at Ascot. He was only fifth behind Enable in the Group 1 King George VI and Queen Elizabeth Stakes at the same venue and a disappointing favourite when unplaced in a mile Group 3 on heavy ground at Haydock in early September. The latter could have been due to the trip or the ground, or both.

Benbatl is a Timeform 125-rated son of Dalham Hall Stud's Dubawi and his sire, who will again command a fee of £250,000 in 2019, was an unbeaten Group 1 winner at two and a classic-winning miler at three, which made him the best of the five stakes winners from the sole crop of tragically ill-fated Timeform 140-rated superstar Dubai Millennium (by Seeking The Gold). This is a branch of the Mr Prospector (by Raise a Native) sire line. He is well established as one of the world's leading stallions, with 38 Group/Grade 1 stars to his name and among more than 100 individual pattern scorers among an overall total in excess of 160 stakes winners.

His earliest stallion sons include Makfi (sire of Make Believe and three other Group 1 winners) and Poet's Voice (sire of Poet's Word and Trap For Fools) – for whom big-race success has been sporadic rather than frequent – but he also has a growing list of younger sons who are in earlier stages of their stud careers, including Hunter's Light (yearlings of 2018), New Bay (foals of 2018), Night Of Thunder (yearlings of 2018), Postponed (first foals in 2019) and Zarak (first foals in 2019), so we will have plenty of opportunities to learn more about his potential to become a source of notable sire sons. And, of course, there are also the Group 1 stars still in training – for example, Quorto, Too Darn Hot, and, of course, Benbatl – and those still to come.

Benbatl is the first foal out of the high-class Nahrain (by Selkirk), whom Roger Varian trained to win five of her 10 starts. She was unraced at two, took the Group 1 Prix de l'Opera by a nose at Longchamp before losing her unbeaten record with a second-place finish to Perfect Shirl in the Grade 1 Breeders' Cup Filly & Mare Turf at Churchill Downs, and added a win in the Grade 1 Flower Bowl Invitational Stakes over 10 furlongs at Belmont Park at four.

A half-sister to dual mile listed scorer Baharah (by Elusive Quality), she is out of Bahr (by Generous), who won the Group 2 Ribblesdale Stakes and Group 3 Musidora Stakes. That talented chestnut also won the Listed Washington Singer Stakes, she was runner-up in the Group 1 Oaks at Epsom and third in both the Group 1 Irish Oaks and Grade 1 Flower Bowl Invitational Handicap, making her one of the best representatives of her sire. Bahr's half-sister Clerio (by Soviet Star) got her best win in the Group 3 Matron Stakes at the Curragh and, in addition to being the dam of a stakes winner, she is the grandam of Our Rokkii (by Roc De Cambres) who won the one-mile Group 1 Toorak Handicap in 2016.

Lady Of The Sea (by Mill Reef), who is the third dam of Benbatl, won just once but was out of New Zealand classic heroine and champion La Mer (by Copenhagen), which made her a half-sister to Listed Ballycorus Stakes winner Cipriani (by Habitat) and to Loughmore (by Artaius), the winning grandam of Group 1 Sires' Produce Stakes scorer Little Jamie (by St Jude).

Benbatl, whose earnings stand at over £3.95 million, looks set for another good year in 2019, and presumably there will be a stallion career ahead of at a future time.

SUMMARY DETAILS

Bred: Darley
Owned: Godolphin
Trained: Saeed bin Suroor
Country: England
Race record: -1320100-112101012-
Career highlights: 7 wins inc Dubai Turf sponsored by DP World (Gr1), Grosser Dallmayr Preis - Bayerisches Zuchtrennen (Gr1), Ladbrokes Stakes (Gr1), Al Rashidiya sponsored by Jebel Ali Port (Gr2), Hampton Court Stakes (Gr3), Singspiel Stakes presented by Longines Ladies Master Collection (Gr3), 2nd Ladbrokes Cox Plate (Gr1), Jebel Hatta sponsored by Emirates Airline (Gr1), Betfred Dante Stakes (Gr2), bet365 Craven Stakes (Gr3)

BENBATL (GB) - 2014 bay colt

Dubawi (IRE)	Dubai Millennium (GB)	Seeking The Gold (USA)
		Colorado Dancer
	Zomaradah (GB)	Deploy
		Jawaher (IRE)
Nahrain (GB)	Selkirk (USA)	Sharpen Up
		Annie Edge
	Bahr (GB)	Generous (IRE)
		Lady Of The Sea

BEST SOLUTION (IRE)

When I reviewed the pedigree of young stallion Invincible Spirit (by Green Desert) for *The Irish Field* in late February 2005, I pointed out the amount of stamina in the distaff side of his family, noted that "the surprise is that he could possess so much speed", that in terms of racing aptitude he was "very much his father's son", all of which made him an intriguing prospect. This was a horse with the potential to get sprinters, milers and middle-distance horses, with the input of the mare likely to be influential.

Two years later, with Invincible Spirit now a record-breaking champion freshman sire, his Group 3-placed half-brother Kodiac (by Danehill) took up stallion duties at Tally-Ho Stud. In my review of his prospects for the same publication, I noted that "one could argue that, of the two brothers, it is Kodiac who is by the stronger sire of sires" – at that time, 16 sons of Danehill (by Danzig) had sired at least one top-level winner compared to just five sons of Green Desert (by Danzig). This was absolutely not any sort of attempt to suggest that Kodiac might become a better sire than Invincible Spirit, but instead to point out that his lack of a stakes-race win on the track was not necessarily an impediment to success at stud given the strength of his pedigree and the support he would likely receive.

Both looked like stallions with the potential to get sprinters and milers, at all levels, and the stamina in the distaff side of their pedigree gave them a chance to get middle-distance horses too, with the right mares. As to which one was perhaps the more likely to get one or more top middle-distance horses, it could have been argued that this would be the younger sibling because Danehill and his line was proven in Group 1s from five to 12 furlongs, but the Green Desert line generally seemed to stop at 10 furlongs. Since then, of course, Green Desert's son Cape Cross has given us 12-furlong champions Sea The Stars, Ouija Board, and Golden Horn – and what the first two have achieved at stud, so far, is well known. Golden Horn, of course, had his first yearlings in 2018.

With 18 Group 1 winners among 118 stakes winners, and counting, versus three Group 1 winners from 47 stakes winners, Invincible Spirit is easily the better stallion of the pair, and his early stallion sons include Group 1 producers Lawman and I Am Invincible, leading 2018 freshmen Kingman and Charm Spirit, and various others who have stakes or pattern winners to their name. Kodiac also has sons at stud, but they are in early stages of those careers and have not yet had runners. The gulf in achievement between the two brothers is also evident by their fees: €120,000 again for Invincible Spirit in 2019 compared to a new high of €65,000 for Kodiac.

Kodiac has been a huge hit in the sales ring in recent seasons but had only one Group 1 scorer on the track before this year – classic-placed Cheveley Park Stakes heroine Tiggy Wiggy. Two of his Group 2-winning sons have been packed off to stud at the end of their juvenile season instead of having a go at the enhanced three-year-old sprint programme – or in one case potentially the mile classics – but he has now achieved something that his brother has, as yet, failed to do. He has a top-class Group 1 performer over 12 furlongs.

Best Solution won the Group 2 Princess of Wales's Stakes at Newmarket in July, the Group 1 Longines Grosser Preis von Berlin at Hoppegarten in August, the Group 1 Longines Grosser Preis von Baden at Baden-Baden in September. In the first-named he beat Mirage Dancer by half a length, whereas both of his German wins were achieved by margins of a neck and half-length, first against Sound Check and Royal Youmzain, and then against Defoe and Iquitos. He then went 'down under' and short-headed Group 1 Underwood Stakes winner Homesman in the Group 1 Stella Artois Caulfield Cup in Australia in mid-October.

The Timeform 125-rated four-year-old, who was a mile Group 3 winner before chasing home Waldgeist in the Group 1 Criterium de Saint-Cloud as a juvenile, and was only beaten by six and a half lengths when out of the frame behind Wings Of Eagles in the Group 1 Investec Derby at Epsom, but his exploits of 2018 have all but guaranteed a place for himself at stud whenever his racing days come to an end.

He was bred by Cecil and Martin McCracken, he is a 90,000gns Tattersalls Book 2 graduate, and he is the second foal of a non-winning mare called Al Andalyya (by Kingmambo). Although one might initially expect a Kodiac - Kingmambo (by Mr Prospector) cross to produce a sprinter or miler, what is in the second and third generations of the pedigree makes it clear that if ever a Kodiac was going to be a top-class 12-furlong horse, then this colt was the one likely to make it happen. It also gives him the potential to become a sire of talented milers and middle-distance horses.

His dam showed limited ability in five starts from six to 10 furlongs although three of her siblings are blacktype earners. Cape Clear Island (by Fastnet Rock) was runner-up in the 11-furlong Group 2 Prix Hocquart before going to Hong Kong where, under the name Gorgeous King, he has won several times over nine furlongs. Squire Osbaldeston (by Mr Greeley) was a listed-placed 10-furlong winner in England, and Kosmische (by Fastnet Rock) won a seven-and-a-half-furlong listed contest in Germany as a two-year-old.

Their dam, Kushnarenkovo (by Sadler's Wells) was runner-up in the Group 3 Noblesse Stakes over 12 furlongs at Cork, her full-sister Kitty O'Shea was a runaway winner of a mile listed race on her second of just two starts, and full-brother Brian Boru, who took the Group 1 Racing Post Trophy as a two-year-old, was the Group 1 St Leger hero of 2003 before going on to become a somewhat successful National Hunt sire. The mare is also a half-sister to Group 2 Prix de Royallieu winner Moon Search (by Rainbow Quest) and a three-parts sister to Burgage Stud stallion Sea Moon (by Beat Hollow), who won a trio of Group 2s over the mile and a half and finished third in the Group 1 St Leger.

Add to all of this that her unraced full-sister, Soviet Moon, came up with Timeform 133-rated Investec Derby and Qatar Prix de l'Arc de Triomphe star Workforce when bred to Kingmambo's Timeform 132-rated 2000 Guineas winner King's Best, that her dam is the Group 3 Park Hill Stakes winner Eva Luna (by Alleged) and that her grandam, Media Luna (by Star Appeal), was placed in the Oaks at Epsom, and the middle-distance potential of Best Solution becomes obvious.

It does not mean, of course, that he is destined to sire only middle-distance horses or stayers. It does seem likely that, in addition to the stamina gene from his dam, he may have got the one that lurks in Kodiac's pedigree, but breeding mares who have, or are likely to have, a speed gene to pass on will allow him to get milers too. Before then, it seems that this triple Group 1 star, who has nine wins and over £2.6 million to his name, may be set to return to action as a five-year-old.

His family's story is far from over too. Al Andalyya had a Timeform rating of just 65 and an official handicap mark of 66, but with her family connections it a case of Kodiac bringing out the best in her bloodlines rather than upgrading her – she always had the potential to produce a Group 1 horse, if clicking with the right sire. Might the lightning strike twice? She had another Kodiac colt in 2018 and the McCrackens sold him for 175,000gns in Newmarket in late November.

The third Group 1 winner for Kodiac, by the way, is the Aidan O'Brien-trained Juddmonte Cheveley Park Stakes heroine Fairyland, the 925,000gns Tattersalls Book 1 graduate whose record of four wins from five starts also includes victory in the Group 2 Sky Bet Lowther Stakes at York and the now six-furlong Listed Cold Move Irish EBF Marble Hill Stakes at the Curragh. She holds an entry in the Group 1 Tattersalls Irish 1000 Guineas and is reviewed elsewhere in this volume.

SUMMARY DETAILS

Bred: Cecil and Martin McCracken
Owned: Godolphin
Trained: Saeed bin Suroor
Country: England
Race record: 313412-40100201-310011110-
Career highlights: 9 wins inc Stella Artois Caulfield Cup (Gr1), Longines Grosser Preis von Baden (Gr1), Longines

BEST SOLUTION (IRE)

Grosser Preis von Berlin (Gr1), Princess of Wales's Arqana
Racing Club Stakes (Gr2), Worthington's "Indigo Leisure" (St
Simon) Stakes (Gr3), Dubai 100 Autumn Stakes (Gr3), Betfred
Derby Trial Stakes (L), 2nd Grosser Dallmayr-Preis
Bayerisches Zuchtrennen (Gr1), Criterium de Saint-Cloud
(Gr1), 3rd International Trakya (Thrace) Trophy (L)

BEST SOLUTION (IRE) - 2014 bay colt

Kodiac (GB)	Danehill (USA)	Danzig (USA)
		Razyana (USA)
	Rafha	Kris
		Eljazzi
Al Andalyya (USA)	Kingmambo (USA)	Mr Prospector (USA)
		Miesque (USA)
	Kushnarenkovo (GB)	Sadler's Wells (USA)
		Eva Luna (USA)

BILLESDON BROOK (GB)

If you pull up the result of this year's Group 1 Qipco 1000 Guineas and let your eye drop to second and below then it reads as having been a good race. Laurens finished a half-length ahead of third-placed Happily, with the same margins back to Wild Illusion in fourth and Altyn Orda in fifth. The winner landed the spoils by one and three-quarter lengths, earning a Timeform rating of 118, but what was a shock result in May remains surprising now. This appears to have been Billesdon Brook's performance-of-a-lifetime effort as she has failed to make the frame in three subsequent starts.

She was a 66/1 shot on the day, a well-exposed, Timeform 99-rated filly who had won three times from eight starts at two – including a three-quarter-length defeat of Whitefountainfairy in the Group 3 Prestige Stakes at Goodwood – and she had been beaten five and a half lengths on her seasonal reappearance, when fourth behind Guineas sixth Soliloquy in the Group 3 Lanwades Stud Nell Gwyn Stakes. The classic was a second attempt at a mile for the Richard Hannon-trained chestnut, and with her pedigree, I expected to see her stepped up in trip possibly going for an Oaks, or two.

Instead, she went to Royal Ascot for the Group 1 Coronation Stakes and finished a well-beaten fourth to Alpha Centauri. She was also well-beaten when fifth to Laurens in the Group 1 Kingdom of Bahrain Sun Chariot Stakes over her classic course and distance in early October, and her best performance was arguably the effort in between those two defeats. She never threatened the principals, but took fourth in the Group 1 Qatar Nassau Stakes over 10 furlongs at Goodwood, which Wild Illusion won by two lengths from Urban Fox and Veracious (who flashed past the post together), with another length-and-a-quarter back the classic heroine. That said, the capable five-year-old Wilamina (official handicap rating of 106) was only a half-length behind in fifth.

Billesdon Brook was bred by Stowell Hill Partners and she is one of the most high-profile representatives of her sire, Champs Elysees (by Danehill). He began his career alongside his full-brother Dansili at Banstead Manor Stud, but although coming up with Group 1 Gold Cup scorer Trip To Paris and the classic-placed pattern scorers Jack Naylor and Xcellence, among others of note, he also attracted the attention of the National Hunt market and he has now completed two seasons as a dual-purpose stallion at Coolmore's Castlehyde Stud. As soon as a stallion switches to dual-purpose or National Hunt there is often an apparent tendency to forget that he still has several flat-bred crops to run and that there is no reason why more blacktype horses will not emerge from those.

His record as a stallion is only part of the equation that suggested that Billesdon Brook might have the potential to become a successful middle-distance filly. In addition to the aforementioned trio, his best also include 10-furlong Australian Group 1 winner Harlem (stayed 12), Grade 1-placed triple US Grade 3 winner Suffused (who has won at up to 15 and a half furlongs), Group 2-placed blacktype scorer Barsanti, stakes-winning stayer Dal Harraild (who was fourth in the Group 1 Goodwood Cup in late July and short-headed in a 12-furlong Group 2 in Australia in November), and talented stayers Low Sun and Withhold. There are also the US Grade 3-winning fillies Elysea's World and Colonia, who are effective at around nine furlongs.

Then there's the distaff side of her family, and the standout name on the page is one of the most brilliant hurdlers of recent years.

Billesdon Brook is a half-sister to the 10-furlong listed race winner Billesdon Bess (by Dick Turpin) – who was sold for 800,000gns at the recent Tattersalls December Mare Sale – and these two fillies are the first two foals out of their dam, a mare whose 2016 Showcasing (by Oasis Dream) filly made 380,000gns from Book 2 of last year's Tattersalls October Yearling Sale, bought by John Gosden. Their dam, Coplow (by Manduro), was placed a few times but is a half-sister to four blacktype earners, notably the Group 3 Prix d'Aumale winner and Group 2 Oaks d'Italia runner-up Middle Club (by Fantastic Light) – whose Frankel (by Galileo) filly foal made 700,000gns in Newmarket at the end of November – and the unbeaten but tragically ill-fated Group 3 Horris Hill Stakes winner Piping Rock (by Dubawi). She is out of Anna Oleanda (by Old Vic), a dual German winner whose full-sister Anno Luce is the pattern-winning dam of Grade 1 Champion Hurdle heroine Annie Power (by Shirocco), one of the most brilliant and popular National Hunt mares of recent years. A half-sister to flat listed scorer Air Trooper (by Monsun), Annie Power is also a half-sister to Angeleno (by Belong To Me), who is the winning dam of US nine-furlong Grade 3 scorer Lady Pimpernel (by Sir Percy).

Anno Luce, meanwhile, is a daughter of the dual German champion Anna Paola (by Prince Ippi), the Group 2 Preis der Diana (German Oaks) heroine whose descendants also include notable performers such as Annus Mirabilis (by Warning), Pozarica (by Rainbow Quest), Annaba (by In The Wings), and Anna Of Saxony (by Ela-Mana-Mou). The Group/Grade 1 scorers Ave (by Danehill Dancer), Anna Monda (by Monsun), Helmet (by Exceed And Excel), and Epaulette (by Commands) all appear in the family too, although they are more distantly connected to this year's Guineas heroine.

It remains to be seen if Billesdon Brook will return to training in 2019 or go to the paddocks. Given that her big win seems likely to remain an isolated success if she races on at the top level in Europe, that it was on fast ground, that her juvenile form included a six-length score over seven furlongs on the Polytrack at Kempton, and that her sire's offspring have been doing well across the Atlantic, it would be interesting to see how she might get on if she made that move.

SUMMARY DETAILS

Bred: Stowell Hill Partners
Owned: Pall Mall Partners & Mrs R J McCreery
Trained: Richard Hannon
Country: England
Race record: 32213110-41440-

Career highlights: 4 wins inc Qipco 1000 Guineas (Gr1), Grosvenor Sport Prestige Stakes (Gr3), 3rd Longines Irish Champions Weekend EBF Stallions Star Stakes (L)

BILLESDON BROOK (GB) - 2015 chestnut filly

Champs Elysees (GB)	Danehill (USA)	Danzig (USA)
		Razyana (USA)
	Hasili (IRE)	Kahyasi
		Kerali
Coplow (GB)	Manduro (GER)	Monsun (GER)
		Mandellicht (IRE)
	Anna Oleanda (IRE)	Old Vic
		Anna Paola (GER)

BLAIR HOUSE (IRE)

Sprint star Pivotal (by Polar Falcon) is about to turn 26 years old but is still an active and popular member of the team at Cheveley Park Stud, the farm where he was bred. He gets his top horses over a wide variety of trips and his tally of 146 stakes winners now includes 28 Group/Grade 1 stars, with Lightning Spear and Blair House the newest additions to that shorter, select list. The latter won the Jebel Hatta at Meydan in March.

Godophin's homebred five-year-old is trained by Charlie Appleby and he seemed to be no more than a smart handicapper before this first step into blacktype company, Timeform-rated just 110 in 2017 and 105 the year before. But he beat Benbatl by three-parts of a length in the nine-furlong feature, with Janoobi a head back in third and another length back to the talented mare Promising Run. He is now on a Timeform figure of 125.

He had won a handicap over the course and distance the month before, was well-beaten behind Benbatl in the Group 1 Dubai Turf three weeks later, and then not seen in action again until late September. This time trainer Charlie Appleby had shipped him to Australia and, although he missed out on blacktype for the effort, he put up an eye-catching performance to finish a two-and-a-half-length fourth to Homesman in the Group 1 Hyland Race Colours Underwood Stakes over nine furlongs at Caulfield, despite never looking like getting to the leaders.

He met his old foe Benbatl in the Group 1 Ladbrokes Stakes over a furlong farther at the same venue 13 days later and, at level weights, failed by just a short-head to beat that younger rival. Humidor was two and a quarter lengths back in third, narrowly pipping the ill-fated Cliffs Of Moher (aka The Cliffsofmoher) and D'Argento in a three-way photo. On the strength of this top-class effort, he was sent off favourite for the Group 1 Seppelt Mackinnon Stakes over 10 furlongs at

Flemington a month later, but this time he disappointed, finishing only seventh as Trap For Fools pipped Irish raider Latrobe and recent Victoria Derby scorer Extra Brut in a three-way photo.

It remains to be seen if this gelding can duplicate his best form and go on to add further pattern race success to his tally in 2019, but there is no doubt that he is bred to be a high achiever. Not only is he by one of Europe's best stallions, but he is a half-brother to Listed Havana Gold Newmarket Stakes winner Key Victory (by Teofilo; official rating of 108), and is out of Patroness (by Dubawi), a placed full-sister to mile Group 1 star and late Dalham Hall Stud stallion Poet's Voice.

That Queen Elizabeth II Stakes winner has not yet sired as many stakes winners as might be hoped at this point of his career, but his tally of 16 includes the aforementioned Trap For Fools, Group 2 Mehl-Mulhens Rennen (German 2000 Guineas) scorer Poetic Dream, 2018's Group 2 Oaks d'Italia heroine Sand Zabeel and Group 2 Derby Italiano winner Summer Festival – who was gelded in September – juvenile Group 3 scorer Arctic Sound, and, of course, Poet's Word. That Timeform 129-rated standout, who is reviewed elsewhere in this volume, won both the Group 1 King George VI and Queen Elizabeth Stakes and Group 1 Prince of Wales's Stakes and is about to start a stallion career at Nunnery Stud in Norfolk, England.

Patroness and Poet's Voice are out of Bright Tiara (by Chief's Crown) and their siblings include four notable broodmares. Best Boot (by Storm Boot) is the winning grandam of Japanese classic-placed Grade 1 Queen Elizabeth II Cup heroine Mozu Katchan (by Harbinger), Queen's Park (by Relaunch) is the stakes-winning dam of Grade 1-placed US Grade 3 scorer Gemswick Park (by Speightstown), Japanese star Gold Tiara (by Seeking The Gold) is the grandam of the multiple Grade 1-placed pattern winner Staphanos (by Deep Impact), and dual juvenile winner Swan Nebula (by Seeking The Gold) is the grandam of 2018's Group 3 Prix Eclipse scorer Sporting Chance (by Kodiac).

Bright Tiara got her only win as a two-year-old, but her full-brother Chief Honcho improved with time, getting his best success in the Grade 1 Brooklyn Handicap at the age of five. Also placed in a string of Grade 1 contests, he had some success at stud, as did his 'nephew' American Chance (by Cure The Blues). That Grade 1-placed Grade 2 Forego Handicap and Grade 2 Jersey Derby winner was out of Bright Tiara's half-sister American Dance (by Seattle Slew), and her siblings also include Dance To Dawn (by Louis Quatorze), the dam of Grade 1 Ballerina Stakes heroine Dance To Bristol (by Speightstown).

Expressive Dance (by Riva Ridge), the third dam of Blair House, won a dozen races, including the Grade 3 Bewitch Stakes, Grade 3 Comely Stakes and Grade 3 Ballerina Stakes, and that daughter of Prioress Stakes winner Exclusive Dancer (by Native Dancer) was a half-sister to classic-placed Grade 1 star and blacktype sire General Assembly (by Secretariat). She was also a half-sister to Mime (by Cure The Blues), who is the third dam of Grade 1 Spinaway Stakes scorer R Heat Lightning (by Trippi), and to the more notable Ten Cents A Dance (by Buckpasser), a Grade 2 Firenze Handicap runner-up who was influential at stud.

The best of that mare's offspring was the multiple Grade 1 star Versailles Treaty (by Danzig), winner of the Alabama Stakes, Test Stakes, Gazelle Stakes and Ruffian Handicap. That celebrity later became the dam of Grade 1 winner and young French stallion George Vancouver (by Henrythenavigator) and of Grade 1-placed Grade 2 scorer Saarland (by Unbridled). Arabian Dancer (by Damascus), who was runner-up in the Grade 1 Matron Stakes, was also a daughter of Ten Cents A Dance and, in addition to being the dam of Grade 3 scorer and successful sire Out Of Place (by Cox's Ridge), she was the grandam of Grade 1 star and stallion Gold Fever (by Forty Niner), third dam of Grade 1 winner Boisterous (by Distorted Humor), and fourth dam of Grade 1 Wood Memorial Stakes scorer Bellamy Road (by Concerto).

Blair House is a gelding, so obviously there's no future stud career for him, but there should be some more good prizes to be won with him before he eventually retires from the track.

SUMMARY DETAILS

Bred: Darley
Owned: Godolphin
Trained: Charlie Appleby
Country: England
Race record: -120212-200-22110420-
Career highlights: 4 wins inc Jebel Hatta sponsored by Emirates Airline (Gr1), 2nd Ladbrokes Stakes (Gr1)

BLAIR HOUSE (IRE) - 2013 chestnut gelding

Pivotal (GB)	Polar Falcon (USA)	Nureyev (USA)
		Marie D'Argonne (FR)
	Fearless Revival	Cozzene (USA)
		Stufida
Patroness (GB)	Dubawi (IRE)	Dubai Millennium (GB)
		Zomaradah (GB)
	Bright Tiara (USA)	Chief's Ceown (USA)
		Expressive Dance (USA)

BLUE POINT (IRE)

Juvenile champion and dual classic star Shamardal (by Giant's Causeway) wasted no time in establishing himself as a top-class international sire, and the Kildangan Stud ace gets leading two-year-olds, high-class sprinters, and top-notch milers and middle-distance runners. He has been represented by 21 Group 1 winners among an overall tally of 124 stakes winners, and Blue Point is one of his many notable performers. That Charlie Appleby-trained bay has been among the leaders of his generation at two, three and four years of age – one among an exceptional group of sprinters that we have seen over the past few years.

He won half of his six starts as a juvenile – including a novice event by 11 lengths at Doncaster and a three-length defeat of Mokarris in the Group 2 Gimcrack Stakes at York – and his three losses that term were runner-up spots to Mehmas in the Group 2 Richmond Stakes and The Last Lion in the Group 1 Middle Park Stakes, and a third-place finish in the Dewhurst Stakes. That seven-furlong Group 1 event went to Churchill, with Lancaster Bomber second and Thunder Snow fourth, so each of the first four home were colts who went on to Group 1 success at three and/or four years of age.

This effort plus his pedigree gave him every chance of staying a mile at three, but such was the speed he had shown over six that it was always on the cards that he would aim for the Group 1 Commonwealth Cup rather than step up in trip for a crack at the 2000 Guineas. Indeed, the Dewhurst remains the only time he has ever been asked to go beyond six.

He kicked off his three-year-old campaign with a one-and-a-half-length defeat of Harry Angel – his rival being known only as the twice-raced Group 2 Mill Reef Stakes winner before lining up that day – and there was only half a length between them when they met again in the Commonwealth Cup. Caravaggio, however, beat the pair of them, taking the prize by three-parts of a length, although the trio pulled three lengths clear of their closest pursuer. It looked like another good edition of the young race, and time only strengthened that impression.

Blue Point disappointed when an eight-length fourth to Harry Angel in the Group 1 Sprint Cup at Haydock, on heavy ground, when next seen in action, but he bounced back to take the Group 3 Bengough Stakes on good-to-soft at Ascot (by half a length from Projection), and put up an encouraging effort when a head runner-up to Ertijaal in the Group 2 Meydan Sprint in February – his first attempt at five furlongs. This set up a potential clash with Timeform 136-rated star Battash, and although that gelding is brilliant on his day, Ascot in June was not one of them.

Battaash was far from disgraced in reaching the line a neck in front of subsequent Group 1 Prix de l'Abbaye de Longchamp heroine Mabs Cross at the end of the Group 1 King's Stand Stakes – the pair almost three lengths clear of their nearest pursuer – but it was not his peak form, and on the day it was Blue Point who came away covered in glory having taken the prize by one and three-quarter lengths, and in a quick time. It was compensation for a very disappointing run in Hong Kong under two months before.

It was disappointing to see him finish down the field behind U S Navy Flag in the Group 1 Darley July Cup at Newmarket – for which he was favourite – and it was something of a surprise to see him come home only third to Alpha Delphini and Mabs Cross in the Group 1 Coolmore Nunthorpe Stakes at York. He remains in training in 2019 and has Meydan's Group 1 Al Quoz Sprint, in March, on his agenda. He had been due to run in the race in 2018 but was withdrawn before being loaded into the stalls due to the presence of blood in his nostrils.

Blue Point was bred by Oak Lodge Bloodstock. He made 110,000gns in Newmarket as a foal and 200,000gns from Book 1 of the Tattersalls October Yearling Sale at the same venue, and he is the best of several winners out of Scarlett Rose (by Royal Applause). Those siblings include a lowly-rated mile winner, but he is also a half-brother to the Group 2 Railway

Stakes winner and Group 2 Mill Reef Stakes runner-up Formosina (by Footstepsinthesand). Indeed, he and Formosina could be described as being three-parts brothers as both are by sons of the prolific Group 1 star and multiple US champion sire Giant's Causeway (by Storm Cat).

Their dam was only placed, as was their grandam Billie Blue (by Ballad Rock), but Scarlett Rose is a half-sister to seven winners, two of whom are of particular note. The track star among them is Tumbleweed Ridge (by Indian Ridge), a prolific seven-furlong specialist whose 10 wins included the Group 3 Horris Hill Stakes, the Group 3 Prix de la Porte Maillot, and three editions of the Group 3 Ballycorus Stakes. The other sibling one made her name at stud because she, the lightly-raced triple sprint winner Tumbleweed Pearl (by Aragon), is the dam of Group 2 Queen Mary Stakes heroine Gilded (by Redback) and grandam of the pattern-placed multiple sprint stakes winner Fort Del Oro (by Lope De Vega), a granddaughter of Shamardal.

Blue Nose (by Windjammer), the third dam of Blue Point, won a listed nursery and earned three other pieces of blacktype, one of which was her fourth-place finish to Monteverdi in the Group 2 National Stakes at the Curragh in 1979. It is, of course, a long time now since finishing fourth in a listed or pattern event awarded any blacktype.

Blue Point was Timeform-rated 118 at two, 124 at three, and, at the time of writing, is a four-year-old rated 129. His juvenile talent and his top-class form beyond that initial season will likely make him a popular addition to the stallion ranks, and it is encouraging that the early handful of Shamardals at stud include notable international sire Lope De Vega. That dual classic hero stands at Ballylinch Stud, has seven Group/Grade 1 stars to his name among 51 stakes winners, and those include Belardo (foals in 2018) who stands at Kildangan Stud, Australian sprint ace Santa Ana Lane, and brilliant US juvenile filly Newspaperofrecord.

SUMMARY DETAILS

Bred: Oak Lodge Bloodstock

Owned: Godolphin
Trained: Charlie Appleby
Country: England
Race record: 112123-1341-20103-
Career highlights: 6 wins inc King's Stand Stakes (Gr1), Irish Thoroughbred Marketing Gimcrack Stakes (Gr2), Merriebelle Stable Pavilion Stakes (Gr3), John Guest Bengough Stakes (Gr3), 2nd Juddmonte Middle Park Stakes (Gr1), Meydan Sprint sponsored by District One Greenery Stretch (Gr2), Qatar Richmond Stakes (Gr2), 3rd Coolmore Nunthorpe Stakes (Gr1), Commonwealth Cup (Gr1), Dubai Dewhurst Stakes (Gr1)

BLUE POINT (IRE)- 2014 bay colt

Shamardal (USA)	Giant's Causeway (USA)	Storm Cat (USA)
		Mariah's Storm (USA)
	Helsinki (GB)	Machiavellian (USA)
		Helen Street
Scarlett Rose (GB)	Royal Applause (GB)	Waajib
		Flying Melody
	Billie Blue	Ballad Rock
		Blue Nose

CALL THE WIND (GB)

Two of the things that we learned from Arc weekend 2018 were that offspring of Frankel (by Galileo) can win a top-level contest over twice the distance over which he excelled and that George Strawbridge's broodmare In Clover (by Inchinor) is on the verge of achieving 'blue hen' status. These things came to light when the Freddy Head-trained Call The Wind won the Group 1 Qatar Prix du Cadran over two and a half miles, beating Holdthasigreen by a length and a quarter on good ground. This victory, a third consecutive one from just seven starts for four-year-old, also highlighted how it can be worth persisting with a promising horse, even if there are problems that keep it off the track at two and three.

Call The Wind has had a variety of issues, including one with stalls, and he was gelded several months before making his debut over eight and a half furlongs in heavy ground at a provincial meeting in France in late March. He finished third there, fifth next time over 12 furlongs, then fourth and third at ParisLongchamp, over 12 and 14 furlongs respectively. It's doubtful that even the most optimistic supporter would have believed this horse would pick up a Group 1 prize by the end of the year.

He won a minor race over 12 furlongs on soft ground at Clairefontaine in early August, followed-up with a two-and-a-half-length over a furlong and a half farther at Deauville a fortnight later, and that was all he had to his name before the first Sunday in October. Now he could have Royal Ascot on his agenda for 2019, with the Group 1 Gold Cup looking like a realistic target. Whether or not he is campaigned with a potential shot at the £1 million Weatherbys Hamilton Stayers' Million bonus remains to be seen.

He is one of five top-level winners to have emerged, so far, from Frankel's first two crops and he the third one for his dam, In Clover. Her daughters We Are (by Dansili) and With You (by Dansili) have won the Group 1 Prix de l'Opera

Longines and Group 1 Prix Rothschild respectively, and she is also the dam of the stakes-winning Oasis Dream (by Green Desert) fillies Dream Clover and Incahoots. Those rare mares who produce at least three Group/Grade 1 winners plus at least one other pattern scorer are the ones usually referred to as 'blue hen' mares. Her three-year-old of 2019 is called Featuring, and that full-sister to We Are and With You finished third in a mile maiden at Chantilly in mid-September, her only start to date. The mare had a bay son of Dansili (by Danehill) in 2017, a chestnut Dubawi (by Dubai Millennium) colt in late April and was then bred to Invincible Spirit (by Green Desert), so that special status is still within her reach.

In Clover won the Group 3 Prix de Flore over 10 and a half furlongs and a listed contest over a mile, and she was only beaten by a total of two and a quarter lengths when fourth to Mandesha in the Group 1 Prix d'Astarte over the latter trip at Deauville. Although out of Group 3 Prix de Royaumont scorer Bellarida (by Bellypha), this was the maximum distance range one would have expected of her given that her sire was the high-class seven-furlong horse and classic sire Inchinor (by Ahonoora). Her pattern-placed, stakes-winning half-sister Bayourida (by Slew O'Gold) is the dam of middle-distance Group 2-placed listed scorer Telluride (by Montjeu), and her half-sister Belesta (by Xaar) is the dam of the middle-distance pattern winners Adjusted (by Montjeu; raced as Assign in Ireland) and Giuseppe Piazzi (by Galileo; Scandinavian champion in 2017), but some of her other siblings are responsible for speedier individuals.

Noyelles (by Docksider), for example, is responsible for the smart fillies Lily's Angel (by Dark Angel) and Zurigha (by Cape Cross), with the former taking the Group 3 Chartwell Stakes in England and the runners-up spot in the Group 1 Matron Stakes at Leopardstown, and the latter taking a listed contest in England plus second place in the Group 2 Cape Verdi Stakes at Meydan.

Bellona (by Bering) won the Listed Prix Rose de Mai and picked up third in the Group 3 Prix Penelope, and her winning daughter Es Que (by Inchinor) – who is very closely related to

In Clover – is the dam of Group 1 Hong Kong Vase winner Dominant (by Cacique) and this year's Group 2 Prix du Conseil de Paris scorer Listen In (by Sea The Stars) over middle-distances but also mile stakes winner Zhui Feng (by Invincible Spirit) and seven-furlong Group 2 scorer Es Que Love (by Clodovil), who got several first-crop juvenile winners in 2018 from just a handful of runners.

Then there's Forty Belles (by Forty Niner). Her daughter Party (by Cadeaux Genereux) was a seven-furlong listed scorer at Newmarket as a two-year-old and went on to produce Australian Group 3 scorer Observational (by Galileo), but more notable is that Jummana, a full-sister to Party, is the dam of 2018's Group 1 Poule d'Essai des Pouliches (French 1000 Guineas) heroine Teppal (by Camacho).

It took time, patience, and persistence to make Call The Wind a winner, and now that he has announced himself as a top stayer it will be interesting to see how the rest of his career unfolds.

SUMMARY DETAILS

Bred: George Strawbridge
Owned: George Strawbridge
Trained: Freddy Head
Country: France
Race record: /3043111-
Career highlights: 3 wins inc Qatar Prix du Cadran (Gr1)

CALL THE WIND (GB) - 2014 chestnut gelding

Frankel (GB)	Galileo (IRE)	Sadler's Wells (USA)
		Urban Sea (USA)
	Kind (IRE)	Danehill (USA)
		Rainbow Lake (GB)
In Clover (GB)	Inchinor (GB)	Ahonoora
		Inchmurrin
	Bellarida (FR)	Bellypha
		Lerida (FR)

CRACKSMAN (GB)

Timeform 147-rated superstar Frankel (by Galileo) has been bred to some of the cream of the world's elite broodmares and, with such support, anything less than a plethora of stakes and pattern winners from the resulting offspring would be disappointing.

So far, 33 members of his first two crops have been stakes winners – most of them successful at least once in pattern company – while his third crop includes the Kevin Ryan-trained Group 3 Prix Thomas Bryon winner and Grade 1 Breeders' Cup Juvenile Fillies Turf runner-up East. He has a champion and classic winner in Japan, colts who have been placed in the Derby at Epsom and Irish Derby (two) at the Curragh, a total of five individual Group 1 winners, and a Timeform 136-rated standout. The latter is a long way clear of the best of the stallion's other representatives, so far, which is a little surprising, given how many blacktype scorers there have been.

That star is, of course, Anthony Oppenheimer's homebred Cracksman, dual wide-margin winner of the Group 1 Qipco Champion Stakes at Ascot and, at the time of writing, rated the joint-top horse in the world, with the great Australian champion Winx, on official handicap figures.

The colt won a mile maiden at Newmarket on his only start at two, and short-headed the ill-fated Permian in a 10-furlong conditions race at Epsom a few weeks before finishing third – as favourite – to Wings Of Eagles and Cliffs Of Moher in the Group 1 Investec Derby, beaten by three-parts of a length and a neck. He looked an unlucky loser when a neck runner-up to Capri in the Group 1 Dubai Duty Free Irish Derby, but then began his sequence of impressive wins.

He powered away from Venice Beach to take the Group 2 Betway Great Voltigeur Stakes by six lengths at York, followed that with a three-and-a-half-length defeat of Avilius in the Group 2 Qatar Prix Niel at Chantilly, and then put up that memorable performance at Ascot, thrashing Poet's Word by seven lengths in the Group 1 Qipco Champion Stakes and pushing his Timeform rating to 136.

He looked as good as ever when easily taking the Group 1 Prix Ganay over 10 and a half furlongs at ParisLongchamp on his seasonal reappearance in April, generating a sense of eager anticipation of a potential clash with his brilliant stable-companion Enable at some point in the year, and likely in the Arc. The Group 1 Investec Coronation Cup was his next stop, but although he won it was a disappointing effort for many. He had to fight to beat Salouen by a head – a well-exposed colt who has never won a stakes race. It emerged, however, that he had hit his head coming out of the stalls and so had likely been running a bit dazed.

He was back in action 19 days later, sent off odds-on (as on all of his starts in 2018) for the Group 1 Prince of Wales's Stakes at Royal Ascot. The ground was perhaps a little quicker than ideal for him, he did not appear to be travelling well during part of the race, and it was reported that he had been quite distracted by some fillies beforehand. Whether his mind was elsewhere or he was just on an off day is open to speculation, but old rival Poet's Word beat him by two and a quarter lengths. The winner went on to confirm his position as a top-class colt with victory in the Group 1 King George VI and Queen Elizabeth Stakes the following month, and it should be noted that the third and fourth on that day in June were Hawkbill and Cliffs Of Moher, and they finished eight lengths and another three-parts of a length behind Cracksman.

There was quite an array of negative comments about the colt on social media. What might those have been had Poet's Word not run that day? Then Cracksman could have been an easy winner of the race and likely heaped with praise, despite his antics before and during the race. But it matters not as he returned to action one more time and, sporting blinkers to help him to concentrate, he swept into the lead about a quarter-mile from home and stormed clear to beat Crystal Ocean by six lengths in the Group 1 Qipco Champion Stakes, a margin that could have been a little wider had Frankie

Dettori not eased off to wave his whip in celebration in the last half-furlong. His retirement from racing was quickly announced, although the location of his new stallion career was not revealed until later.

Cracksman is a half-brother to the Group 3 Solario Stakes winner Fantastic Moon (by Dalakhani), and he is the fourth foal out of Rhadegunda (by Pivotal), a triple winner whose tally includes the Listed Prix Solitude over nine furlongs on heavy ground at Fontainebleau, the final start in a nine-race career for the John Gosden-trained bay. Her half-brother Halla San (by Halling) earned his blacktype with third-place finishes in 14-furlong listed contests at Nottingham and York, he was beaten by just a head when runner-up in the two-mile Northumberland Plate and then went on to some success over hurdles.

His stamina stands out in contrast to the aptitude of his sister, to his dam's Listed Sirenia Stakes-winning half-brother Art Of War (by Machiavellian), and to the classic speed of his grandam, On The House (by Be My Guest), the Group 1 1000 Guineas and Group 1 Sussex Stakes heroine of 1982. That Timeform 125-rated star is also the grandam of Group 2 Royal Lodge Stakes winner Leo (by Pivotal) and of dual Italian listed scorer Balkenhol (by Polar Falcon), and she is the third dam of Irish Field (by Dubawi), who won the Group 2 Prix Robert Papin and was runner-up in the Group 3 Prix du Bois.

In terms of optimal distance, Cracksman could have gone either way – miler or middle-distance horse. These first three generations are mostly about talent at up to nine furlongs, with Halla San an exception. That gelding, however, is by a stallion often noted for getting horses who excel from 12 furlongs to two miles, and so one could argue that this was the source of his stamina.

Frankel was bred to stay a mile and a half – something his triple Group 1-winning full-brother Noble Mission did – and so, with the right mares, it was always going to happen that some of his offspring would also be suited to that trip, and a bit farther. And we are seeing his stakes winners coming over a wide range of distances, from sprints up to the Cup races.

Cracksman is not the first member of his extended family to achieve hit the top over middle-distances. That's because his fourth dam is Lora (by Lorenzaccio), the unraced grandam of Nuryana (by Nureyev) and Littlewick (by Green Desert). The latter is the dam of the Chilean-bred Grade 1 Premio St Leger heroine Fontanella Borghese (by Roy), but in addition to being the stakes-winning dam of Group 1 Coronation Stakes winner Rebecca Sharp (by Machiavellian), Nuryana is a half-sister to 11 and a half-furlong Group 3 scorer and Derby sixth Mystic Knight (by Caerleon) and grandam of Golden Horn (by Cape Cross).

That Oppenheimer-bred, Timeform 134-rated champion won the Group 1 Derby, Group 1 Coral-Eclipse, Group 1 Irish Champion Stakes, and Group 1 Prix de l'Arc de Triomphe in 2015, he stands at Dalham Hall Stud, will be a freshman sire of 2019, and his first yearlings have proved very popular in the auction ring this year. His string of six-figure lots includes a colt who made 550,000gns from Book 1 of the Tattersalls October Yearling Sale. Of course, his relationship to Crackman is remote, as are that of Nuryana, Fontanella Borghese, New Zealand-bred dual Group 1 mile star Obsession (by Bachelor Duke; grandam a half-sister to Nuryana), and Australian Group 1 scorers Kidnapped (by Viscount) and Hauraki (by Reset; their grandam is another half-sister to Nuryana).

Cracksman lived up to the star potential he first showed at York and went on to become the best horse that his immediate and broad family has produced. He has now been retired to stand at Dalham Hall Stud in Newmarket, at a fee of £25,000, and he looks sure to prove very popular in that new role. We can expect his offspring to prove effective from a mile and upwards, with some of them showing talent in the latter half of their juvenile year.

SUMMARY DETAILS

Bred: Hascombe and Valiant Studs
Owned: A E Oppenheimer
Trained: John Gosden

Country: England
Race record: 1-132111-1121-
Career highlights: 8 wins inc Qipco Champion Stakes (Gr1-twice), Investec Coronation Cup (Gr1), Prix Ganay (Gr1), Qatar Prix Niel (Gr2), Betway Great Voltigeur Stakes (Gr2), 2nd Prince of Wales's Stakes (Gr1), Dubai Duty Free Irish Derby (Gr1), 3rd Investec Derby (Gr1)

CRACKSMAN (GB) - 2014 bay colt

Frankel (GB)	Galileo (IRE)	Sadler's Wells (USA)
		Urban Sea (USA)
	Kind (IRE)	Danehill (USA)
		Rainbow Lake (GB)
Rhadegunda (GB)	Pivotal (GB)	Polar Falcon (USA)
		Fearless Revival
	St Radegund (GB)	Green Desert (USA)
		On The House

CROSS COUNTER (GB)

Pay attention to those juvenile maidens on the all-weather tracks if you want to find Group 1 stars of the future!

In the past few years we have seen an increasing number of top performers emerge who got their first win(s) on one of the artificial tracks, and they include Derby runner-up and Irish Derby winner Jack Hobbs (Wolverhampton), Irish Oaks heroine Covert Love (Chelmsford), classic and multiple Group 1 star Winter (Dundalk), Grand Prix de Saint-Cloud scorer Silverwave (Pornichet La Baule), recently retired dual Group 1 star Hawkbill (Kempton and Lingfield), and the mighty Enable (Newcastle).

Irish Oaks heroine Seventh Heaven (Dundalk), Group 1 Pretty Polly Stakes scorer Nezwaah (Chelmsford), French mile Group 1 star Zelzal (Deauville), and 2018's top-level winners Lightning Spear (Kempton) and Mabs Cross (Newcastle) also got their maiden success on an artificial track, although it was at the start of their three-year-old season. Among the younger age group, this year's Grade 1 Natalma Stakes winner La Pelosa made a winning debut on the Polytrack at Kempton in May, whereas Group 1 Moyglare Stud Stakes heroine Skitter Scatter got her first win at Dundalk. And to all of these, we can add Group 1 Lexus Melbourne Cup hero Cross Counter.

Godolphin's homebred began his career at Wolverhampton in early December of his juvenile year and took that eight-and-a-half-furlong novice race by two and a quarter lengths. He returned to the venue just over six weeks later and ran away with a similar contest over the same trip, this time coming home eight lengths clear. He was gelded two months after that, was runner-up in a 10-furlong novice event at Sandown on his turf debut at Sandown in early June, and then put up an eye-catching performance at Royal Ascot, finishing a two-and-a-half-length fourth to Baghdad in the valuable King George V Stakes (handicap).

He was another handicap over that course and distance in July, taking his official handicap mark up to 108, and then put up the first performance that stamped him as a potential Group 1 horse in the making. It may sound as though the Group 3 Qatar Gordon Stakes at Goodwood was something of a non-event as only four lined-up and two of those were beaten out of sight, plus the favourite has still not lived up to the promise he showed when chasing home Masar in the Group 1 Investec Derby, but the clock told a different story. Cross Counter took it up after a quarter of a mile and was never headed, eventually eased down to beat Dee Ex Bee by four and a half lengths in a course record time that saw his Timeform rating shoot up from 115p to 123.

York was his next stop and he was sent off favourite there to take the Group 2 Sky Bet Great Voltigeur Stakes, also over 12 furlongs. This time he didn't get to the front, but he remained full of promise after this head defeat by his stablemate Old Persian (gave 3lbs), with prior and subsequent Group 1 star Kew Gardens (gave 5lbs) a length and a half back in third. Both this race and the Gordon Stakes are often viewed as being trials for the St Leger, but of course, geldings are barred from the classics, so an alternative plan had to be hatched for this exciting prospect.

Three-year-olds receive a favourable weight allowance in the Group 1 Lexus Melbourne Cup and the race went to the Joseph O'Brien-trained Group 2 winner and Group 1 St Leger fourth Rekindling in 2017. That colt remained in Australia but has not run since that day and it was reported recently that he's returning to Ireland to resume his career in 2019. It was decided that Cross Counter would bid to make it a double for the younger generation.

He flew to Australia and was an ante-post favourite for the big race, but three weeks before it he met with a setback that gave connections a brief scare; he needed veterinary attention and two days of box rest after sustaining a cut to a leg. The Aidan O'Brien-trained Yucatan posted an impressive Group 2 win shortly after his arrival 'down under' and it was he who went off favourite on the first Tuesday in November, just ahead of the Ian Williams-trained Group 3 Henry II Stakes winner Magic Circle and then Cross Counter. That first pair finished down the field as Godolphin's charge, who met with some trouble in running, stayed on strongly in the straight, hit the front in the final 50 yards, and beat the Hughie Morrison-trained Marmelo by a length. Prince Of Arran, trained by Charlie Fellowes in Newmarket, made it a historic one-two-three for England, with the ex-French colt Finche fourth and the Aidan O'Brien-trained Rostropovich fifth.

Cross Counter is one of 16 Group 1 winners from an overall tally of 83 blacktype scorers for Kildangan Stud's Teofilo (by Galileo), a tally that includes also December's Group 1 Longines Hong Kong Vase scorer Exultant, who was classic-placed in Ireland in 2017 – third to Churchill in the Irish 2000 Guineas – under the name Irishcorrespondent. The stallion is mostly responsible for milers and middle-distance horses, although Voleuse De Coeurs won the Group 1 Irish St Leger over 14 furlongs and Quest For More took the two-and-a-half-mile Group 1 Qatar Prix du Cadran. However, the latter is out of a daughter of Rainbow Quest (by Blushing Groom) whereas Cross Counter is from a famous family of sprinters and milers, with the occasional 12-furlong horse. That said, he is not its only big winner at around two miles.

He is the second foal of his dam, Waitress (by Kingmambo), and his older sibling is the Saeed bin Suroor-trained filly Right Direction (by Cape Cross) who, although unraced at two and three, won twice over seven furlongs this year, from just six starts. The mare was listed-placed over seven furlongs and unplaced in a blacktype sprint after that, and she is a half-sister to Woven Lace (by Hard Spun) who chased home subsequent classic star Beauty Parlour in the Group 3 Prix de la Grotte over a mile at Longchamp back in 2012.

Their dam is the Group 3 Prix de Meautry winner Do The Honours (by Highest Honor) and that half-sister to Listed Chesham Stakes winner and Grade 1 Mother Goose Stakes third Seba (by Alzao) is among the 11 winners produced from Persian Secret (by Persian Heights), a mile listed scorer in

France and half-sister to Group 2 King's Stand Stakes and Group 2 Temple Stakes heroine Cassandra Go (by Indian Ridge). This family has also hit the Group 1 jackpot with two other horses in 2018, namely Qipco British Champions Filly and Mare Turf heroine and Breeders' Cup Turf runner-up Magical (by Galileo) and her Juddmonte Lockinge Stakes-winning full-sister Rhododendron. They are out of Cassandra Go's top-class daughter Halfway To Heaven (by Pivotal), who completed the Group 1 treble of Irish 1000 Guineas, Nassau Stakes and Sun Chariot Stakes in 2008.

Magical is one of this family's rare 12-furlong horses, and it is one of Persian Secret's descendants who is another to do well over that trip, and farther, in 2018. In addition to being the third dam of Cross Counter, she is also the third dam of Brundtland (by Dubawi). His dam, Future Generation (by Hurricane Run), won the Group 3 Desmond Stakes over a mile, and his unraced grandam Posterity is a daughter of Indian Ridge (by Ahonoora), but he went off favourite for the Group 1 Prix Royal-Oak at ParisLongchamp in late October following wins in the Group 2 Prix Niel and Group 2 Prix Chaudenay. The latter is, like the Group 1, over a mile and seven, and Brundtland was somewhat unlucky to finish only fourth in the Royal-Oak, beaten a total of one length by the winner, Holdthasigreen, despite having met with some trouble during the race.

Cross Counter, now rated 124 by Timeform, is an exciting prospect for 2019. His Goodwood performance showed that he is almost top-class over 12 furlongs and his victory at Flemington produced an almost identical rating. The latter was over farther than one would expect a horse of his pedigree to stay, and if he is to go the Cup route, then it's possible that the extra half-mile of the Group 1 Gold Cup could be beyond him.

SUMMARY DETAILS

Bred: Godolphin
Owned: Godolphin
Trained: Charlie Appleby

Country: England
Race record: 1-1241121-
Career highlights: 5 wins inc Lexus Melbourne Cup (Gr1), Qatar Gordon Stakes (Gr3), 2nd Sky Bet Great Voltigeur Stakes (Gr2)

CROSS COUNTER (GB) - 2015 bay gelding

Teofilo (IRE)	Galileo (IRE)	Sadler's Wells (USA)
		Urban Sea (USA)
	Speirbhean (IRE)	Danehill (USA)
		Saviour (USA)
Waitress (USA)	Kingmambo (USA)	Mr Prospector (USA)
		Miesque (USA)
	Do The Honours (IRE)	Highest Honor (FR)
		Persian Secret (FR)

DESERT ENCOUNTER (IRE)

It is something of a surprise that Desert Encounter managed to pick up a top-level win in 2018, and he was among the fancied horses too when he beat Thundering Blue by a length in the Grade 1 Pattison Canadian International Stakes over 12 furlongs on good ground at Woodbine in mid-October. Yes, he was a 50/1 third to Ulysses and Barney Roy in the Group 1 Coral-Eclipse in 2017 – beaten a nose and three and a half lengths – but he beat only one home behind Hawkbill in the Group 1 Longines Dubai Sheema Classic at Meydan in March and had been well-beaten in a Group 1 Qipco Champion Stakes, a Group 1 Prince of Wales's Stakes, and in two editions of the Group 1 King George VI and Queen Elizabeth Stakes. In short, he is a highly capable gelding who has done his connections proud and earned over £575,000 to date, but he is not a true Group 1-calibre one.

He achieved a Timeform rating of 121 as a five-year-old – up from 109p the previous year – and he had a career-best official handicap mark of 114 before his trip to Canada. He returned with that figure raised to 119. He had been a half-length third to Young Rascal and Mirage Dancer in the Group 3 Dubai Duty Free Legacy Cup Stakes at Newbury on his previous start, won a listed contest at Windsor the time before that, and his two other placings in 2018 are a listed second at Newbury and third to Poet's Word in the Group 3 Brigadier Gerard Stakes at Sandown, the horse who won the two Ascot Group 1s in which he was well-beaten.

Desert Encounter is the fifth top-level winner for the late Dalham Hall Stud stallion Halling (by Diesis), the Timeform 133-rated 10-furlong star whose 58 blacktype scorers featured Jack Hobbs (Irish Derby), Cavalryman (Grand Prix de Paris), Cutlass Bay (Prix Ganay), and Empoli (Preis von Europa). His various Group 1-placed horses included dual Group 3 winner and National Hunt stallion Norse Dancer (sire of Yanworth), classic runners-up Romsdal (St Leger), Something Exciting

(Oaks) and The Geezer (St Leger), and also Bauer, an Australian Group 3 winner who was a nose runner-up in the Group 1 Melbourne Cup.

The gelding made 32,000gns when consigned by his breeders, Tally-Ho Stud, to the 2013 edition of Tattersalls' Book 1 sale in Newmarket, he is a half-brother to the multiple sprint winners Fast Enough (by Kodiac) and Shaheen (by Society Rock), and his juvenile half-brother Desert Land (by Kodiac) – whom David Simcock also trains, finished fourth in the Yarmouth maiden won by subsequent Group 1 scorer Royal Meeting on his only start of 2018.

Their dam is an Invincible Spirit (by Green Desert) mare called La Chicana, and she is a full-sister to a high-class 12-furlong horse. Yes, you read that right. The Irish National Stud's flag bearer is a leading sire of sprinters and milers, but the distaff side of his pedigree gave him the chance to get a good middle-distance horse with the right mare, and Always Friendly (by High Line) was very much a likely candidate for 'right mare'. She was by a noted stamina influence, and she won the Group 3 Princess Royal Stakes over 12 furlongs, chased home Assessor in the Group 1 Prix Royal-Oak over a half-furlong short of two miles, and was third to Magic Night in the Group 2 Prix de Pomone over 13 and a half furlongs. Her final race was an unplaced finish in Urban Sea's Prix de l'Arc de Triomphe.

When bred to Danehill (by Danzig) – proven as a source of Group 1 stars from five to 12 furlongs – she got the Group 2-winning Italian miler Dane Friendly. He later sired the mile and 10-furlong Group 1 scorer Priore Philip. When bred to Invincible Spirit, however, she came up with Allied Powers who won the Group 2 Grand Prix de Chantilly plus two editions of the Group 3 Prix d'Hedouville, all over 12 furlongs.

Another striking aspect of Desert Encounter's pedigree is that the full-brother Diesis (his grandsire) and Kris (Invincible Spirit's broodmare sire) both feature within the first four generations of his pedigree, making him inbred to their parents, Sharpen Up (by Atan) and Doubly Sure (by Reliance).

It may have no bearing on his talent, but it catches the eye nonetheless.

Desert Encounter hit a new peak at the age of six, so it will be interesting to see what this talented gelding can do if he returns to training in 2019.

SUMMARY DETAILS

Bred: Tally-Ho Stud
Owned: Abdulla Al Mansoori
Trained: David Simcock
Country: England
Race record: 42-31-11132-123010-03020131-
Career highlights: 8 wins inc Pattison Canadian International Stakes (Gr1), Dubai Duty Free Legacy Cup Stakes (Gr3), Sri Lanka August Stakes (L), Carey Group Buckhounds Stakes (L), 2nd bet365 Stakes (L), Smarter Bets At Matchbook Tapster Stakes (L), Betway Stand Cup (L), 3rd Coral-Eclipse (Gr1), Dubai Duty Free Legacy Cup Stakes (Gr3), Matchbook Brigadier Gerard Stakes (Gr3)

DESERT ENCOUNTER (IRE) - 2012 bay gelding

Halling (USA)	Diesis	Sharpen Up
		Doubly Sure
	Dance Machine	Green Dancer (USA)
		Never A Lady
La Chicana (IRE)	Invincible Spirit (IRE)	Green Desert (USA)
		Rafha
	Always Friendly (GB)	High Line
		Wise Speculation (USA)

ENABLE (GB)

Emotion should never be part of the equation when it comes to assessing the merit or potential of a horse, although sometimes it is hard to remain fully objective. And if Enable is fit, happy, and healthy come the first Sunday in October 2019, then many hearts will likely be willing her home. Few horses have won the Group 1 Prix de l'Arc de Triomphe twice; no horse has won it three times. Enable is brilliant, she's popular, she has just one loss to her name, is currently on a nine-race winning streak, and she landed her second Arc despite having had just a single prior run since her first one. Then she became the first Arc winner to add the Grade 1 Breeders' Cup Turf, pushing her earnings past the £8 million mark in the process. Timeform-rated 134 at three and at four years of age, Enable is one of the great fillies of the Turf.

The brilliant French mare Treve came close to pulling off the Arc hat-trick and carried an unbeaten five-year-old season into the race when finishing fourth to Golden Horn in 2015, something that Enable could also be taking with her to Paris. The runner-up that day was Flintshire, the horse she'd beaten in the race 12 months before, and that Group 1 star went on to further fame in North America the following year before taking up stallion duties in Kentucky. He landed both the Grade 1 Woodford Reserve Manhattan Handicap and Grade 1 Sword Dancer Stakes that final season and closed out what had been a glittering international career by chasing home Highland Reel in the Grade 1 Breeders' Cup Turf. The Juddmonte homebred, a five-time scorer at the highest level, rated 128 by Timeform, and earner of over £6.2 million, could be described, in human terms, as being a first cousin of Enable.

His dam is Dance Routine (by Sadler's Wells), and she won the Group 2 Prix de Royallieu. She was a runner-up in the Group 1 Prix de Diane (French Oaks), her offspring also include the Group 2-placed middle-distance stakes winner

Dance Moves (by Dansili) and she is the grandam of Projected (by Showcasing), a former French-trained gelding who has been a Grade 2 scorer over a mile in the USA. That Chad Brown-trained six-year-old, who still carries his owner-breeder's famous green, pink, and white colours, has been out of luck in 2018 – a nose runner-up in a Grade 3 at Laurel Park in September and just a few weeks after he finished third, beaten a nose and a nose, in an eight-and-a-half-furlong Grade 2 at Saratoga.

Dance Routine is the best of four stakes winners out of Apogee (by Shirley Heights), a mare who won the Group 3 Prix de Royaumont. They include dual Group 3 scorer Apsis (by Barathea; sire of Group 1 Prix Royal-Oak scorer Les Beaufs) and, of course, Enable's dam, Concentric. She was unraced at two, made a five-length winning debut over 10 furlongs on very soft ground at Longchamp in April of her three-year-old season, picked up a listed contest at Chantilly in early October and then chased home La Boum in the Group 3 Prix de Flore at Saint-Cloud. Timeform rated her 107.

Concentric's second foal is the triple mile winner Tournament (by Oasis Dream), and her third is Contribution (by Champs Elysees), who was already a very valuable broodmare prospect for Juddmonte before her star sibling's career began. The Andre Fabre-trained bay won over 15 furlongs at Maisons-Laffitte as a three-year-old but dropped down in trip at four, picking up blacktype when third in the Group 3 Prix Allez France over 10 furlongs at Chantilly and when third to Highlands Queen in the Group 2 Prix de Pomone over 12 and a half furlongs at Deauville. Her final start was in a Saint-Cloud listed contest in mid-November, in which she was unplaced, and that was 10 days before her John Gosden-trained half-sister caught the eye with a winning debut over a mile on Tapeta at Newcastle. The race was a maiden contested by some well-bred fillies and the manner in which the winner pulled clear to score by three and three-quarter lengths suggested group potential.

All-weather tracks have been a tremendous addition to the racing programmes of England, Ireland, and France. They have always been an outlet for low-level horses to have more chances to compete, for smaller yards to keep going over the winter months, and for apprentices to develop their skills and acquire much-needed experience. But, in recent years, the standard of the best horses competing has risen considerably, there are a growing number of blacktype races held on those tracks, and they are now a recognised source of early opportunities for potential Group 1 stars. For those who have only come into the industry in the past decade or so, it must be hard for them to imagine what it was like before we had these venues.

Horses who have got their first win, or an early one, on an artificial track include classic-winning miler Ghanaati (Kempton), Derby runner-up and Irish Derby winner Jack Hobbs (Wolverhampton), Irish Oaks heroine Covert Love (Chelmsford), classic and multiple Group 1 ace Winter (Dundalk), Grand Prix de Saint-Cloud scorer Silverwave (Pornichet La Baule), Irish Oaks star Seventh Heaven (Dundalk), Group 1 Pretty Polly Stakes scorer Nezwaah (Chelmsford), and French mile Group 1 winner Zelzal (Deauville). Among top-level winners of 2018, Hawkbill (Dubai Sheema Classic), La Pelosa (Natalma Stakes), Skitter Scatter (Moyglare Stud Stakes), Lightning Spear (Sussex Stakes), Mabs Cross (Prix de l'Abbaye de Longchamp), and Cross Counter (Melbourne Cup) got their maiden wins at Lingfield, Kempton, Dundalk, Kempton, Newcastle, and Wolverhampton respectively.

Enable's second start was in a 10-furlong conditions race at Newbury in April 2017 and it was her stablemate Shutter Speed who was the favourite and carried the first colours of owner-breeder Khalid Abdullah. That daughter of Dansili had narrowly won a one-mile maiden on soft ground at Yarmouth the previous October, and she went on to take the Group 3 Tattersalls Musidora Stakes several weeks later before finishing only fourth to Senga in the Group 1 Prix de Diane (French Oaks) and unplaced behind Ulysses in the Group 1 Juddmonte International Stakes at York. She won that conditions race by two and a half lengths from subsequent Group 3 scorer

Raheen House, with Enable a head back in third and a six-length gap back to the fourth.

Enable beat Alluringly by one and three-quarter lengths to take the Listed Cheshire Oaks on her next start, then trounced Rhododendron by five lengths in the Group 1 Investec Oaks at Epsom, with her Chester victim another six lengths back in third. A wide-margin defeat of Rain Goddess in the Group 1 Darley Irish Oaks followed, her reputation now so strong that she was sent off favourite against the colts and older horses in the Group 1 King George VI and Queen Elizabeth Stakes at Ascot a fortnight later. She stayed on strongly there to beat Ulysses by four and a half lengths, with Idaho third and Highland Reel fourth, and then it was on to York for the Group 1 Darley Yorkshire Oaks, back against her own sex. There she made all to beat Coronet by five lengths, with Queen's Trust third and Nezwaah fourth, and that was her prep race for her first Arc.

Partnered as usual by Frankie Dettori, who had taken the mount since her third start, she hit the front a quarter-mile from home, and it was quickly evident that she was not going to be caught. She stayed on strongly on the soft ground to beat Cloth Of Stars by two and a half lengths, with Ulysses a length-and-a-quarter back in third, a length and a half in front of Order Of St George. In a season that had been witness to some brilliant performances from a number of different horses – including the runaway Group 1 Qipco Champion Stakes victory of her Timeform 136-rated stablemate Cracksman – there really was only one choice for Horse of the Year. And the prospect of her bidding for Arc glory again as a four-year-old was an exciting one.

Early-season bulletins were encouraging but then, in early May, came the shock news that she had acquired a problem with a knee and would be in a race against time to make it to the Arc. There would likely be, at most, time for a single prep race before the big one, and some began to speculate that we would never see her back on the track. Spring passed to summer, and then as autumn approached we got the news we had been waiting for – Enable was ready to return to action.

Her comeback would be in the Group 3 188Bet September Stakes over a mile and a half on the Polytrack at Kempton, one month before the Arc.

Only three lined-up against her, and although two of those were capable handicappers with no prayer of getting anywhere near her at the finish, even if she turned up a stone below her best, the other one was the top-class middle-distance colt Crystal Ocean. That Sir Michael Stoute-trained four-year-old won the Group 2 Hardwicke Stakes at Ascot in June, was a neck runner-up to Poet's Word in the Group 1 King George VI and Queen Elizabeth Stakes at that same venue a month later, and under the conditions of the Kempton race, he had to carry a 5lb penalty. It made no difference to the result. Enable made all, was briefly pressed by the colt a quarter-mile from home but easily brushed him aside. It was a hands-and-heels ride by Dettori, and the filly was eased down to win by three and a half lengths.

There is a phenomenon of which American race fans speak, called 'the bounce effect', and it now cropped up in conversation about Enable's upcoming Arc bid. It refers to how a horse who runs especially well on their first start after a long break, especially after a lay-off, can disappoint the second time. The filly would be going to Europe's top race without the race-fit edge that all of her rivals would possess, and this would, as always, be a large start-list full of top-class horses for whom a case for victory could be made for many. Dual classic star Capri took over the lead from stablemate Nelson about a furlong and a half from home, but almost immediately Enable swept past him and went clear. The previous year's runner-up Cloth Of Stars was staying on to be placed again, but three-year-old filly Sea Of Class, the exciting Group 1 Darley Irish Oaks and Group 1 Darley Yorkshire Oaks heroine, was storming down the track having overcome some trouble in running. It was close, but the post came just in time for Enable. The official margin was a short-neck, with three-quarters of a length back to Cloth Of Stars, who was the same distance ahead of fourth-placed Waldgeist.

Her great trainer John Gosden surprised everyone with a post-race comment that she'd had a "slight hiccup" between the Kempton race and the Arc – an elevated temperature. Then came the announcement that she would have one more race in 2018, the Grade 1 Longines Breeders' Cup Turf at Churchill Downs in early November. No Arc winner had ever completed that double, and the Timeform 140-rated great Dancing Brave was among those who tried, but it comes at the end of a long season for most European runners whereas Enable had run just twice. She was an odds-on favourite to beat a dozen rivals, but from the time the field swung into the stretch, it became just a two-horse race. Enable and the Aidan O'Brien-trained Magical came down the centre of the track and thrilled the crowds as the pair pulled farther and farther clear of the field. Enable beat her younger rival by three-parts of a length. There was a nine-length gap back to the third, Sadler's Joy.

Enable represents the first crop of the top-class middle-distance horse Nathaniel (by Galileo), and in 2018 the Newsells Park Stud stallion was also represented by Group 1 Premio Lydia Tesio scorer God Given, Group 2 Lillie Langtry Stakes winner Pilaster, pattern scorers Chasedown, Highgarden, and Precious Ramotswe, and several who won at listed level. She is, therefore, inbred 3x2 to Sadler's Wells (by Northern Dancer), which may or may not have any bearing on her talent.

Her dam had a Frankel (by Galileo) filly in 2017, a Sea The Stars (by Cape Cross) colt in 2018, and was then bred back to Nathaniel, whereas her talented half-sister Contribution's first foal is a Lope De Vega (by Shamardal) colt who arrived in early January of 2018. That mare was then bred to Dubawi (by Dubai Millennium).

The family has been a top Juddmonte one for a long time, and in addition to the highlights of the first two generations noted above, Enable's third dam is their homebred Bourbon Girl (by Ile De Bourbon), who chased home Unite in both the Group 1 Oaks and Group 1 Irish Oaks in 1987. In addition to Apogee, she also gave us Daring Miss (by Sadler's Wells), who could be described as being a three-parts sister to Concentric and Dance Route. She won the Group 2 Grand Prix de Chantilly three weeks before chasing home Montjeu in the Group 1 Grand Prix de Saint-Cloud. And she is the grandam of the talented full-siblings Spanish Moon (by El Prado) and Spanish Sun who won the Group 1 Grand Prix de Saint-Cloud and Group 2 Ribblesdale Stakes respectively. Lightly raced fourth dam Fleet Girl (by Habitat) was an easy winner of nine-furlong and 12-furlong races at Tramore as a three-year-old, in 1978, and she was bought by Juddmonte. She was later sold-on by them and the best of her subsequent foals was Sleet Skier (by Niniski) who won a trio of listed races, over 12 and 14 furlongs, for the Dermot Weld stable.

Both Enable and Sea Of Class are confirmed as returning to training in 2019, and hopefully Magical will do so too, although there has been no announcement yet on plans for her. Another significant candidate for next season's Group 1 Qatar Prix de l'Arc de Triomphe emerged in late November and raises the possibility that the 2019 renewal could repeat the feat seen in 1983, when it was fillies and mares who filled the first four places in the race: All Along, Sun Princess, Luth Enchantee, and Time Charter. That contender is the Sakae Kunieda-trained Almond Eye, the first-crop daughter of Lord Kanaloa (by King Kamehameha) who comes from the immediate family of European champion El Gran Senor (by Northern Dancer). She swept all three legs of the Japanese Fillies' Triple Crown (Satsuki Sho, Yushun Himba, Shuka Sho) and then smashed the track record with an impressive defeat of colts and older horses in the Grade 1 Japan Cup at Tokyo.

Win, lose, or draw – no matter how Enable's five-year-old season turns out, there can be no doubt that she is among the great fillies of European racing. She also represents one of the world's greatest owner-breeders, one of the world's greatest trainers, and with the pedigree she possesses there is every reason to hope that she can eventually go on to continue her story with a notable career at stud.

SUMMARY DETAILS

Bred: Juddmonte Farms Ltd
Owned: Khalid Abdullah
Trained: John Gosden
Country: England
Race record: 1-3111111-111-
Career highlights: 10 wins inc Qatar Prix de l'Arc de
Triomphe (Gr1-twice), Longines Breeders' Cup Turf (Gr1),
King George VI and Queen Elizabeth Stakes (sponsored by
Qipco) (Gr1), Investec Oaks (Gr1), Darley Irish Oaks (Gr1),
Darley Yorkshire Oaks (Gr1), 188bet September Stakes (Gr3),
Arkle Finance Cheshire Oaks (L)

ENABLE (GB) - 2014 bay filly

Nathaniel (IRE)	Galileo (IRE)	Sadler's Wells (USA)
		Urban Sea (USA)
	Magnificient Style (USA)	Silver Hawk (USA)
		Mia Karina (USA)
Concentric (GB)	Sadler's Wells (USA)	Northern Dancer (CAN)
		Fairy Bridge (USA)
	Apogee (GB)	Shirley Heights
		Bourbon Girl

EQTIDAAR (IRE)

The Group 1 Commonwealth Cup, a six-furlong event for three-year-olds, has been one of the best additions to the European racing calendar in recent years and the 2018 edition, its fourth one, had a tough act to follow. The inaugural running went to sprint champion Muhaarar, who was chased home by subsequent Group 1 scorer Limato, and the second edition went to star filly Quiet Reflection, from Kachy. In 2017, Caravaggio led home the subsequent Group 1 winners Harry Angel and Blue Point.

The impression on the day was that the 2018 edition may have been the weakest one yet – it was a blanket finish among the first eight home – and by the end of the season that was confirmed. The winner, fourth and seventh were unplaced in all of their subsequent outings, the third did not run again, the fifth managed third in a four-horse race after a couple of unplaced runs, the sixth has not won since returning to the USA, and the only placing in three subsequent runs by the eighth was when a well-beaten last of three in a conditions race. The one saving grace for the race was the surprise Group 1 British Champions Sprint victory of runner-up Sands Of Mali, which came after three unplaced finishes in other Group 1 events.

Eqtidaar is an early May foal and, indeed, his physical third birthday was not until two days after chasing home Invincible Army in the Group 3 Merriebelle Stable Pavilion Stakes at Ascot, so if he returns to action as a four-year-old then we could see an improved colt. The Shadwell homebred is trained by Sir Michael Stoute, who is no stranger to having horses excel as four-year-olds and older.

Eqtidaar is one of 18 Group 1 winners for the Irish National Stud's flag bearer Invincible Spirit (by Green Desert), a stallion who has 118 stakes winners to his name, and who also supplied Commonwealth Cup third Emblazoned. He has emerged as a source of successful sire sons – something that will add to the attraction of this newest star when his time to retire comes about – although not yet enough notable ones to deserve the descriptor 'sire of sires'.

The colt is the third foal and third winner out of Madany (by Acclamation), and the better of those siblings is Massaat (by Teofilo), the Owen Burrows-trained colt who chased home Galileo Gold in the Group 1 2000 Guineas at Newmarket before going on to win the Group 2 Hungerford Stakes over seven at Newbury, beating Librisa Breeze by one and three-quarter lengths. Massaat's only runs after that victory have been his third-place finish to Ribchester and Taareef in the Group 1 Prix du Moulin de Longchamp at Chantilly in September and his runners-up spot to Limato in the Group 2 Challenge Stakes at Newmarket a month later, and he will start his stallion career at Mickley Stud in Shropshire in 2019.

Madany was trained by Barry Hills, won six-furlong contests at Haydock in July of her juvenile year, was runner-up in the valuable Tattersalls Millions 3YO Sprint at Newmarket, and missed out on blacktype when only fifth to Perfect Tribute in the Pavilion Stakes at Ascot, which carried listed status that year. The mare is among a string of winners produced from one-time scorer Belle De Cadix (by Law Society), and her siblings include two horses of particular note.

Dolled Up (by Whipper) won the Group 3 Prix de Bois, was placed in the Group 2 Prix Robert Papin and Group 2 Criterium de Maisons-Laffitte, and her second foal – the first one died as a yearling – is French three-year-old Fou Rire (by Iffraaj). That Fabrice Chappet-trained filly has won twice and finished fourth in the seven-furlong listed contest won by Intello Kiss at San Siro in May.

Madany's other notable sister is four-time stakes winner and successful broodmare Zeiting (by Zieten). She is the dam of the Group 2-winning miler Combat Zone (by Refuse To Bend), of Group 3 Geoffrey Freer Stakes winner Royal Empire (by Teofilo), of Group 3 Strensall Stakes scorer and Group 1 Caulfield Cup runner-up Scottish (by Teofilo), and three stakes-placed daughters. That trio includes Zut Alors (by Pivotal), the Group 3 Prix Miesque third whose daughter

Precieuse (by Tamayuz) won last year's Group 1 Poule d'Essai des Pouliches (French 1000 Guineas).

There is plenty of blacktype to be found also under the third generation of the pedigree, but those stakes winners out of and descended from Gourgandine (by Auction Ring) achieved their honours in India, and although those include classic wins and places in that country, and horses who showed plenty of stamina, it is connections under the fourth dam that tell us more about the strength of the family.

That mare is Group 2 Ribblesdale Stakes runner-up North Forland (by Northfields) and, in addition to Gourgandine, she was the dam of Group 3 Prix des Chene heroine and Group 1 Prix Marcel Boussac third Harmless Albatross (by Pas De Seul), of Group 2 Prix d'Harcourt scorer Fortune's Wheel (by Law Society), and of Group 2 winner Libertine (by Hello Gorgeous) who was third in the Group 1 Poule d'Essai des Pouliches.

Fortune's Wheel could be described as being a three-parts brother to Belle De Cadix, Libertine has additional note as having Group 2 Lowther Stakes winner Infamous Angel (by Exceed And Excel) among her descendants, and Harmless Albatross excelled at stud. Her star son is Grade 2 winner Volochine (by Soviet Star), she was also responsible for the listed scorers Almass (by Elnadim), Ghataas (by Sadler's Wells), Kahtan (by Nashwan) and Sakha (by Wolfhound), and for two others who were blacktype placed.

North Forland, in turn, was a half-sister to Group 1 Prix Ganay and Group 1 Gran Premio del Jockey Club Coppa d'Oro heroine Infra Green (by Laser Light), and that star filly was both the dam of Group 3 scorers Ecologist (by Rainbow Quest), Green Reef (by Mill Reef) and Infrasonic (by Dancing Brave), and of Group 1 St James's Palace Stakes runner-up Greensmith (by Known Fact), and grandam of 1991's Group 1 St Leger hero Toulon (by Top Ville).

Eqtidaar is a Group 1-winning sprinter from a prolific blacktype family and is by a stallion who has a couple of top sire sons. His birth date and connections suggest that he could be capable of further improvement, and it will be interesting to see how his future works out.

SUMMARY DETAILS

Bred: Shadwell Estate Company Limited
Owned: Hamdan Al Maktoum
Trained: Sir Michael Stoute
Country: England
Race record: 14-24100-
Career highlights: 2 wins inc Commonwealth Cup (Gr1), 2nd Merriebelle Stable Pavilion Stakes (Gr3)

EQTIDAAR (IRE) - 2015 bay colt

Invincible Spirit (IRE)	Green Desert (USA)	Danzig (USA)
		Foreign Courier (USA)
	Rafha	Kris
		Eljazzi
Madany (IRE)	Acclamation (GB)	Royal Applause (GB)
		Princess Athena
	Belle De Cadix (IRE)	Law Society (USA)
		Gourgandine

EXPERT EYE (GB)

With so much hype and focus every year on young and largely unproven stallion prospects who peaked in their two-year-old season – horses who may sparkle for their first two or three years at stud before fizzling out – it is good to see that reliable veterans who continue to get good horses without challenging for championship honours not only retain support but build their profile in their later years. Acclamation (by Royal Applause) is a fine example, and such has been the way the market views sprinters these days he may have struggled if he was retiring to stud now, especially having an unfashionable pedigree.

He won three of his five starts at two, including a sales race, and he was listed placed, but he ran only twice at three and had added just a conditions race by August of his four-year-old season, and that was in a dead-heat. It was after that win that his best form emerged – a third-place finish to Oasis Dream in the Group 1 Nunthorpe Stakes, listed success at Goodwood, victory in the Group 2 Diadem Stakes at Ascot, then fourth to Patavellian in the Group 1 Prix de l'Abbaye de Longchamp. He has spent his stallion career at Rathbarry Stud, has risen from an initial €10,000 fee to the €40,000 he will command in 2019 – his 16th season – and he now has five Group 1 winners to his name, two of whom are stallions of note and two of whom look likely to earn that description in the not too distant future. The fifth one is his Nunthorpe Stakes and Prix de l'Abbaye heroine Marsha.

Both he and his hugely popular son Dark Angel have sired 49 stakes winners, and counting, with the latter being responsible for the top-level stars Battash, Harry Angel, Hunt, Lethal Force, Mecca's Angel, Persuasive, and December's Grade 1 Hollywood Derby scorer Raging Bull. Equiano's double-digit tally of stakes winners is headed by triple Group 1 standout The Tin Man, whereas Aclaim covered 160 mares in his first season at the National Stud in Newmarket, so has a large initial crop due to arrive in the coming months.

All of this augurs well for the prospects of the fourth top-level-winning son of Acclamation and he is, of course, Grade 1 Breeders' Cup Mile hero Expert Eye, the Juddmonte homebred who is joining the small but mighty stallion team at Banstead Manor Stud in Newmarket, to stand alongside the established duo Frankel and Oasis Dream, rising star Kingman, and blacktype sire Bated Breath, son of the now retired long-time team member Dansili.

Expert Eye was trained by Sir Michael Stoute and he wasted no time in advertising his star potential, kicking off his career with an eye-catching debut win over six and a half furlongs at Newbury in mid-June of his juvenile year and then putting up a performance in the Group 2 Qatar Vintage Stakes that was both visually exciting and good on the clock. He took up the running more than a quarter-mile from home and dismissed Zaman, Mildenberger, James Garfield and Seahenge by four and a half lengths and more. Although a big disappointment when coming home last behind U S Navy Flag in the Group 1 Darley Dewhurst Stakes on his final outing, he went into winter quarters with a Timeform rating of 117p, a figure he raised to 124 by the end of this year.

He was beaten by three-parts of a length by James Garfield in the Group 3 Al Basti Equiworld Supporting Greatwood Greenham Stakes at Newbury on his seasonal reappearance, having pipped Hey Gaman – a neck runner-up in the Group 1 Poule d'Essai des Poulains (French 2000 Guineas) next time – on the line. It was even more disappointing when he finished down the field behind Saxon Warrior in the Group 1 Qipco 2000 Guineas a fortnight later, but then he stormed home by four and a half lengths in the Group 3 Jersey Stakes at Royal Ascot, chased home Lightning Spear in the Group 1 Qatar Sussex Stakes at Goodwood, and beat Gordon Lord Byron by a length and a quarter in the Group 3 Sky Bet City of York Stakes in late August.

The latter and the Ascot race are over seven furlongs, but he returned to a mile for his final two starts. He didn't have the clearest of runs in the Group 1 Prix du Moulin de Longchamp at ParisLongchamp in early September but stayed on well to take third to Recoletos and Wind Chimes, beaten a head and one and a quarter lengths. Two months later he guaranteed his future stallion career with victory in the Grade 1 Breeders' Cup Mile at Churchill Downs, again staying on well in the final furlong. He won by half a length from Catapult with a trio flashing past the post together just a neck behind, and the previous month's Group 1 Prix de la Foret heroine One Master coming off worst in that photo, having to settle for fifth place.

There was some speculation afterwards as to what the 2019 plans would be for Expert Eye as, if he remained in training, he looked a natural for races such as the Group 1 Juddmonte Lockinge Stakes, Group 1 Queen Anne Stakes and Group 1 Qatar Sussex Stakes. But the decision came quite soon, and he looks certain to be a very busy member of the Banstead Manor team, especially with a starting fee of £20,000. Might he be a future mate for Enable? It would be an interesting cross.

Although Acclamation tends to be associated with sprinters, there is no surprise that this star son excelled over a mile. He is a half-brother to a mile winner, he's out of Exemplify (by Dansili), who is a mile-winning half-sister to Group 1 1000 Guineas and Group 1 Poule d'Essai des Pouliches (French 1000 Guineas) scorer Special Duty (by Hennessy), and related to a string of horses who achieved fame at a mile and upwards.

Special Duty, who also won the Group 1 Cheveley Park Stakes over six furlongs at two, had the unusual although not unique distinction of having got two of her Group 1 wins in the stewards' room. She was pipped in photo finishes for both the 1000 Guineas and Poule d'Essai des Pouliches, but Jacqueline Quest (Line of Duty's dam) was dropped to second at Newmarket, Liliside to sixth at Longchamp, and Juddmonte's filly got both races. In 2001, Vahorimix was awarded both the Poule d'Essai des Poulains and Prix Jacques le Marois after Noverre failed the post-race test at Longchamp and Proudwings was thrown out at Deauville for interference caused.

Quest For Peak (by Distant View), the grandam of Expert Eye, is out of the pattern-placed dual stakes winner Viviana (by Nureyev) and that makes her both a full-sister to seven-time Grade 1 heroine Sightseek and half-sister to dual Grade 1 scorer Tates Creek (by Rahy), a pair of Bobby Frankel-trained Juddmonte-bred standouts. Sightseek's blacktype-placed son Raison D'Etat (by A.P. Indy) stands at Calumet Farm in Kentucky and has sired winners from a small number of early runners.

Viviana's winning full-sister Willstar has produced two blacktype winners and is the grandam of several blacktype earners – the latter group featuring Group 3 Prix de Fontainbleau winner Glaswegian (by Selkirk) and dual listed scorer Preferential (by Dansili) – but the standout among them all is her excellent daughter Etoile Montante (by Miswaki). Runner-up in the Group 1 Prix Marcel Boussac as a juvenile, she was third in the Group 1 Poule d'Essai des Pouliches, took second in the Group 1 Prix Maurice de Gheest and then won the Group 1 Prix de la Foret before crossing the Atlantic where, at the age of four, she added the Grade 2 Palomar Handicap and Grade 3 Las Cienegas Handicap and finished runner-up in the Grade 1 Matriarch Stakes. Etoile Montante, another Juddmonte homebred, died at the age of 15, but her offspring include Starformer (by Dynaformer), who was Group 3-placed at Longchamp before going to the USA where she won the Grade 2 New York Stakes over 10 furlongs at Belmont Park and a trio of Grade 3 contests at 11-12 furlongs.

Viviana and Willstar are half-sisters to the Grade 1-placed Grade 2 scorer Revasser (by Riverman) and Grade 1-placed stakes winner Hometown Queen (by Pleasant Colony), the latter being the dam of Grade 2 winner and successful sire Bowman's Band (by Dixieland Band). They are out of Nijinsky Star (by Nijinsky), an unraced daughter of triple Grade 1-winning standout Chris Evert (by Swoons Son) and so are related to a host of talented horses, including Grade/Group 1 stars Chief's Crown (by Danzig), Classic Crown (by Mr

Prospector), Excellent Art (by Pivotal) and Winning Colors (by Caro). The latter famously beat the colts to take the Kentucky Derby in 1988. Chief's Crown's 47 stakes winners included seven who won at the highest level, notably Grand Lodge whose dozen Group 1-winning offspring featured the late Arc and dual Derby hero – and classic sire – Sinndar.

With family connections like these, it is clear why Expert Eye was effective over slightly farther than are many by his sire, and his combination of pedigree, performance and expected breeder support also give him every chance of becoming another notable sire son of Acclamation.

SUMMARY DETAILS

Bred: Juddmonte Farms Ltd
Owned: Khalid Abdullah
Trained: Sir Michael Stoute
Country: England
Race record: 110-2012131-
Career highlights: 5 wins inc Breeders' Cup Mile (Gr1), Qatar Vintage Stakes (Gr2), Sky Bet City of York Stakes (Gr3), Jersey Stakes (Gr3), 2nd Qatar Sussex Stakes (Gr1), Al Basti Equiworld Supporting Greatwood Greenham Stakes (Gr3), 3rd Prix du Moulin de Longchamp (Gr1)

EXPERT EYE (GB) - 2015 bay colt

Acclamation (GB)	Royal Applause (GB)	Waajib
		Flying Melody
	Princess Athena	Ahonoora
		Shopping Wise
Exemplify (GB)	Dansili (GB)	Danehill (USA)
		Hasili (IRE)
	Quest To Peak (USA)	Distant View (USA)
		Viviana (USA)

FAIRYLAND (IRE)

Tally-Ho Stud stallion Kodiac (by Danehill) never won a stakes race, but the pattern-placed horse has risen through the ranks to become one of the most sought-after stallions in Europe. He is a slightly closer than half-brother to Group 1 winner and leading international sire Invincible Spirit (by Green Desert) – representing a different branch of the mighty Danzig (by Northern Dancer) line – and although his stats lag behind those of his sibling his new fee of €65,000 is easy to understand and was not unexpected.

His early success, which included classic-placed juvenile Group 1 star Tiggy Wiggy, led to improved books, which have led to greatly increased prices for his most choice foals and yearlings, reaching a pinnacle when a filly made 925,000gns from Book 1 of the Tattersalls October Yearling Sale in Newmarket in 2017. That filly was among his juvenile stakes winners of 2018, a list that included Group 2 scorers Hello Youmzain and Kessaar, and she is a potential classic challenger for 2019.

Fairyland was bred by Tally-Ho Stud, she is trained by Aidan O'Brien, and when she beat The Mackem Bullet by a neck in the Group 1 Juddmonte Cheveley Park Stakes at Newmarket in late September she took her record to four wins from five starts, and gave her Timeform rating a boost to 112. That is quite low for a top-level winner, but this filly is bred to improve as a three-year-old, so it would be no surprise to see her increase that figure by quite a bit. The Mackem Bullet was also her immediate victim when she scored a nose victory in the Group 2 Sky Bet Lowther Stakes at York in August, and it was subsequent pattern winner Van Beethoven who chased her home when she won the Listed Cold Move Irish EBF Marble Hill Stakes at the Curragh in late May. That race is now over six furlongs, having previously been over five and, for a long time, was the first juvenile stakes race of the year in Europe – it's not now.

Her winning debut came at Naas 19 days before, and her only defeat is her third-place finish in what turned out to be a surprisingly strong edition of the Group 3 Albany Stakes at Royal Ascot in June. It was won by Main Edition, La Pelosa was a neck second, there was half a length back to Fairyland, who was another length and a quarter in front of Angel's Hideaway, who was a neck ahead of Pretty Pollyanna. The fifth arguably improved most of all and, like La Pelosa and Fairyland, she won at the highest level. The other pair went on to pick up Group 3 races.

Fairyland is by the sire of top-class mile-and-a-half horse Best Solution and she is out of a half-sister to the pattern-placed dual middle-distance stakes winner Into The Dark (by Rainbow Quest), but both of those horses are exceptions to the general rules of what you would expect of their respective sire and distaff line, and so there is no reason to expect that their young relation will match their distance preference and become a potential Oaks filly. The odds of that seem remote. Indeed, there is a chance that she may not even stay the mile of the Group 1 Tattersalls Irish 1000 Guineas – in which she holds an entry.

Kodiac gets predominately sprinters and milers, and this daughter of his is out of Group 2 Flying Childers Stakes scorer Land Of Dreams (by Cadeaux Genereux). That mare is a daughter of Group 3 Molecomb Stakes winner Sahara Star by Green Desert), who was out of Group 1 July Cup runner-up Vaigly Star (by Star Appeal), and, of course, Land Of Dreams is best known as being the dam of Timeform 133-rated sprint star Dream Ahead (by Diktat). He was a brilliant winner of the Group 1 Prix Morny and Group 1 Middle Park Stakes at two, went on to add the Group 1 July Cup, Group 1 Sprint Cup, and the seven-furlong Group 1 Prix de la Foret, and his best offspring tend to be sprinters and milers.

He began his stallion career at Ballylinch Stud, in Ireland, and is about to start his third season at Haras de Grandcamp in France, while his classic-placed, Group 1-winning miler Al Wukair is entering his second one at Haras de Bouquetot.

Queenofthefairies (by Pivotal), who is a half-sister to Dream Ahead and Into The Dark, is the dam of Fairyland and also of Now Or Never (by Bushranger). The fillies are slightly closer than half-sisters as the latter is a granddaughter of Danetime (by Danehill). She began her career with Michael O'Callaghan, in Ireland, easily winning a seven-furlong Galway maiden before chasing home Herald The Dawn in the Group 2 Futurity Stakes over the same trip at the Curragh. She then won the one-mile Group 3 Derrinstown Stud 1000 Guineas Trial Stakes at Leopardstown before finishing third in the Group 1 Irish 1000 Guineas, albeit finishing 10 lengths behind Jet Setting and Minding, who flash past the post with only a head between them. She was then a two-and-a-half-length fourth to Qemah in the Group 1 Coronation Stakes at Ascot, only beaten five lengths when fourth to Alice Springs in the Group 1 Matron Stakes at Leopardstown, and later won a seven-furlong Group 2 contest at Flemington, after being exported to Australia.

That sibling's record gives hope that Fairyland will also stay the mile, but it is not guaranteed, and if she is not a classic filly then she could be one for the Group 1 Commonwealth Cup.

The Fozzy Stack-trained Zihba (by Choisir) is another member of the family whose record could be used as an argument for her chance of staying the trip. He too represents a speedy member of the Danehill sire line, his grandam, Starchy (by Cadeaux Genereux), is a full-sister to Land Of Dreams, and he won the Group 3 Amethyst Stakes over a mile at Leopardstown in May. It must, however, be pointed out that he is out of a daughter of Galileo (by Sadler's Wells) and it is possible that his ability to stay beyond sprints comes from there.

Princess Noor is another of the stakes winners on the page and she was a Timeform 109-rated juvenile of 2013 when she won the Group 3 Princess Margaret Stakes and was runner-up in the Group 1 Cheveley Park Stakes, both over six furlongs. She was unplaced in the Group 1 1000 Guineas on her only start at a mile, but that was also her only run at three and so lack of stamina is just one possible reason for that effort. She is a daughter of classic sire Holy Roman Emperor (by Danehill) and of Land Of Dreams's half-sister Gentle Night (by Zafonic), and she was bought by the famous Barronstown Stud for 675,000gns at the recent Tattersalls December Mare Sale in Newmarket, due to Decorated Knight (by Galileo) on a mid-March cover..

We won't know if Fairyland stays a mile until she tries it, but regardless of how her three-year-old campaign turns out, it seems a fair bet that this well-related daughter of Kodiac will eventually go on to a successful career at stud.

SUMMARY DETAILS

Bred: Tally-Ho Stud
Owned: Mrs E M Stockwell, Michael Tabor & Derrick Smith
Trained: Aidan O'Brien
Country: Ireland
Race record: 11311-
Career highlights: 4 wins inc Juddmonte Cheveley Park Stakes (Gr1), Sky Bet Lowther Stakes (Gr2), Cold Move Irish EBF Marble Hill Stakes (L), 3rd Albany Stakes (Gr3)

FAIRYLAND (IRE) - 2016 bay filly

Kodiac (GB)	Danehill (USA)	Danzig (USA)
		Razyana (USA)
	Rafha	Kris
		Eljazzi
Queenofthefairies (GB)	Pivotal (GB)	Polar Falcon (USA)
		Fearless Revival
	Land Of Dreams (GB)	Cadeaux Genereux
		Sahara Star (GB)

FLAG OF HONOUR (IRE)

I came into the industry from a non-racing background, and much of my early education on the subject was from watching television broadcasts and from reading whatever books I could get as gifts, written by a generation now mostly retired or dead, in some cases long dead. I am someone who is, of course, willing and able to change her mind as more data come to hand on a subject, but fashion or popularity of a thing do not change underlying fact. This cringe-inducing 'on debut' thing is bad grammar unworthy of any serious writer, those famous marathons at Ascot and Aintree are called the Gold Cup and the Grand National respectively, that historic big race in Surrey is called the Derby, and the European classics are for three-year-olds only, with geldings excluded.

My later study of Timeform Annuals from the 1950s and 1960s solidified the latter position, with more than one essay noting that the purpose of the classics was to identify the best candidates among each crop who would hopefully go on to become the leading progenitors of future generations. Geldings were excluded for the obvious reason of being unable to breed. Indeed, geldings were excluded from all Group 1 races in Europe until 1986, when Teleprompter and Bedtime made history by being allowed to take part in the Coral-Eclipse Stakes at Sandown, finishing third and sixth respectively behind Dancing Brave and Triptych.

Geldings are still excluded from the classics, they are still excluded from all juvenile Group 1 races in Europe and, in France, they remain barred from taking part in the Prix de l'Arc de Triomphe, Prix du Moulin de Longchamp, Prix Jacques le Marois, Prix Jean Prat, and Grand Prix de Paris.

Both the Irish St Leger and Prix Royal-Oak gave up their classic status when they were opened up to older horses and to geldings, and yet the former is still referred to under that label, with those of us who consider it a non-classic since 1983 – when the four-year-old filly Mountain Lodge took the race –

called 'traditionalists'. The Prix Royal-Oak had been opened to older horses back in 1979, and geldings since 1986.

As a Group 1-winning son of prolific champion sire Galileo, Flag Of Honour will likely find a place at stud when his racing days are over, and having won the Group 1 Comer Group International Irish St Leger over 14 furlongs, that will probably be a National Hunt slot, with promotional material proclaiming him to be a classic winner because of that success, in which he beat Irish Derby scorer Latrobe by two and three-quarter lengths, for a Timeform rating of 123. It was his third consecutive pattern win over the trip, it added to a nine-furlong Group 3 success at two, and his streak ended when he finished fourth to Stradivarius in a slowly-run Group 2 Qipco British Champions Long Distance Cup over two miles at Ascot in October. That was eight days before he finished fifth behind Holdthasigreen in the Group 1 Prix Royal-Oak, a position that should have been closer to the front yet still meritorious given that he almost ran out at an earlier part of the race.

So, although I do not consider him to be a classic winner, I do consider him to be potentially a leading player in the Cup races of 2019. Whether or not he can stay the full two and a half miles of the Group 1 Gold Cup at Ascot remains to be seen because, although a son of Galileo, he comes from the immediate family of horses who are typically best at up to 10 furlongs. Those who stay a bit farther are more distant relations.

His half-sister Slip Dance (by Celtic Swing) stayed a mile but got her listed wins over five and six furlongs and her Group 3 placing over seven. Half-brother Misu Bond (by Danehill Dancer), who has sired quite a few sprint handicappers, got his listed wins over six and seven and he was only beaten by five and a quarter lengths when fifth to George Washington in the Group 1 2000 Guineas. His dual sprint-winning full-brother Foxtrot Romeo sprang a 33/1 surprise when picking up second to Power in the Group 1 Irish 2000 Guineas, whereas Air Chief Marshal – another full-brother – won the Group 3 Minstrel Stakes over seven and chased home

Alfred Nobel in the Group 1 Phoenix Stakes over six. That one's star son – then named Mont Ormel – put up a performance-of-a-lifetime effort to take the Group 1 Grand Prix de Paris two years ago, over 12 furlongs.

They are all out of mile winner Hawala, a daughter of Timeform 136-rated miler Warning (by Known Fact), but she got her distance preference from her sire, unlike her siblings Zack Hall (by Muhtathir), Afaf (by Spectrum) and Zack Dream (by Dream) who were all middle-distance blacktype performers, as could have been expected of the offspring of a daughter of the Timeform 140-rated great Dancing Brave (by Lyphard).

That mare, Halawa, won over 10 furlongs in France and was out of Hanzala (by Akarad), who won a trio of listed races from 10 to 12 and a half furlongs. That made Halawa a half-sister to Listed Trigo Stakes scorer Hasainiya (by Top Ville), and in addition to being the dam of Listed Ballycullen Stakes winner Hasanka (by Kalanisi), that one is also notable as being the third dam of Group 2-winning Italian miler Amore Hass (by Azamour).

Overall, this is a family that you could expect to produce middle-distance horse or stayer when crossed with Galileo – and that gives Flag Of Honour a chance of staying the trip at Ascot in June – but just what his dam has passed on could be crucial, as it is comparative speed that the best of her other offspring got. If he got some of that too, then a strongly-run mile and six or perhaps two miles may be as far as he'll really want to go.

SUMMARY DETAILS

Bred: Barronstown Stud
Owned: Mrs John Magnier, Michael Tabor & Derrick Smith
Trained: Aidan O'Brien
Country: Ireland
Race record: 0101-30011140-
Career highlights: 5 wins inc Comer Group International Irish St Leger (Gr1), Comer Group International Curragh Cup (Gr2), Comer Group International Irish St Leger Trial Stakes

(Gr3), TheTote.com Eyrefield Stakes (Gr3), 3rd Prix Noailles (Gr3)

FLAG OF HONOUR (IRE) - 2015 bay colt

Galileo (IRE)	Sadler's Wells (USA)	Northern Dancer (CAN)
		Fairy Bridge (USA)
	Urban Sea (USA)	Miswaki (USA)
		Allegretta
Hawala (IRE)	Warning	Known Fact (USA)
		Slightly Dangerous (USA)
	Halawa (IRE)	Dancing Brave (USA)
		Hanzala (FR)

FOREVER TOGETHER (IRE)

Winners of most of the better juvenile contests get ante-post classic quotes for the following spring. Then, when the early-season trials come around, a considerable amount of time and space is devoted to an examination of those who enhanced their prospects following a victory, or perhaps unlucky defeat, in the events expected to pinpoint the so-to-be-crowned classic stars. Even when a longshot surprises on the day, that classic scorer will at least have taken a maiden en route to their big moment. But not Forever Together.

She finished fourth and third in the mile maidens won by Who's Steph and the ill-fated Contingent on her only starts at two – well-beaten both times – and chased home stablemate Magic Wand in the Listed Cheshire Oaks on her seasonal reappearance. Then she headed to Epsom to contest the Group 1 Investec Oaks. The classic came just one week after her physical third birthday – she is a May 25th foal – and there did not appear to be any fluke about the way she stormed home to beat Wild Illusion by four and a half lengths. There was a gap of three and a half lengths back to the front-running Bye Bye Baby, who was another three clear of Magic Wand, this pair – like the winner – trained by Aidan O'Brien.

Aside from the margins and the style of her victory, it was also striking that this was her maiden success. She is, of course, not the first horse to get off the mark in a classic, or even to do so in the Oaks. Sun Princess routed the opposition by 12 lengths and more in the 1983 edition of that classic before going on to take high rank among the best middle-distance fillies of the modern era, Group 1-placed Snurge opened his winning account in the Group 1 St Leger at Doncaster in 1990, and both Ballymore and Lady Capulet were making their racecourse debuts when taking the Group 1 Irish 2000 Guineas and Group 1 Irish 1000 Guineas in 1972 and 1977 respectively.

After her classic success, Forever Together dropped back to 10 furlongs for the Group 1 Juddmonte Pretty Polly Stakes at the Curragh, but performed well below the standard and promise of her Epsom win, chasing home exposed four-year-old Urban Fox, who won by three and a quarter lengths. She returned to the venue three weeks later for the Group 1 Darley Irish Oaks and, wearing cheekpieces for the first time, she again met with defeat. Of course, her neck second to Sea Of Class looks much better now than perhaps it did on the day, although it is fair to say that her chestnut rival has improved since that July afternoon.

Forever Together was touted as a potential Group 1 Qatar Prix de l'Arc de Triomphe candidate, and she was entered in the Group 1 Qipco British Champions Fillies & Mares Stakes but was not seen out again. Her late foaling date adds an eye-catching dimension to her profile, and it would be no surprise to see her return to action as a four-year-old when the physical advantage enjoyed by many of her rivals would not be so pronounced.

She is one of 75 Group 1 scorers among a total of 288 stakes winners by Coolmore Stud's dual Derby hero and prolific champion sire Galileo (by Sadler's Wells). The great stallion beat his own great sire's tally of 73 top-level winners from 294 blacktype scorers when Magical won the Group 1 Qipco British Champions Fillies & Mares Stakes at Ascot in mid-October, then added another when Line of Duty landed the Grade 1 Breeders' Cup Juvenile Turf at Churchill Downs in early November. He is, however, still some way short of the final figures achieved by the mighty Danehill (by Danzig) – 83 Group 1 winners from 348 stakes winners.

She is inbred 3x4 to Northern Dancer (by Nearctic) and 4x4 to Special (by Forli), which may or may not have any bearing on her talent. More significant is that her big win has elevated her dam to that elite club of broodmares who have produced at least three Group/Grade 1 winners.

Green Room (by Theatrical) was unraced but as a granddaughter of Rare Treat Handicap scorer Chain Store (by Nodouble) there was always the chance that she could excel at stud, especially given what some of her relations had achieved. Hitting the Group 1 target so many times, however, could not be expected of any mare. Her unraced half-sister Rusty Back (by Defensive Play) came up with Grade 1 Santa Anita Handicap winner Heatseeker (by Giant's Causeway), half-sister Dayville (by Dayjur) is the grandam of Group 1 Gran Criterium scorer Hearts Of Fire (by Firebreak), but sadly their half-sister Spanish Fern (by El Gran Senor), who won the Grade 1 Yellow Ribbon Handicap at Santa Anita, died before getting the chance to go to stud.

They are all out of the unraced Chain Fern (by Blushing Groom), a half-sister to Peplum (by Nijinsky) and Bloudan (by Damascus). The latter is the dam of Group 2 Prix Eugene Adam winner Radevore (by Generous) and third dam of both Group 2 Hungerford Stakes scorer Richard Pankhurst (by Raven's Pass) and 2018's Group 1 Derrinstown Stud Flying Five Stakes winner Havana Grey (by Havana Gold). Peplum won the Listed Cheshire Oaks, finished third in the Group 3 Princess Royal Stakes, and her pattern-winning descendants include Hong Kong top-level mile scorer Giant Treasure (by Mizzen Mast) and US Grade 2 winners Jibboom (by Mizzen Mast) and Aviate (by Dansili).

Of course, also notable is that Chain Fern is a full-sister to Al Bahathri, the Group 1 Irish 1000 Guineas and Group 2 Coronation Stakes heroine whose sons feature Group 1 2000 Guineas and Group 1 Champion Stakes star Haafhd (by Alhaarth) and Group 2 Challenge Stakes winner Munir (by Indian Ridge), and whose descendants include four top-level stars. Triple 10-furlong Group 1 ace Military Attack (by Oratorio) did most of his racing in Hong Kong, Gladiatorus (by Silic) got his best win in the Group 1 Dubai Duty Free Stakes at Nad Al Sheba, star stayer Big Orange (by Duke Of Marmalade) landed the Group 1 Gold Cup at Ascot in 2017, and ill-fated multimillionaire Red Cadeaux (by Cadeaux Genereux) was a popular globetrotter whose tally included the Group 1 Hong Kong Vase at Sha Tin.

As for Green Room, in addition to her classic heroine, she is also responsible for Lord Shanakill (by Speightstown) and

Together Forever (by Galileo). The latter was also trained by Aidan O'Brien and the Group 1 Fillies' Mile heroine was not seen out again after finishing fourth (no blacktype) to Covert Love in the Group 1 Irish Oaks at the Curragh three years ago. Lord Shanakill, on the other hand, was trained by the late Sir Henry Cecil. He won the Group 2 Mill Reef Stakes and was short-headed by Intense Focus in the Group 1 Dewhurst Stakes at two, took the Group 1 Prix Jean Prat over a mile at Chantilly at three, and added the Group 2 Lennox Stakes over seven furlongs at Goodwood at four. He began his stallion career at the Irish National Stud, from where he sired Group 1 Prince of Wales's Stakes scorer and young Bridge House Stud sire My Dream Boat, and he is now based in Pennsylvania.

Forever Together, who has immense potential as a broodmare, was bred by Vimal and Gillian Khosla. She is a €900,000 Goffs Orby Sale graduate, and that price was easily eclipsed by her full-sister who made €3,200,000 at the 2018 edition of that auction, both consigned by Ballylinch Stud.

SUMMARY DETAILS

Bred: Vimal and Gillian Ghosla
Owned: Michael Tabor, Derrick Smith & Mrs John Magnier
Trained: Aidan O'Brien
Country: Ireland
Form: 43-2122-
Career highlights: 1 win inc Investec Oaks (Gr1), 2nd Darley Irish Oaks (Gr1), Juddmonte Pretty Polly Stakes (Gr1), Arkle Finance Cheshire Oaks (L)

FOREVER TOGETHER (IRE) - 2015 bay filly

Galileo (IRE)	Sadler's Wells (USA)	Northern Dancer (CAN)
		Fairy Bridge (USA)
	Urban Sea (USA)	Miswaki (USA)
		Allegretta
Green Room (USA)	Theatrical	Nureyev (USA)
		Tree Of Knowledge
	Chain Fern (USA)	Blushing Groom (FR)
		Chain Store (USA)

GOD GIVEN (GB)

Top-class middle-distance horse Nathaniel is among the 14 sons of Galileo (by Sadler's Wells) who have sired at least one top-level winner so far and the Newsells Park Stud stallion made it two Group 1 scorers from his first crop when God Given won the Premio Lydia Tesio Sisal Matchpoint over 10 furlongs on heavy ground at Capannelle in early November. This is the only race left in Italy to hold that status and wonders for how much longer as, once again, it was a weak affair for the grade.

God Given holds an official handicap mark of 110 – and a Timeform rating of 112 – and she had won the 14-and-a-half-furlong Group 2 DFS Park Hill Stakes on her penultimate start, beating Horseplay by a neck. In Italy, she beat the well-exposed Nyaleti by the same margin. That three-year-old picked up the Group 2 German 1000 Guineas at Dusseldorf in late May, was a distant fourth to Alpha Centauri in the Group 1 Coronation Stakes at Ascot, and beaten by a total of six lengths when third in a nine-furlong Grade 1 at Keeneland in October.

What is particularly noteworthy about her successful career finale is that she has been running over 12 furlongs and farther since she turned three, having been placed in both races over a mile at two. On the human side of things, the victory gave now-retired trainer Luca Cumani his 50th Group 1 success and British champion apprentice Jason Watson his first.

God Given has tremendous potential as a broodmare and not just because she is a multiple pattern-winning daughter of the regally related sire of dual Timeform 134 superstar Enable. She is out of one-time winner Ever Rigg (by Dubai Destination), her grandam is Group 1 Moyglare Stud Stakes heroine Bianca Nera (by Salse), and the best of her siblings is Timeform 130-rated multiple Group 1 star Postponed (by Dubawi), who is about to start his second season at Dalham Hall Stud.

He began his career with Cumani, won over seven furlongs at two, took the Group 2 Great Voltigeur Stakes at three, and added the Group 1 King George VI and Queen Elizabeth Stakes at four. It was two months after that, and shortly after he won the Group 2 Prix Foy at Longchamp, that he moved to the Roger Varian stable. He won his first four races for his new base, all as a five-year-old and including the Group 1 treble of Dubai Sheema Classic, Coronation Cup, and Juddmonte International Stakes. He then finished fifth to Found – whom he'd beaten by four and a half lengths at Epsom – in the Group 1 Prix de l'Arc de Triomphe.

He stayed in training at the age of six but only ran twice. He was a neck runner-up to Prize Money in the Group 2 Dubai City of Gold – which he'd won by three lengths the year before – and then finished third to Jack Hobbs and Seventh Heaven in the Group 1 Longines Dubai Sheema Classic. An injury ended his career, and by mid-May he had already moved into Dalham Hall Stud to recover and prepare for a stallion career that would start the following spring. He covered 112 mares in 2018.

Bianca Nera did not produce any stakes-winning offspring, but two of her daughters were listed-placed and one of those, Pietra Dura (by Cadeaux Genereux), became the dam of Grade 1-placed US Grade 3 scorer Turning Top (by Pivotal). Bijou A Moi (by Rainbow Quest) – another daughter of Bianca Nera – has done her part for the family by coming up with Group 3 Winter Derby winner Robin Hoods Bay (by Motivator).

Hotelgenie Dot Com (by Selkirk) did not quite emulate her half-sister on the track but she picked up second in the Group 1 Moyglare Stud Stakes and third in the Group 1 Fillies' Mile before going on to become the dam of Group 1 Falmouth Stakes and Group 1 Fillies' Mile star Simply Perfect (by Danehill). That classic-placed filly is the dam of nine-furlong Group 3 winner Mekong River (by Galileo) and grandam of a listed scorer in France, whereas her full-sister One Moment In Time is best-known as being the dam of Bondi Beach (by Galileo). He won the Group 3 Curragh Cup and Group 3

Vintage Crop Stakes and was narrowly beaten by Simple Verse in the Group 1 St Leger at Doncaster. It was he who was briefly awarded the classic in the stewards' room only to have the original result reinstated on appeal.

Bianca Nera also has a noteworthy sibling in Crackling (by Electric) as that granddaughter of Blakeney (by Hethersett) is the dam of Listed Warwickshire Oaks scorer Ronaldsay (by Kirkwall), grandam of classic-placed Group 3 Jersey Stakes winner and young Irish National Stud stallion Gale Force Ten (by Oasis Dream) and of dual US Grade 3 scorer Pickle (by Piccolo). She is also the direct ancestor of the listed-race winners Gusto (by Oasis Dream) and Beauly (by Sea The Stars). Birch Creek (by Carwhite), the third dam of God Given, was Group 3-placed in Italy and a half-sister to sprinter Great Deeds (by Forzando), who won the Group 3 Ballyogan Stakes and took second place in the Group 2 Flying Childers Stakes.

With her racing record, pedigree and connections, there is every reason to hope that God Given can become a broodmare of note and it would be no surprise to see her appearing in the pedigree of one or more Group 1 or classic horses in the future.

SUMMARY DETAILS

Bred: St Albans Bloodstock Llp
Owned: St Albans Bloodstock Limited
Trained: Luca Cumani
Country: England
Race record: 33-21110-4123101-
Career highlights: 6 wins inc Premio Lydia Tesio Sisal Matchpoint (Gr1), DFS Park Hill Stakes (Gr2), Betway Pinnacle Stakes (Gr3), Prix Minerve (Gr3), Betbright Aphrodite Stakes (L), 2nd bet365 Lancashire Oaks (Gr2), 3rd Darley Prix de Pomone (Gr2)

GOD GIVEN (GB) - 2014 bay filly

Nathaniel (IRE)	Galileo (IRE)	Sadler's Wells (USA)
		Urban Sea (USA)
	Magnificient Style (USA)	Silver Hawk (USA)
		Mia Karina (USA)
Ever Rigg (GB)	Dubai Destination (USA)	Kingmambo (USA)
		Mysterial (USA)
	Bianca Nera (GB)	Salse (USA)
		Birch Creek

HAVANA GREY (GB)

Like his sire before him, Galileo (by Sadler's Wells) has had an enormous influence, and there are already 14 of his sons who have sired at least one top-level winner in one of the world's Category I-listed countries. Of those, Frankel, New Approach and Teofilo have established themselves as being important stallions, and now the test of the line is to see through how many more generations the influence can extend. The latter pair have a few sons at stud, and both have one who has made a promising start with his first runners. For Teofilo, that is his Group 1-winning miler Havana Gold, a member of the team at Tweenhills Farm & Stud in Gloucestershire, and now that young son has a stallion son of his own.

Havana Grey represents his first crop and could hardly have given his sire a better start as, following a five-length maiden success in early May of his two-year-old campaign, he won two of the season's earliest juvenile stakes races, then added a one-and-three-quarter-length defeat of Invincible Army in the Group 3 Molecomb Stakes before chasing home Unfortunately in the Group 1 Prix Morny – the only time he ever tried six furlongs. He rounded off that first year with a second-place finish to Group 2 Queen Mary Stakes winner Heartache in the Group 2 Flying Childers Stakes, and he went into winter quarters with a 112 Timeform rating.

In terms of the number of races won, the Karl Burke-trained colt's second season was not as fruitful – he notched two wins and six unplaced finishes from eight starts – but he advertised himself in fine style to Irish mare owners by beating Caspian Prince by a length in the Group 2 Sapphire Stakes at the Curragh in July before returning there two months later to beat Son Of Rest by half a length in the newly promoted Group 1 Derrinstown Stud Flying Five Stakes. A patchy win-run record is not uncommon for sprinters, and this pale grey goes to stud as a Timeform 118-rated top-level winner.

He can also lay claim to being the fastest representative of the Galileo sire line, and he looks sure to prove popular in his new home at Whitsbury Manor Stud in Hampshire, the home of Group 1 sire and rising star Showcasing (by Oasis Dream). His initial fee has been set at £8,000.

Although one might be tempted to attribute his five-furlong speed to being out of a daughter of Dark Angel (by Acclamation), it should not be forgotten that the sire of a horse contributes half of the genetic make-up and his sire is out of the talented sprinter Jessica's Dream (by Desert Style) – a Group 3 Ballyogan Stakes winner who was third in the Group 2 Flying Five.

Havana Grey, who was bred by the partnership of Mickley Stud and Lady Lonsdale, made 42,000gns in Newmarket as a foal and €70,000 when reoffered as a yearling in Deauville. He is the first foal of five-furlong winner Blanc De Chine, and that half-sister to Group 3 Molecomb Stakes runner-up and triple sprint scorer Fast Act (by Fast Company) is a half-sister to the prolific duo Desert Opal (by Cadeaux Genereux) and Kuanyao (by American Post) – who won 28 races between them – and out of Nullarbor. This makes him inbred 4x3 to that mare's sire, Green Desert (by Danzig). No surprise then that sprinting was his game, and it will likely be the area in which many of his offspring also excel. He will also sire milers.

Nullarbor's half-brother Radevore (by Generous) won the Group 2 Prix Eugene Adam over 10 furlongs at Saint-Cloud and finished third to Helissio in the Group 2 Prix Niel over 12, and his dam's half-sister Peplum (by Nijinsky) won the Listed Cheshire Oaks before taking third to Always Friendly in the Group 3 Princess Royal Stakes at Ascot. It's no surprise, of course, for horses by their sires to prove effective over middle-distances, but there is plenty of mile and 10-furlong talent in the family too because the fourth dam of Havana Grey is Chain Store (by Nodouble), the stakes-winning dam of 1985's Group 1 Irish 1000 Guineas heroine Al Bahathri (by Blushing Groom).

She also won the Group 2 Coronation Stakes and Group 3 Child Stakes that year, she was the middle one in that memorable three-way photo-finish of short-heads in the Group 1000 Guineas at Newmarket, splitting Oh So Sharp and Bella Colora, and her record also included victory in the Group 2 Lowther Stakes as a juvenile. She was the dam of Group 1 2000 Guineas and Group 1 Champion Stakes star Haafhd (by Alhaarth), and she lived in retirement at Derrinstown Stud until her death, at the age of 32.

Al Bahathri was also the dam of seven-furlong Group 2 scorer Munir (by Indian Ridge), and grandam of eight and nine-furlong Group 1 star Gladiatorus (by Silic) and of Hong Kong's 10-furlong Group 1 standout Military Attack. In stark contrast, her descendants also include Group 1 Gold Cup hero Big Orange (by Duke Of Marmalade) and Group 1 Hong Kong Vase scorer and triple Group 1 Melbourne Cup runner-up Red Cadeaux (by Cadeaux Genereux).

But that's not all you'll find on the page because Bloudan (by Damascus) – the third dam of Havana Grey – was also a half-sister to Chain Fern (by Blushing Groom) and that unraced filly achieved fame as the dam of ill-fated US Grade 1 star Spanish Fern (by El Gran Senor), grandam of Grade 1 Santa Anita Handicap scorer Heatseeker (by Giant's Causeway), and of one of this year's European classic stars. Chain Fern's unraced daughter Green Room (by Theatrical) is the mare who has given us Group 1 Prix Jean Prat winner and sire Lord Shanakill (by Speightstown), Group 1 Fillies' Mile scorer Together Forever (by Galileo), and 2018's Group 1 Investec Oaks heroine Forever Together (by Galileo).

Their relationship to Havana Grey is remote, even though they're by Galileo and share a direct ancestor in Chain Store, but their presence on the page does show some of the depth there is to this famous family. He is an interesting addition to the stallion ranks, and I look forward to seeing what he can do as a sire.

SUMMARY DETAILS

Bred: Mickley Stud & Lady Lonsdale
Owned: Global Racing Club & Mrs E Burke
Trained: Karl Burke

Country: England
Race record: 21101122-00100100-
Career highlights: 6 wins inc Derrinstown Stud Flying Five
Stakes (Gr1), Sapphire Stakes (Gr2), Bombay Sapphire
Molecomb Stakes (Gr3), Allied World Dragon Stakes (L),
Better Odds With Matchbook National Stakes (L), 2nd Darley
Prix Morny (Gr1), Wainwrights Flying Childers Stakes (Gr2)

HAVANA GREY (GB) - 2015 grey colt

Havana Gold (IRE)	Teofilo (IRE)	Galileo (IRE)
		Speirbhean (IRE)
	Jessica's Dream (IRE)	Desert Style (IRE)
		Ziffany (GB)
Blanc De Chine (IRE)	Dark Angel (IRE)	Acclamation (GB)
		Midnight Angel (GB)
	Nullarbor (GB)	Green Desert (USA)
		Bloudan (USA)

HAWKBILL (USA)

The all-weather tracks have been a huge benefit to the racing industry in Britain, Ireland and France, and the number of Group 1 stars who got their maiden success on one of the artificial surfaces has been on the increase over the past few years.

Jack Hobbs, who was a three-length winner over eight and a half furlongs at Wolverhampton on his only juvenile start, chased home Golden Horn in the Derby at Epsom before taking the Irish Derby at the Curragh, and Covert Love, whose first start at three was a winning one at Chelmsford, went on to take the Irish Oaks at the Curragh, one of two Group 1 races the filly won that season. Classic and multiple Group 1 stars Seventh Heaven and Winter got their first wins at Dundalk (also the venue of Skitter Scatter's first win), Pretty Polly Stakes winner Nezwaah got off the mark at Chelmsford, Grand Prix de Saint-Cloud scorer Silverwave broke his maiden at Pornichet La Baule in France, mile Group 1 ace Zelzal won a maiden on Deauville's Polytrack, 2018's Melbourne Cup hero Cross Counter won both his first two starts at Wolverhampton, Lightning Spear won his maiden at Kempton, and even the mighty Enable began her career on an artificial surface, scoring on her debut at Newcastle, as did this year's Group 1 St James's Palace Stakes scorer Without Parole.

Hawkbill is another. He began his career with a forgettable effort over five furlongs at Newbury in mid-April of his juvenile season but showed some promise when third over seven furlongs on the Polytrack at Kempton two months later. Several weeks after that he narrowly won a maiden at Lingfield, and both his subsequent outings of 2015 were back at Kempton, an easy win in a seven-furlong nursery followed by a narrow defeat of subsequent listed scorer Steel Of Madrid in a four-runner contest over a mile.

Three all-weather wins from a total of five starts, with an official handicap rating of 98, was not a typical profile of a potential Group 1 star, but Hawkbill showed that he had improved over the winter when springing a 14/1 surprise in the Listed Newmarket Stakes over 10 furlongs, on turf, on his reappearance in late April of his three-year-old year and then took another step up in grade and added the Group 3 Tercentenary Stakes over the same trip at Ascot. The ground was soft that day, as it was at Sandown when the white-faced chestnut extended his winning sequence to six with a half-length defeat of Group 1 Poule d'Essai des Poulains (French 2000 Guineas) winner The Gurkha in the Group 1 Coral-Eclipse, thereby becoming the first Group 1 winner in Europe for his sire, Kitten's Joy (by El Prado).

It was only a matter of time before that US champion sire achieved such a feat as the grandson of Sadler's Wells (by Northern Dancer) was not only a top turf horse himself, but he is arguably the premier source of turf horses in North America. His array of stars also includes Grade 1 Breeders' Cup Turf Sprint scorer Bobby's Kitten, who ran away with a listed sprint at Cork on his only start in Europe and is now a popular member of the stallion team at Lanwades Stud in Newmarket (first foals in 2018), and, of course, 2018's Cartier Horse of the Year, Roaring Lion, whose four Group 1 wins and Timeform rating of 130 made him a shining light in what was a very good year. He is now about to embark on a stallion career at Tweenhills Farm & Stud in Gloucestershire.

Hawkbill's best win at four was the Group 2 Princess of Wales's Stakes at Newmarket, in which he beat Frontiersman by three-parts of a length, and that came a month before he chased home Timeform 125-rated German star Dschinghis Secret in the Group 1 Longines Grosser Preis von Berlin at Hoppegarten. Another month after that he was in action in Canada and failed by just a head to beat Johnny Bear the Grade 1 Northern Dancer Turf Stakes. Those three races are all over 12 furlongs, as are the two big races he won at Meydan in March of this year. First, he beat old rival Frontiersman by a head in the Group 2 Dubai City of Gold and then he trounced an admittedly not yet fully tuned-up Poet's Word by three lengths in the Group 1 Longines Dubai Sheema Classic.

When he returned to Europe, he finished third to Poet's Word and Cracksman in the Group 1 Prince of Wales's Stakes, eight lengths behind the latter, but three-parts of a length in front of the tragically ill-fated Derby-placed Group 2 scorer colt Cliffs Of Moher. He then went to Sandown for another crack at the Coral-Eclipse, but had to settle for fourth while Roaring Lion and Saxon Warrior fought out a memorable finish. Cliffs Of Moher was third. He had one final run before his retirement was announced, but although sent off favourite and leading for the early part of the race, he finished down the field as Johnny Bear won a second edition of the Grade 1 Northern Dancer Turf Stakes, this time beating Mekhtaal by half a length.

His sire was bred by Kenneth and Sarah Ramsey and spent all of his career at their Ramsey Farm until transferring to Hill 'N Dale Farms, also in Kentucky, where will soon start his second season. Of course, many in Europe will remember his sire, El Prado, who was trained by the great Vincent O'Brien and was one of the early Group 1 winners and juvenile stars for Sadler's Wells. He stood at Adena Springs in Kentucky and his total of 83 stakes-winning progeny also includes Grade 1 scorers such as Artie Schiller, Asi Siempre, Borrego, Paddy O'Prado, Spanish Moon and major US sire Medaglia d'Oro – the Jonabell Farm stallion who has given us Rachel Alexandra, Songbird, Talismanic, and many others of note.

As a Group 1-winning son of a champion sire who represents the Sadler's Wells sire line, Hawkbill will likely draw plenty of attention in his new role at Dalham Hall Stud in Newmarket, especially as he can also boast the attraction of coming from the immediate family of a champion sire whose Group/Grade 1-winning offspring include another winner of the Eclipse Stakes.

Hawkbill, one of three Kitten's Joy Grade 1 winners who are out of mares that represent the Storm Cat (by Storm Bird) sire line, was bred by the Helen K Groves Revokable Trust. The $350,000 graduate of the Keeneland September Yearling Sale was trained by Charlie Appleby, he is the second foal out of Trensa (by Giant's Causeway), and his younger half-brother,

Free Drop Billy (by Union Rags), is also about to begin a stallion career. He beat Bravazo by four lengths to take the Grade 1 Claiborne Breeders' Futurity over eight and a half furlongs on the dirt at Keeneland last year, and he is joining the roster at Spendthrift Farm in Kentucky in 2019.

Trensa was a winner at three, four and five years of age and her multiple blacktype placings included the runners-up spot in a Grade 3 handicap at Del Mar. Her half-sister Batique (by Storm Cat) was also durable, notching up seven wins from two to six years of age, and that triple Grade 3-scorer's credentials also include setting a new course record over nine furlongs at Monmouth Park. Indeed, multiple successes, above-average form, and an ability to win at the age of four or older are frequently seen attributes in the family.

Tejida (by Rahy), who is out of Batique, won only four of her 23 starts, but she was Grade 3-placed over nine furlongs and over a mile and a half as a five-year-old, and three times Grade 3-placed at the age of six.

The grandam of Hawkbill is Serape (by Fappiano), whom Helen Groves bred and raced, and the best of her five wins, from two to four years of age, came in the Grade 1 Ballerina Handicap over seven furlongs at Saratoga. Although her dam did not win at the highest level, she did beat Serape by win total and accumulated earnings. That mare, Mochila (by In Reality), was a nine-time scorer from two to four years of age, a Grade 1 Ruffian Handicap runner-up, and half-sister to the Grade 1 Breeders' Cup Mile hero and Eclipse Award winner Cozzene (by Caro).

He spent his stallion career at Gainesway Farm in Kentucky, was US champion sire in 1996 when his son Alphabet Soup won the Grade 1 Breeders' Cup Classic, and his other top-level winners include Mizzen Mast, Tikkanen, Star Of Cozzene, and the popular grey Environment Friend, whom Clive Brittain trained to win the Group 1 Coral-Eclipse Stakes in 1991. Coming from the immediate family of a champion sire boosts the prospects of both Hawkbill and Free Drop Billy doing well in their second careers.

Mochila, who was out of the unraced Ride The Trails (by Prince John), was also a half-sister to the Grade 2 Del Mar Oaks winner Movin' Money (by Dr Fager) and to listed scorer Ivy Road (by Dr Fager), with the latter being the dam of the blacktype earners Addled (by Foolish Pleasure), Devil On Ice (by Devil's Bag) and Yurtu (by Fappiano), who won 23 races between them. Her three-time winning half-sister Mesabi (by Minnesota Mac) was the dam of the blacktype-placed eight-time winner Kunjar (by Fappiano), of Wakonda (by Fappiano) – a dual blacktype scorer who got the bulk of her dozen wins from four to six years of age – and of their full-sister Funistrada, who was Grade 1-placed at two, won the Grade 2 Fall Highweight Handicap at three, was a Grade 1-placed dual stakes winner at four, and a listed race winner at five. The talented Conte Di Savoya (by Sovereign Dancer), who missed out on classic placing when fourth in the Kentucky Derby, and the Grade 2 La Prevoyante Handicap heroine Krisada (by Kris S) feature among Funistrada's progeny.

Hawkbill was an admirable and much-travelled horse who won 10 of his 24 starts, struck twice at the highest level, earned over £3.5 million in prize money, and earned Timeform ratings of 125, 123 and 123 at three, four and five years of age respectively. He is by a champion sire who represents the Sadler's Wells line, he is a half-brother to a mile Grade 1 winner in the US, and he comes from the family of a champion sire. All of this makes him an interesting new addition to the stallion ranks, and he looks like great value at an introductory fee of just £7,500. Some of his offspring may be more prominent as juveniles than he was – depending on the contribution of their dams – and his long-term potential would appear to be as a sire of milers and middle-distance horses.

SUMMARY DETAILS

Bred: Helen K Groves Revokable Trust
Owned: Godolphin
Trained: Charlie Appleby
Country: England

Race record: 03111-11103-0130122-110340-
Career highlights: 10 wins inc Longines Dubai Sheema Classic (Gr1), Coral-Eclipse (Gr1), Dubai City of Gold sponsored by Emirates SkyCargo (Gr2), Al Rayyan Stakes (Gr3), Tercentenary Stakes (Gr3), Havana Gold Newmarket Stakes (L), 2nd Northern Dancer Turf Stakes (Gr1), 127th Longines Grosser Preis von Berlin (Gr1), 3rd Prince of Wales's Stakes (Gr1), Investec Coronation Cup (Gr1), Pastorius Grosser Preis von Bayern (Gr1)

HAWKBILL (USA) - 2013 chestnut horse

Kitten's Joy (USA)	El Prado (IRE)	Sadler's Wells (USA)
		Lady Capulet (USA)
	Kitten's First (USA)	Lear Fan (USA)
		That's My Hon (USA)
Trensa (USA)	Giant's Causeway (USA)	Storm Cat (USA)
		Mariah's Storm (USA)
	Serape (USA)	Fappiano (USA)
		Mochila (USA)

HOLDTHASIGREEN (FR)

The Storm Cat (by Storm Bird) line and its various branches are typically associated with sprinters, milers and some who do well at 10 furlongs, but it is not usually a source of stayers. Holdthasigreen, however, is one of the leading performers in France at 15 furlongs and above. The prolific gelding, whom Timeform rated 116 at four and 118 at five – when trained by his co-breeder Claude Le Lay – had his most significant season at the age of six, beating Marmelo by two and a half lengths in the Group 2 Darley Prix Kergorlay two months before landing a dramatic edition of the Group 1 Prix Royal-Oak at Chantilly, after which he remained on his 2018 Timeform figure of 122.

Both of those races are over the mile and seven, the listed contest he won in July and the Group 3 Qatar Prix Gladiateur – in which he was short-headed by Called To The Bar in early September – are over a half-furlong farther, whereas the Group 1 Qatar Prix du Cadran is, of course, over two and a half miles. In that race, at ParisLongchamp in October, he was sent off favourite but chased home one-and-a-quarter-length winner Call The Wind.

Jean Gilbert's homebred gelding is trained by Bruno Audouin and he is a son of Hold That Tiger (by Storm Cat). That $1.1 million foal purchase was trained by Aidan O'Brien, won the Group 1 Grand Criterium and Group 3 Railway Stakes and finished in the Grade 1 Breeders' Cup Juvenile, but disappointed at three. He did chase home Mineshaft in the Grade 1 Woodward Stakes at Belmont Park and take fourth to Zafeen in the Group 1 St James's Palace Stakes, but classic success had been hoped for, and he was a well-beaten favourite for that year's Group 1 2000 Guineas, won by Refuse To Bend.

He spent four seasons at Ashford Stud in Kentucky, then moved to Haras de la Haie Neuve in France, and his brightest star, among a small number of blacktype horses, is the triple Grade 1-winning US sprinter Smiling Tiger. There was some stamina in the distaff side of his family, however, and his half-brother Editor's Note (by Forty Niner) won both the Grade 1 Belmont Stakes over 12 furlongs and the Grade 1 Super Derby over 10.

Holdthasigreen is out of eight to 10-furlong winner Greentathir who is, as her name suggests, a daughter of the top-class miler Muhtathir (by Elmaamul). That stallion is by a top 10-furlong horse whose siblings featured Group 1 Oaks heroine Reams Of Verse (by Nureyev), and it has been notable that some of his best offspring stay farther than he did. Dual 12-furlong Group 1 scorer Doctor Dino and 2015's Group 1 Prix du Cadran star Mille Et Mille are shining examples. So it would seem that the stamina elements from both Hold That Tiger and Muhtahtir came together to give us the French stayers' division's latest Group 1 winner, helped, of course, by the presence of some middle-distance stamina in the distaff line.

The mating had been a repeat of the previous year's one and the multiple scorer that resulted from that, Holdgreen, has won at up to two miles. Their half-sister Srilandagreen (by Sri Putra) has won over 12 furlongs, and their dam's half-sister Lady Dolpour (by Dolpour) has produced Lady Lox (by Loxias), a blacktype-placed dual winner over hurdles. Grandam Lady Honorgreen (by Hero's Honor) is by a stallion who got record-breaking sprinters as well as talented middle-distance horses, and that half-sister to middle-distance listed scorers Kingren (by King Of Macedon) and Kadgreen (by Kadrou) was out of a mare who won over obstacles in France in the early 1960s.

Holdthasigreen is an admirable stayer, albeit one who will remain vulnerable to a top-class one should he return to action as a seven-year-old, and it would be no surprise to see him add more good prizes to his record before he eventually retires. His current earnings, including breeders' premiums, stand at over €939,000 (€690,000 without them) so reaching the €1 million mark is also on the cards in 2019.

SUMMARY DETAILS

Bred: Jean Gilbert & Claude Le Lay
Owned: Jean Gilbert & Claude Le Lay
Trained: Bruno Audouin
Country: France
Race record: -40-1041113013-10123231-1011221-
Career highlights: 12 wins inc Prix Royal-Oak (Gr1), Darley
Prix Kergorlay (Gr2), Grand Prix de Lyon Etape du Defi
Galop (L), Prix du Carrousel (L), Prix Max Sicard Etape du
Defi du Galop (L) Grand Prix de Nantes Etape du Defi Galop
(L), Prix Right Royal (L-twice), Prix Hubert Baguenault de
Puchesse (L), 2nd Qatar Prix du Cadran (Gr1), Qatar Prix
Gladiateur (Gr3-twice), Prix Hubert Baguenault de Puchesse
(L), 3rd Prix Royal-Oak (Gr1), Darley Prix Kergorlay (Gr2),
Prix Max Sicard Etape du Defi du Galop (L), Grand Prix de la
Ville de Craon-Mayenne (L)

HOLDTHASIGREEN (FR) - 2012 chestnut gelding

Hold That Tiger (USA)	Storm Cat (USA)	Storm Bird (CAN)
		Terlingua (USA)
	Beware Of The Cat (USA)	Caveat (USA)
		T.C. Kitten (USA)
Greentathir (FR)	Muhtathir (GB)	Elmaamul (USA)
		Majmu (USA)
	Lady Honorgreen (FR)	Hero's Honor (USA)
		Homer Green

INTELLOGENT (IRE)

Prolific champion sire Galileo (by Sadler's Wells) has developed a good record as a sire of sires, and his promising young stallion sons include Intello, the French champion and Group 1 Prix du Jockey Club winner who is back at Cheveley Park Stud following two seasons at Haras du Quesnay. His racing and pedigree profile suggested that he would get some promising two-year-olds but excel with three-year-olds and older horses running over a mile and upwards, and so far he is on track to fulfil that potential. Listed Prix Saraca scorer Sonjeu was among his juvenile winners in 2017, and now that first crop has yielded three pattern winners: Intellogent, Regal Reality and Young Rascal, in addition to three others who were listed race winners in 2018.

Intellogent's first pattern success came in the Group 3 Prix de Guiche over nine furlongs at Chantilly. He beat Patascoy and Glorious Journey by a head and half a length, and this trio finished five lengths clear of the fourth, Efraan. A mile winner on his only start at two, the Fabrice Chappet-trained chestnut was runner-up in a listed contest at Fontainebleau in March and also only beaten by half a length when third in a conditions event over the same trip at ParisLongchamp in May. His pattern success came on his first time running on good ground – his other runs had been on soft or very soft.

It was soft at Chantilly for the Group 1 Prix du Jockey Club (French Derby) and Intellogent ran well to finish fourth in a blanket finish, beaten a half-length, a head and a head by Study Of Man, Patascoy, and Louis D'Or the latter another first-crop son of Intello. After this, he dropped back to the mile at Deauville and narrowly beat Cascadian to take the Group 1 Qatar Prix Jean Prat. His next two starts were his toughest tasks to date and he was found wanting – finishing well-beaten behind Alpha Centauri in the Group 1 Prix du Haras de Fresney-le-Buffard Jacques le Marois at Deauville and behind Recoletos in the Group 1 Prix du Moulin de Longchamp at ParisLongchamp.

Intellogent was bred by Ecurie Des Monceaux and he is a €320,000 graduate of the Arqana August yearling sale in Deauville. He is inbred 4x4 to Danzig (by Northern Dancer), his stakes-placed half-sister Lightupthenight (by Dutch Art) has won at up to a mile, and the pair are among the first three foals out of Nuit Polaire (by Kheleyf). The mare won once, as did grandam Night Teeny (by Platini), but she comes from a famous German classic family that also added to its Group 1 tally in 2018.

Nuit Polaire's siblings include listed scorer Night Serenade (by Golan) but, more notably, also the full-sisters Night Of Magic (by Peintre Celebre) and Neele. The latter was Group 3-placed in Germany before becoming the dam of Group 1 Deutsches Derby scorer Nutan (by Duke Of Marmalade) of Group 1 Grosser Preis von Berlin heroine and Group 1 Preis der Diana (German Oaks) runner-up Nymphea (by Dylan Thomas). Night Of Magic, on the other hand, won the Group 2 Oaks d'Italia, was runner-up in the all-aged Group 3 Deutsches St Leger and is the dam of classic and multiple Group 1-placed dual Group 1 Preis von Europa star Nightflower (by Dylan Thomas).

Night Teeny, in turn, was out three-time German winner Nightrockettte (by Rocket) and that makes her a half-sister to the Group 2 Preis der Diana winner Night Petticoat (by Petoski), who went on to become the dam of Group 1 Deutsches Derby star Next Desert (by Desert Style) and Group 1 Preis der Diana scorer Next Gina (by Perugino). And it is here that the latest top-level winner in the family comes in as Next Gina's dual 10-furlong stakes-winning daughter Nina Celebre (by Peintre Celebre) is the dam of the enigmatic Pakistan Star (by Shamardal). He was a three-length winner of the Group 1 Audemars Piguet QEII Cup over 10 furlongs at Sha Tin, in Hong Kong, in late April and added a one-and-three-quarter-length score in the Group 1 Standard Chartered Champions & Chater Cup over 12 furlongs a month later.

This is a solid middle-distance blacktype family and it would be no surprise to see Intellogent step up again to 10 furlongs, or even to 12 furlongs next season.

SUMMARY DETAILS

Bred: Ecurie Des Monceaux
Owned: Fiona Carmichael
Trained: Fabrice Chappet
Country: France
Race record: 1-2314100-
Career highlights: 3 wins inc Qatar Prix Jean Prat (Gr1), Prix de Guiche (Gr3), 2nd Prix Omnium II (L)

INTELLOGENT (IRE) - 2015 chestnut colt

Intello (GER)	Galileo (IRE)	Sadler's Wells (USA)
		Urban Sea (USA)
	Impressionnante (GB)	Danehill (USA)
		Occupandiste (IRE)
Nuit Polaire (IRE)	Kheleyf (USA)	Green Desert (USA)
		Society Lady (USA)
	Night Teeny (GB)	Platini (GER)
		Nightrockette (GER)

IQUITOS (GER)

Anatevka (by Espresso) raced in Germany in 1971 and 1972, winning four times and earning blacktype when runner-up in a listed contest. She was a full-sister to stakes winner Algarve and Group 3 Oettingen-Rennen scorer Antuco, her third dam was 1949's Deutsches Derby and Preis der Diana (German Oaks) heroine Asterblüte (by Pharis), and she left the world quite a legacy through the exploits of her many descendants. Her sons Anatas (by Priamos) and Anno (by Lombard) were notably talented, a Group 1-placed Group 2 scorer and a Group 2-winning champion respectively, but it is because of her daughters that we still talk about her today.

Amethysta (by Gulf Pearl) gave us the classic-placed pattern winner Apollonios (by Lombard) and was the grandam of Azzurro (by Bluebird), who won the Group 1 1000 Guineas in Australia. Stakes-placed Anna Charlotta (by Charlottown) is the third dam of multiple Group 2 scorer Alianthus (by Hernando) and fourth dam of this year's Breeders' Cup-placed US Grade 1 star A Raving Beauty (by Mastercraftsman), but it is two of Anno's full-sisters who are most significant. Allegretta, who was Group 3 placed in an Oaks Trial in England, is the dam of Timeform 132-rated Group 1 2000 Guineas winner and classic sire King's Best (by Kingmambo), of Group 3 scorer and influential broodmare Allez Les Trois (by Riverman) and, of course, of Group 1 Prix de l'Arc de Triomphe heroine Urban Sea (by Miswaki), one of the greatest broodmares the world has ever seen.

Her legacy is covered elsewhere in this volume – her descendants Athena (by Camelot) and Masar (by New Approach) won at the highest level in 2018 – and, as surely everyone in the industry knows, she is the dam of the Derby heroes and outstanding stallions Galileo (by Sadler's Wells) and Sea The Stars (by Cape Cross), among many others of note.

Allegretta's full-sister Alya was runner-up in the Group 2 Preis der Diana, and although none of her offspring was a stakes winner, she is the third-dam of Group 2 scorer Auvray (by Le Havre), grandam of Group 1-placed Group 2 winner Arrigo (by Shirocco), and grandam of Adlerflug (by In The Wings). That Group 1 Deutsches Derby star of 2007 is somewhat closely related to Galileo, so it is no surprise that he too has become a stallion of note.

Also a winner of the Group 1 Deutschland-Preis and placed in both the Group 1 Prix Ganay and two editions of the Group 1 Grosser Preis von Baden, the Timeform 123-rated chestnut spent seven years at Gestut Harzburg before moving to his breeders' Gestut Schlenderhan in 2017, with a more than doubling of his fee. His dozen stakes winners include Group 1 Grosser Preis von Bayern winner Ito, Group 1 Preis der Diana scorer Lacazar, classic-placed Group 2 winner Savoir Vivre, Group 1-placed Group 3 Prix Chloe scorer Wunder, and triple Group 1 star Iquitos. Rated 121 by Timeform as a four-year-old and 123 at five, Germany's Horse of the Year for 2016 got his latest top-level victory when trouncing Defoe by four lengths in the Grosser Preis von Bayern over 12 furlongs on soft ground at Munich in early November.

He is the best of three winners from four foals out of four-time scorer Irika (by Areion), his dam is a full-sister to a stakes-placed triple winner called Inanya, and his grandam Ingrid (by Nebos), who won once as a two-year-old, is a full-sister to Group 2 Grosser Preis von Dusseldorf third Inkognito, who won eight times. They are out of Iracema (by Konigsstuhl), who was an unraced half-sister to multiple stakes winner Illampu (by Athenagoras) and out of pattern-placed juvenile Ipameri (by Pentathlon).

The Hans-Jurgen Groschel-trained bay has now been retired and it was announced in mid-November that he will begin his stallion career at Gestut Ammerland near Munich, with an initial fee of €6,000. The stud's owner, Dietrich von Beetticher, has bought a 51% share in the horse. He was bred by Dr Erika Buhmann, and there are blacktype horses under each of the first few generations of his pedigree, but it is fair to say that the bulk of his talent seems to be due to his sire, which will make him an interesting prospect in his new role.

SUMMARY DETAILS

Bred: Dr Erika Buhmann
Owned: Stall Mulligan
Trained: Hans-Jurgen Groschel
Country: Germany
Race record: 1112-41241040-2212020-104321-
Career highlights: 8 wins inc Bayerische Hausbau - Grosser Preis von Bayern (Gr1), Grosser Dallmayr Preis Bayerisches Zuchtrennen (Gr1), Longines Grosser Preis von Baden (Gr1), Grosser Preis der Badischen Wirtschaft (Gr2), 2nd Grosser Preis von Bayern (Gr1), Grosser Preis von Baden (Gr1), Grosser Hansa Preis (Gr2), Grosser Preis der Badischen Wirtschaft (Gr2), pferdewetten.de 28th Preis der Deutschen (Gr3), Grosser Preis der Sparkasse Krefeld (Gr3), 3rd Longines Grosser Preis von Baden (Gr1)

IQUITOS (GER) - 2012 bay horse

Adlerflug (GER)	In The Wings	Sadler's Wells (USA)
		High Hawk
	Aiyana (GER)	Last Tycoon
		Alya (GER)
Irika (GER)	Areion (GER)	Big Shuffle (USA)
		Aerleona (IRE)
	Ingrid (GER)	Nebos (GER)
		Iracema (GER)

IRIDESSA (IRE)

Ruler Of The World (by Galileo) is by one of the greatest and most influential sires, he is a half-brother to a classic sire, and he comes from the famous stallion-producing family of A.P. Indy (by Seattle Slew), Summer Squall (by Storm Bird), Al Mufti (by Roberto) and Lemon Drop Kid (by Kingmambo). That made him one of the most promising new additions to the stallion ranks in 2015. The Timeform 128-rated Derby hero is a member of the Coolmore team – standing at Castlehyde Stud in Co Cork – his 2018 fee of €8,000 was down from his first-year price of €15,000, and his foal and yearling sale prices have been surprisingly poor. This made it likely that his best early runners would come from homebreds.

His fortunes may be about to pick up now that a small selection of his first crop have completed their two-year-old season on the track as he is one of two freshman sires of 2018 who have a Group 1 winner to their name. The other one is fellow Coolmore horse No Nay Never (by Scat Daddy), whose large number of winners is headed by unbeaten Group 1 Middle Park Stakes star Ten Sovereigns, plus five other blacktype scorers. Ruler Of The World, on the other hand, is responsible for Iridessa, who shot to the top end of the ante-post market for the Group 1 Investec Oaks when landing the Group 1 bet365 Fillies' Mile Stakes at Newmarket in October.

A homebred winner for Anne Marie O'Brien when she scored by four lengths over a mile at Killarney on her debut in mid-July, the filly changed hands before her next start. She was only fifth to Skitter Skatter in the Group 2 Debutante Stakes at the Curragh and then third to the ill-fated Sparkle'n'joy in a listed contest at Leopardstown – also over seven furlongs – but the return to a mile saw her storm home a length and a half clear of Hermosa at Newmarket on her final start, with Pretty Pollyanna, who may not quite have stayed the trip, another three-parts of a length back in third, followed by large gaps back to the fourth and fifth.

Timeform rated Iridessa 113p for this performance, placing her joint second among all juvenile fillies in Europe in 2018 – on their figures – equal with Group 1 Moyglare Stud Stakes heroine Skitter Scatter and 3lbs below Group 1 Prix Morny scorer Pretty Pollyanna. She holds entries in both the Group 1 Tattersalls Irish 1000 Guineas and Group 1 Darley Irish Oaks – as you'd expect – and she could be a leading middle-distance and staying three-year-old of 2019, a potential Oaks and St Leger candidate.

Her young sire – a half-brother to Duke Of Marmalade by Danehill) – also deserves a large amount of the credit for her talent because, with the notable exception of her grandam, there is nothing of note in the family for several generations.

She is the sixth foal of an unraced mare named Senta's Dream (by Danehill), she is a half-sister to two minor winners. Her dam – who is the first of only two foals out of the top-class Starine (by Mendocino) – had an Australia (by Galileo) colt in 2017, a Camelot (by Montjeu) filly in March and was then bred to Australia, so her young star may not remain her only stakes winner for long.

Starine, whose four winning siblings include Group 3 Prix Minerve third Pearlescence (by Pleasantly Perfect), died in late 2005 and the foal she had earlier that year, Media Stars (by Green Desert), won three times at up to 13 furlongs, including a seller and a claimer. This was disappointing given how talented the mare had been during her racing days, notching up 10 wins and a seven-figure earnings total, including victories in the Grade 1 Breeders' Cup Filly & Mare Turf at Arlington International, the Grade 1 Matriarch Stakes at Hollywood Park, and the Grade 2 Diana Handicap at Saratoga. She had been a multiple listed-placed stakes winner in France before that.

Starine's dam, Grisonnante (by Kaldoun) ran six times without success, her grandam, Lady Cherie (by Sir Gaylord) failed to win in seven starts, and the most striking thing about her pedigree was that she was inbred 3x3 to Caro (by Fortino). He won the Group 1 Prix d'Ispahan and Group 1 Prix Ganay, was awarded the Group 1 Poule d'Essai des Poulains (French

2000 Guineas) in the stewards' room, was runner-up in the Group 1 Eclipse Stakes, third in the Group 1 Prix du Jockey Club (French Derby) and fourth in the Group 1 Prix de l'Arc de Triomphe, and his 78 stakes-winning offspring featured standouts such as Cozzene, With Approval, Dr Carter, Crystal Palace, and Kentucky Derby heroine Winning Colors.

Another eye-catching aspect of the mare's pedigree is her little-known sire, Mendocino (by Theatrical). He won the Listed Prix Herod over a mile at Evry on his final start at two, finished a three-quarter-length third in the Group 3 Prix du Lys over 12 furlongs at Chantilly at three, and his record at stud is pretty much Starine plus little else.

All of this makes Iridessa an intriguing prospect for 2019 and, later, as a broodmare. Her victory at Newmarket made her the latest top-level winner for her 25-year-old trainer, Joseph O'Brien. He also sent out Latrobe to win the Group 1 Dubai Duty Free Irish Derby at the end of June and, in prior seasons, he won the Group 1 Melbourne Cup with Rekindling and the Group 1 Moyglare Stud Stakes with Intricately.

SUMMARY DETAILS

Bred: Whisperview Trading Ltd
Owned: Mrs C C Regalado-Gonzalez
Trained: Joseph O'Brien
Country: Ireland
Race record: 1031-
Career highlights: 2 wins inc bet365 Fillies' Mile (Gr1), 3rd Ballylinch Stud Irish EBF Ingabelle Stakes (L)

IRIDESSA (IRE) - 2016 bay filly

Ruler Of The World (IRE)	Galileo (IRE)	Sadler's Wells (USA)	
		Urban Sea (USA)	
	Love Me True (USA)	Kingmambo (USA)	
		Lassie's Lady (USA)	
Senta's Dream (GB)	Danehill (USA)	Danzig (USA)	
		Razyana (USA)	
	Starine (FR)	Mendocino (USA)	
		Grisonnante (FR)	

JUNGLE CAT (IRE)

When you have a horse who has been placed in as many stakes and pattern events as Jungle Cat has, it comes as something of a surprise that a first win at that level comes so late in his career. Godolphin's homebred six-year-old began his career in the Mark Johnston stable, winning a six-furlong Goodwood maiden and being placed in each of the Group 2 Coventry Stakes, Group 2 July Stakes, Group 2 Richmond Stakes and Group 2 Gimcrack Stakes – beaten just a nose by the following year's sprint champion Muhaarar in the latter!

At three, and now with Charlie Appleby, he chased home Adaay in the Listed Carnarvon Stakes at Newbury from just three starts, and he had been off the track for seven months when easily taking a six-furlong handicap at Meydan on his first start at four. He was then beaten by a nose in a Group 3 contest at the same venue, was fourth in the Group 1 Al Quoz Sprint, runner-up to Profitable in the Group 3 Palace House Stakes at Newmarket and then fourth behind that same horse in the Group 1 King's Stand Stakes at Ascot.

In 2017, he won a conditions race over seven furlongs at Haydock and was multiple blacktype-placed, and when he took the Group 2 Al Fahidi Fort over that same trip at Meydan at the start of the February of this year, it was his first outing since August. He beat Janoobi by three-parts of a length there and followed that with a two-and-a-quarter-length defeat of Timeform 127-rated star Ertijaal in a six-furlong conditions race at the same venue. It was no surprise, therefore, that Jungle Cat notched up his first Group 1 win shortly afterwards.

He beat now dual Grade 1 Breeders' Cup Turf Sprint star Stormy Liberal by half a length in the Group 1 Al Quoz Sprint over six furlongs, also at Meydan, and with that one's stablemate Conquest Tsunami another length and a half back in third and Irish raider Washington DC fourth. Jungle Cat was then off the track until late September when, on the first of the Group 1 outings in Australia, he short-headed Dollar For Dollar in the Sir Rupert Clarke Invitation Stakes over seven furlongs. The mile was perhaps to blame for his disappointing performance next time, but then be bounced back over six furlongs to force a dead-heat with Pierata for third in the Group 1 VRC Sprint Classic at Flemington, just a neck and one and a half lengths behind Santa Ana Lane and In Her Time, and with Redzel three-parts of a length back in fifth.

Jungle Cat is one of nine Group 1 stars for Darley's notable international sire Iffraaj (by Zafonic), a horse who himself did not even earn any blacktype until he was four years old. He took the Group 2 Park Stakes over seven furlongs at Goodwood that year, repeated the feat at five, added the Group 2 Lennox Stakes at Goodwood, and failed narrowly to beat Les Arcs in the Group 1 July Cup. He stands at Dalham Hall Stud, his four-time Group 1-winning miler Ribchester is about to start his second season at Kildangan Stud, and his son Wootton Bassett came up with classic star and young fellow Haras d'Etreham-based stallion Almanzor from his first crop. Iffraaj also has the Group 1-placed, Group 2-winning sprinter Hot Streak at stud (Tweenhills Farm & Stud) and that chestnut's first crop made up to 220,000gns at the yearling sales in October.

All of this augurs well for the prospects of Jungle Cat who, like mile Group 1 star Rizeena, is out of a mare from the Storm Cat (by Storm Bird) line.

His siblings include the dual Grade 3-placed six-figure earner Texas Wildcatter (by Monarchos), and his dam is Mike's Wildcat (by Forest Wildcat), a lightly raced and speedy juvenile stakes winner whose blacktype-placed dam, Mistyray (by In Reality), won seven times from two to four years of age. There are some blacktype horses in the next generation of the pedigree, including Mistyray's listed-winning half-sister Speier's Hope (by Minnesota Mac) and a pair of South American graded scorers, but it would seem fair to say that Jungle Cat is the best horse the family has produced in some time and that Iffraaj upgraded the page.

Jungle Cat looks likely to get some speedy and precocious juveniles – as he was at that age – and to become a source of sprinters and milers. The contribution of the mares will likely be influential in how many he can get who win over 10 furlongs, and it would be no surprise to see him get one or more classic runners in not too distant future.

SUMMARY DETAILS

Bred: Darley
Owned: Godolphin
Trained: Charlie Appleby
Country: England
Race record: 3132320-020-1242400-2214022100-111103-
Career highlights: 8 wins inc Al Quoz Sprint (Gr1), Sir Rupert Clarke Invitation Stakes (Gr1), Al Fahidi Fort Stakes (Gr2), 2nd Gimcrack Stakes (Gr2), July Stakes (Gr2), Palace House Stakes (Gr3), Meydan Sprint (Gr3-twice), Criterion Stakes (Gr3), City Plate Stakes (L), 3rd VRC Sprint Classic (Gr1), Coventry Stakes (Gr2), Richmond Stakes (Gr2)

JUNGLE CAT (IRE) - 2012 bay horse

Iffraaj (GB)	Zafonic (USA)	Gone West (USA)
		Zaizafon (USA)
	Pastorale (GB)	Nureyev (USA)
		Park Appeal
Mike's Wildcat (USA)	Forest Wildcat (USA)	Storm Cat (USA)
		Victoria Beauty (USA)
	Old Flame (USA)	Black Tie Affair
		Mistyray (USA)

KEW GARDENS (IRE)

He was well-beaten in the Derby and a four-length seventh to Enable in the Qatar Prix de l'Arc de Triomphe, but Kew Gardens, a Group 2-placed 10-furlong listed scorer at two, was one of the best three-year-olds in Europe in 2018. Timeform rated him 127, placing him fifth in the running order, behind Roaring Lion (130), Sea Of Class (129), Alpha Centauri (128) and Magical (128), and so the second-best colt of his age group.

He was a well-beaten third in the Listed Feilden Stakes on his seasonal reappearance and then chased home Knight To Behold in the Listed Derby Trial at Lingfield before finishing down the field at Epsom, but then his form took a leap forward. He trounced Southern France by four and a half lengths in the Group 2 Queen's Vase over 14 furlongs at Royal Ascot in June, beat Neufbosc by a length and a quarter to take the Group 1 Juddmonte Grand Prix de Paris at ParisLongchamp in July, then finished an honourable third to Old Persian (received 2lbs) and subsequent Group 1 Melbourne Cup hero Cross Counter (received 5lbs) in the Group 2 Sky Bet Great Voltigeur Stakes at York. He was only beaten by a head and one and a half lengths, and he had Wells Farhh Go another three lengths behind in fourth.

This made the son of Galileo (by Sadler's Wells) a leading contender for the final classic of the year – the Group 1 William Hill St Leger Stakes at Doncaster – and he duly landed the spoils in style, hitting the front a quarter of a mile from home and beating rising star and race favourite Lah Ti Dar by two and a quarter lengths, with old rival Southern France another four and a half lengths back in third, ahead of Derby runner-up Dee Ex Bee and Old Persian. His good performance in the Arc followed three weeks later.

Yet another top-class horse bred by the famous Barronstown Stud in Ireland, Kew Gardens is a half-brother to Group 3-winning sprinter and Group 1 Prix Maurice de

Gheest runner-up Thawaany (by Tamayuz), and he is out of Chelsea Rose (by Desert King), the Group 1 Moyglare Stud Stakes heroine of 2004. She went on to wins stakes races at nine and 12 furlongs at three, she was Group 1-placed over 10 furlongs in Italy, and gave Alexander Goldrun a fright in the Group 1 Pretty Polly Stakes at the Curragh as a four-year-old, getting within a neck of the multiple Group 1 star at the line.

The mare's half-brother European (by Great Commotion) won the Listed Amethyst Stakes over a mile at Leopardstown and was Grade 3 placed at Keeneland, and they were among 10 winners out of one-time scorer Cinnamon Rose (by Trempolino), a half-sister to Group 2 Prix Eugene Adam winner and Grade 1 San Juan Capistrano Invitational Handicap runner-up River Warden (by Riverman). There are several other stakes winners under that third generation of the family, and its branches, including Cinnamon Rose's eight-and-a-half-furlong, Grade 3-winning half-sister Sweettuc (by Spectacular Bid), and if you go back another generation then you will find that third dam Sweet Simone (by Green Dancer) was a half-sister to Serenita (by Lyphard), a stakes-placed mare whose many blacktype descendants include several who won at Group/Grade 2 level.

Although each ancestor in the fifth generation of a pedigree contributes only 1.125% of the genetic make-up of the current individual, it is worth noting that the fifth dam of Kew Gardens is Prix Penelope scorer Senones (by Prince Bio) and she was a full-sister to Timeform 135-rated champion Sicambre. His only defeat in nine starts was when runner-up in the Prix Morny in 1950, he won the Grand Criterium that same year, and his string of wins at three featured the Prix du Jockey Club (French Derby) over 12 furlongs and the Grand Prix de Paris over 15 furlongs. He then went on to a hugely successful stallion career in which his roll of honour featured classic stars such as Ambergris (Irish Oaks), Belle Sicambre (Prix de Diane), Cambremont (Poule d'Essai des Poulains), Celtic Ash (Belmont Stakes), Hermieres (Prix de Diane) and Sicarelle (Oaks), among others of note.

Kew Gardens is a classic winner, a dual Group 1 star with a Timeform rating to match, and he has accumulated more than £920,000 in prize money, so far. There would not appear to be any reason why he won't be at least as good as a four-year-old, and he could be one of Europe's top older horses from 12 furlongs and upwards in 2019. Beyond that, there will no doubt be a stallion career in his future, and being a Galileo horse with a direct ancestor who was a full-sister to a major sire will make him an interesting prospect.

SUMMARY DETAILS

Bred: Barronstown Stud
Owned: Derrick Smith, Mrs John Magnier & Michael Tabor
Trained: Aidan O'Brien
Country: Ireland
Race record: 01241-32011310-
Career highlights: 5 wins inc William Hill St Leger Stakes (Gr1), Juddmonte Grand Prix de Paris (Gr1), Queen's Vase (Gr2), Godolphin Flying Start Godolphin Stakes (L), 2nd Willis Towers Watson Champions Juvenile Stakes (Gr3), Betfred Derby Trial Stakes (L), 3rd Sky Bet Great Voltigeur Stakes (Gr2), bet365 Feilden Stakes (L)

KEW GARDENS (IRE) - 2015 bay colt

Galileo (IRE)	Sadler's Wells (USA)	Northern Dancer (CAN)
		Fairy Bridge (USA)
	Urban Sea (USA)	Miswaki (USA)
		Allegretta
Chelsea Rose (IRE)	Desert King (IRE)	Danehill (USA)
		Sabaah (USA)
	Cinnamon Rose (USA)	Trempolino (USA)
		Sweet Simone (FR)

KHAN (GER)

Khan was fourth in a listed contest at Dusseldorf a month before he won his maiden – an almost 12-furlong contest on very soft ground at Strasbourg in early May of his three-year-old season – and since then he has been highly tried and often found wanting. He picked up third place in the all-aged Group 3 Deutsches St Leger over a mile and six at Dortmund last year, was fifth behind Guignol in the Group 1 Grosser Preis von Bayern – he was Timeform-rated 114 in 2017 – and then managed just one placing from seven starts in 2018.

Those recent defeats included fifth to Dschingis Secret in the Group 2 Grosser Hansa-Preis at Hamburg in July and finishing well-beaten behind Best Solution in both the Group 1 Grosser Preis von Berlin at Hoppegarten in August and Group 1 Grosser Preis von Baden at Baden-Baden in early September, but then he somehow managed to put up a performance-of-a-lifetime effort at Cologne three weeks later, also over 12 furlongs. The ground was soft, he hit the front three and a half furlongs from home, fought off a determined challenge from Walsingham, and then pulled away to win by six lengths. The race was the Group 1 Preis von Europa, last year's Group 1 Deutsches Derby scorer, Windstoss, was third, and the *Star Trek* fan in me cannot help but smile at the idea of a longshot with his name spoiling the day of some better-fancied rivals.

The Henk Grewe-trained colt ran once more, this time in the Grade 1 Pattison Canadian International Stakes over 12 furlongs on good ground at Woodbine, but he beat only one home as Desert Encounter and Thundering Blue led home a one-two for British-trained horses.

Khan is the first Group 1 winner for his sire in a Category I-listed country and that stallion is the German-based Santiago (by Highest Honor), who got his best win the Group 2 Premio Ribot over a mile in Italy. He is not, however, the only one of his sire's sons to catch the attention on the international stage.

Some will remember Chopin, who ran away with a Group 3 contest over eight and a half furlongs at Krefeld before finishing seventh to Ruler Of The World in the Group 1 Investec Derby at Epsom, beaten less than four lengths. He was unplaced at Royal Ascot next time but made another trip to England the following spring to finish fourth to Olympic Glory in the Group 1 Lockinge Stakes at Newbury. The horse then spent a season with Ger Lyons in Ireland – although was unplaced in all four starts – before moving to Asia, where he was a winner over 10 furlongs in Bahrain before running out a four-length winner of the prestigious H.H. The Emirs Trophy over 12 furlongs at Doha, in Qatar – a local Group 1.

But back to Khan, a horse for whom there may possibly be a chance at stud now that he's a Group 1-winning half-brother to Group 1 Deustches Derby, Group 1 Grosser Preis von Baden and Group 1 Rheinland-Pokal star Kamsin (by Samum). That horse moved to Haras d'Etreham in 2017 and his roll of honour is headed by this year's Grade 1 Grande Steeple-Chase de Paris hero On The Go.

Their dam is the German Group 3 scorer Kapitol (by Winged Love), their siblings also include Group 1-placed pattern winner Kapitale (by Dubawi) and listed scorer Kashmar (by Samum) – both fillies – and their dam's winning half-sister Kamakura (by Exit To Nowhere) is the dam of Kamellata (by Pomellato), a four-time winner whose pieces of blacktype include a listed win and a Group 2 third. Karlshorst (by Surumu), the winning grandam of Khan and Kamsin, is a half-sister to Cheltenham Festival scorer Kadi (by Shareef Dancer), who won the 1995 edition of the Mildmay of Flete Challenge Cup Chase.

Khan's Group 1 win appears to have been something of a fluke, but with his pedigree, there will no surprise if he goes on to become a successful National Hunt stallion.

SUMMARY DETAILS

Bred: Gestut Karlshof
Owned: Darius Racing
Trained: Henk Grewe

Country: Germany
Race record: -41003230-0000010-
Career highlights: 2 wins inc 56th Preis von Europa (Gr1),
3rd 133rd Deutsches St Leger (Gr3)

KHAN (GER) - 2014 bay colt

Santiago (GER)	Highest Honor (FR)	Kenmare (FR)
		High River (FR)
	Serenata (GER)	Lomitas (GB)
		Secret Energy (USA)
Kapitol (GER)	Winged Love (IRE)	In The Wings
		J'ai Deux Amours (FR)
	Karlshorst (GB)	Surumu (GER)
		Kaisertreue (GER)

KITESURF (GB)

Classic-winning miler Dubawi (by Dubai Millennium) is well established among the world's leading stallions and the Dalham Hall Stud veteran has now had 38 individual Group/Grade 1 winners among an overall total of 161 blacktype scorers. In 2018, his top-level winners were Benbatl, North America, Wild Illusion, the undefeated juvenile stars Quorto and Too Darn Hot, and Godolphin's four-year-old filly Kitesurf.

She was unraced at two, began her career with a couple of middle-distance runs at Compiegne, and then stepped up into blacktype company, a level at which she has remained for every one of her 11 subsequent outings over two years. She was runner-up in that initial one – an 11-furlong listed contest at Chantilly – but then won the Group 3 Prix de Royaumont over a furlong farther at the same venue before finishing down the field behind Senga in the Group 1 Prix de Diane (French Oaks). She was also unplaced behind Bateel at Deauville next time and behind Ice Breeze in the Group 1 Prix Royal-Oak at Saint-Cloud, but between those runs she was third to The Juliet Rose and Listen In – beaten by a short-neck and a head – in the Group 2 Qatar Prix de Royallieu on soft ground at Chantilly.

There may be a temptation to retire a well-bred filly with good blacktype credentials at the end of her three-year-old season, but Godolphin kept Kitesurf in training for another season and was rewarded with Group 1 success at ParisLongchamp in September when she beat Magic Wand by a head in the Qatar Prix Vermeille. This came a month after she had run out a three-and-a-half-length winner of the Group 2 Darley Prix de Pomone over a half-furlong farther at Deauville, and added to her earlier Group 3 Prix Allez France victory over 10 furlongs in April when she beat old rival Listen In by two lengths.

Her final start was her also her first international trip as she headed to Ascot for the Group 1 Qipco British Champions Fillies & Mares Stakes at Ascot. The ground came up soft – she'd won and been pattern-placed in similar conditions in the past – but although she looked briefly as though she might get involved in the finish, she weakened in the final furlong to finish fourth. Magical won by a length from Coronet, with Lah Ti Dar three-parts of a length back in third, but three and a half lengths clear of Kitesurf.

Kitesurf was bred by Peter Winkworth and she has a great deal of potential as a future broodmare. Her sire has already established himself as a successful damsire – 2018's Group 1 Jebel Hatta scorer Blair House (by Pivotal) is just one example – and she comes from a prolific blacktype family whose notable winners include a classic star. She is the first foal of her dam, her Derby-entered two-year-old half-brother Surfman (by Kingman) was an odds-on winner of an eight-and-a-half-furlong Nottingham maiden in early November, and her dam is the talented middle-distance runner Shimmering Surf (by Danehill Dancer).

That mare won the Group 3 Pinnacle Stakes at Haydock and was runner-up in the Group 2 Lancashire Oaks, and she is out of 10-furlong listed scorer and Group 2 Ribblesdale Stakes fourth (no blacktype) Sun On The Sea (by Bering), a half-sister to the pattern-placed stakes winner Beau Temps (by Mtoto). They are out of Group 3 Prix de Psyche runner-up Shimmer (by Green Dancer) who is, in turn, a daughter of Group 3 Prix Corrida winner and Group 3 Prix de Royallieu second Radiance (by Blakeney). This is clearly a middle-distance family.

Shimmer, the third dam of Kitesurf, has three winning siblings and one of those is Shining Water (by Riverman). She won just once, in France as a three-year-old, and her four successful offspring included the successful full-siblings Norton Sound (by Bering) and Blue Water. The former was third in the Group 3 Prix La Force but the latter was a listed race winner who finished third in the Group 3 Prix de Flore. They could be described as being three-parts siblings to Sun

On The Sea, and what makes that interesting is Blue Water's broodmare record.

She had just five foals, but three of those are relevant here. Indian Creek was best of them on the track, and he had the distinction of being a rare middle-distance star for long-time Irish National Stud flag bearer Indian Ridge (by Ahonoora) – High Pitched and Sights On Gold were others. He won the Group 2 Hardwicke Stakes, Group 3 Earl of Sefton Stakes, and Group 3 Gordon Richards Stakes, the races in which he was placed included the Group 1 Prince of Wales's Stakes and two editions of the Group 1 Champion Stakes, and Timeform rated him 117 at three plus 119 at four and five.

His full-brother Desert Dew was runner-up in the Group 3 Dee Stakes at Chester, and the third sibling of note is their three-time winning half-sister Honorine (by Mark Of Esteem, the mare whose four blacktype offspring are headed by Group 1 Irish Derby and Grade 1 Secretariat Stakes winner Treasure Beach (by Galileo). He was a champion in Ireland, was runner-up in the Group 1 Investec Derby at Epsom, Grade 1 placed in both the USA and Canada, and the Florida-based stallion shuttles to Argentina, where he recently got his first Grade 1 winner when daughter Mirta landed a top-level contest over 10 furlongs at San Isidro.

Treasure Beach's half-brother Elidor (by Cape Cross) has won a 14-furlong listed contest in England and been third in the Group 2 Curragh Cup in Ireland, half-sister Honor Bound (by Authorized) on the Listed Oaks Trial Stakes at Lingfield, and four-year-old Count Octave (by Frankel) has been placed in both the Group 2 Queen's Vase and Group 2 Jockey Club Stakes, over 14 furlongs and two miles respectively.

With the amount of stamina in her pedigree, combined with her own racing record over middle-distances, it would be no surprise to see Kitesurf bred to milers at stud, possibly ones who also had enough speed to win or be placed in good company over six or seven furlongs. She is the sort of filly who could go on to produce a classic winner.

SUMMARY DETAILS

Bred: Peter Winkworth
Owned: Godolphin SNC
Trained: Andre Fabre
Country: France
Race record: -31210030-104114-
Career highlights: 5 wins inc Qatar Prix Vermeille (Gr1), Darley Prix de Pomone (Gr2), Prix Allez France Longines (Gr3), Prix de Royaumont (Gr3), 2nd Prix de la Seine (L), 3rd Qatar Prix de Royallieu (Gr2)

KITESURF (GB) - 2014 bay filly

Dubawi (IRE)	Dubai Millennium (GB)	Seeking The Gold (USA)
		Colorado Dancer
	Zomaradah (GB)	Deploy
		Jawaher (IRE)
Shimmering Surf (IRE)	Danehill Dancer (IRE)	Danehill (USA)
		Mira Adonde (USA)
	Sun On The Sea (IRE)	Bering
		Shimmer (FR)

LA PELOSA (IRE)

Classic-placed Group 1 sprint star Danehill (by Danzig) not only forged one of the two most powerful branches of his great sire's line, but the dynasty-maker set and holds the world record for both the number of Group/Grade 1 winners sired (83) and the number of individual stakes winners (348). His sons have long been prized as stallions, and there was plenty of excitement about the addition of classic-placed European sprint champion Mozart to Coolmore's stallion team. Sadly, the Group 1 July Cup and Group 1 Nunthorpe Stakes star died in May of that first season – 2002. Eight of the 100 foals by him who arrived the following year went on to become stakes winners.

Amadeus Wolf won the Group 1 Middle Park Stakes, Group 2 Duke of York Stakes and Group 2 Gimcrack Stakes but has had only moderate success at stud, Rebellion was a seven-furlong Grade 2 scorer at Keeneland and won the Breeders' Cup Dirt Mile before going on to sire winners in Canada – as Grade 3 winner Stratham did in Argentina – whereas Mozart's daughters include the stakes-winning sprinter Absolutelyfabulous, dam of Group 1 Irish 2000 Guineas and Grade 1 Breeders' Cup Turf star Magician (by Galileo) who will be standing in France in 2019.

Mozart's sole crop also included Dandy Man. A stakes winner at two, Group 3 Palace House Stakes winner at three, and Group 1-placed stakes winner at four, the talented sprinter has spent his stallion career at Ballyhane Stud in Ireland and got his second top-level winner when the Charlie Appleby-trained juvenile La Pelosa won the Grade 1 Natalma Stakes over a mile on firm turf at Woodbine in mid-September. The form of that Canadian race appears to be below what one would expect of the level here, but this filly had been placed three times in blacktype company in England, including when runner-up in what turned out to be a remarkably strong edition of Royal Ascot's Group 3 Albany Stakes.

This came a month after her three-length winning debut over six furlongs on the Polytrack at Kempton – adding her name to a long and growing list of European-trained top-level winners who have got their initial score on an artificial track (see the essay on Cross Counter) – and she was a neck runner-up to Main Edition. That filly went on to further pattern success later in the year – as did fourth-placed Angel's Hideaway – half-length third Fairyland went on to take the Group 1 Cheveley Park Stakes, and subsequent Group 1 Prix Morny star Pretty Pollyanna was a close fifth.

She had a chance to put her newfound form to the test in the Grade 1 Breeders' Cup Juvenile Fillies Turf over the same trip at Churchill Downs in early November, on ground described as yielding, but she finished only tenth, as exciting Irish-born US filly Newspaperofrecord stormed home by almost seven lengths from the Kevin Ryan-trained pattern winner East, with the Aidan O'Brien-trained Just Wonderful another length back in fourth.

La Pelosa will likely bounce back from that performance and, given that we already know that she stays a mile, it would be no surprise to take up her entry in the Group 1 Tattersalls Irish 1000 Guineas in May. She will need to improve on what she achieved at two, but she could have a rewarding season at seven furlongs and a mile, even if she may need to travel a bit. Being a daughter of Dandy Man and out of a Bushranger (by Danetime) mare, however – which makes her inbred 3x4 to Danehill – it seems unlikely that she will stay farther, even though some of her relations have done so.

She was bred by Elton Lodge Stud, made €52,000 in Goffs as a foal, and joined Godolphin after being bought for 280,000gns at the Tattersalls Craven Breeze-Up Sale in mid-April. The first foal out of an unraced mare called Lauren's Girl, her Hallowed Crown (by Street Sense) half-sister made €62,000 at the Tattersalls Ireland September Yearling Sale, and they have a first-crop Mehmas (by Acclamation) half-sister who was born in February.

Grandam Piacenza (by Darshaan) won once as a three-year-old in France, and the best of her six winners are the

Group 3 Prix Eclipse scorer Perugina (by Highest Honor) and Group 3 Prix Minerve third Sovana (by Desert King). That pair have produced a dozen winners between them at stud, but it is the latter who has excelled as she is the dam of Bocca Baciata (by Big Bad Bob), Kalsa (by Whipper), and Topeka (by Whipper). The latter won the Group 3 Prix Miesque and finished third in the Group 1 Poule d'Essai des Pouliches (French 1000 Guineas), her full-sister won the Group 3 Prix Edmond Blanc over a mile, and their younger sibling was a high-class filly in Ireland.

Bocca Baciata was trained by Jessica Harrington, her five wins included the Group 2 Kilboy Estate Stakes and Group 3 Dance Design Stakes – both over nine furlongs at the Curragh – and the races in which she was placed featured the Group 1 Pretty Polly Stakes and Group 2 Blandford Stakes, both over 10 furlongs. It should be noted, however, that one would expect the offspring of the late Big Bad Bob (by Bob Back) to stay that trip, and farther, whereas Whipper (by Miesque's Son) is associated with sprinters and milers.

Stakes-placed Kahara (by Habitat), the third dam of La Pelosa, is the dam of dual Danish Eclipse Stakes winner Silvestro (by Zino), a prolific middle-distance star in Scandinavia, and her various blacktype-earning descendants include King Air (by Kingsalsa), who won the Group 2 Premio Ribot over a mile. Starina (by Crepello) is the fourth dam, she won the Listed Prix Finlande, was out of Falmouth Stakes winner Caprera (by Abernant) and is a direct descendant of 1933's July Cup heroine and 1000 Guineas third Myrobella (by Tetratema). That star is the ninth dam of La Pelosa, so makes no contribution to the current filly, but what her presence in the lineage shows is that this is a distaff line that has a very long history of being associated with speed at up to a mile.

It will, therefore, be interesting to see how La Pelosa's career on the track turns out, and she also has the potential to do well as a broodmare. As for Dandy Man, his current career total of just nine stakes winners also included Group 1 Hong Kong Sprint winner Peniaphobia plus Grade 2 Twilight Derby scorer River Boyne, who was a half-length runner-up to

Raging Bull in the Grade 1 Hollywood Derby at the start of December, and two-year-old Comedy, who won the Group 3 Darley Prix de Cabourg at Deauville.

SUMMARY DETAILS

Bred: Elton Lodge Stud
Owned: Godolphin
Trained: Charlie Appleby
Country: England
Race record: 1203210-
Career highlights: 2 wins inc Natalma Stakes (Gr1), 2nd german-thoroughbred.com Sweet Solera Stakes (Gr3), Albany Stakes (Gr3), 3rd British Stallion Studs EBF Star Stakes (L)

LA PELOSA (IRE) - 2016 bay filly

Dandy Man (IRE)	Mozart (IRE)	Danehill (USA)
		Victoria Cross (USA)
	Lady Alexander (IRE)	Night Shift (USA)
		Sandhurst Goddess
Lauren's Girl (IRE)	Bushranger (IRE)	Danetime (IRE)
		Danz Danz (GB)
	Piacenza (IRE)	Darshaan
		Kahara

LANCASTER BOMBER (USA)

It's hard to believe that Lancaster Bomber won only twice in his 18-race career. He was multiple Group 1-placed at two and three years of age – Timeform-rated 113 and 122 respectively – and retired to the National Stud in Newmarket as the earner of over £1 million in prize money to go with a profile that was developed in four countries on two continents. Timeform raised him to 125 after his two-length defeat of ill-fated Derby-placed Group 2 scorer Cliffs Of Moher in the Group 1 Tattersalls Gold Cup at the Curragh in late May, what proved to be his final start.

His dam Sun Shower (by Indian Ridge) was only placed, but his triple Group 3-winning half-brother Mull Of Killough (by Mull Of Kintyre), who was her first foal, won nine times in his career, one ahead of the final tally of his multiple Group 1-winning half-brother Excelebration (by Exceed And Excel), a Timeform 133-rated star who had the misfortune to run up against the great Frankel several times. Their dam had been exported to India after he was born and the second of her multiple winners out there was prolific blacktype scorer Shivalik Showers (by Dancing Forever), who has won a total of 14 times to date. But Lancaster Bomber won just two. The mare moved to the US in 2012 and had full-brothers to her latest star in 2017 and 2018.

He chased home World Approval in both the Grade 1 Breeders' Cup Mile at Del Mar and the Grade 1 Ricoh Woodbine Mile Stakes in Canada, he was runner-up to his brother's star son Barney Roy in the Group 1 St James's Palace Stakes at Ascot and to Churchill in the Group 1 Dewhurst Stakes at Newmarket, fourth behind that same star in the Group 1 2000 Guineas, and third this year to Rhododendron and Lightning Spear in the Group 1 Juddmonte Lockinge Stakes at Newbury. It is an admirable record and one that fully entitles him to his place at stud.

Lancaster Bomber is one of 19 Group/Grade 1 winners by Claiborne Farm's outstanding stallion War Front (by Danzig), a horse who could possibly forge a third branch of his sire's mighty line in the coming years. For so long it has been just his classic-placed, Group 1-winning sprinters Danehill and Green Desert who have made their own dynasties – War Front was among his late representatives. It is too early in that potential development yet to make it better than perhaps a 66/1 shot, but the signs are promising as his early stallion sons include Declaration Of War (Olmedo) and The Factor (Noted And Quoted) who have one top-level winner apiece. Data Link has disappointed so far, War Command got a listed scorer among his high double-digit tally of first-crop winners in 2018, Air Force Blue's first crop arrived in 2018, Darley Japan-based American Patriot will have his first foals in 2019, and U S Navy Flag will start his stallion career in the spring.

Sun Shower was out of Miss Kemble (by Warning), a non-winning daughter of Group 1 Irish 1000 Guineas and Group 1 Yorkshire Oaks heroine Sarah Siddons (by Le Levanstell), and that made that mare a half-sister to record-breaking Group 1 Irish Oaks star Princess Pati (by Top Ville) and to Group 2 Great Voltigeur Stakes winner Seymour Hicks (by Ballymore), the sire of Cheltenham Gold Cup and dual King George VI Chase star See More Business. Sarah Siddons was also responsible for dual stakes winner Sidara (by Golden Fleece) – grandam and third dam of Group 3-winning juvenile fillies Athlumney Lady (by Lycius) and Princess Iris (by Desert Prince) respectively – and of three other fillies who went on to make their name at stud.

Dansara (by Dancing Brave) became the grandam of Group 2 Prix de Royallieu winner Sea Of Heartbreak (by Rock Of Gibraltar) and of Group 3 Ballysax Stakes scorer Puncher Clynch (by Azamour), whereas Princess Pati's full-sister Cantanta gave us Cantilever (by Sanglamore), the Group 2-placed, Group 3 Prix de Royaumont winner whose star grandson Wicklow Brave (by Beat Hollow) has won the Group 1 Irish St Leger. Then there's Gertrude Lawrence, a full-sister to Seymour Hicks but dam of the speedy stakes winner Lady Ambassador (by General Assembly). That one, in turn, became the dam of Group 1 Prix Vermeille heroine and Group 1 Prix de l'Arc de Triomphe runner-up Leggera (by Sadler's Wells) and of Group 2-placed dual middle-distance pattern winner Lucido (by Royal Academy).

Stallions from the Danzig line have clicked well with Sun Shower, and the other Group 1 winner of 2018 out of an Indian Ridge mare was Irish 2000 Guineas scorer Romanised (by Holy Roman Emperor). She already has one son who has sired a Group 1 star and other stakes winners at stud, so it's no stretch of the imagination to think that she could do it again, with Lancaster Bomber. He looks likely to get his best juveniles over seven furlongs and a mile, and to get talented milers and middle-distance horses, and possibly some stayers, among his three-year-olds and older horses. His initial fee is £8,500.

SUMMARY DETAILS

Bred: Sun Shower Syndicate
Owned: Michael Tabor, Derrick Smith & Mrs John Magnier
Trained: Aidan O'Brien
Country: Ireland
Race record: 014022-440202020-031-
Career highlights: 2 wins inc Tattersalls Gold Cup (Gr1), 2nd Breeders' Cup Mile (Gr1), St James's Palace Stakes (Gr1), Ricoh Woodbine Mile Stakes (Gr1), Dubai Dewhurst Stakes (Gr1), Breeders' Cup Juvenile Turf (Gr1), 3rd Al Shaqab Lockinge Stakes (Gr1)

LANCASTER BOMBER (USA) - 2014 bay colt

War Front (USA)	Danzig (USA)	Northern Dancer (CAN)
		Pas De Nom (USA)
	Starry Dreamer (USA)	Rubiano (USA)
		Lara's Star (USA)
Sun Shower (IRE)	Indian Ridge	Ahonoora
		Hillbrow
	Miss Kemble (GB)	Warning
		Sarah Siddons (FR)

LATROBE (IRE)

US racing welcomed its 13th Triple Crown hero in June when Justify took the Grade 1 Belmont Stakes in style in New York, just three years after American Pharoah swept the classic series. The previous horse to achieve the feat had been Affirmed, back in 1978, one year after Seattle Slew. The original Triple Crown is the English series of the 2000 Guineas, Derby and St Leger, and no horse has successfully completed it since Nijinsky in 1970. In 1985, Oh So Sharp won the 1000 Guineas, Oaks and St Leger – called the Fillies' Triple Crown – something that had not been done since Meld, in 1955, and has not been achieved since.

There have been horses who have won two legs, and since Nijinsky, those have been Nashwan, Reference Point and Sea The Stars. Nashwan, whom Timeform rated 135, bypassed the St Leger in favour of an Arc attempt that ultimately did not happen, whereas many believed that, like Blue Peter in 1939, it was sheer bad luck that denied the Sir Henry Cecil-trained Reference Point his chance at history in 1987. The Timeform 139-rated champion missed the Guineas due to illness, leaving Don't Forget Me to pick up the first leg of what was a classic double for him. Sea The Stars, of course, did win the Prix de l'Arc de Triomphe after bypassing Doncaster; Timeform rated him 140.

Camelot, however, ran in all three classics and, in 2012, he came so close to becoming the 13th winner of the Triple Crown (16th if you include the three who won the races when they were all held at Newmarket during World War I). A mile Group 1 winner at two, he won the 2000 Guineas by a neck from French Fifteen, trounced Main Sequence by five lengths at Epsom, and failed by just three-parts of a length to beat the ill-fated Encke at Doncaster. In between those latter two classics he added the Irish Derby at the Curragh, beating Born To Sea by two lengths.

Camelot won the Group 3 Mooresbridge Stakes and chased home Al Kazeem in the Group 1 Tattersalls Gold Cup from four starts at four, and he retired to Coolmore Stud with a top Timeform rating of 128. In 2018 he was a star member of Europe's sophomore stallions. His first two seasons with runners have yielded 13 stakes winners, three of whom have won at the highest level. The Aidan O'Brien-trained Athena is one of that trio and she gained her top-level success in the Grade 1 Belmont Oaks Invitational Stakes in New York just days after finishing third in the Group 1 Pretty Polly Stakes at the Curragh. Juvenile filly Wonderment is another, and the third is Latrobe.

That Joseph O'Brien-trained colt beat Rostropovich and Saxon Warrior by a half-length and neck in the Group 1 Dubai Duty Free Irish Derby at the Curragh, ridden by the trainer's brother, Donnacha, who had a phenomenal season and was crowned champion jockey in Ireland.

The colt had been runner-up to James Cook in a mile maiden on soft ground at Leopardstown on his only start at two, was a neck second to Hunting Horn over 10 furlongs on softer ground at Naas in April, then chased home Platinum Warrior in the Group 3 Gallinule Stakes before running away with a 12-furlong Curragh maiden three weeks before his classic success. Since then he has disappointed in the Group 1 Juddmonte International Stakes at York but put up a good effort to chase home Flag Of Honour in the Group 1 Comer Group International Irish St Leger.

He was then shipped to Australia for a potential Group 1 Lexus Melbourne Cup bid and was among the ante-post favourites for the two-mile feature, but in the last week of October, it was announced that he would bypass that race in favour of the 10-furlong Group 1 Mackinnon Stakes, also at Flemington. The ground was good, he settled near the rear of the field, was under pressure from three furlongs out, but stayed on well and failed by just a head to land the spoils. Five-year-old Trap For Fools held on to win by a head, the previous week's Group 1 AAMI Victoria Derby Extra Brut was third, and there was a gap of one and three-quarter lengths back to the fourth, Prized Icon. It was announced shortly afterwards that Latrobe would return to Ireland for a four-year-old campaign, but before that, he had one final run, this time in Hong Kong. There was a minor scare when he was found to be mildly lame after work a few days before the Grade 1 Longines Hong Kong Vase, reported as showing sensitivity in the heel bulbs of his left fore. A veterinary inspection the day before the race cleared him. But he was always in rear and never looked dangerous, finishing down the field behind Exultant, who had been classic-placed in Ireland in 2017 under the name Irishcorrespondent.

Latrobe, who was bred by Sweetmans Bloodstock, was originally bought by Margaret O'Toole for €88,000 in Goffs as a foal and then sold on to Joseph O'Brien for 65,000gns from Book 1 of the Tattersalls October Yearling Sale in Newmarket.

He is the third foal of six-furlong, three-year-old Polytrack winner Question Times (by Shamardal), who earned her blacktype when runner-up in a listed contest over six furlongs at Newmarket as a two-year-old, and both of his older siblings are multiple winners. Entangling (by Fastnet Rock) won over 10 furlongs at Yarmouth and 12 furlongs on the Polytrack at Kempton last year, whereas that one's full-sister Diamond Fields won the Group 3 Gladness Stakes at Naas first time out as a four-year-old having been Grade 2-placed in the USA the previous season.

Forever Times (by So Factual), the grandam of Latrobe, won six times from five to seven furlongs, all on turf and mostly on good or fast ground, and that mare's other offspring include Group 3 Sceptre Stakes winner and Group 1 Cheveley Park Stakes runner-up Sunday Times (by Holy Roman Emperor), and this family has also struck at the highest level in the USA in 2018. Classical Times (by Lawman), a four-year-old daughter of Sunday Times and, like her dam, trained by Peter Chapple-Hyam, won the Listed Cecil Frail Stakes at Haydock in late May and was third in the Group 3 Chipchase Stakes over six furlongs on the Tapeta at Newcastle shortly after that. But, more notably, that one's two-year-old half-sister is Newspaperofrecord (by Lope De Vega).

The rising star was bred by Times Of Wigan Ltd, who sold her for 200,000gns from Book 1 of the Tattersalls October Yearling Sale in Newmarket, she was bought by Klaravich Stables Inc and sent into training with Chad Brown. She has been favourite on all three of her starts to date, ran away with an eight-and-a-half-furlong maiden on turf at Saratoga in mid-August, was a wide-margin winner of the Grade 2 Miss Grillo Stakes over the same trip at Belmont Park six weeks later, and then made all for an impressive six-and-three-quarter-length defeat of East in the Grade 1 Breeders' Cup Juvenile Fillies Turf over a mile at Churchill Downs in early November. There was some ease in the ground on each occasion.

As you might expect of a daughter of Group 1 Nunthorpe Stakes scorer So Factual (by Known Fact), Forever Times is a half-sister to some speedy horses, and although Majestic Times (by Bluebird) won a listed sprint, Welsh Emperor (by Emperor Jones) is the more notable of her half-brothers. That 13-time scorer was trained by Tom Tate, he won the Group 2 Hungerford Stakes, the Group 3 Bentinck Stakes, and two listed contests, he chased home Toylsome in the Group 1 Prix de la Foret, failed by just a neck to beat Caradak in another edition of that same contest, and he was short-headed by Group 1 Lockinge Stakes heroine and subsequent Group 1-producer Red Evie when bidding for a repeat success in the Hungerford.

The distance was a reason given for the decision to bypass the Melbourne Cup, the 3200 metres considered to be a bit too far for Latrobe at this stage of his career. Might he stay the trip with another year behind him?

If only his sire mattered then you would have little doubt that such distances would be within his compass, but the amount of speed on the distaff side of his family casts a shade of doubt. He clearly stays 14 furlongs, however, and that suggests that it is not the speed element of the female side of his family that he has inherited from his dam but, instead, possibly the middle-distance side of his broodmare sire, Shamardal (by Giant's Causeway). That stallion, the son of a star mile to 10-furlong colt and grandson of an Irish Oaks heroine, gets his best winners over a wide range of trips.

It will be interesting to see how the racing career of Latrobe turns out, and with a Timeform rating of 119 he still has a lot of progress to make if he is going to hit the very top in Europe, but he is progressive, stays at least 14 furlongs, and he could do well on the international circuit in 2019.

SUMMARY DETAILS

Bred: Sweetmans Bloodstock
Owned: N C Williams & Mr & Mrs Lloyd J Williams
Trained: Joseph O'Brien
Country: Ireland
Race record: 2-22110220-
Career highlights: 2 wins inc Dubai Duty Free Irish Derby (Gr1), 2nd Seppelt Mackinnon Stakes (Gr1), Comer Group International Irish St Leger (Gr1), Airlie Stud Gallinule Stakes (Gr3)

LATROBE (IRE) - 2015 brown colt

Camelot (GB)	Montjeu (IRE)	Sadler's Wells (USA)
		Floripedes (FR)
	Tarfah (USA)	Kingmambo (USA)
		Fickle (GB)
Question Times (GB)	Shamardal (USA)	Giant's Causeway (USA)
		Helsinki (GB)
	Forever Times (GB)	So Factual (USA)
		Simply Times (USA)

LAURENS (FR)

Winning a Group 1 race is something that most horses will never even come close to achieving, but in 2018 we have had three who have notched up four Group 1 wins for the year. All are three-year-olds, two are fillies, and they are, of course, Roaring Lion, Alpha Centauri, and Laurens.

The first two are now retired to stud, but Laurens may return to action as a four-year-old, and that could be an interesting move. Although new Tweenhills Farm & Stud stallion recruit Roaring Lion is Timeform-rated 130, and prospective broodmare Alpha Centauri is on 128 from the same organisation, both Timeform and the official BHA handicappers have Laurens on just 116, and Racing Post ratings have her just 1lb higher. She will need to improve from three to four or she will be vulnerable to the next batch of classic-generation fillies coming through, and from late developers among her cohort.

The expert time analysts have explained their figure in various places, and her official handicap mark makes sense when you take even a cursory glance at each of her races in 2018 – all of them Group 1s.

She chased home Billesdon Brook – who failed to be placed in three subsequent outings – in the Qipco 1000 Guineas, scraped home by a short-head from With You in the Prix Saint-Alary and from Musis Amica in a blanket finish (instant indicator of weak form at this level) in the Prix de Diane (French Oaks). She failed to stay in the Yorkshire Oaks, then benefitted from the career-ending injury sustained by Alpha Centauri when beating that champion by three-parts of a length in the Coolmore Fastnet Rock Matron Stakes over the mile at Leopardstown. Then she beat Happily (disappointing at three and raised to a BHA mark of 113 after this) in the Kingdom of Bahrain Sun Chariot Stakes.

The race that could have shown her to be a genuine Group 1-quality horse (120+ official handicap mark; 125+ Timeform

142

rating) was the Queen Elizabeth II Stakes at Ascot, but she was a well-beaten eighth behind Roaring Lion.

Her connections and her many fans can be justifiably proud of her and what she has achieved. Trainer Karl Burke has done an outstanding job with her, and who would not love to own such an admirable filly? But in terms of her place in history – judged on facts, stripped of emotion – she is a long way down in the pecking order, one of those lucky horses whose CV outshines their actual merit. She is tough, genuine, popular, and very talented, and she also has a short-head defeat of September (well-beaten on her only start in 2018) in the Group 1 Fillies' Mile to her name from 2017, with an impressive balance of over £1.4 million in earnings to date. But unless she can improve next year then she will again be reliant on finding races soft for the grade if she is to add to her Group 1 tally.

Laurens, who was bred by Bloodstock Agency Ltd, is a £220,000 graduate of the Goff UK Premier Yearling Sale in Doncaster and she is the second classic and multiple Group 1 star for her sire, Siyouni. One of 28 Group 1 winners by Cheveley Park Stud's sprint star and outstanding stallion Pivotal (by Polar Falcon), he achieved his top win at the age of two, taking the Group 1 Prix Jean-Luc Lagardere-Grand Criterium over seven furlongs at Longchamp. He failed to win from six starts as a three-year-old but was placed in both the Group 1 Prix Jean Prat and Group 1 Prix du Moulin de Longchamp and improved his Timeform rating from 117 to 122. Being a high-class son of the sire of Kyllachy and out of a stakes-winning half-sister to Group 1 star Slickly (by Linamix), he went to stud as a promising prospect.

The fee for his first four years at Haras de Bonneval was just €7,000, but since then it has soared. He was busy this year at €75,000 and will likely be so again in 2019 at his new fee of €100,000. Ervedya is the other champion among his 26 stakes winners, a roll of honour that also includes the Group 1-placed pattern winners City Light, Le Brivido, Siyoushake, Spectre and Volta. Those who have won pattern races for him in 2018 include Australian Group 2 scorer Aylmerton, US

Grade 3 winner La Signare, and Group 3 Prix Vantaux winner Barkaa.

Laurens, a half-sister to two National Hunt winners, is the fourth foal out of Recambe (by Cape Cross), which makes her inbred 4x4 to Danzig (by Northern Dancer). Her dam's siblings include Listed Newmarket Stakes winner and notable Hong Kong performer Salford Mill (by Peintre Celebre), and her grandam is the stakes-placed Razana (by Kahyasi). That daughter of triple winner Raysiya (by Cure The Blues) is a half-sister to four blacktype producers, one of whom was herself a listed winner and two of whom are of particular note.

Profit Alert (by Alzao), a full-sister to stakes winner and blacktype producer Raysiza, is the dam of the high-class miler Shifting Power (by Compton Place). He won the Listed European Free Handicap and Listed Royal Windsor Stakes, chased home Kingman in the Group 1 Irish 2000 Guineas, was a one-length runner-up to Charm Spirit in the Group 1 Prix Jean Prat, and was third to Custom Cut in the Group 2 bet365 Mile at Sandown.

Ribot's Guest (by Be My Guest), the other mare of note, was unraced, but her son Mickdaam (by Dubawi) won the Group 3 Chester Vase and her daughter Kinnaird (by Dr Devious) won the Group 1 Prix de l'Opera. That filly is, in turn, the dam of Group 2 Royal Lodge Stakes winner Berkshire (by Mount Nelson), who has completed his first season at Haras de Sorelis in France, and she is the grandam of young Coolmore stallion Ivawood (by Zebedee). That grandson of Invincible Spirit (by Green Desert) won both the Group 2 July Stakes and Group 2 Richmond Stakes as a two-year-old, was a nose runner-up to Charming Thought in the Group 1 Middle Park Stakes that autumn, and filled third place in the Group 1 2000 Guineas and Group 1 Irish 2000 Guineas the following spring, both won by Gleneagles. His first-crop yearlings have made up to €80,000.

Laurens is worth a considerable amount as a prospective broodmare, but before then there should be more good prizes to be won with her.

SUMMARY DETAILS

Bred: Bloodstock Agency Ltd
Owned: John Dance
Trained: Karl Burke
Country: England
Race record: 1211-2110110-
Career highlights: 7 wins inc Prix de Diane Longines (Gr1),
Coolmore Fastnet Rock Matron Stakes (Gr1), Kingdom of
Bahrain Sun Chariot Stakes (Gr1), The Gurkha Coolmore Prix
Saint-Alary (Gr1), bet365 Fillies' Mile (Gr1), William Hill May
Hill Stakes (Gr2), 2nd Qipco 1000 Guineas (Gr1), Shadwell
Prix du Calvados (Gr3)

LAURENS (FR) - 2015 bay filly

Siyouni (FR)	Pivotal (GB)	Polar Falcon (USA)
		Fearless Revival
	Sichilla (IRE)	Danehill (USA)
		Slipstream Queen (USA)
Recambe (IRE)	Cape Cross (IRE)	Green Desert (USA)
		Park Appeal
	Razana (IRE)	Kahyasi
		Raysiya

LIGHTNING SPEAR (GB)

If at first you don't succeed, try, try, try again. It's an often-quoted motivational statement, but even the most enthusiastic could be forgiven for calling a halt when the number of misses reaches double digits. Lightning Spear's connections persevered, they got within a short-head of taking the Group 1 Juddmonte Lockinge Stakes at Newbury in May – pipped by Rhododendron – and just reward finally came at Goodwood on August 1st, the entire's 16th attempt at the highest level. He beat high-class three-year-old Expert Eye by one and a half lengths in the Qatar Sussex Stakes, with Lord Glitters another half-length back in third, a nose and neck ahead of Gustav Klimt and Beat The Bank.

The dual Group 2 Celebration Mile winner has six Group 1 placings to his name, including third to Accidental Agent in this year's Queen Anne Stakes at Ascot, but when he starts his first season the stallion team at Tweenhills Farm & Stud, in 2019, he will do so as a Group 1-winning son of a leading international sire.

He was bred by Newsells Park Stud, is a good-looking horse who made 260,000gns from Book 1 of the Tattersalls October Yearling Sale, he is by the sire of multiple Group 1-siring stallions Kyllachy (Sole Power, Twilight Son, etc) and Siyouni (Ervedya, Laurens, etc), and he comes from the family of a European champion sire – which makes him a likely candidate to get stakes and pattern-winning offspring at all levels, mostly in the six to 12-furlong range.

Lightning Spear was trained by Ralph Beckett when he won his only start as a juvenile, over seven furlongs on Polytrack at Kempton in August, making him yet another top-level scorer who got an early winning start on the artificial tracks (see the essay on Cross Counter). He was in the Olly Stevens stable when taking his only race at three, an eight-and-a-half-furlong contest at Nottingham. He won two more handicaps at four, lost his unbeaten record when chasing home Arod in the Group 2 Summer Mile at Ascot, and was fourth to Esoterique in the Prix Jacques le Marois at Deauville a month later, his first Group 1 attempt.

Timeform rated him 125 as a five-year-old when he won his first Group 2 Celebration Mile – now trained by David Simcock – before taking third to Minding and Ribchester in the Group 1 Queen Elizabeth II Stakes, and that organisation had him on 124 for this year before his Goodwood success. The win saw him raised to 126, but then he put in three below-par performances. First, he was a two-and-a-half-length fifth to Recoletos in the Group 1 Prix du Moulin de Longchamp, then over seven lengths behind Roaring Lion when seventh in the Group 1 Queen Elizabeth II Stakes at Ascot, although he was beaten by less than three lengths when seventh to Expert Eye in the Grade 1 Breeders' Cup Mile at Churchill Downs.

The best of four blacktype earners out of multiple stakes-winning sprinter Atlantic Destiny (by Royal Academy), the half-brother to 10-furlong listed scorer Ocean War (by Dalakhani) is out of a half-sister to Make No Mistake (by Darshaan), who did well for the Dermot Weld stable. That talented colt carried the famous Moyglare Stud colours to victory in the Group 2 Royal Whip Stakes and Group 3 Meld Stakes at the Curragh, he was third in the Group 1 Tattersalls Gold Cup at the same venue and was also a Grade 2-placed dual Grade 3 winner in the USA.

Grandam Respectfully (by The Minstrel) was unplaced in a single start in France, and third dam Treat Me Nobly (by Vaguely Noble) – who made a record 1,300,000 francs as a yearling – was unraced, but the latter was out of What A Treat (by Tudor Minstrel), the US three-year-old filly champion of 1965, and so she was a half-sister to Be My Guest (by Northern Dancer). What A Treat, whose 11 wins included the Beldame Stakes, Alabama Stakes, and Gazelle Handicap, was out of the prolific Rare Treat (by Stymie) – which made her a half-sister to the dam of ill-fated Derby hero Golden Fleece (by Nijinsky) – and her star son was one of the early standout stallions for Coolmore Stud.

Be My Guest first came to prominence when setting a short-lived European record yearling price of 127,000gns when topping the Goffs Premier Yearling Sale in 1975. The Vincent O'Brien-trained, white-faced chestnut won the second of his two starts at two, kicked off his three-year-old campaign with an easy win in the Blue Riband Trial over eight and a half furlongs at Epsom, but was beaten twice when stepping up in trip – including in the Derby – before returning to a mile. He easily won the Desmond Stakes at the Curragh before, on soft ground at Goodwood, he fought to hold off the challenge of Don in the Waterford Crystal Mile. A bruised foot denied him the chance to run in the Queen Elizabeth II Stakes, and he went to stud as a Timeform 126-rated son of leading sire Northern Dancer (by Nearctic), whose growing list of major winners included that year's Derby hero, The Minstrel.

Be My Guest was crowned European champion sire in 1982 when his first crop of three-year-olds featured Group 1 Prix du Jockey Club (French Derby), Group 1 Benson & Hedges Gold Cup (now Juddmonte International Stakes) and runaway Group 1 Irish Derby hero Assert, and star miler On The House, who took both the Group 1 1000 Guineas and Group 1 Sussex Stakes. His career roll of honour also featured Group 1 aces Double Bed, Go And Go, Luth Enchantee, Pelder, Pentire, and Valentine Waltz, and Group 2 Lockinge Stakes winner and Group 1 Derby runner-up Most Welcome, and although his sons met with mixed success at stud, many of his daughters excelled in that role.

If you go back farther on the page then you find that the sixth dam of Lightning Spear was the speedy stakes winner Rare Perfume (by Eight Thirty), which made his fifth dam a half-sister to 1962's Belmont Stakes winner and US three-year-old champion Jaipur (by Nasrullah), whose progeny included dual Group 1 scorer and sprint champion Amber Rama, and Timeform 120-rated sprint juvenile Mansingh (sire of Petong).

Lightning Spear, the winner of seven of his 26 starts and over £1.3 million in prize money, has a pedigree that could see him do well as a sire, and he will be among the brightest new prospects joining the stallion ranks in 2019. His fee is £8,500.

SUMMARY DETAILS

Bred: Newsells Park Stud
Owned: Qatar Racing Ltd
Trained: David Simcock
Country: England
Race record: 1-1-112430-30013-20031000-231000-
Career highlights: 7 wins inc Qatar Sussex Stakes (Gr1),
Celebration Mile (Gr2-twice), 2nd Al Shaqab Lockinge Stakes
(Gr1-twice), Fred Cowley MBE Memorial Summer Mile (Gr2),
3rd Queen Anne Stakes (Gr1-twice), Qatar Sussex Stakes
(Gr1), Queen Elizabeth II Stakes (Gr1), Clipper Logistics
Boomerang Stakes (Gr2)

LIGHTNING SPEAR (GB) - 2011 chestnut horse

Pivotal (GB)	Polar Falcon (USA)	Nureyev (USA)
		Marie D'Argonne (FR)
	Fearless Revival	Cozzene (USA)
		Stufida
Atlantic Destiny (IRE)	Royal Academy (USA)	Nijinsky (CAN)
		Crimson Saint (USA)
	Respectfully (USA)	The Minstrel (CAN)
		Treat Me Nobly (USA)

149

LILY'S CANDLE (FR)

Getting a first Group 1 winner is an important career landmark for any stallion and Haras de Bouquetot's classic-winning miler Style Vendome (by Anabaa) achieved the feat when Lily's Candle landed the Qatar Prix Marcel Boussac - Criterium des Pouliches over a mile at ParisLongchamp in early October. This was a second blacktype success for the Fabrice Vermeulen-trained filly, and it is something of a surprise that this second-crop representative is currently the only stakes winner for her young sire. That will surely change before long.

She was unplaced over seven furlongs on soft ground at Saint-Cloud on her debut in mid-June but was a two-length winner over a mile on good ground at Marseille Borely a month later and then added a nose success in the Listed Prix des Jouvenceaux et des Jouvencelles over seven at Vichy. It was also soft there, but a bit more solid underfoot when she finished a one-length fourth to The Black Album on the Group 3 Prix de la Rochette next time.

She was sold for €390,000 at the Arqana Arc Sale the day before her Group 1 success, which represented a nice return on investment for both her previous and new owners. She had been a €15,000 buy at the Arqana Deauville October yearling sale and earned that back several times over by the time of her resale, whereas her prize at ParisLongchamp covered a large chunk of what Martin Schwartz had to fork out on her behalf. Two months later she was back in the ring, this time selling for €1,100,000 to Katsumi Yoshida.

Her Group 1 win also appears to have been somewhat lucky as, with just over three lengths covering the entire field of eight runners at the line, and a gap of just three-parts of a length between first and fourth, this does not appear to have been a strong renewal of the race. There were some well-bred and promising types in the field, so something may emerge as a divisional star in 2019, but right now it would appear that the odds of Lily's Candle winning another Group 1 in Europe – if she stays here – are similar to those with which her backers were rewarded in October – 28/1.

She was well-beaten when finishing down the field behind exciting Irish-bred, US-trained filly Newspaperofrecord in the Grade 1 Breeders' Cup Juvenile Fillies Turf at Churchill Downs on her final start, but if she were to return to North America, on a visit or to stay, then it would be no surprise to see her do well there. Indeed, it may be her best prospect of getting another top-level win to her name.

Lily's Candle was bred by Mme P Lepaudry and she is easily the best of her dam's first seven foals, but she is not the first member of her family to make the frame at the highest level. Her dam, Golden Lily (by Dolphin Street) was only placed, albeit on a string of occasions, but that mare's seven successful siblings include the stakes-winning full-sisters Liliside (by American Post) and Lily America as well as a multiple Group 3-placed filly – The Wise Lady (by Ganges) – who has done well at stud.

Liliside was actually a bit better than her blacktype record appears because what it cannot show is that she was first past the post in the Group 1 Poule d'Essai des Pouliches (French 1000 Guineas). It was a blanket finish and a rough race, and not a particularly strong edition of the classic, but she fought her way into the lead and had her head in front on the line, pipping the almost unbelievably fortunate Special Duty before being thrown out and placed sixth. That rival had been short-headed at Newmarket a fortnight before only to be handed the Group 1 1000 Guineas in the stewards' room when Jacqueline Quest was disqualified. So there's the answer to the trivia questions: What filly won two classics in the stewards' room? And who were the pair who lost those two races?

Liliside was only fifth to Joanna – who had had been promoted to third in the classic – in the Group 2 Prix de Sandringham over the same trip at Chantilly a few weeks later but then won her third listed race on what turned out to her penultimate start. She was also back in the news again in mid-November of 2018 when her daughter Lys Gracieux (by

Heart's Cry) won the Grade 1 Queen Elizabeth II Cup over 11 furlongs on firm ground at Kyoto in Japan. It was a third pattern success for the Yoshito Yahagi-trained four-year-old and it came six months after she'd failed by just a nose to take a mile Grade 1 at Tokyo. She was also a Grade 1-placed pattern winner at two and was runner-up in two classics at three.

The Wise Lady, on the other hand, was placed in the Group 3 Prix Miesque, Group 3 Prix du Calvados and Group 3 Prix de Ris-Orangis during her racing days, and in addition to juvenile listed scorer Melodyman (by Green Tune) and stakes-placed Good Bye My Friend (by Kendor), she is the dam of mile Group 3 and dual listed scorer Ming Zhi Cosmos (by Duke Of Marmalade) and the grandam of Group 1 Criterium de Saint-Cloud winner Robin Of Navan. That much-travelled chestnut is trained by Harry Dunlop, his wins also include the Group 3 Prix de Conde and Group 3 La Coupe, the races in which he has been placed include the Group 1 Prix d'Ispahan and Group 1 Premio Roma.

Robin Of Navan is out of Cloghran (by Muhtathir), a placed half-sister to Golden Lily, and as he is a son of American Post (by Bering), that makes him closely related to Liliside and also to the American Post-sired half-sister to Lily's Candle who made €230,000 at this year's Arqana Deauville October Yearling Sale.

With her pedigree and connections, it will be interesting to see how Lily's Candle's racing and eventual stud careers turn out. She may struggle to add to her Group 1 tally if remaining in Europe and she seems the type who could do well from a mile to 10 furlongs in North America, but with her new owner being the person behind the famous Northern Farm in Japan, it is possible that she will be heading there instead. Her sale happened the day before publication and details of the plan for her were not yet available.

SUMMARY DETAILS
Bred: Mme P Lepaudry
Owned: Martin S Schwartz Racing

Trained: Fabrice Vermeulen
Country: France
Race record: 011410-
Career highlights: 3 wins inc Qatar Prix Marcel Boussac - Criterium des Pouliches (Gr1), Prix des Jouvenceaux et des Jouvencelles (L)

LILY'S CANDLE (FR) - 2016 grey filly

Style Vendome (FR)	Anabaa (USA)	Danzig (USA)
		Balbonella (FR)
	Place Vendome (FR)	Dr Fong (USA)
		Mediaeval (FR)
Golden Lily (FR)	Dolphin Street (FR)	Bluebird (USA)
		Or Vision (USA)
	Millers Lily (FR)	Miller's Mate
		Lymara (FR)

LINE OF DUTY (IRE)

Is this the Investec Derby winner of 2019?

Ante-post quotations for the following year's classic appear often before a juvenile pattern winner has even left the winners' enclosure, and many times for horses that barely look like genuine Group 1 prospects, but there was something about the way that Line of Duty won the Grade 1 Breeders' Cup Juvenile Turf that just screamed Derby.

The merit of the bare form shown that day is open to question, with Anthony Van Dyck disappointing and finishing only ninth and Arthur Kitt taking fourth, just two and a half lengths behind the winner. The latter, a Listed Chesham Stakes winner who chased home Too Darn Hot in the Group 3 Solario Stakes at Sandown, had been well-beaten behind Mohawk in the Group 2 Royal Lodge Stakes, but he is a son of Camelot (by Montjeu) and so could be open to quite a bit of improvement next year. Line of Duty was behind horses after the field swung into the straight, he had to be pulled wide to challenge, and once he got going he stormed home. He did not steer a straight course in the final furlong, and he beat the promising sprint stakes winner Uncle Benny by half a length.

Timeform rated the performance 112p, an increase of 5lbs from his previous start. That had been the nine-furlong Prix de Conde at Chantilly, which he won by a length and a quarter from once-raced maiden winner Syrtis, with another once-raced maiden winner a short-neck back in third. But that form then got a boost almost four weeks later when that placed horse, the Camelot filly Wonderment, beat Sydney Opera House by a neck in the Group 1 Criterium de Saint-Cloud over 10 furlongs.

There is no doubt that Line of Duty is a colt of considerable promise and that he was one of the best staying juveniles of 2018, but will he stay 12 furlongs? He's out of a miler and several of the stakes winners in the first few generations of the family were sprinters, so he could be a top mile to 10-furlong colt who comes cruising two out at Epsom only to falter, or he could have the stamina to go all the way to the line, there or at any other venue where he might be asked to try the distance. But there are others in his immediate family who were middle-distance horses, and one who was a runaway winner over two miles and a furlong. This tilts the balance in favour of the son of Galileo (by Sadler's Wells) staying the distance.

His full-brother World War won over nine and a half furlongs at Gowran Park, has one 13-furlong second among a bunch of well-beaten efforts over 12 furlongs, 14, furlongs and two miles, and has shown little in two tries over hurdles. He achieved a peak handicap mark of 92 on the flat, so the issue may be stamina-related rather than a lack of ability. Their full-sister Hibiscus was raised to a career-high handicap mark of 95 after she finished a three-quarter-length third-past-the-post in a 12-furlong listed contest at the Curragh – promoted to second after a stewards' enquiry – and although she stayed-on to pick up that spot, the time of the race was slow for the conditions, which suggests that it might not have been a true test. Her only win came over 10 furlongs and she was well-beaten in her three subsequent blacktype outings.

Their dam is the quirky Jacqueline Quest (by Rock Of Gibraltar), the filly who pipped Special Duty in the Group 1 1000 Guineas only to lose the race in the stewards' room. She was then third to Lillie Langtry in the Group 1 Coronation Stakes and, at four, short-headed by Libranno in the Group 3 Supreme Stakes over seven furlongs at Goodwood. She also refused to race on two occasions and was beaten in races that even at 7-10lbs below her best she should have won.

Her half-sister Mam'Selle (by Teofilo) won three times last year at up to 12 furlongs, picked up some blacktype when third in a listed contest over that trip at Goodwood in May and was only beaten by four lengths when taking third in a valuable 14-furlong handicap on heavy ground at Haydock in September. She was then sold for 300,000gns at the Tattersalls December Mare Sale. The William Haggas-trained four-year-old is rated 90, just 3lbs below the career-high mark achieved by her dam, Coquette Rouge (by Croco Rouge). That mare is by a top middle-distance horse, she is out of a daughter of Sadler's Wells (by Northern Dancer), and her second start was a 20-length victory in a two-mile, one-furlong maiden at Killarney, eased down. The Kevin Prendergast-trainee 'only' won by two lengths over 12 furlongs on heavy ground at Tipperary a few weeks later, and she chased home Al Eile in the valuable two-mile Leopardstown November Handicap.

Coquette Rouge's half-sister Salut D'Amour (by Danehill Dancer) won the Listed National Stakes over five furlongs in May of her two-year-old year and was runner-up in both the Group 2 Queen Mary Stakes – run at York that year – and the Group 2 Cherry Hinton Stakes. That is quite a remarkable contrast for two talented flat siblings. Then consider that their half-brother Regime (by Golan) won the Group 3 Mooresbridge Stakes and Group 3 Classic Trial over 10 furlongs, and the ill-fated Fearless Falcon (by Pivotal) was a Grade 1-placed winner over hurdles, and one could be left puzzled by the sprint two-year-old among this clearly stamina-laden family.

But then you take a look at the next generation of the family and Salut D'Amour makes sense. Their dam, Juno Madonna, got the stamina gene from her sire, Sadler's Wells, and a speed one from her dam, Tough Lady (by Bay Express), and it was the latter that she passed on to that daughter, who probably got a matching one from her sire. The mare's best siblings, however, got a likely double dose of the speed gene too. They were Group 3 King George Stakes winner Title Roll (by Tate Gallery), dual sprint stakes winner Northern Express (by Northern Guest), and Group 3 Anglesey Stakes third El Zorro Dorado (by Tate Gallery). And their non-winning half-sister Maimiti (by Goldhill) did her part for the family by producing five-furlong listed scorer My-O-My (by Waajib).

This was a speed family but the addition of a Sadler's Wells covering led to the emergence of a middle-distance and staying branch, one that can still throw up the occasional sprinter or miler. Being a Galileo colt from that line, and inbred 2x4 to

Sadler's Wells, makes it likely that Line of Duty will stay 12 furlongs.

There is another branch of the family that has already yielded a three-year-old middle-distance Grade 1 winner, albeit the 10 furlongs of the American Oaks Stakes at Hollywood Park. Tough Lady's daughter Starring Role (by Glenstal) went to Arc hero Peintre Celebre (by Nureyev) and the resulting filly, named Await, became the unraced dam of Cambina (by Hawk Wing), a now Japan-based broodmare who was listed-placed over a mile at two in Ireland before her string of US graded race wins, from six and a half furlongs to 10 furlongs.

Should Line of Duty go on to win the Derby, and/or other top races, and eventually join the roster at Dalham Hall Stud or Kildangan Stud, then this horse would almost represent something of a storybook success for his connections. Having bypassed the elite Coolmore stallions for so long at the sales, Godolphin finally relented in 2017 and bought this 400,000gns colt and four other Galileos from Book 1 of the Tattersalls October Yearling Sale, and a €1,200,000 Galileo filly at Goffs. He is the first of those purchases to run in their colours.

SUMMARY DETAILS

Bred: Triermore Stud
Owned: Godolphin
Trained: Charlie Appleby
Country: England
Race record: 22111-
Career highlights: 3 wins inc Breeders' Cup Juvenile Turf (Gr1), Prix de Conde (Gr3)

LINE OF DUTY (IRE) - 2016 chestnut colt

Galileo (IRE)	Sadler's Wells (USA)	Northern Dancer (CAN)
		Fairy Bridge (USA)
	Urban Sea (USA)	Miswaki (USA)
		Allegretta
Jacqueline Quest (IRE)	Rock Of Gibraltar (IRE)	Danehill (USA)
		Offshore Boom
	Coquette Rouge (IRE)	Croco Rouge (IRE)
		Juno Madonna (IRE)

MABS CROSS (GB)

There is an obsession within the industry for early two-year-old speed, which will also require quite early foaling dates, and yet the best sprinters are almost always three-year-olds and older horses. Indeed, some of the brightest stars in the sprinting ranks only hit their peak at four or five years of age. A horse born on June 6th was never going to be a 'two-year-old type', and this may have been partly why the homebred filly that Highfield Farm Llp offered at the DBS November Yearling & H-i-T Sale in 2015 fetched only £3,000. She didn't run at two, she was unplaced and then third in six-furlong maidens run a few weeks before her physical third birthday, and then she dropped down to the minimum trip, won easily at Newcastle – making her yet another top-level scorer who got an early winning start on an artificial track (see the essay on Cross Counter or Enable) – and has never looked back in her now two-year quest to become a Group 1 star.

Mabs Cross has improved with almost every run in her now 13-start career, and having come agonisingly close to taking the Group 1 Coolmore Nunthorpe Stakes at York in August – a long examination of the photo resulted in a nose verdict to Alpha Delphini – she closed out her four-year-old season a winner, taking the Group 1 Prix de l'Abbaye de Longchamp Longines in France. That overlooked early June-born, £3,000 filly has now earned almost £400,000 for her connections and is worth a considerable amount as a prospective broodmare.

Her birth date is not the only thing that would have left many passing her by as a yearling. For many, the low strike rate of winners to foals born within the first four generations of the family would have been off-putting, as would the lack of blacktype in the second and third generations and only a Belgian stakes winner under the fourth dam. On the plus side, however, was that she was by Cheveley Park Stud stallion Dutch Art (by Medicean) –sire of Group 1 stars Garswood

158

and Slade Power – her dam won the Listed Hilary Needler Trophy as a two-year-old and that mare had already produced Charlie Em (by Kheleyf), who had been listed-placed in Germany at two, won a Grade 3 contest over a mile on turf in California at three and a middle-distance stakes race there at four. Charlie Em's first foal is a Kodiac (by Danehill) filly who made £110,000 at the Goffs UK Premier Yearling Sale in August. She was born on January 23rd. Miss Meggy's latest foal, on the other hand, is an Oasis Dream (by Green Desert) filly born on June 2nd. Can lightning strike twice? Sure, why not?

After Mabs Cross won her maiden, which was also just before her physical third birthday, she remained at five furlongs, adding handicaps at Windsor and Haydock before taking a listed contest at Musselburgh, finishing that season on a Timeform rating of 112. She was runner-up to Mrs Gallagher in a listed race at Bath first time out in 2018, then beat Judicial by a neck in the Group 3 Palace House Stakes before finishing an honourable fourth Battaash, Washington DC and Kachy in the Group 2 Temple Stakes at Haydock, beaten a total of just three-parts of a length.

Royal Ascot was next on her agenda and this time she put up the best performance of her career to that point, taking third in the Group 1 King's Stand Stakes. Blue Point starred that day, taking the prize by one and three-quarter lengths from Battaash, and although it's fair to say that the runner-up was nowhere near his brilliant best on that occasion, it was still a good effort to get within a neck of him at the line.

She was sent off favourite for the Group 2 Sapphire Stakes at the Curragh the following month but had to settle for third as three-year-old Havana Grey beat nine-year-old Caspian Prince by a length, with the filly another half-length behind. It was probably that somewhat flat effort that saw her largely overlooked next time in the Group 1 Coolmore Nunthorpe Stakes at York in August. Blue Point and Battaash both ran some way below their best, finishing third and fourth, and the seven-year-old gelding Alpha Delphini chose that day for his performance-of-a-lifetime effort, but it was also an excellent try by Mabs Cross and a loss so narrow that a dead-heat would have been the kinder call.

It was something of a surprise to see the now Timeform 119-rated filly sent off at double-figures again in the Group 1 Prix de l'Abbaye de Longchamp on her final start, but not to see her staying on well in the final furlong and getting her head in front near the line. This time It was the French-trained gelding Gold Vibe who had a better than expected day, taking second, with the talented two-year-old Soldier's Call a short-head back in third.

Like the now-retired Timeform 129-rated dual Group 1 Nunthorpe Stakes heroine Mecca's Angel, Mabs Cross has been trained throughout her career by Co Durham-based Michael Dods. She is not yet in the same league as that brilliant grey, but she is admirable, could still be improving, and may have an even more rewarding 2019 than she had in this year.

SUMMARY DETAILS

Bred: Highfield Farm Llp
Owned: David W Armstrong
Trained: Michael Dods
Country: England
Race record: -031111-2143321-
Career highlights: 6 wins inc Prix de l'Abbaye de Longchamp Longines (Gr1), Longholes Palace House Stakes (Gr3), EBF Musselburgh Fillies' Sprint Stakes (L), 2nd Coolmore Nunthorpe Stakes (Gr1), Whitsbury Manor Stud / British EBF Lansdown Stakes (L), 3rd King's Stand Stakes (Gr1), Sapphire Stakes (Gr2)

MABS CROSS (GB) - 2014 bay filly

Dutch Art (GB)	Medicean (GB)	Machiavellian (USA)
		Mystic Goddess (USA)
	Halland Park Lass (IRE)	Spectrum (IRE)
		Palacegate Episode (IRE)
Miss Meggy (GB)	Pivotal (GB)	Polar Falcon (USA)
		Fearless Revival
	Selkirk Rose (IRE)	Pips Pride (IRE)
		Red Note

MAGICAL (IRE)

It is not uncommon for horses to show marked improvement in the autumn of their three-year-old campaign. There are various reasons why this happens, and in the case of Magical there are three possible explanations. One is that the step up to a mile and a half suited her better than being a miler, another is that the cloud under which some of the Ballydoyle horses had been for the summer had now lifted, and the other is her date of birth. A horse born on May 18th was always going to be likely a candidate to take an autumnal leap forward.

She was already well established as a talented performer before the final third of the year, but it is fair to say that she was a bit disappointing. This regally-related bay had been a seven-furlong Group 2 scorer as a juvenile, was short-headed by Happily in the Group 1 Moyglare Stud Stakes and then finished fourth to Laurens in the Group 1 Fillies' Mile at Newmarket, and this identified her as a leading classic contender for 2018. The distance over which she might excel was not certain, even though she by the phenomenal stallion Galileo (by Sadler's Wells), and that's because of the amount of speed in her family.

Her Guineas-placed full-sister Rhododendron appeared to run out of stamina when chasing home Enable in the Group 1 Investec Oaks but rounded off that campaign with a victory in the Group 1 Prix de l'Opera over 10 furlongs at Chantilly and a one-length second in the Grade 1 Breeders' Cup Filly & Mare Turf over nine at Del Mar. Their full-brother Flying The Flag got his pattern success over 10 furlongs, their top-class dam was a star at eight and 10 furlongs, and their grandam won the Group 2 King's Stand Stakes and Group 2 Temple Stakes. The Galileos from a speed family often prove best at a mile and/or 10 furlongs.

Magical kicked off her second season with a disappointing fourth in a Group 3 contest over a mile in France and then bypassed the mile classics. She was next seen out in mid-July when, on fast ground, she beat I'm So Fancy by two and three-quarter lengths in the Group 2 Kilboy Estate Stakes over nine furlongs at the Curragh, this win coming two months after her sister had pipped Lightning Spear in the Group 1 Juddmonte Lockinge Stakes over a mile at Newbury. Her final run over a mile was in the Group 1 Matron Stakes at Leopardstown on Irish Champions Weekend, and although she finished a three-length fourth to Laurens – a good effort – there was still a feeling that she had not yet lived up to full strength of her early potential.

The decision to run her in the Group 1 Qatar Prix de l'Arc de Triomphe a few weeks later was eye-catching, and with the excitement generated by the repeat victory of Enable, and how Sea Of Class had gone so close to toppling her, the performance of Magical was somewhat overlooked. Yes, having a 40/1 longshot finish in 10th place in a championship event is hardly newsworthy material, but it was her proximity to the winner that was interesting. She had only been beaten by a total of five and a quarter lengths, and this suggested that another go at the 12-furlong trip was worth a shot.

The ground was soft at Ascot 13 days later, but Magical stayed on well to hold off the late challenge of Coronet in the Group 1 Qipco British Champions Fillies & Mares Stakes, beating the grey by a length. Classic-placed rising star Lah Ti Dar was another three-parts of a length back in third and finished three and a half lengths clear of fourth-placed Kitesurf.

Magical's Timeform rating rose from 118 to 122, but even better was to come. She gave Enable a few moments of concern in the Grade 1 Longines Breeders' Cup Turf on good ground at Churchill Downs, staying on strongly in the last of those 12 furlongs and finishing a three-quarter-length runner-up to the history-making dual Prix de l'Arc de Triomphe champion. Sadler's Joy, Arklow and Waldgeist led home the separate race that took place nine lengths behind these outstanding fillies.

Timeform raised Magical to 128 for that effort, putting her equal with Alpha Centauri and 1lb behind their divisional champion, Sea Of Class – the top three-year-old fillies of the year.

Does it represent a performance-of-a-lifetime effort or has this Aidan O'Brien-trained truly made such a leap forward? If the latter, and hoping that she remains in training in 2019, then we could be for a memorable middle-distance division, one that – right now – looks set to be dominated by fillies, because Enable and Sea Of Class are due to return to action for another crack at the Arc, and Japanese champion Almond Eye also has her sights set on that first Sunday in October at ParisLongchamp.

Magical is one of many top horses bred by Orpendale, Chelston & Wynatt, and that top-class dam alluded to above is, of course, Halfway To Heaven (by Pivotal). She won the Group 1 Irish 1000 Guineas and Group 1 Sun Chariot Stakes over a mile, and she beat Lush Lashes by a head in the Group 1 Nassau Stakes over 10 furlongs. That was as far as she was asked to try, and being a daughter of Pivotal (by Polar Falcon) and Cassandra Go (by Indian Ridge), that was to be expected. There are some by Pivotal who excel at 12 furlongs – dual Oaks heroine Sariska is a notable example – but not when the dam is a July Cup-placed five-furlong star whose star sibling is a Group 3 Coventry Stakes winner who managed to pick up second in an Irish 2000 Guineas. That horse is Verglas (by Highest Honor), who went on to sire several Group 1 winners in a stallion career cut short by his premature death. His three-parts sister Do The Honours (by Highest Honor) – out of listed scorer Persian Secret (by Persian Heights) – was also a sprint pattern winner.

In addition to Halfway To Heaven, Cassandra Go has been responsible for the pattern-winning sprinters Tickled Pink (by Invincible Spirit) and Theann (by Rock Of Gibraltar), and the latter has emerged as a broodmare of note. Her son Land Force (by No Nay Never) finished third in the Group 2 Norfolk Stakes over five furlongs at Ascot in June, won a listed contest over the same trip at Tipperary in July, and added the Group 2 Richmond Stakes over six furlongs at Goodwood in early August. He appears to have inherited the speed of both of his parents and could be a potential Group 1 Commonwealth Cup candidate in 2019.

His older half-sister, Photo Call (by Galileo), was never going to be a sprinter, and although she was blacktype-placed over 12 furlongs, a Grade 3 scorer over 11, and winner of the Grade 1 Rodeo Drive Stakes over 10 furlongs at Santa Anita, her most memorable performance was her defeat of Tepin in the Grade 1 First Lady Stakes over a mile at Keeneland. This was not Tepin at her best, of course, but this two-and-three-quarter-length score was impressive.

Magical always had a chance, on pedigree, to stay 12 furlongs well, even if the odds were tilted slightly in favour of 10 furlongs being as far as she would want to go.

She is one of seven European Group 1 winners for her sire in 2018, one of a remarkable eight top-level stars out of Pivotal mares, and she and her sister are not the only Group 1 stars of the year for their family. Do The Honours, the aforementioned three-parts sister to Verglas, is the grandam of November's Group 1 Lexus Melbourne Cup hero Cross Counter (by Teofilo). Indeed, Brundtland (by Dubawi) was somewhat unlucky not to have made it four family members – the 15-furlong Group 2 scorer was favourite but hampered badly in running in the Group 1 Prix Royal-Oak at Chantilly in late October, eventually passing the line just a length behind the winner, Holdthasigreen. His Group 3 Desmond Stakes-winning dam Future Generation (by Hurricane Run) is out of a half-sister to Do The Honours.

It would be great to see her return to action as a four-year-old, and she looks like one who would do well at that age, but she is, of course, also a potential broodmare of considerable value. Whatever her path in 2019, Magical could become a future dam of Group 1 horses.

SUMMARY DETAILS

Bred: Orpendale, Chelston & Wynatt
Owned: Derrick Smith, Mrs John Magnier & Michael Tabor

MAGICAL (IRE)

Trained: Aidan O'Brien
Country: Ireland
Race record: 211244-414012-
Career highlights: 4 wins inc Qipco British Champions
Fillies & Mares Stakes (Gr1), Kilboy Estate Stakes (Gr2),
Breast Cancer Research Debutante Stakes (Gr2), 2nd Longines
Breeders' Cup Turf (Gr1), Moyglare Stud Stakes (Gr1)

MAGICAL (IRE) - 2015 bay filly

Galileo (IRE)	Sadler's Wells (USA)	Northern Dancer (CAN)
		Fairy Bridge (USA)
	Urban Sea (USA)	Miswaki (USA)
		Allegretta
Halfway To Heaven (IRE)	Pivotal (GB)	Polar Falcon (USA)
		Fearless Revival
	Cassandra Go (IRE)	Indian Ridge
		Rahaam (USA)

MAGNA GRECIA (IRE)

Irish National stud flag bearer Invincible Spirit (by Green Desert) added three new Group 1 winners to his tally in 2018: Eqtidaar won the Commonwealth Cup at Ascot in June and Royal Meeting took the Criterium International at Chantilly the day after Magna Grecia won the Vertems Futurity Trophy Stakes at Doncaster. The latter pair are, of course, two-year-olds, and the colt who won in England is trained in Ireland by Aidan O'Brien. It was his second win in three starts, came a fortnight after he failed by just a neck to beat Persian King in the Group 3 Masar Godolphin Autumn Stakes over a mile at Newmarket, and so almost a month after he had made a three-and-a-half-length winning debut over seven furlongs at Naas.

As you would expect, he holds entries in next year's classics, but what catches the eye about those is that one is in the Group 1 Dubai Duty Free Irish Derby. Can a son of Invincible Spirit win at the highest level of 12 furlongs?

It hasn't happened, yet, but Born To Sea was runner-up to Camelot in that Curragh classic in 2012, the same year that Allied Powers won his second edition of the Group 3 Prix d'Hedouville over 12 furlongs at Longchamp, and two years after that gelding took the Group 2 Grand Prix de Chantilly. It hasn't happened yet, but there is no reason why it can't, and it is the contribution from the distaff side of the individual's pedigree that will be influential.

Of that pair, Born To Sea is out of Group 1 Prix de l'Arc de Triomphe heroine and phenomenal broodmare Urban Sea (by Miswaki), the mare who gave us Galileo (by Sadler's Wells), Sea The Stars (by Cape Cross) and so many more. Allied Powers, on the other hand, is a son of Always Friendly (by High Line) who, in addition to being by a noted source of stamina, was a dual Group 3 scorer over 12 furlongs in England and chased home Assessor in the Group 1 Prix Royal-Oak.

So, what does the distaff side of Magna Grecia's pedigree have to offer? Is he likely to be an eight to 10-furlong colt in 2019 or might he have the stamina to give Invincible Spirit what that stallion's three-parts brother achieved in 2018 – a first Group 1 star over a mile and a half? That Kodiac (by Danehill) horse is, of course, Godolphin's triple top-level winner Best Solution.

Magna Grecia was bred by Woodnook Farm Pty Ltd and he was snapped up by Coolmore partners for 340,000gns at the Tattersalls December Foal Sale of 2016. The late February-born bay is a full-brother to the triple seven-furlong Dundalk scorer Invincible Ryker, a Michael Halford-trained colt who has never tried beyond a mile. Their dam, Cabaret, won the Group 3 Silver Flash Stakes over seven at Leopardstown as a juvenile but was then well-beaten in all four subsequent career starts, which came over a mile, 10 furlongs, and twice over 12, but she is a daughter of Galileo (by Sadler's Wells) and so an immediate reaction would likely be that the issue was something other than stamina.

Of course, not every Galileo is a middle-distance horse, even though it is the stamina gene that he passes on, and that's because receipt of the speed gene from the dam reduces their outer range to 10 furlongs, and sometimes to the mile. Cabaret's siblings include several middle-distance horses, and two seven-furlong blacktype scorers – Drumfire (by Danehill Dancer) and Ho Choi (by Pivotal) – and her own dam was by a mile star. Drumfire, however, stayed 10 furlongs at three, and their dam is Listed Sweet Solera Stakes third Witch Of Fife (by Lear Fan), a mare whose siblings include the dam of Group 3 C L Weld Park Stakes winner and Group 1 Moyglare Stud Stakes runner-up Ugo Fire (by Bluebird).

This family can clearly produce some horses who have speed rather than stamina, but with Cabaret being a Galileo mare whose grandam was placed over 14 furlongs, and that grandam was a half-sister to El Conquistador (by Shirley Heights) – a colt who was runner-up in the Group 3 Goodwood Cup in the days when it was run over two miles, five furlongs – then the odds that Magna Grecia may have what's needed to stay the Derby distance look greatly reduced.

Fife (by Lomond) and El Conquistador also had a notable sibling in Piffle (by Shirley Heights) and that one-time scorer produced two top-level 12-furlong winners: Hollywood Turf Handicap scorer Frenchpark (by Fools Holme) and Prix Vermeille heroine Pearly Shells (by Efisio). The latter, who also won the Group 2 Prix de Mallaret and Group 3 Prix de la Nonette before going on to a successful stud career, was, like Magna Grecia, by a stallion noted for sprinters and milers, yet excelled over a mile and a half. She also passed on that stamina to several of her offspring, including her Group 3-winning daughter Pearl Banks (by Pivotal) and stakes-placed filly Pearly Avenue (by Anabaa).

There are other stakes winners to be found within the branches of these first four generations of the pedigree, but their connection to next year's potential classic contender is remote.

There are no guarantees, of course, but there is more than enough evidence here to suggest that, like Born To Sea and Allied Forces, the Timeform 116p-rated Magna Grecia may have what it takes to become a son of Invincible Spirit who excels over a mile and a half, and that could make him a very interesting prospect.

SUMMARY DETAILS

Bred: Woodnook Farm Pty Ltd
Owned: D Smith, Mrs J Magnier, M Tabor & Flaxman Stables
Ireland
Trained: Aidan O'Brien
Country: Ireland
Race record: 121-
Career highlights: 2 wins inc Vertem Futurity Trophy Stakes (Gr1), 2nd Masar Godolphin Autumn Stakes (Gr3)

MAGNA GRECIA (IRE) - 2016 bay colt

Invincible Spirit (IRE)	Green Desert (USA)	Danzig (USA)
		Foreign Courier (USA)
	Rafha	Kris
		Eljazzi
Cabaret (IRE)	Galileo (IRE)	Sadler's Wells (USA)
		Urban Sea (USA)
	Witch Of Fife (USA)	Lear Fan (USA)
		Fife (IRE)

MASAR (IRE)

Juvenile champion and classic star New Approach (by Galileo) made a lightning-quick start to his stallion career and, in addition to Royal Ascot two-year-olds, his first crop included champion and 2000 Guineas ace Dawn Approach – now a promising young sire with two Group 1 classic-placed fillies in his first crop – and Oaks heroine Talent. His current Group 1 tally stands at seven, and Masar is the most recent new addition to the list.

Godolphin's homebred won two of his five starts as a juvenile, including a two-length defeat of Romanised in the Group 3 BetBright Solario Stakes at Sandown, and he finished third to Happily and Olmedo in the Group 1 Qatar Prix Jean-Luc Lagardere (Grand Criterium) over a mile at Chantilly before finishing an eye-catching sixth to Mendelssohn in the Grade 1 Breeders' Cup Juvenile Turf at Del Mar. He was odds-on first time out at three, but that run can be ignored – it was on dirt at Meydan and what we learned there is that he should stick to turf. His first European outing of the year was in the bet365 Craven Stakes over a mile on good ground at Newmarket and it was a stunning effort. One hopes to see something emerge from the classic trials as a potential star – and not blanket finishes – and Masar made all, quickened a quarter-mile from home, and came home nine lengths clear of his closest pursuer.

Whether or not he returns to action as a four-year-old – and it is to be hoped that he will do so and will live up to his potential – that Newmarket victory is one that should be kept in mind by breeders eventually looking to send him mares. Ignore the fact that Roaring Lion – the odds-on favourite that day and a Timeform 130-rated, four-time Group 1 star subsequently – was third. He was not 'the' Roaring Lion there. And it is true that neither the runner-up nor fourth have turned out to be as good as they could have been. But this was a subsequent Derby hero showing impressive pace over a mile at three.

He was only beaten by one and a half lengths and a head when third to Saxon Warrior and Tip Two Win in the Group 1 Qipco 2000 Guineas just 16 days later, and despite being a classic-placed runaway pattern winner, and bred to be a middle-distance star, he was largely overlooked by punters on the first Saturday in June. He was sent off at 16/1 for the Group 1 Investec Derby but powered home to take the world's most famous classic by a length and a half from Dee Ex Bee, who outstayed Roaring Lion for third.

It is unfortunate that a setback ended his season so early, but in addition to his obvious potential as a top-class four-year-old, Masar also has a pedigree that could see him become a stallion of significance whenever his racing career comes to a close.

His sire's first stallion son – the aforementioned classic-winning miler Dawn Approach – made notable progress in 2018 with the emergence of the classic-placed, blacktype-winning fillies Musis Amica and Mary Tudor from his first crop, and he has a potential classic contender for 2019 in Madhmoon, a Group 2 winner at Leopardstown on Irish Champions Weekend.

Then there's the all-important distaff side of the pedigree, and it gives Masar the potential to sire classic and other Group 1 stars. One of his relations is a prolific champion sire, another has sired a Derby hero of his own, and neither of those stallions showed the precocity that Masar did.

He is the second foal out of Group 2 UAE Derby heroine Khawlah (by Cape Cross), and that half-sister to Group 2 Prix Guillaume d'Ornano winner and Group 1 Jebel Hatta runner-up Vancouverite (by Dansili) is out of Villarrica (by Selkirk). Her immediate relations are her pattern-winning half-brothers Masterstroke (by Monsun) and Moonlight Magic (by Cape Cross) and her Group 2-placed, stakes-winning half-sister Hidden Gold (by Shamardal), and they are all out of Melikah (by Lammtarra), the dual Oaks-placed daughter of Group 1

171

Prix de l'Arc de Triomphe heroine and phenomenal broodmare Urban Sea (by Miswaki).

This makes Masar inbred 3x4 to one of the greatest broodmares of all time, the matriarch who gave us Galileo (by Sadler's Wells), Sea The Stars (by Cape Cross) and their Group/Grade 1-winning siblings Black Sam Bellamy (by Sadler's Wells) and My Typhoon (by Giant's Causeway), and whose many notable descendants include her Group 1 Irish Oaks-winning granddaughter Bracelet (by Montjeu) and that filly's three-parts sister Athena (by Camelot) who took the Grade 1 Belmont Oaks Invitational in July.

Urban Sea's half-brother King's Best (by Kingmambo) won the Group 1 2000 Guineas before going on to become a classic sire – his star son Workforce ran away with the Derby at Epsom before adding the Arc at Longchamp – her three-parts brother Tertullian (by Miswaki) has sired a Group 1 winner, and the stallions who also descend from her dam, Allegretta (by Lombard), include the Group 1 winners and Group 1 sires Anabaa Blue (by Anabaa) and Tamayuz (by Nayef).

If you go back another generation, you find a branch that leads to Group 1 Deutsches Derby star and leading German sire Adlerflug (by In The Wings), among others of note. The plethora of talented horses in the family also include last year's Group 2-winning fillies Tusked Wings (by Adlerflug) and Armande (by Sea The Stars), and this year's notable French sprinter Tantheem (by Teofilo), each of whom also show inbreeding to mares from this female line.

It is to be hoped that Masar can return to action in 2019 to show us what he can do in the broad mile-to-12-furlong range. And with this pedigree behind him, he will make a fascinating stallion prospect.

SUMMARY DETAILS

Bred: Godolphin
Owned: Godolphin
Trained: Charlie Appleby
Country: England

Race record: 13130-0131-
Career highlights: 4 wins inc Investec Derby (Gr1), bet365 Craven Stakes (Gr3), BetBright Solario Stakes (Gr3), 3rd Qipco 2000 Guineas (Gr1), Qatar Prix Jean-Luc Lagardere (Grand Criterium) (Gr1), Chesham Stakes (L)

MASAR (IRE) - 2015 chestnut colt

New Approach (IRE)	Galileo (IRE)	Sadler's Wells (USA)
		Urban Sea (USA)
	Park Express	Ahonoora
		Matcher (CAN)
Khawlah (IRE)	Cape Cross (IRE)	Green Desert (USA)
		Park Appeal
	Villarrica (USA)	Selkirk (USA)
		Melikah (IRE)

MERCHANT NAVY (AUS)

Leading Australian sprinter Merchant Navy, who was an unbeaten listed scorer from three starts as a juvenile, was sent to Ireland to be prepared by Aidan O'Brien for a crack at the Group 1 Diamond Jubilee Stakes at Royal Ascot before the colt would then return 'down under' to begin his stallion career immediately at Coolmore Australia.

There was a possible hitch due to the weight he would have to carry in Europe. When running in the northern hemisphere, he counted as being a four-year-old as he was born before 1st January 2015. But his actual date of birth is 14th November 2014, making him a late-season three-year-old in his native land, yet not entitled to that weight allowance when running here. So, in effect, he was carrying penalties in both his European starts, which makes his performances more meritorious. Calculating that discrepancy based on what a three-year-old receives from an older horse in May and June is not the accurate way to do it as, again, he did it as a late-season three-year-old, just shy of being classed as a four-year-old in his home territory.

With this in mind, he put up an outstanding performance first time out, beating Spirit Of Valor by a length in the Group 2 Weatherbys Ireland Greenlands Stakes at the Curragh. Tasleet was another length-and-a-quarter back in third, with a neck more back to Brando in fourth, each of them receiving weight from him due to his Group 1 penalty.

His effort at Ascot was not as impressive. It was close, very close, and also quite fortunate given how the race went for the runner-up, but Merchant Navy held on by a short-head to take the Ascot feature from the French colt City Light, with American challenger Bound For Nowhere third and English runner The Tin Man fourth. Mission accomplished. There was some brief speculation about whether or not he would remain a bit longer, to take up his entry in the Group 1 Darley July

Cup at Newmarket, but that soon ended. Merchant Navy went into quarantine for a return trip to Australia.

But now he was heading home with a European top-level win to add to his six-furlong Group 1 success at Flemington, and a 126 rating from Timeform that placed him behind only Battaash (133), Harry Angel (131) and Blue Point (129) among sprinters who raced on this continent in 2018. His status was enhanced, he did it as a late-season three-year-old forced to compete as if a four-year-old, and he has no doubt caught the attention of mare owners in this part of the world too.

A listed and Group 3 scorer for trainer Ciaron Maher, he switched to Aaron Purcell and then got up on the line to take the six-furlong Group 1 Coolmore Stud Stakes at Flemington in November 2017. He was only beaten by half a length when Group 2-placed on his next start, then by a neck when third to Redkirk Warrior in the Group 1 Newmarket Handicap in March, over the course and distance of his major win.

He was bred by Chris Barnham, and although there as aspects of the distaff side of his family that won't be familiar to many here, his sire needs no introduction. Fastnet Rock (by Danehill) is one of the most successful of all the reverse-shuttle stallions and his global tally of 142 stakes winners includes 36 who have won at the highest level, including the European-trained Group 1 stars Diamondsandrubies, Fascinating Rock (first foals in 2018), Intricately, Laganore, One Master (Qatar Prix de la Foret in 2018), Qualify, Rivet, and Zhukova.

All but two of that list are fillies, Fascinating Rock is a member of the stallion team at Ballylinch Stud, and this male line got another advertisement at the Curragh this year when Urban Fox, a daughter of Australian Group 1 scorer Foxwedge (by Fastnet Rock) – who reverse-shuttled to Whitsbury Manor Stud for four seasons – sprang a surprise in the Group 1 Juddmonte Pretty Polly Stakes.

Merchant Navy is out of the Group 1-placed, Group 3-winning sprinter Legally Bay (by Snippets) and that makes him a full-brother to Jolie Bay. Also bred by Barnham, she was a short-head winner of the Group 2 Roman Consul Stakes over six furlongs at Randwick a month before chasing home Nechita in the Group 1 Coolmore Stud Stakes over the same trip at Flemington.

Their dam is among a string of winners produced from the seven-furlong and mile scorer Decidity (by Last Tycoon) and those siblings include three of note. The prolific Bonaria (by Redoute's Choice) won the Group 1 VRC Myer Classic over a mile, Time Out (by Rory's Jester) was a six-furlong Group 3 scorer as a juvenile, and four-time sprint winner Chatoyant (by Flying Spur) made her name at stud. That mare's best are by stallions who are very familiar to those in this part of the world. Smart two-year-old Montsegur (by New Approach) won a five-and-a-half-furlong Group 3 at Caulfield and one over six furlongs at Flemington, whereas Tessera (by Medaglia d'Oro), who was stakes-placed at seven, got his best win in a five-and-a-half-furlong juvenile Group 3 contest at Rosehill.

Decidity was out of Class (by Twig Moss), which made her a half-sister to nine-furlong Group 2 scorer Classy Fella (by Kenmare) and what could be described as being a three-parts sister to 12-furlong Group 3 winner Vestey (by Last Tycoon).

It is not impossible that some of the talented future offspring of Merchant Navy will also stay that distance, although it seems likely – given his racing profile and the achievements of those most closely related to him – that he will mostly get sprinters and milers, along with some who will be effective at 10 furlongs. He already has a southern hemisphere breeding season behind him, and he will stand the northern hemisphere half of that first year at Coolmore Stud in 2019, where his fee has been set at €20,000.

SUMMARY DETAILS

Bred: C Barhan, Qld
Owned: Merchant Navy Syndicate / Smith / Magnier / Tabor
Trained: Aidan O'Brien
Country: Ireland
Form: 111-1013311-

Career highlights: 7 wins inc Diamond Jubilee Stakes (Gr1),
Coolmore Stud Stakes (Gr1), Weatherbys Ireland Greenlands
Stakes (Gr2), H.D.F. McNeil Stakes (Gr3), ANZAC Day
Stakes (L), 3rd Lexus Newmarket Handicap (Gr1), Schweppes
Rubiton Stakes (Gr2)

MERCHANT NAVY (AUS) - 2014 bay colt

Fastnet Rock (AUS)	Danehill (USA)	Danzig (USA)
		Razyana (USA)
	Piccadilly Circus (AUS)	Royal Academy (USA)
		Gatana (AUS)
Legally Bay (AUS)	Snippets (AUS)	Lunchtime
		Easy Date (AUS)
	Decidity (AUS)	Last Tycoon
		Class (AUS)

NONZA (FR)

It is an interesting aspect of French racing how many of their homebred stakes and pattern winners carry somewhat unfashionable pedigrees. Sometimes it is even Group 1 and classic stars who emerge from what are, from a pedigree perspective, humble origins. One could not call the distaff side of Nonza's pedigree humble, as it has yielded prior top-level winners, but it is fair to say that it is one of those female lines that has clicked with less fashionable stallions. And in the case of this year's Darley Prix Jean Romanet heroine, that sire is Zanzibari (by Smart Strike).

That lightly-raced grandson of Mr Prospector (by Raise a Native) is out of the speedy Zinziberine (by Zieten), he won the Group 3 Prix de Cabourg over six furlongs at Deauville and was then last of five in Arcano's Group 1 Prix Morny. His dam won over four and a half furlongs in June of her juvenile year, added the Group 2 Criterium de Maisons-Laffitte and Group 3 Prix Eclipse – both over six furlongs – that October, and she clearly got her sire's speed rather than the stamina aspect of the family that yielded her dam's full-brother Amilynx (by Linamix), winner of the Group 1 Prix Royal-Oak.

Zanzibari began his stallion career for a €1,000 fee at Haras du Mesnil and moved to Haras de Grandcamp four years later. In addition to Nonza, he has been represented by the pattern-placed nine-furlong stakes winner Thank You Bye Bye – who stays a bit farther – by multiple stakes-placed sprinter Fastidious – who will be four in 2019 – and also high earner Joyful Trinity. That gelding has won a seven-furlong Group 3 in Hong Kong, was runner-up in a mile Group 1 there, and was previously a winner of the Group 3 Prix de la Porte Maillot when racing in France under the name Baghadur. Those are the shining highlights of his career so far, and clearly not the sort of profile one would expect to see in the sire of a Group 1 star.

Nonza made a winning debut over 10 furlongs on soft ground at Chateaubriant in late April of her three-year-old year and was not seen out for seven months. By then she had moved from the Étienne Leenders team to join the Henri-François Devin one. She ran twice before the end of the year, finishing second and third on Polytrack, at Chantilly and Deauville. In 2018, however, she went undefeated in four starts, kicking off with a pair of nine-and-a-half-furlong events on the artificial track at Chantilly before switching to turf at Maisons-Laffitte in July. There she beat Morgan Le Faye by a length in a 10-and-a-half-furlong listed contest. Deauville and her neck defeat of Group 1 Pretty Polly Stakes winner Urban Fox in the 10-furlong Prix Jean Romet came next, and she was not seen out again after that.

She is out of an unplaced mare Terra Alta, who is by a stallion who has had two stars but mostly minor success aside from those, but one of those standouts is this mare's full-sister Terre A Terre (by Kaldounevees). She won seven times, headed by the Group 1 Dubai Duty Free and Group 1 Prix de l'Opera, and she is the dam of the pattern-placed multiple winner Terra Incognita (by Rock Of Gibraltar). Their full-brother Kachagi was effective from six to 10 furlongs and his 13 wins included a listed race success at Chantilly. Their sire's other big star was Group 1 Hong Vase and dual Group 1 Grand Prix de Saint-Cloud scorer Ange Gabriel, who has no connection to them on his distaff side.

Nonza's grandam, Toujours Juste (by Always Fair), won once as a three-year-old and was placed several times, the next dam is an unraced mare called Soloist (by Alleged), and that makes the Grade 2-placed multiple US stakes winner Solo Haina (by Solo Landing) the fourth dam. She won 13 times from two to five years of age, her son Polished Brass (by Dixie Brass) won a juvenile Grade 3 contest, his half-brother Horatio Luro (by El Gran Senor), and both sired winners – the latter being a classic sire in Hungary. The mare is also notable as being the grandam of Grade 1 Secretariat Stakes third and triple Grade 2 winner Tizdejavu (by Tiznow) –

179

another sire of winners – and she also has some blacktype-earning descendants in Japan.

If you take another step back on the page then you will find that Solo Haina had a half-sister named Silk And Wrapper (by Jontilla), who was a stakes-placed winner of 21 of her 88 starts, and that tough filly went on to become the dam of Grade 1 Vosburgh Stakes winner Birdonthewire (by Proud Birdie), the most successful stallion in these first few generations of the pedigree.

Nonza is a 10-furlong Group 1 winner who represents a family that has done very well without becoming 'fashionable', and all of this will make her a fascinating broodmare prospect, especially if she continues the family trend of visiting stallions who lack a high profile.

SUMMARY DETAILS

Bred: Mme H Devin
Owned: Mme H Devin
Trained: Henri-François Devin
Country: France
Race record: -123-1111-
Career highlights: 5 wins inc Darley Prix Jean Romanet (Gr1), Prix de la Pepiniere - Fonds Europeen de l'Elevage (L)

NONZA (FR) - 2014 bay filly

Zanzibari (USA)	Smart Strike (CAN)	Mr Prospector (USA)
		Classy 'N Smart (CAN)
	Zinziberine (USA)	Zieten (USA)
		Amenixa (FR)
Terra Alta (FR)	Kaldounevees (FR)	Kaldoun (FR)
		Safaroa (FR)
	Toujours Juste (FR)	Always Fair (USA)
		Soloist (USA)

OLMEDO (FR)

We have long been able to say that there are two major branches of the Danzig (by Northern Dancer) line, those forged by his classic-placed, Group 1-winning sprint sons Danehill and Green Desert. It is still too early to know for certain, but the early signs are that a third branch may develop thanks to one of the last of the Danzigs, War Front.

A six-furlong Grade 2 scorer who was Grade 1-placed at six and seven furlongs, the Claiborne Farm resident has become one of the most expensive stallions in the world thanks to a growing string of top-level winners on both sides of the Atlantic. Many of his best are colts, they are going to stud, and now two of them have sired a Group/Grade 1 winner of their own. Two promising sons in early stages of their careers do not make a sire line, but this is an encouraging beginning. The Factor, who returns to Lane's End Farm in Kentucky in 2019 after a single year in Japan, was the first of the War Fronts to hit the Grade 1 mark at stud, and now Ashford Stud stallion Declaration Of War (who will be in Japan in 2019) has done it too.

Winner of the Group 1 Queen Anne Stakes and Group 1 Juddmonte International Stakes for the Aidan O'Brien stable, Declaration Of War spent one season at Coolmore in Ireland before moving to their US branch. His first crop are three-year-olds, they include Group/Grade 3 scorers Actress and Speed Franco, plus pattern-placed, listed race winner Eirene, and also Olmedo. His second crop contains the Todd Pletcher-trained, eight-and-a-half-furlong turf Grade 3 winner Opry, and six-furlong Belmont Park listed scorer Uncle Benny.

Olmedo made a winning debut over seven and a half furlongs at Deauville in August of his juvenile season, he was short-headed by Stage Magic in the Group 3 Prix des Chenes over a mile at Chantilly a month later and then chased home Happily in the Group 1 Qatar Prix Jean-Luc Lagardere (Grand Criterium) over the same course and distance in early October.

This was enough to see him crowned champion French two-year-old colt, and although he was again runner-up when pipped by Wootton in the Group 3 Prix de Fontainebleau over a mile on heavy ground at ParisLongchamp on his seasonal reappearance, he came home in front in the Group 1 Poule d'Essai des Poulains (French 2000 Guineas) on good ground at the same venue in May.

Four lengths covered the first seven home, with longshots in sixth and seventh, but there was every reason to believe that this colt could improve further. For the record, he beat Hey Gaman by a neck, with Dice Roll a nose back in third, then one and three-quarter lengths back to fourth-placed Wootton, who was a length in front of Europe's overall champion juvenile of 2017, U S Navy Flag, who subsequent dropped in distance and landed the Group 1 Darley July Cup at Newmarket.

Unfortunately, Olmedo disappointed in his next two starts, but that does not mean that he can't come back to form and fulfil his potential. He was sent off favourite for the Group 1 Qipco Prix du Jockey Club (French Derby) over 10 and a half furlongs at Chantilly in early June, but he beat only three of the 16 runners. Then he finished last of nine in the Group 1 Qatar Prix Jean Prat over a mile at Deauville in early July and was not seen out again.

Olmedo is trained by Jean-Claude Rouget, he was bred by the Dream With Me Stable Inc and he is a €100,000 graduate of the Arqana August Yearling Sale. He is the second foal of his dam, Super Pie (by Pivotal), and is a half-brother to multiple winner Super Mac (by Makfi). The mare won once at Deauville, her half-brother Art Contemporain (by Smart Strike) was third in the Group 2 Prix Noailles, and her dam, Super Lina (by Linamix), is a Group 3 Prix Penelope runner-up whose siblings feature Super Celebre (by Peintre Celebre). That colt won the Group 2 Prix Noailles and was runner-up in the Group 1 Prix du Jockey-Club (French Derby) and Group 1 Prix Lupin.

Southern Seas (by Jim French) is the fourth dam of Olmedo, and that four-time scorer is best known as being the dam of multiple US Grade 1 star Steinlen (by Habitat) – who won the Breeders' Cup Mile and Arlington Million, among other top races – and grandam of runaway Group 1 Irish Derby star Zagreb (by Theatrical). She is also a more distant ancestor of Stacelita (by Monsun), and not only did that champion win the Group 1 Prix de Diane (French Oaks), Group 1 Prix Saint-Alary, Group 1 Prix Vermeille, Group 1 Prix Jean Romanet, Grade 1 Flower Bowl Invitational Stakes, and Grade 1 Beverley D Stakes, but she is the dam of Japanese champion and classic heroine Soul Stirring (by Frankel).

A berth at stud likely awaits Olmedo when his racing career ends. It is to be hoped that he will have enhanced his record on the track before that time comes.

SUMMARY DETAILS

Bred: Dream With Me Stable Inc
Owned: Ecurie Antonio Caro & Gerard Augustin-Normand
Trained: Jean-Claude Rouget
Country: France
Race record: 122-2100-
Career highlights: 2 wins inc The Emirates Poule d'Essai des Poulains (Gr1), 2nd Qatar Prix Jean-Luc Lagardere (Grand Criterium) (Gr1), Prix de Fontainebleau (Gr3), Prix des Chenes (Gr3)

OLMEDO (FR) - 2015 bay colt

Declaration Of War (USA)	War Front (USA)	Danzig (USA)
		Starry Dreamer (USA)
	Tempo West (USA)	Rahy (USA)
		Tempo (USA)
Super Pie (USA)	Pivotal (GB)	Polar Falcon (USA)
		Fearless Revival
	Super Lina (FR)	Linamix (FR)
		Supergirl (USA)

ONE MASTER (IRE)

If the dam won the Group 3 Molecomb Stakes, the grandam was a champion two-year-old filly in Europe, and other stars on the page include a Group 1 Racing Post Trophy scorer and other talented juveniles, then surely the talented filly who represents their lineage must at least win at that age, right? Not necessarily. And to presume so could lead to a high-class racehorse being written off too soon. Some horses take longer than others, for various reasons, and Lael Stables' homebred One Master (by Fastnet Rock) is a fine example of patience rewarded.

In addition to the Molecomb, her dam, Enticing (by Pivotal), won the Group 3 King George Stakes at Goodwood, was placed in another edition of the five-furlong contest and a trio of other pattern sprints. The Timeform 116-rated mare has produced a trio of winners. Superstar Leo (by College Chapel), the champion, won the Group 3 Norfolk Stakes at Royal Ascot, chased home Minardi in the Group 1 Phoenix Stakes at Leopardstown, then beat Misty Eyes in the Group 2 Flying Childers Stakes before taking on the older horses in France, finishing an honourable length-and-a-half runner-up to Namid in the Group 1 Prix de l'Abbaye de Longchamp. She finished that initial season on a Timeform rating of 114, but was not as talented at three (Timeform 104), with second to Danehurst at Chester and fourth to Invincible Spirit at Newbury – both listed races – the pick of her form. Her nine winning offspring also include mile listed scorer and Group 3 Jersey Stakes runner-up Sentaril (by Danehill Dancer).

Superstar Leo's half-sister Starship (by Galileo) is the one who is responsible for the classic-placed Racing Post Trophy winner Rivet (by Fastnet Rock) and his blacktype-winning, fellow Hong Kong-based full-brother Out And About, in addition to the Group 3 Gallinule Stakes winner and Group 2 King Edward VII Stakes third Alexander Pope (by Danehill Dancer). And that mare's siblings include Rocking (by Oasis

Dream) – whose stakes-winning grandson Son Donato (by Lope De Vega) could become a notable sprinter in 2019 – and New York, the grandam of Australian 10-furlong Group 1 scorer December Draw (by Medecis).

With relations like these, it is no surprise that One Master has shown her best form from six furlongs to a mile, even if she did not even begin her career on the track until mid-August of her three-year-old season.

That debut was in a six-furlong maiden at Doncaster, in which she finished third, she was an odds-on winner over the same trip, on soft ground, at Yarmouth a month later, and then earned a Timeform rating of 107p following a surprise victory in a seven-furlong listed contest at Ascot. The William Haggas-trained bay ran six times in 2018, in four different countries, and always in pattern company. Her first big win of the campaign came on a visit to Tipperary, where she beat Dan's Dream by half a length in the Group 3 Coolmore Stud Fairy Bridge Stakes over seven and a half furlongs, and then she sprang something of a mild shock in France.

She had finished fourth in seven-furlong pattern events at Lingfield and Goodwood earlier in the year, and been only third to Actress in the Group 3 Ballyogan Stakes over six at the Curragh, and even with her recent win in Ireland there did not appear to be any reason to suspect that she could take the Group 1 Qatar Prix de la Foret. But she did. She stayed on strongly in the final furlong of the race and put her nose in front on the line, beating Inns Of Court and Dutch Connection in a three-way photo.

Her next run was arguably an even better performance and one that could make her an interesting contender for races such as the Group 1 Lockinge Stakes, Group 1 Queen Anne Stakes and Group 1 Sussex Stakes if she returns to action as a five-year-old. Once again she was doing her best work in the final furlong, and this time it was in the Grade 1 Breeders' Cup Mile at Churchill Downs where she was beaten by a total of just a length while finishing fifth to Expert Eye. Her final outing was at Sha Tin in December where, although finishing a five-and-a-half-length eighth in the Grade 1 Longines Hong

Kong Mile, she was not disgraced. The race was won easily by local champion Beauty Generation, for whom a possible trip to Europe in 2019 has been mentioned.

One Master is among 36 top-level winners for leading international sire Fastnet Rock (by Danehill), a reverse shuttle stallion who has been champion sire in Australia and has sired sprinters, milers and classic middle-distance horses in both hemispheres. Indeed, his offspring also include the high-class European stayer Torcedor, so they can prove effective at any distance.

She also promises to become a notably successful broodmare, one whose future sons could include a blacktype sire or two – if they prove worthy of a place at stud. Why? Her fourth dam is the Group 2 Nassau Stakes winner Dancing Rocks (by Green Dancer) and so her third dam, Council Rock (by General Assembly), is a half-sister to Glatisant (by Rainbow Quest). That filly won the Group 3 Prestige Stakes over seven furlongs at Goodwood as a juvenile, and her star sons are Footstepsinthesand (by Giant's Causeway) and Pedro The Great (by Henrynavigator). The former is Coolmore's lightly raced but unbeaten Group 1 2000 Guineas winner whose six Group 1 scorers from 56 stakes winners include Chachamaidee. His brother won the Group 1 Phoenix Stakes, stands at Haras de la Haie Neuve in France, and has 2018's Grade 1 Del Mar Oaks heroine Fatale Bere among his first crop.

Also of note is that Glatisant's daughters include Frappe (by Inchinor) and that one-time winner is responsible for classic-placed Grade 1 E.P. Taylor Stakes heroine Curvy (by Galileo), for Group 2 Ribblesdale Stakes winner Thakafaat (by Unfuwain), and for Group 1 Irish 2000 Guineas and Group 1 National Stakes scorer Power (by Oasis Dream). The latter's handful of stakes winners include Group 1-placed juvenile Group 3 scorer Peace Envoy, a Worsall Grange stallion whose first foals will arrive in 2019.

Whether she goes to stud in the spring or returns to training for another year, it seems that there are still more chapters to be written in the story of One Master.

SUMMARY DETAILS

Bred: Lael Stables
Owned: Lael Stables
Trained: William Haggas
Trained: England
Race record: -311-4341100-
Career highlights: 4 wins inc Qatar Prix de la Foret (Gr1), Coolmore Stud Fairy Bridge Stakes (Gr3), totepool British EBF October Stakes (L), 3rd TRM Ballyogan Stakes (Gr3)

ONE MASTER (IRE) - 2014 bay filly

Fastnet Rock (AUS)	Danehill (USA)	Danzig (USA)
		Razyana (USA)
	Piccadilly Circus (AUS)	Royal Academy (USA)
		Gatana (AUS)
Enticing (IRE)	Pivotal (GB)	Polar Falcon (USA)
		Fearless Revival
	Superstar Leo (IRE)	College Chapel (GB)
		Council Rock

POET'S WORD (IRE)

A surprising number of stallions died in the first few months of 2018 and although some of them were, as one might expect, elderly horses living in retirement, several were much younger. The latter include Group 1-winning miler and Dalham Hall Stud resident Poet's Voice, one of the early sire sons of Dubawi (by Dubai Millennium). His initial foals and yearlings lit up the auction ring, his eldest offspring are five years old, he shuttled to Australia and has accumulated a double-digit tally of stakes winners.

But, before the start of 2018, he had no Group 1 winner to his name, and the best of blacktype scorers included Group 2 Mehl-Mulhens Rennen (German 2000 Guineas) winner Poetic Dream and Italian Group 3 mile classic scorers Mi Raccomando (Premio Regina Elena) and Poeta Diletto (Premio Parioli). His southern hemisphere stint had yielded the Group 1-placed Group 2 Roman Consul Stakes winner Viridine – who is out of an Anabaa (by Danzig) mare – three listed race scorers, and also Group 1 Australian Oaks runner-up Perfect Rhyme, who is out of a daughter of Danehill (by Danzig).

For a horse of whom so much was expected, this was a disappointing overall record, but there was one among the 13 whose 2017 form suggested he could go on to strike at the highest level. And, of course, it is all but guaranteed that there are more stakes and pattern winners still to emerge from his younger offspring, some of whom could become racehorses of real note, so the story of Poet's Voice certainly did not end with his premature death. Indeed, in 2018 his blacktype tally included Australian Group 1 winner Trap For Fools, Group 2 Derby Italiano scorer Summer Festival, Group 2 Oaks d'Italia heroine Sand Zabeel, and juvenile Group 3 winner Arctic Sound.

Poet's Word was that promising son from 2017 and he did indeed fulfil his potential by hitting the very top in 2018. The

Sir Michael Stoute-trained bay represents his late sire's first crop, and he is now about to embark on a new phase of his career because he has joined the stallion team at Nunnery Stud in Norfolk, with an initial fee of £7,000. The new recruit excelled as a middle-distance horse, but that does not mean that he will be a source of only similar types at stud, as he's the son of a miler and from the family of a speedy horse who went on to sire several Group 1 stars from six to 10 and a half furlongs, including a classic winner, despite dying at a young age.

Poet's Word was bred by Woodcote Stud, was fourth over seven furlongs on his only start at two, won handicaps over 10 and 11 furlongs at Nottingham and Goodwood from five starts at three, and was among the leading older horses in Europe at the age of four. He began that campaign with handicap success at Chelmsford, was only beaten a neck by Deauville in the Group 3 Huxley Stakes over the extended 10 furlongs at Chester and then landed the Group 3 Betfred Glorious Stakes over 12 on soft ground at Goodwood, beating Second Step by a length and a half. That was a useful effort but it is what he did after in the latter part of that season that was impressive, even though those three runs all ended in defeat.

First, he failed by just half a length to beat Decorated Knight in the Group 1 Qipco Irish Champion Stakes at Leopardstown, he chased home Cracksman in the Group 1 Qipco Champion Stakes at Ascot, was only beaten about five lengths when sixth to Time Warp in the Group 1 Longines Hong Kong Cup at Sha Tin. Timeform rated him 124. His sire received a figure of 126 from that same organisation but the son now has the father beaten as he retired to stud with a Timeform mark of 132.

Poet's Word kicked off his 2018 campaign by chasing home Hawkbill in the Group 1 Longines Dubai Sheema Classic at Meydan in late March, was an odds-on winner of the Group 3 Matchbook Brigadier Gerard Stakes over 10 furlongs at Sandown two months later, and then caused something of a sensation when taking the Group 1 Prince of Wales's Stakes over the same trip at Royal Ascot in June, beating the brilliant Cracksman by two and a quarter lengths and with old rival Hawkbill another eight lengths back in third.

It was an exceptionally good performance, even allowing for the fact that Cracksman did not run up to his best (and had reportedly sustained a head injury coming out of the stalls). The third, also now retired, is a good horse and proven multiple Group 1 star for whom this was the ideal distance. A month later, over a quarter-mile farther at the same venue, Poet's Word proved that his newfound level of talent was no one-off performance as he beat Crystal Ocean by a neck to take the Group 1 King George VI and Queen Elizabeth Stakes, also on fast ground. This time the additional margin back to the third was nine lengths, with the spot being filled by the high-class filly Coronet.

After this, it was on to York for the Group 1 Juddmonte International Stakes over 10 and a quarter furlongs and he was sent off favourite to complete a top-level hat-trick. This day, however, he had to settle for the runners-up spot as Roaring Lion, who had won the Coral-Eclipse on his previous start, powered to victory by three and a quarter lengths. Thundering Blue, the only non-Group 1 winner in the line-up, ran a huge race to be third, with 2000 Guineas hero and Eclipse runner-up Saxon Warrior fourth.

A rematch with Roaring Lion – now finally showing the full potential he had promised – was eagerly anticipated, but while that colt went on to add the Group 1 Qipco Irish Champion Stakes and Group 1 Queen Elizabeth II Stakes en route to a new stallion career at Tweenhills Farm and Stud in Gloucestershire, Poet's Word did not make it back to the track. He had been among the ante-post favourites for the Group 1 Qipco Champion Stakes and Grade 1 Breeders' Cup Turf at Churchill Downs but sustained an injury shortly after York. His retirement was announced in mid-September.

The first point of note about the distaff side of his pedigree is that he is the sixth foal of Whirly Bird (by Nashwan) and that makes him a half-brother to two fillies of note: the talented former Mick Channon-trainee Malabar (by Raven's

Pass) and two-time scorer Whirly Dancer (by Danehill Dancer). The latter is the dam of last year's Group 2 Railway Stakes winner Beckford (by Bated Breath), who was runner-up in the Group 1 National Stakes and Group 1 Phoenix Stakes for the Gordon Elliott stable before moving to the USA, where he has won a five-furlong turf listed race for trainer Brendan Walsh, on his only start to date.

Malabar, on the other hand, won the Group 3 Prestige Stakes over seven furlongs at two, added the Group 3 Thoroughbred Stakes over a mile at three – both at Goodwood – and although the performances do not count for blacktype, she was fourth in each of the Group 1 1000 Guineas, Group 1 Prix Marcel Boussac and Group 1 Moyglare Stud Stakes.

Their dam was trained by Amanda Perrett, won five of her seven starts, and earned her blacktype when finishing third in the Listed Harvest Stakes over 11 and a half furlongs at Windsor on her final outing, so it is no surprise that Poet's Word stayed middle-distances. Her half-brother Ursa Major (by Galileo) won a 14-furlong Group 3 contest at the Curragh a month before finishing fourth to Encke, Camelot, and Michelangelo in the Group 1 St Leger at Doncaster, and the pair also have two half-sisters of note.

Inchiri (by Sadler's Wells) won a listed contest over 12 furlongs, and Inchberry (by Barathea) was a maiden in eight starts but listed-placed over a mile at Pontefract and missed out on a more notable accolade – classic placing – when finishing a two and a half-length fourth to Casual Look in the Group 1 Oaks at Epsom. She is also the dam of Measuring Time (by Dubai Destination) who was placed in several middle-distance pattern events.

They are all out of one-time scorer Inchyre (by Shirley Heights) and so the third dam of Poet's Word is Inchmurrin (by Lomond). A stakes-winning sprinter at two, she went on to beat classic-placed Dabaweyaa by five lengths in the Group 2 Child Stakes (now Falmouth Stakes) at Newmarket, shortly after chasing home Magic Of Life in the Group 1 Coronation Stakes at Ascot, and her final start resulted in a fourth-place finish to Sudden Love in the Grade 1 E P Taylor Stakes at Woodbine. The best of her offspring was the Group 1-placed triple Group 3 scorer Inchinor (by Ahonoora) – who died at the age of 13 – and so Poet's Word's grandam is a half-sister to the sire of Group 1 stars Cape Of Good Hope, Latice, Notnowcato, Silca's Sister and Summoner.

Inchinor's stakes-winning half-sister Ingozi (by Warning) is the dam of Grade 1 E P Taylor Stakes heroine Miss Keller (by Montjeu) and grandam of Group 1 St Leger star Harbour Law (by Lawman), and the long list of stakes and pattern winners among Inchmurrin's descendants also include Agent Murphy (by Cape Cross), Ayaar (by Rock Of Gibraltar), Blue Bayou (by Bahamian Bounty), Fantastic Pick (by Fantastic Light), Hatta Fort (by Cape Cross), and Venus De Milo (by Duke Of Marmalade). This selection represents a mixture of speed and stamina.

If you go back another step and take a look at the record of the fourth dam On Show (by Welsh Pageant) then you find that Inchmurrin was a half-sister to Group 2 Mill Reef Stakes winner Welney (by Habitat) and full-sister to Balnaha, the winning dam of Group 1 Coronation Stakes scorer Balisada (by Kris). However, it is Poet's Word's relationship to Inchinor that is most eye-catching when it comes to considering his prospects as a stallion.

Stud success sometimes skips a generation in mares – so, given his relationship to Inchinor, might we see this in Poet's Word? Seeking The Gold (by Mr Prospector) was an excellent stallion, but his brilliant son Dubai Millennium got just five stakes winners from his sole crop. One of the five was Group 1 winner and outstanding sire Dubawi, whose son Poet's Voice has done okay without qualifying for the label 'a good sire', but has among his 16 stakes winners a peak Timeform 132-rated son who has joined the team at a famous stud farm. Time will tell.

SUMMARY DETAILS

Bred: Woodcote Stud Ltd
Owned: Saeed Suhail

Trained: Sir Michael Stoute
Country: England
Race record: 4-31412-121220-21112-
Career highlights: 7 wins inc King George VI and Queen Elizabeth Stakes (sponsored by Qipco) (Gr1), Prince of Wales's Stakes (Gr1), Matchbook Brigadier Gerard Stakes (Gr3), Betfred Glorious Stakes (Gr3), 2nd Juddmonte International Stakes (Gr1), Longines Dubai Sheema Classic (Gr1), Qipco Irish Champion Stakes (Gr1), Qipco Champion Stakes (Gr1), sportingbet.com Huxley Stakes (Gr3)

POET'S WORD (IRE) - 2013 bay horse

Poet's Voice (GB)	Dubawi (IRE)	Dubai Millennium (GB)
		Zomaradah (GB)
	Bright Tiara (USA)	Chief's Crown (USA)
		Expressive Dance (USA)
Whirly Bird (GB)	Nashwan (USA)	Blushing Groom (FR)
		Height Of Fashion (FR)
	Inchyre (GB)	Shirley Heights
		Inchmurrin (IRE)

POLYDREAM (IRE)

July Cup hero and Banstead Manor Stud-based Oasis Dream has long been established as one of Europe's leading sires, and he had already secured his name on the protected list before the 2018 season began. This feat requires a stallion getting a minimum of 15 individual Group/Grade 1 winners, and from his initial crop – born in 2005 – to his 2012 crop – which contained Charming Thought and Muhaarar – he had hit that target. It is odd that, as yet, no top-level winner has emerged from either his 2013 or 2014 crop, and his fee has dropped in recent seasons, falling to just £30,000 in 2018. It is remaining at that level for 2019.

Some of his stock improve with time, so those blanks could yet be filled in, but he already has one from each of the next two batches: two-year-old star Pretty Pollyanna and three-year-old French ace Polydream.

The latter is a Wertheimer brothers' homebred and first caught the eye at the end of July 2017 when taking a six-furlong race for newcomers at Deauville. She followed that with a one-and-three-quarter-length defeat of the subsequent multiple Group 1 star Laurens in the Group 3 Prix du Calvados over seven at the same venue, and then chased home Wild Illusion in the Group 1 Prix Marcel Boussac over a mile. That race was on soft ground and she also won on that type of surface in 2018, when beating Inns Of Court by a length and a quarter in the Group 3 Prix du Palais Royal. That seven-furlong victory came a few weeks after a disappointing run in the Group 1 Poule d'Essai des Pouliches (French 1000 Guineas) and it preceded her half-length defeat of James Garfield in the Group 1 Prix Maurice de Gheest at Deauville.

That six-and-a-half-furlong contest has been won by some outstanding horses in the past, and there was every reason to hope that Polydream would also become one of its high-profile winners. She was sent off favourite for the Group 1 Qatar Prix de la Foret at ParisLongchamp two months later but encountered trouble in running, and by the time she got clear and charged home, it was too late. She finished seventh to One Master, beaten a total of three and a half lengths. The Grade 1 Breeders' Cup Mile was to have been her next start but in a decision that trainer Freddy Head called "a disgrace", Kentucky Horse Racing Commission vets deemed her lame in a foreleg and ordered her scratched from the race the day before the race. She had been one of the ante-post favourites. Head pointed out that the filly has offset knees, and that this is why she has an awkward trot, but the decision was final.

It would be great to see Polydream back in action as a four-year-old, and it will also be fascinating to follow her eventual career at stud. She is by a leading sire, her first three dams were all stakes winners, her fourth dam was Group 1 placed, and there are plenty of other blacktype winners on the page too.

Evaporation (by Red Ransom) is the better of her two blacktype siblings, and that filly's five wins included listed races at Maisons-Laffitte and Compiegne. She was also placed in a string of pattern contests, including the Group 2 Prix de Sandringham, Group 2 Prix du Muguet, and Group 2 Prix Daniel Wildenstein. Their half-brother Ankle (by Shamardal) is a stakes-placed winner and their half-sister Big Brothers Pride (by Invincible Spirit) could be one to note for 2019. That François Rohaut-trained juvenile made a winning debut over six furlongs at Chantilly in mid-October and had a listed entry in November (didn't run), so she would appear to be held in high regard.

They are out of Polygreen (by Green Tune), who was sold in a €200,000 private transaction at the Arqana December Sale just months after Polydream was born. Her listed success came over a mile at Saint-Cloud, she missed out on pattern placing when fourth to Turtle Bow in the Group 2 Prix d'Astarte, and her successful siblings include the dual stakes-placed sprinter Perfect Blessings (by Kheleyf). Her dam, Yxenery (by Sillery) won the Listed Prix Saraca at Evry and Listed Prix La Camargo at Saint-Cloud, and that smart miler is out of Polyxena (by Lyphard), a listed scorer at eight and 10 furlongs.

The fourth dam of Polydream is, therefore, Group 1 Criterium des Pouliches runner-up Minstrel Girl (by Luthier), with her third dam being a half-sister to Truculent (by Val De l'Orne). He was a Group 3 winner at eight, nine and 10 furlongs in France in the early 1980s, was runner-up in the Group 1 Grand Criterium at two, finished fourth to Darshaan in the Group 1 Prix du Jockey Club over 12 furlongs, and was later a stakes winner in California.

If you go back another generation then you will find that the fifth dam of Polydream is 1968's Cheveley Park Stakes heroine Mige (by Saint Crespin), which makes her sixth dam Midget II (by Djebe). That pair were owned and bred by Pierre Wertheimer, and the latter – a half-sister to classic-placed King George VI and Queen Elizabeth Stakes winner Vimy (by Wild Risk) – was a filly of exceptional talent. She earned a Timeform rating of 130 after her impressive victory in the Cheveley Park Stakes in 1955 and went on to add the Coronation Stakes, Prix Maurice de Gheest, Prix de la Foret, Queen Elizabeth Stakes and Prix de Meautry, as well as being placed in both the 1000 Guineas and Prix de Diane (French Oaks). Her Timeform rating at three was 'only' 125.

Polydream, therefore, represents a branch of the family that has produced the Group 1 stars Ma Biche (by Key To The Kingdom), Kistena (by Miswaki) and Belardo (by Lope De Vega), and also the successful Irish stallion Mujadil (by Storm Bird) among others of note, although those particular horses are remotely connected to her.

SUMMARY DETAILS

Bred: Wertheimer et Frere
Owned: Wertheimer et Frere
Trained: Freddy Head
Country: France
Race record: 112-0110-
Career highlights: 4 wins inc LARC Prix Maurice de Gheest (Gr1), Prix du Palais Royal (Gr3), Shadwell Prix du Calvados (Gr3), 2nd Total Prix Marcel Boussac - Criterium des Pouliches (Gr1)

POLYDREAM (IRE) - 2015 bay filly

Oasis Dream (GB)	Green Desert (USA)	Danzig (USA)
		Foreign Courier (USA)
	Hope (IRE)	Dancing Brave (USA)
		Bahamian
Polygreen (FR)	Green Tune (USA)	Green Dancer (USA)
		Soundings (USA)
	Yxenery (IRE)	Sillery (USA)
		Polyxena (USA)

PRETTY POLLYANNA (GB)

In 1990, Stetchworth Park Stud sent a filly to the sales in Newmarket, but she failed to meet her reserve, a figure that Timeform later quoted as being 25,000gns. Owner-breeder Bill Gredley kept the daughter of runaway Derby hero Slip Anchor (by Shirley Heights), put her in training with Clive Brittain, and in late April of her three-year-old season, she sprang a 25/1 surprise with a debut success over 10 furlongs at Sandown.

She won the Listed Oaks Trial at Lingfield two weeks later and then went to Epsom where she notched up the first leg of the Group 1 four-timer that would see her earn the accolade Racehorse of the Year and a Timeform rating of 128. User Friendly took up the running three furlongs from home and stayed on well to beat subsequent mile Group 1 star All At Sea by three and a half lengths in the Oaks – the pair finishing 20 lengths clear of third-placed longshot Pearl Angel. Next stop was the Group 1 Irish Oaks at the Curragh, where she defeated subsequent Group 1 scorer Market Booster and Arrikala by a neck and half-length. Bineyah, who finished fourth in that classic, was the one who chased her home when she took the Group 1 Yorkshire Oaks by two and a half lengths on the Knavesmire the following month.

The Group 1 St Leger was the obvious target and she was sent off favourite to beat six rivals. George Duffield sent her to the front two out, looked around for dangers, and then rode her out to the line for a three-and-a-half-length victory over Sonus, with Bonny Scot a neck back third and Shuailaan fourth. Her unbeaten record came to an end in the Group 1 Prix le d'Arc de Triomphe when, having taken up the running from St Jovite in the straight, she got into a lengthy battle with Subotica, who won by a neck. She was not quite as good at four, yet still won the Group 1 Grand Prix de Saint-Cloud, and, after being sold to Gary Tanaka, a spell in the US at five yielded just a listed race win over eight and a half furlongs at Del Mar.

The daughter of Group 3 Ormonde Stakes fourth (did count for blacktype in those days) Rostova (by Blakeney) disappointed as a broodmare, although she did get the ill-fated Group 3 Give Thanks Stakes winner Downtown (by Danehill) and she is the grandam of current Chris Waller-trained ace Youngstar (by High Chaparral). That one landed the Group 1 Queensland Oaks in May, chased home the great Winx in the Group 1 Turnbull Stakes over 10 furlongs at Flemington in early October and then finished sixth to Cross Counter in the Group 1 Lexus Melbourne Cup a month later, beaten by less than six lengths.

Indeed, Rostova only produced three winners from 11 foals – the other pair were User Friendly's multiple-winning full-brothers Sea Freedom and Williamshakespeare – but it is their unraced half-sister Friendlier (by Zafonic) who has kept the family going in the northern hemisphere. She is the dam of Listed Pretty Polly Stakes third Madame Defarge (by Motivator) and of Gender Agenda (by Holy Roman Emperor), a five-time winner who landed a nine-furlong Grade 3 contest at Santa Anita and finished third in a Grade 2 at Del Mar. The mare is also responsible for Unex Mona Lisa (by Shamardal).

That filly was unraced but has produced three winners from three foals of racing age. The third of them was offered for sale from Tattersalls' Book 1 last year, but she was bought back for 50,000gns and put into training by her owner-breeders, the Gredleys of Stetchworth & Middle Park Studs. The Michael Bell-trained bay sprang a 14/1 surprise on her debut in a six-furlong Sandown maiden in mid-June, finished fifth (to Main Edition, La Pelosa, Fairyland, and Angel's Hideaway) in what turned out to be an usually strong edition of the Group 3 Albany Stakes at Royal Ascot eight days later, and then put up one of the most visually impressive performances of the year from a juvenile.

Pretty Pollyanna trounced subsequent easy pattern winner Angel's Hideaway by seven lengths to take the Group 2 Duchess of Cambridge Stakes at Newmarket, with third-placed Chaleur another six lengths behind. She went to France the following month and beat Group 2 Queen Mary Stakes and Group 2 Prix Robert Papin heroine Signora Cabello by three-parts of a length in the Group 1 Darley Prix Morny, with True Mason four lengths back in third and another two-and-a-half-length gap to Land Force.

Her final two runs of the year were disappointing in comparison – she was a one-and-three-quarter-length fourth to Fairyland in the Group 1 Juddmonte Cheveley Park Stakes and then looked as though not quite lasting the trip when third to Iridessa in the Group 1 bet365 Fillies' Mile – but she finished her first season as the most highly ranked juvenile filly of the year on Timeform ratings. Her 116 is some way behind overall juvenile champion Too Darn Hot's 127p, but she is 3lbs clear of the next-best fillies: Iridessa and Skitter Scatter.

One would imagine that an Oasis Dream (by Green Desert) filly out of a Shamardal (by Giant's Causeway) mare from the family of User Friendly would have a good chance of staying a mile at three, and she does hold an entry in the Group 1 Tattersalls Irish 1000 Guineas. But the amount of speed that she showed during the summer, combined with how she ran in the Fillies' Mile, suggests that perhaps she may be more of a Commonwealth Cup filly than a classic one. It will be good to see her back in action in 2019 and fascinating to see how her career turns out, both on the track and, eventually, at stud.

SUMMARY DETAILS

Bred: Stetchworth & Middle Park Studs Ltd
Owned: W J and T C O Gredley
Trained: Michael Bell
Country: England
Race record: 101143-
Career highlights: 3 wins inc Darley Prix Morny (Gr1) Duchess of Cambridge Stakes (Gr2), 3rd bet365 Fillies' Mile (Gr1)

PRETTY POLLYANNA (GB) - 2016 bay filly

Oasis Dream (GB)	Green Desert (USA)	Danzig (USA)
		Foreign Courier (USA)
	Hope (IRE)	Dancing Brave (USA)
		Bahamian
Unex Mona Lisa (GB)	Shamardal (USA)	Giant's Causeway (USA)
		Helsinki (GB)
	Friendlier (GB)	Zafonic (USA)
		Rostova

QUORTO (IRE)

A Godolphin-owned colt made a promising debut over six furlongs in June, followed that with victory in the Superlative Stakes over seven furlongs at Newmarket, and then advertised his classic potential with an impressive win in the Group 1 National Stakes over the same trip at the Curragh. Timeform rated the unbeaten bay 123p. He was out of a mare who was a high-class middle-distance performer, one who had classic form to her name despite being by a promising yet unfashionable sire, and there was much anticipation about what he might achieve as a three-year-old. Further Group 1 success would surely come his way. That was 14 years ago.

The Saeed bin Suroor-trained Dubawi (by Dubai Millennium) went on to take the Group 1 Irish 2000 Guineas by two lengths from Oratorio, he finished an honourable third to Motivator in the Derby at Epsom, then beat Whipper by a length and a half to take the Group 1 Prix Jacques le Marois at Deauville before finishing runner-up to Starcraft in the Group 1 Queen Elizabeth II Stakes at Newmarket on his final start. He retired to Dalham Hall Stud with a Timeform rating of 129. The top-class miler, a son of Group 1 Oaks d'Italia winner Zomaradah (by Deploy), is now one of the world's most sought-after stallions, with 38 Group 1 stars to his name among an overall total of 161 stakes winners, and 14 offspring who have earned in excess of £1 million on the track, so far.

In 2018, a Godolphin homebred won a six-furlong maiden in June and followed that with an impressive three-and-three-quarter-length success in the Group 2 Superlative Stakes at Newmarket before going to the Curragh where he beat Anthony Van Dyck by one and a quarter lengths in the Group 1 Goffs Vincent O'Brien National Stakes. Quorto is an unbeaten son of Dubawi, he is out of a mare who had middle-distance classic form yet is by a somewhat unfashionable stallion, and this Timeform 122p-rated colt is one of the most exciting prospects for 2019.

The Charlie Appleby-trained bay is the first foal of Volume, whose Group 1 Coral-Eclipse Stakes-winning sire Mount Nelson (by Rock Of Gibraltar) stood at Newsells Park Stud before being switched to a dual-purpose role at Boardsmill Stud in 2017. She was trained by the recently retired Luca Cumani, won a maiden and nine-furlong nursery at two, and added listed success over 10 furlongs at Newbury before taking third to Taghrooda in the Group 1 Investec Oaks at Epsom and a closer third to Bracelet and Tapestry in the Group 1 Darley Irish Oaks at the Curragh, beaten by a neck and the same having tried to make all.

Her half-brother Velox (by Zamindar) has been Group 3-placed over 10 furlongs in Australia, her dam won over a mile at Chantilly, and that mare – Victoire Finale (by Peintre Celebre) – is a half-sister to classic-placed stayer Vertical Speed (by Bering). He won the Group 2 Prix Hubert de Chaudenay and Group 3 Prix du Lys and lost his unbeaten record on his final start, when chasing home Silver Patriarch in the Group 1 St Leger at Doncaster. He has had some success as a National Hunt stallion.

It is going to be interesting to see just how far Quorto will stay in 2019. Dubawi was by a Timeform 140-rated 10-furlong champion and out of a middle-distance mare but was a miler, and his son appears to have inherited his speed. The big question is what the colt has got from his dam. She is a granddaughter of an outstanding miler – Rock Of Gibraltar (by Danehill) – and there are some notable six to 10-furlong horses in her family. But Victoire Finale's aforementioned half-brother got their dam's stamina, and that mare – Victoire Bleue (by Legend Of France) – won the Group 1 Prix du Cadran over two and a half miles.

The fourth dam of Quorto is, therefore, Group 1 Prix Vermeille third Vosges (by Youth), and his fifth dam is Group 3 Prix de Mallaret winner, Group 1 Yorkshire Oaks runner-up and Group 1 Prix de Diane (French Oaks) third Virunga (by Sodium). The latter's high-class sons Vin De France (by Foolish Pleasure) and Vacarme (by Lyphard) – who won the Group 1 Prix Jacques le Marois and Group 2 Mill Reef Stakes respectively – are distantly related to Quorto, and those who descend from their unraced half-sister Venise (by Nureyev) are even more so, although the best of them must be mentioned because they include the Group 1 stars Volga (by Caerleon), Vallee Enchantee (by Peintre Celebre) and Vespone (by Llandaff).

Some like to go farther back in time to look for answers, but although that will show that the ninth dam of Quorto is 1933's juvenile filly champion and subsequent 1000 Guineas heroine and Champion Stakes runner-up Campanula (by Blandford), each member of her generation of the pedigree contributes 0.195% to the current horse, so her presence on the extended page is not really anything more than an 'oh, that's interesting' moment. What really matters is what's there in the first few generations of the pedigree, and what they tell us is that the odds lean towards the colt staying at least 10 furlongs, and possibly also the Derby distance. He is a highly promising colt, and it will be fascinating to find out just how good he is, and what distance suits him best.

SUMMARY DETAILS

Bred: Godolphin
Owned: Godolphin
Trained: Charlie Appleby
Country: England
Race record: 111-
Career highlights: 3 wins inc Goffs Vincent O'Brien National Stakes (Gr1), bet365 Superlative Stakes (Gr2)

QUORTO (IRE) - 2016 bay colt

Dubawi (IRE)	Dubai Millennium (GB)	Seeking The Gold (USA)
		Colorado Dancer
	Zomaradah (GB)	Deploy
		Jawaher (IRE)
Volume (GB)	Mount Nelson (GB)	Rock Of Gibraltar (IRE)
		Independence (GB)
	Victoire Finale (GB)	Peintre Celebre (USA)
		Victoire Bleue (FR)

RECOLETOS (FR)

Multiple Group 1 star Whipper (by Miesque's Son) looked full of promise when he retired to stud, and not just because of his considerable talent as a racehorse. He is by a full-brother to leading sire Kingmambo (by Mr Prospector), he could be described as being a three-parts brother to the top-class filly Divine Proportions (by Kingmambo), and his grandam was a full-sister to dual Derby hero and influential stallion Shirley Heights (by Mill Reef). He has three top-level winners among a total of 26 blacktype scorers, but that is from 10 crops of racing age, which is below the level of achievement that would have hoped of him.

He spent five years at Ballylinch Stud in Ireland, then five at Haras du Mezeray, two at Haras de Gelos, and he moved to Haras de Treban in 2018. His best before this year were Group 1 Prix d l'Abbaye de Longchamp heroine Wizz Kid, Italian mile Group 1 scorer Waikika, and the Group 1-placed Group 2 winners Pollyana, Royal Bench, and Recoletos. The latter had taken both the Group 2 Prix Greffulhe and Group 3 Prix du Prince d'Orange in 2017, finished third to Brametot in the Group 1 Prix du Jockey Club (French Derby), and fourth to Cracksman in the Group 1 Qipco Champion Stakes. Timeform rated him 118.

In 2018, Recoletos became a dual Group 1 winner, and the Timeform 125-rated star is now about to embark on a stallion career of his own, at the famous Haras du Quesnay. He kicked off the season with a near two-length defeat of Jimmy Two Times in the Group 2 Prix du Muguet over a mile at Saint-Cloud and followed that with victory in the Group 1 Prix d'Ispahan at ParisLongchamp, this time beating Almodovar by a length and three-quarters. He disappointed when only seventh behind Accidental Agent in the Group 1 Queen Anne Stakes at Royal Ascot in June, but bounced back from that to chase home Alpha Centauri in the Group 1 Prix du Haras de Fresney-le-Buffard Jacques le Marois at Deauville in August.

He then grabbed a second top-level win when getting up almost on the line to beat Wind Chimes by a head in the Group 1 Prix du Moulin de Longchamp – in which Expert Eye was another length and a half back in third – before heading to Ascot for what would be his final race. The Timeform 125-rated colt was beaten just under two lengths when fifth to Roaring Lion in the Group 1 Queen Elizabeth II Stakes. Although both his pattern wins of 2017, plus his first one of 2018 came on soft ground, his second top-level victory came on good, so plenty of ease in the underfoot conditions was not a requisite for him. That said, the one time that he ran on fast ground resulted in the disappointing seventh-place finish at Royal Ascot.

Sarl Darpat France's homebred Recoletos stays farther than his sire did, but as he comes from the direct family of a Timeform 135-rated dual Derby hero, that's not really a surprise. He is trained by Carlos Laffon-Parias, and he is the best of several winners for his dam, Highphar (by Highest Honor). His half-sister and stablemate Castellar (by American Post) won both the Group 2 Shadwell Prix de la Nonette and Group 3 Prix Cleopatre in 2018, and his dam is an unraced daughter of the Grade 2 Garden City Breeders' Cup Handicap and Group 3 Prix de Sandringham scorer Pharatta (by Fairy King). That talented filly, whose top wins came over nine and eight furlongs respectively, is out of the unraced Sharata (by Darshaan), which makes her a half-sister to Group 2 Premio Ribot and Group 3 September Stakes scorer Crimson Tide (by Sadler's Wells), a successful sire in Brazil.

The next dam is triple winner Shademah (by Thatch) and so Sharata, the third dam of Recoletos, is a half-sister to the Aga Khan's homebred dual Derby hero but poor stallion Shahrastani (by Nijinsky). He won the Group 3 Guardian Classic Trial and Group 2 Dante Stakes before that somewhat fortunate defeat of Dancing Brave at Epsom, and then ran away with the Group 1 Irish Derby before finishing fourth behind his old rival in both the Group 1 King George VI and Queen Elizabeth Stakes at Ascot and Group 1 Prix de l'Arc de Triomphe at Longchamp in what was a vintage year – 1986.

His dam was a half-sister to Group 1 Grand Prix de Saint-Cloud winner Shakapour (by Kalamoun), to Grade 1 Bowling Green Handicap scorer Sharannpour (by Busted), and to Shashna (by Blakeney) – the unplaced dam of Group 1 Prix de Diane (French Oaks) heroine Shemaka (by Nishapour) – and they were out of Shamim (by Le Haar), a winning half-sister to the classic-placed Group 2 Prix du Conseil de Paris winner Kamaraan (by Tanerko).

Recoletos is not in the same league as his most famous relation – but then, few horses are. He is a classic-placed dual Group 1 winner, and although his best form came as a four-year-old, it is possible that this is at least in part due to him dropping down in distance this year rather than being entirely about maturity. He is to stand at one of France's most famous studs, and it would be no surprise to see him become a successful sire. His fee has been set at €8,000.

SUMMARY DETAILS

Bred: Sarl Darpat France
Owned: Sarl Darpat France
Trained: Carlos Laffon-Parias
Country: France
Race record: 0-1113014-110210-
Career highlights: 7 wins inc Prix du Moulin de Longchamp (Gr1), Churchill Coolmore Prix d'Ispahan (Gr1), Prix du Muguet (Gr2), Prix Greffulhe (Gr2), Prix du Prince d'Orange (Gr3), 2nd Prix du Haras de Fresney-le-Buffard Jacques le Marois (Gr1), 3rd Qipco Prix du Jockey Club (Gr1)

RECOLETOS (FR) - 2014 bay colt

Whipper (USA)	Miesque's Son (USA)	Mr Prospector (USA)
		Miesque (USA)
	Myth To Reality (FR)	Sadler's Wells (USA)
		Millieme
Highphar (FR)	Highest Honor (FR)	Kenmare (FR)
		High River (FR)
	Pharatta (IRE)	Fairy King (USA)
		Sharata (IRE)

RHODODENDRON (IRE)

The phrase 'breed the best to the best and hope for the best' has long been used by many thoroughbred producers. All too often it soon becomes apparent that the dreams of stardom have been dashed, but there are, of course, many Group 1 performers who are the product of Group 1-winning parents. Rhododendron, a daughter of Derby hero and prolific champion sire Galileo (by Sadler's Wells) and of the triple Group 1 ace Halfway To Heaven (by Pivotal), is just one notable example of where it succeeded.

The Aidan O'Brien-trained bay was bred by Orpendale, Chelston & Wynatt and she achieved her top first billing with an impressive two and a quarter-length defeat of Hydrangea in the Group 1 Dubai Fillies' Mile at Newmarket as a two-year-old. It was her fifth start of the season, she had beaten that same rival by a head in the Group 2 Debutante Stakes over seven furlongs at the Curragh about seven weeks before, and between those outings she took third in the Group 1 Moyglare Stud Stakes, beaten a total of one and three-quarter lengths by Intricately and Hydrangea, who passed the post together.

All of this made her a leading classic contender for 2017, and the obvious question was this: how far would she stay? Some presume that if it's by Galileo then it will stay middle-distances, and maybe a little farther, but as was the case with his great sire, Sadler's Wells (by Northern Dancer), some of the Galileos out of speed-oriented mares turn out to be milers who may, or may not, stay 10 furlongs.

Rhododendron's top-class dam won the Group 1 Irish 1000 Guineas and Group 1 Sun Chariot Stakes over a mile, and she beat Lush Lashes by a head in the Group 1 Nassau Stakes on the first of two tries over 10 furlongs. She was not asked to attempt farther, even though there are some notable offspring of sprint star Pivotal (by Polar Falcon) who stay the mile and a half, and the decision made sense.

Halfway To Heaven is out of Cassandra Go (by Indian Ridge), the Group 2 King's Stand Stakes and Group 2 Temple Stakes winner who chased home Mozart in the Group 1 July Cup, and whose star half-brother is the classic-placed speedster Verglas (by Highest Honor). Cassandra Go is also the dam of the Group 3 Abernant Stakes and Group 3 Coral Charge Sprint Stakes winner Tickled Pink (by Invincible Spirit) and of Theann (by Rock Of Gibraltar), the six-furlong Group 3 scorer whose daughter Photo Call (by Galileo) has been a Grade 1 star at eight and 10 furlongs in the USA, but has also had blacktype success at 11 furlongs and been placed at 12.

The aforementioned Verglas won the Group 3 Coventry Stakes and chased home Desert King in the Group 1 Irish 2000 Guineas before going on to a successful stud career, and his stakes-winning half-sister Persian Secret (by Persian Heights) became the dam of the pattern-winning sprinter Do The Honours (by Highest Honor) and of Grade 1 Mother Goose Stakes third Seba (by Alzao), as well as being the grandam of Group 3 Desmond Stakes scorer Future Generation (by Hurricane Run) and third dam of this year's Group 2 Prix Niel and Group 2 Prix Chaudennay scorer Brundtland (by Dubawi). An even more notable grandson of Do The Honours emerged in the latter half of 2018, but more on him below, and elsewhere in this volume.

Combining that distaff line with Pivotal could have yielded a sprinter or a miler, with the latter having a chance, while by no means guaranteed, to stay up to 10 and a half furlongs. What she would then pass on to her offspring would likely determine their distance range, especially when bred to Galileo.

Rhododendron proved at two that a mile was no problem to her, and this boosted the chance that she would stay at least the Prix de Diane trip. Her full-brother, Flying The Flag, got his best win in the Group 3 International Stakes over 10 furlongs at the Curragh and was unplaced both times he tried farther. But, of course, her year-younger full-sister proved that the cross could yield a 12-furlong Group 1 winner when, on soft ground at Ascot in October, she beat Coronet by a length to take the Qipco British Champions Filly and Mare Turf over that distance, before going on to make Enable fight for victory in the Grade 1 Breeders' Cup Turf at Churchill Downs. Magical is reviewed elsewhere in this book.

Rhododendron kicked off her three-year-old campaign by chasing home stablemate Winter in the Group 1 Qipco 1000 Guineas at Newmarket – another Galileo filly with a speed-oriented distaff side to her pedigree. The impression she created that day led to her going off at odds-on for the Group 1 Investec Oaks at Epsom the following month, but although her evidently limited stamina could have seen her through in some years, she had what turned out to be an impossible task as this was the race that launched Enable's career into orbit.

She has never been asked to try 12 furlongs again. Her two outings over 10 and a half furlongs produced contrasting results, as she was pulled up and dismounted in the Group 1 Prix de Diane at Chantilly last year but finished a five-and-a-half-length fourth to Cracksman in the Group 1 Prix Ganay at ParisLongchamp in April. She won 2017's Group 1 Prix de l'Opera over 10 furlongs at Chantilly shortly before chasing home Wuheida in the Grade 1 Breeders' Cup Filly & Mare Turf over nine at Del Mar but has been unplaced in each of her last six starts, five of them over the mile and a quarter.

Indeed, aside from her promising run behind Cracksman, the only shining light in an eight-race campaign for her as a four-year-old has been her short-head defeat of subsequent Group 1 scorer Lightning Spear in the Group 1 Al Shaqab Lockinge Stakes over a mile on fast ground at Newbury in May.

Rhododendron retires a triple Group 1 winner, and she will make an exciting addition to the broodmare ranks. It will be interesting to see to whom she is bred as there is a chance that she could throw a sprinter to a sprint sire while getting a 10-to-12-furlong horse to a miler or middle-distance performer.

In addition to the talented horses noted above, this is also the family of Group 1 Lexus Melbourne Cup hero Cross Counter (by Teofilo). Winner of his only juvenile start and a runaway scorer first time out at three – both races at

Wolverhampton – he was gelded before his first run on turf, at Sandown in June. Several weeks later, he won a competitive 12-furlong handicap at Ascot, followed that with an impressive four-and-a-half-length defeat of Dee Ex Bee in the Group 3 Qatar Gordon Stakes at Goodwood, then failed by a head to beat Old Persian (gave 3lbs) in the Group 2 Sky Bet Great Voltigeur Stakes at York –where Kew Gardens (gave 5lbs) was a length and a half back in third. Despite a minor setback shortly after arriving in Australia, the Charlie Appleby-trained three-year-old put up an outstanding performance over two miles at Flemington to take the Group 1 Lexus Melbourne Cup a couple of weeks later, beating Marmelo by a length. He is a grandson of Do The Honours, is bred on very similar lines to Rhododendron, but is only distantly related to her.

It is also noteworthy that the third dam of Rhododendron is the winning grey Rahaam (by Secreto) and that half-sister to Group 3 Prix Thomas Bryon winner and Group 1 Poule d'Essai des Poulains (French 2000 Guineas) third Glory Forever (by Forever Casting) was also a half-sister to the ancestor of some interesting horses. That mare is Queen Caroline (by Chief's Crown), who was placed a few times, and she is the grandam of Remus De La Tour (by Stormy River), who is at stud in France. He is a grandson of Verglas, so is inbred 4x3 to Rahaam's unraced dam Fager's Glory (by Mr Prospector), and both his Group 3 success and Group 2 placing came over 12 furlongs. His three-parts sister Chill (by Verglas) won the nine-furlong Listed Prix Finlande and was runner-up in the 10 and a half-furlong Group 3 Prix Cleopatre before going on to produce Childa (by Duke Of Marmalade), a listed scorer who finished third in the Group 2 Prix du Conseil de Paris at Longchamp.

Rhododendron was a very good filly on her day, and with her pedigree and connections, there is every reason to hope that she could become a broodmare of note.

SUMMARY DETAILS
Bred: Orpendale, Chelston & Wynatt
Owned: Mrs John Magnier, Michael Tabor & Derrick Smith

Trained: Aidan O'Brien
Country: Ireland
Race record: 21131-22P012-41000000-
Career highlights: 5 wins inc Al Shaqab Lockinge Stakes
(Gr1), Prix de l'Opera Longines (Gr1), Dubai Fillies' Mile
(Gr1), Breast Cancer Research Debutante Stakes (Gr2), 2nd
Breeders' Cup Filly & Mare Turf (Gr1), Investec Oaks (Gr1),
Qipco 1000 Guineas (Gr1), 3rd Moyglare Stud Stakes (Gr1)

RHODODENDRON (IRE) - 2014 bay filly

Galileo (IRE)	Sadler's Wells (USA)	Northern Dancer (CAN)
		Fairy Bridge (USA)
	Urban Sea (USA)	Miswaki (USA)
		Allegretta
Halfway To Heaven (IRE)	Pivotal (GB)	Polar Falcon (USA)
		Fearless Revival
	Cassandra Go (IRE)	Indian Ridge
		Rahaam (USA)

ROARING LION (USA)

The phenomenal legacy left by triple Group 1 star and prolific champion sire Sadler's Wells (by Northern Dancer) has been felt around the world. In Europe, many will immediately identify his sons Galileo and Montjeu as having forged mighty branches of his line, with some of us who have been around for a while also naming In The Wings – the first of the major Sadler's Wells sire sons here – as having had an influence too.

In North America, however, it is the former Vincent O'Brien-trained Group 1 National Stakes winner El Prado who achieved lasting fame. The grey came from the fourth crop of Sadler's Wells, he stood at Adena Springs in Kentucky, his 83 stakes winners included eight who won at the highest level, and two of his Grade 1-winning sons have become titans: Medaglia d'Oro and Kitten's Joy. The latter, a Ramsey Farm homebred who was a Grade 1 winner over 10 and 12 furlongs on turf, commanded a fee of $100,000 from 2014 to 2017 and now, at 17, completed his first season at Hill 'N Dale Farms in Kentucky, covering for $60,000, and will be available at $75,000 in 2019.

His is not a profile of a horse who would have been expected to make such an impact on that side of the Atlantic, and yet this champion sire has achieved progeny earnings in excess of $10 million every year from 2013 to 2018 and gets a high number of individual stakes winners each season. At the time of writing, he is leading the overall title race for champion sire in the USA, his more than $18.3 million in progeny earnings placing him ahead of Candy Ride ($17.6 million) and the late Scat Daddy ($15.2 million), with Mendelssohn's half-brother Into Mischief ($13.3 million) in fourth.

His Grade 1 Breeders' Cup Turf Sprint winner Bobby's Kitten – who was a runaway winner of a listed sprint at Cork on his only start in Ireland, and had his first foals in 2018 – stands at Lanwades Stud in Newmarket, and he has two Group 1-winning sons and a Group 2 scorer joining the

European stallion ranks in 2019. The latter is the high-class miler Taareef, who will stand at Haras Du Mezeray in France, and the other pair are Hawkbill and Roaring Lion.

Hawkbill added 2018's Group 1 Dubai Sheema Classic at Meydan, in which he beat Poet's Word by three lengths, to his half-length defeat of The Gurkha in the Group 1 Coral-Eclipse at Sandown in 2016. Godolphin's widely travelled chestnut was trained by Charlie Appleby. He bowed out with a record of 10 wins from 24 starts and over £3.5 million in prize money and has joined the team at Dalham Hall Stud.

Qatar Racing Ltd's Roaring Lion, however, is best of all of their sire's European runners, and quite possibly his best anywhere in the world. The Timeform 130-rated grey, who was crowned Cartier Horse of the Year, has retired to Tweenhills Farm & Stud in Gloucestershire as a four-time Group 1 star whose eight wins from 13 starts yielded over £2.7 million in earnings. His initial fee has been set at £40,000 and he looks sure to be very popular in his new role.

The John Gosden-trained colt made a winning debut over a mile at Newmarket's July course in mid-August of his juvenile season, followed that with a six-length score over the same trip on the Polytrack at Kempton, and then gamely beat Nelson by a neck in the Group 2 Juddmonte Royal Lodge Stakes. A month later he looked set for victory in the Group 1 Racing Post Trophy at Doncaster before veering off a straight course and then losing out by a neck to Saxon Warrior.

The pair met again in the Group 1 Qipco 2000 Guineas at Newmarket in early May, which Saxon Warrior won by a length and a half and a head from Tip Two Win and Masar, with Roaring Lion another three-parts of a length back in fifth. Of course, both he and Masar improved considerably after that. The Masar who won the Group 1 Investec Derby at Epsom was more like the Masar who ran away with the Group 3 bet365 Craven Stakes at Newmarket – where Roaring Lion finished a rusty third – whereas the grey's impressive Group 2 Betfred Dante Stakes victory at York and his Derby third – where Saxon Warrior was fourth – were just a hint of what was to come.

Roaring Lion and Saxon Warrior renewed their rivalry at Sandown a month after Epsom, and this time the grey won the battle, by a neck from the bay, taking their personal score to two apiece. The pair pulled two and a half lengths clear of third-placed Cliffs Of Moher who was, in turn, a length and a quarter in front of Hawkbill.

Round five was eagerly anticipated and it came about in the Group 1 Juddmonte International Stakes at York. Dual Group 1 star Poet's Word was sent off favourite ahead of Roaring Lion and Saxon Warrior, the line-up was completed by Group 1 winners Benbatl, Latrobe, Thunder Snow and Without Parole and the improving Group 2 scorer Thundering Blue, making it the toughest test yet for the three-year-old rivals. And it was arguably the brightest moment of Roaring Lion's career as powered to a three-and-a-quarter-length victory from the favourite, with Thundering Blue running a huge race in third, a length and a quarter ahead of Saxon Warrior.

Three-two became four-two when the colts met for the sixth and final time, in the Group 1 Qipco Irish Champion Stakes over 10 furlongs at Leopardstown. Saxon Warrior went to the front under a quarter of a mile from home and looked briefly like he might hold on as Roaring Lion began his challenge, but the grey got there to win by a neck. It soon emerged that the runner-up had sustained an injury and would be retired immediately, which was unfortunate. That colt is now on the Coolmore roster for 2019.

Although a Timeform 130-rated star over 10 furlongs, Roaring Lion's connections made the decision to bypass the Group 1 Qipco Champion Stakes in favour of the one-mile Group 1 Queen Elizabeth Stakes on the same card, at the Qipco British Champions day at Ascot in October. It was the right call as there was no horse in Europe – possibly in the world – who could have beaten Cracksman that day as the Timeform 136-rated champion ran away with the race for the second consecutive year.

The bare form of beating I Can Fly by a neck, with Century Dream a half-length back in third and another three-parts of a length to Stormy Antarctic, is some way below the heights he achieved in his other top-level wins, but Roaring Lion stayed on gamely to land the spoils and complete his Group 1 four-timer over a trip just short of his best distance. His final outing, when never a factor in the Grade 1 Breeders' Cup Classic on dirt at Churchill Downs, can be ignored. He's not a dirt horse – which is typical for offspring of Kitten's Joy – and it takes nothing away from his exceptional talent on turf.

Roaring Lion was bred by Ranjan Racing Inc, he is a $160,000 graduate of the Keeneland September Yearling Sale, and he is related to a string of high-class performers, most of whom did well at around a mile. The first foal of Vionnet (by Street Sense), who was a three-quarter-length third in the 10-furlong Grade 1 Rodeo Drive Stakes on turf at Santa Anita, he is a grandson of the prolific Cambiocorsa (by Avenue Of Flags), a dual Grade 3 scorer over six and a half furlongs on the downhill turf course at that same venue.

That mare, who won nine of her 18 starts, has excelled at stud, coming up with five blacktype offspring from six runners, and in addition to Vionnet, they are nine-furlong Grade 2 winner Moulin De Mougin (by Curlin), Grade 2-winning miler Schiaparelli (by Ghostzapper), and mile listed scorers Alexis Tangier (by Tiznow) and Bronson (by Medaglia d'Oro) – all turf horses. Cambiocorsa also has the distinction of being a full-sister to the high-class sprinter California Flag, whose double-digit tally included three editions of the six and a half-furlong Grade 3 Morvich Handicap at Santa Anita.

They, in turn, are out of Ultrafleet (by Afleet), who failed to make the frame in four attempts, and that daughter of multiple stakes-placed six-time winner Social Conduct (by Vigors) is a half-sister to Social Service (by Green Forest), the five-time winning dam of multiple stakes-winning filly Princess Deelite (by Afternoon Deelites).

All of this pointed to Roaring Lion as being a potentially high-class mile-to-10-furlong horse who, depending on the amount of stamina he had received from his sire, could stay the Derby distance – and that's how he turned out. It also makes him a fascinating new addition to the stallion ranks. He represents a cross of the El Prado branch of the Sadler's Wells

(by Northern Dancer) line with the Machiavellian branch of
the Mr Prospector (by Raise a Native) line, he never ran over
less than a mile, and he went from being a Timeform 120p-
rated juvenile to a four-time Group 1 star rated 130. His two-
year-olds will likely be seen to best effect over seven furlongs
and upwards, and his best offspring are likely to do well
anywhere in the broad seven-to-14-furlong range.

SUMMARY DETAILS

Bred: Ranjan Racing Inc
Owned: Qatar Racing Ltd
Trained: John Gosden
Country: England
Race record: 1112-301311110-
Career highlights: 8 wins inc Queen Elizabeth II Stakes
(Gr1), Qipco Irish Champion Stakes (Gr1), Juddmonte
International Stakes (Gr1), Coral-Eclipse Stakes (Gr1), Betfred
Dante Stakes (Gr2), Juddmonte Royal Lodge Stakes (Gr2),
2nd Racing Post Trophy (Gr1), 3rd Investec Derby (Gr1)

ROARING LION (USA) - 2015 grey colt

Kitten's Joy (USA)	El Prado (IRE)	Sadler's Wells (USA)
		Lady Capulet (USA)
	Kitten's First (USA)	Lear Fan (USA)
		That's My Hon (USA)
Vionnet (USA)	Street Sense (USA)	Street Cry (IRE)
		Bedazzle (USA)
	Cambiocorsa (USA)	Avenue Of Flags (USA)
		Ultrafleet (USA)

ROMANISED (IRE)

"A stallion with the potential to sire classic winners" – that was my assessment of Holy Roman Emperor (by Danehill) in the *Irish Racing Yearbook 2010*, which was published several months before Coolmore's juvenile star had his first runners. On May 26th of this year, he notched up his fourth Group 1 classic star when Romanised put up an impressive performance to beat last year's two-year-old champion U S Navy Flag by two and a quarter lengths in the Tattersalls Irish 2,000 Guineas at the Curragh. Then, just over two months later, he made it five when Well Timed landed the Group 1 Henkel-Preis der Diana (German Oaks) at Dusseldorf.

Before his year, his daughter Homecoming Queen had run away with the 1000 Guineas at Newmarket in 2012, several months before Rollout The Carpet won the New Zealand 1000 Guineas, and followed by triple Group 1 ace Mongolian Khan who took both the New Zealand Derby and Australian Derby in 2015. His overall tally stands at 79 stakes winners worldwide, of whom 13 have won at least once at the highest level – including 2018's Grade 1 Sword Dancer Stakes winner Glorious Empire. Much of his most notable success has come abroad – including with Hong Kong standouts Designs On Rome and Beauty Only – his fee for this year was just €15,000, and it will be that price again in 2019. His yearlings made up to 210,000gns in 2017 and up to €300,000 in 2018, and the earlier of those two transactions, at the Tattersalls October Yearling Sale, came just under two months before his seven-year-old daughter Inca Princess changed hands for €1,900,000 in Goffs. Holy Roman Emperor stands at Castlehyde Stud in Co Cork.

Romanised, whom Timeform rated 104 at two and 122 after his classic success, has always been held in high regard by trainer Ken Condon. He made a winning debut over six furlongs at Navan last April, was only beaten just over two lengths when unplaced behind Rajasinghe in the Group 2 Coventry Stakes at Ascot, and by over three lengths when out of the frame behind Sioux Nation in the Group 1 Phoenix Stakes at the Curragh. His final outing of 2017, however, was full of promise and that second-place finish looks even better now when you consider that the colt who beat him by two lengths in the Group 3 Solario Stakes over seven furlongs at Sandown was none other than Masar, this year's Group 1 Investec Derby hero and runaway Group 3 Craven Stakes winner.

Had Romanised not run in the Listed Tetrarch Stakes at Naas on his seasonal reappearance in early May then it is likely that, with his Sandown performance being most recent on his record, he would have been sent off at shorter than the 25/1 at which he returned at the Curragh. He was unplaced behind Imaging that first day, but given his pedigree it is no surprise that he showed such marked improvement when stepped up to a mile. It was disappointing, however, that he failed to reproduce that level of form in three subsequent outings – he was unplaced in the Group 1 St James's Palace Stakes, in the Group 1 Prix Jacques le Marois, and in the Group 1 Queen Elizabeth II Stakes.

He held an entry in the Group 1 Commonwealth Cup at Ascot, but there is not really anything in his pedigree or race record that suggests sprinting might be his game. He is a three-parts brother to the aforementioned Timeform 130-rated Hong Kong four-time 10-furlong Group 1 star Designs On Rome, so is bred to be a miler who is likely stay 10 furlongs – and the way he stormed home at the Curragh bears that out. It would be interesting, therefore, to see how he might get on if stepped up in trip in 2019.

Might he stay a mile and a half? It is possible. Horses such as Mongolian Khan and notable Irish filly Banimpire – who won the Group 2 Ribblesdale Stakes and was short-headed by Blue Bunting in the Group 1 Irish Oaks – prove that offspring of Holy Roman Emperor can be fully effective at that trip. And then there's all the stamina in the distaff side of Romanised's pedigree.

The best of his siblings are Rock On Romance (by Rock Of Gibraltar) and Fictional Account (by Stravinsky), both of whom stayed two miles. The former, who won the all-aged Group 3 St Leger Italiano over 14 furlongs, ran away with a two-mile listed contest on heavy ground at Hamburg, whereas Fictional Account, who sprang a surprise when beating Fame And Glory by a neck in a 14-furlong listed event at the Curragh, won the Listed Fenwolf Stakes over two miles at Ascot 11 months before. That pair were sired by a mile champion and by a sprint champion respectively, which suggests that their dam, Romantic Venture (by Indian Ridge), has been passing on a stamina influence rather than the speed shown by her sire and grandam. And that probably comes via Alleged (by Hoist The Flag), sire of her non-winning dam, Summer Trysting.

Romantic Venture, who was a four-length debut winner of an eight and a half-furlong Galway maiden as a three-year-old, is a full-sister to Sights On Gold, who was a Group 3 scorer over 10 and 11 furlongs in England and only beaten by half a length when runner-up to Phoenix Reach in the Group 1 Hong Kong Vase over 12 furlongs at Sha Tin. Their half-brother Simple Exchange won the Listed Magnolia Stakes over 10 furlongs on the Polytrack at Kempton and the Grade 2 American Derby over a half-furlong less at Arlington, they all share a dam with Designs On Rome, and they were all bred by Moyglare Stud. So too was Fictional Account. Romanised, on the other hand, was bred by Monica Aherne, and Rock On Romance was bred by Brendan Corbett.

Rekindled Affair (by Rainbow Quest), an unraced half-sister to Summer Trysting, has also done her part for the family as her three stakes-winning offspring are headed by Australian 10-furlong Group 2 scorer Rekindled Interest (by Redoute's Choice) and the Moyglare Stud-bred filly Where We Left Off (by Dr Devious), who won a nine-furlong Grade 3 at Monmouth Park a month before failing by just half a length to add a similar contest over 11 furlongs at Saratoga. The mare's other one is 11-furlong French listed scorer Porticcio (by Lomitas) who later won over hurdles in Ireland.

The third dam of Romanised is stakes-winning sprinter Seasonal Pickup (by The Minstrel), and while one could suggest that her speed could combine with that of Holy Roman Emperor to produce a sprinter, the particular branch of her line that has yielded the recent classic star is one that has more stamina, a fairly reliable source of milers and middle-distance horses, with some who can stay farther. She was among the quickest representatives of her Derby-winning sire, she was out of 10-furlong filly Bubinka (by Nashua), and those produced by her siblings include Group 1 Irish Derby hero Grey Swallow (by Daylami).

Farther back it is the family of Group 2-placed Taufan (by Stop The Music) – who sired Group 1 stars Tagula and Taufan's Melody – and of Best In Show (by Traffic Judge), the US Grade 3 scorer who went on to found a hugely influential female family of her own. And, as a Danehill-line (by Danzig) representative from a branch of the family of Taufan and, remotely, of the many notable male descendants of Best In Show (El Gran Senor, Redoute's Choice, Xaar, Try My Best, Bated Breath, Cityscape, etc) there is every reason to hope that a successful stallion career awaits Romanised whenever his racing days come to an end.

SUMMARY DETAILS

Bred: Monica Aherne
Owned: Robert Ng
Trained: Ken Condon
Country: Ireland
Race record: 1002-01000-
Career highlights: 2 wins inc Tattersalls Irish 2000 Guineas (Gr1), 2nd BetBright Solario Stakes (Gr3)

ROMANISED (IRE) - 2015 bay colt

Holy Roman Emperor (IRE)	Danehill (USA)	Danzig (USA)
		Razyana (USA)
	L'On Vite (USA)	Secretariat (USA)
		Fanfreluche (CAN)
Romantic Venture (IRE)	Indian Ridge	Ahonoora
		Hillbrow
	Summer Trysting (USA)	Alleged (USA)
		Seasonal Pickup (USA)

ROYAL MARINE (IRE)

Many prolific blacktype sires will get at least one Group 1 winner at some point in their career and for Kildangan Stud's Grade 1 Breeders' Cup Classic hero Raven's Pass (by Elusive Quality) that omission from his record was finally erased in October. The Saeed bin Suroor-trained Royal Marine hit the front a furlong and a half from home in the Group 1 Qatar Prix Jean-Luc Lagardere at ParisLongchamp on Arc weekend and gamely held off the challenge of Broome by a neck, with odds-on favourite Anodor another three-parts of a length back in third.

The winner had run only twice before, and it will be interesting to see how he turns out in 2019. He was unruly in the stalls on his debut at Newmarket in July and finished a well-beaten sixth in that six-furlong novice race, but then beat subsequent dual winner Turgenev by two and a quarter lengths in a seven-furlong Doncaster maiden almost three weeks later. He is bred to be effective at anywhere from a mile to 12 furlongs, and should he do enough to earn a place at stud then the record of one of his relations would make him an interesting prospect.

Raven's Pass was a top-class mile-to-10-furlong horse, rated 133 by Timeform, and his best include sprinters like Raven's Lady, milers like Tower Of London, and middle-distance horses like Big Duke (aka Swashbuckling) and Secret Number – all Group 2 scorers. Misfortune may have robbed him of the chance of a Group 1 star in 2017 as Timeform 115-rated pattern winner Via Ravenna died shortly after failing by just a short-neck to beat Roly Poly in the Group 1 Prix Rothschild over a mile at Deauville. And, like Royal Marine, she was out of a daughter of Singspiel (by In The Wings).

Royal Marine is the fourth foal and fourth winner out of Inner Secret, and each of the quartet has shown above-average ability. Secret Ambition (by Exceed And Excel) is the eldest and is a Group 3-placed prolific winner at seven and eight furlongs in the UAE. Crystal River (by Dubawi) came next, and having been fifth in a Newcastle maiden on her only start at two, she joined the William Haggas stable the following summer, ran away with an eight-and-a-half-furlong Hamilton maiden and then won a nine-furlong listed contest at Chantilly, both on soft ground. Midnight Meeting (by Dubawi) is the mare's third foal and won two of his four starts for the bin Suroor-stable this year, the latter one by two and a half lengths over 10 furlongs at Salisbury in late July. This is a promising start for the once-raced mare, she had an early May-born Dark Angel (by Acclamation) colt in 2017, and a son of Dawn Approach (by New Approach) in late April of 2018.

There is no surprise that Inner Secret has become a successful broodmare given that she is by Group 1 star and leading sire Singspiel (by In The Wings) and out of Mysterial (by Alleged), a half-sister to Group 1 July Cup and Group 1 Prix de l'Abbaye de Longchamp hero Agnes World (by Danzig). He proved to be a disappointing stallion, but two of Mysterial's sons have had moments of success in that role. Librettist (by Danzig), who could be described as being a three-parts brother to Agnes World, won the Group 1 Prix du Moulin de Longchamp and Group 1 Prix Jacques le Marois, and he has sired some prolific winners, albeit among horses rated in the 80-99 range, with one standout among them. Libranno won the Group 2 Park Stakes, Group 2 Richmond Stakes, Group 2 July Stakes, the Group 3 Supreme Stakes, and two editions of the Group 3 Criterion Stakes.

Dubai Destination (by Kingmambo), on the other hand, beat Rock Of Gibraltar by an eased-down length in the Group 2 Champagne Stakes at two and went on to take the Group 1 Queen Anne Stakes by four lengths. He started well at stud, with Group 1 scorer Ibn Khaldun in his first crop, added a variety of other stakes and pattern winners, and eventually got transferred to a dual-purpose role, but has become prized as a broodmare sire. This year's top-level winners God Given (by Nathaniel) and Thunder Snow (by Helmet) are just two of the Group 1 winners who have been produced from his daughters.

Mysterial's offspring also include a talented performer who may serve as a guide to the potential distance range that Royal Marine might show, and that's because Secret Number (by Raven's Pass) is what can be described as being his three-parts brother. He beat subsequent Group 1 Coronation Cup scorer Pether's Moon by a neck on his only start at two and followed that mile Polytrack win with victory in a nine-and-a-half-furlong listed contest on Tapeta at Meydan. He was then third in the Group 2 UAE Derby, returned to Europe, was beaten by less than four lengths when sixth to Leading Light in the Group 1 St Leger, won the Group 3 Cumberland Lodge Stakes over 12 furlongs at Ascot and a listed contest over a half-furlong farther at Chester, and later added Group 2 success over a mile and a half at Veliefendi, in Turkey.

Royal Marine ended his first season on a Timeform rating of 113p, he holds entries in the Group 1 Tattersalls Irish 2000 Guineas and Group 1 Dubai Duty Free Irish Derby, and it would be no surprise to see him become a well-known member of the three-year-old crop of 2019.

SUMMARY DETAILS

Bred: Godolphin
Owned: Godolphin
Trained: Saeed bin Suroor
Country: England
Race record: 011-
Career highlights: 2 wins inc Qatar Prix Jean-Luc Lagardere sponsorise par Manateq (Gr1)

ROYAL MARINE (IRE) - 2016 bay colt

Raven's Pass (USA)	Elusive Quality (USA)	Gone West (USA)
		Touch Of Greatness (USA)
	Ascutney (USA)	Lord At War (ARG)
		Right Word (USA)
Inner Secret (USA)	Singspiel (IRE)	In The Wings
		Glorious Song (CAN)
	Mysterial (USA)	Alleged (USA)
		Mysteries (USA)

ROYAL MEETING (IRE)

The first thing that catches the eye when you look at a five-generation pedigree chart for Royal Meeting is the curious inbreeding that resulted in his grandam. She was a daughter of leading South African sire Al Mufti (by Roberto) and out of Swinging Girl, a daughter of Roberto's full-brother Mullineaux (by Hail To Reason). Drummer Girl never raced, but her daughter Rock Opera was a champion two-year-old. She won a six-furlong Grade 1 and an almost-six-furlong Grade 2 contest in her native country, she finished third in the Listed UAE 1000 Guineas, and with so many blacktype relations to her name there was every reason to expect that she could become a broodmare of note.

She is a daughter of the Seeking The Gold (by Mr Prospector) stallion Lecture and that makes her a full-sister to juvenile Grade 2 scorer Hit Song, to Grade 1-placed and blacktype producer Rock Concert, and Royal Drummer, a four-time scorer became the dam of the five-and-a-half-furlong Grade 1 star Gulf Storm (by Sail For Seattle). His dam is a daughter of Kilconnel (by Mr Prospector) – a half-brother to Group 1 Irish Oaks heroine Alydaress (by Alydar) – and that stallion was trained by Dermot Weld to win handicaps at Leopardstown and Bellewstown.

Royal Opera, however, came to Europe and she has made an excellent start to her broodmare career. Her first foal, a colt named Frankenfurter (by Singspiel), won in Australia, and her fifth is this year's Newcastle and Lingfield scorer Night Castle (by Dubawi), a Charlie Appleby-trained gelding – a miler. The mare's second and sixth foals, however, are horses of significance.

Star UAE-based miler Heavy Metal (by Exceed And Excel) is the elder sibling. He was Timeform-rated 118 in 2017 and added three pattern races to his tally in 2018, starting with a four-and-a-half-length defeat of Thunder Snow in the Group 2 Al Maktoum Challenge R1 at Meydan in January. Just over a month later he ran away with the Group 3 Firebreak Stakes over the same course and distance, and to that he added a two-length score in the Group 2 Godolphin Mile at the end of March – all on dirt.

His younger sibling promises to be even better, and having made a winning debut over seven furlongs at Yarmouth in mid-September, the Saeed bin Suroor-trained juvenile followed-up with a three-quarter-length defeat of Hermosa in the Group 1 Criterium International over the same trip at Chantilly in late October. The runner-up is trained by Aidan O'Brien, had won a Group 3 at Naas on her previous start, and been third to Skitter Scatter in the Group 1 Moyglare Stud Stakes the time before that.

Royal Meeting earned a rating of 114p from Timeform. He was the second Group 1-winning juvenile for his Irish National Stud-based sire Invincible Spirit (by Green Desert) in the space of 24 hours, following the narrow victory of Magna Grecia in the Vertem Futurity Trophy Stakes over a mile at Doncaster. The stallion is primarily a source of sprinters and milers, so it is no surprise to see the colt entered in the Group 1 Tattersalls Irish 2000 Guineas, but his entry in the Group 1 Dubai Duty Free Irish Derby catches the eye.

As discussed in the essay on Magna Grecia, what the few middle-distance Invincible Spirit horses have in common is stamina in the distaff side of their pedigrees. Royal Meeting, however, comes from a family associated with sprinters and milers, and that makes it unlikely that he would stay the Derby distance.

SUMMARY DETAILS

Bred: Godolphin
Owned: Godolphin
Trained: Saeed bin Suroor
Country: England
Race record: 11-
Career highlights: 2 wins inc Criterium International (Gr1)

ROYAL MEETING (IRE) - 2016 bay colt

Invincible Spirit (IRE)	Green Desert (USA)	Danzig (USA)
		Foreign Courier (USA)
	Rafha	Kris
		Eljazzi
Rock Opera (SAF)	Lecture (USA)	Seeking The Gold (USA)
		Narrate (USA)
	Drummer Girl (SAF)	Al Mufti (USA)
		Swinging Girl (SAF)

SANDS OF MALI (FR)

There has been an increasing tendency to view pattern-winning juvenile colts as prospective stallions, and many of them have plenty of positives about their pedigree that could be used to promote their appeal. But every now and then you get one who is less fashionably bred and whose speed and precocity come as something of a surprise. Sands Of Mali is such a horse and as a Timeform 125-rated Group 1 star who was also talented at two, the Richard Fahey-trained colt has proved that he deserves a chance at stud some day.

He achieved a Timeform rating of 116 as a juvenile – surpassing the career peak of both his sire (Panis, 112) and broodmare sire (Indian Rocket, 115) – and that level of attainment was just a few pounds ahead of the best of his siblings, Timeform 112-rated half-brother Kadrizzi (by Hurricane Cat), who won 2016's Shergar Cup Sprint. The performance that earned Sands Of Mali his rating was his two-and-three-quarter-length defeat of Invincible Army in the Group 2 Gimcrack Stakes over six furlongs at York.

He had beaten subsequent stakes winner Eirene by almost four lengths over the same trip at Nottingham on his previous start, and although he finished last in the Group 1 Middle Park Stakes and only ninth in the Grade 1 Breeders' Cup Juvenile Turf on his final two runs of the year, the latter performance was better than it might sound. He was only three and a half lengths behind the winner, Mendelssohn, and it was the only time he has tried a mile.

He kicked off his three-year-old campaign with a narrow win in the Group 3 Prix Sigy on heavy ground at Chantilly in mid-April, followed that with a nose defeat of old rival Invincible Army in the Group 2 Sandy Lane Stakes on good at Haydock, and then chased home Eqtidaar in the Group 1 Commonwealth Cup on fast ground at Ascot in June, beaten just half a length. This year's edition of that race was its weakest to date, and it looked that way on the day as the first eight home were covered by less than three lengths. The winner, fourth and seventh have been unplaced in all of their subsequent outings, the fifth was unplaced in each of his next three starts, and the eighth in his next two. Only his final run of the year saved Sands Of Mali from being included among those.

He beat only one home in the Group 1 July Cup, was 16th of 20 in the Group 1 Prix Maurice de Gheest at Deauville, and then unplaced in the Group 1 Sprint Cup at Haydock. The latter was a more promising effort than his previous two tries, as he finished a three-and-a-half-length fifth to The Tin Man on heavy ground, but his final run of the year was still a surprise. He made all to beat Harry Angel by a length in the Group 1 Qipco British Champions Sprint on soft ground at Ascot, with Donjuan Triumphant third, Brando fourth, and Sir Dancealot fifth. This career-beat saw his official handicap mark rise to 118, but his Timeform rating increased to 125. The latter put him equal with U S Navy Flag and so made him the joint-top three-year-old sprinter of the year.

Sands Of Mali was bred in France by Simon Urizzi, and in addition to the aforementioned Kadrizzi, he is also a half-brother to Flawless Jewel (by Kheleyf). Also trained by Fahey, she made €70,000 at the Osarus September Yearling Sale, the auction at which Sands Of Mali made €20,000 in 2016, and she was snapped up by her current connections for 95,000gns at the Tattersalls Craven Breeze-Up Sale in April. She was runner-up at York on her debut in mid-July, followed that with a 16-length romp over five furlongs at Pontefract two weeks later, but was then unplaced in both the Group 2 Lowther Stakes and Listed Harry Rosebery Stakes, the former on fast ground and the latter on heavy. Stroud Coleman Bloodstock bought then her for 85,000gns at the Tattersalls December Mare Sale.

With so many sprint stallions representing a limited number of notable sires and sire lines, and some showing inbreeding to one or more of those, Sands Of Mali will offer breeders something different whenever he goes to stud, and that could be valuable for those striving to avoid further inbreeding. It is true that he has outrun his modest pedigree, and that adds an element of risk, but he is a better racehorse than some more fashionable types who have not yet lived up to the support they've received, and representing a broad Miswaki - Indian Ridge cross, he could work with some of those speedier Sadler's Wells-line and Danzig-line mares.

What's more, his pedigree is an outcross – a term that is often inaccurately used these days. It means that the horse has no inbreeding within the first five generations of its pedigree. If your mare has no duplicated ancestors within the first four generations of her pedigree and the sire to whom you want to send her is similarly free of any duplications within his chart, and if none of her four-generation ancestors matches any of his, then the foal will have no inbreeding within the first five generations of its pedigree. It will be an outcross because all 62 names in its five-generation pedigree chart will be different.

So no stallion with any inbreeding in his pedigree can be called an outcross for anything, it does not mean that he represents a different sire line to that of your mare, or that his sire line "nicks" with that of your mare. A large proportion of the thoroughbred population here carries at least one duplication within the first five generations of their pedigrees, and many carry multiple duplications. They are not and cannot be outcrosses.

Before Sands Of Mali came along the only stakes winner in the first four generations of his family was one remotely connected to him both in genetics and aptitude – a winner of the Lonsdale Stakes descended from his fourth dam. His unraced dam Kadiania (by Indian Rocket) is out Kapi Creek (by Sicyos), which makes her a half-sister to the multiple winners Majik Charly (by Soave) and Such A Maj (by Soave). Kirigane (by Vitiges), his third dam, won once and finished third in a listed contest, and that half-sister to Mexican blacktype earner Ladakh (by Sir Gaylord) was also a half-sister to Kumari (by Luthier), the one-time winning dam of Listed Lonsdale Stakes winner and Group 3 Prix de Lutece third Angel City (by Carwhite).

The fifth dam is the listed race winner and 1967 Cheshire Oaks fourth All Hail (by Alcide), who has had some notable descendants in South America, but there is nothing in the first few generations of the family to suggest why Sands Of Mali could have become a Group 1 winning sprinter or a high-class two-year-old. His sire has, obviously, played an important part and that horse is the dual pattern-winning miler Panis (by Miswaki), an Haras des Faunes stallion with just a handful of stakes winners to his name – two of whom are the Group 3-winning sprinters Myasun and Out Of Time – plus the Group 1 Poule d'Essai des Poulains (French 2000 Guineas) runner-up Veneto (renamed Californiavitality in Hong Kong).

Sands Of Mali stays in training in 2019 and it was announced at the end of November that, with Phoenix Thoroughbreds having bought into the horse, he would have the Group 1 Al Quoz Sprint at Meydan, in March, as a major early target.

SUMMARY DETAILS

Bred: Simon Urizzi
Owned: The Cool Silk Partnership
Trained: Richard Fahey
Country: England
Race record: 01100-1120001-
Career highlights: 5 wins inc Qipco British Champions Sprint Stakes (Gr1), Armstrong Aggregates Sandy Lane Stakes (Gr2), Al Basti Equiworld Gimcrack Stakes (Gr2), Prix Sigy (Gr3), 2nd Commonwealth Cup (Gr1)

SANDS OF MALI (FR) - 2015 bay colt

Panis (USA)	Miswaki (USA)	Mr Prospector (USA)
		Hopespringseternal (USA)
	Political Parody (USA)	Doonesbury (USA)
		Urakawa (USA)
Kadiania (FR)	Indian Rocket (GB)	Indian Ridge
		Selvi
	Kapi Creek (FR)	Sicyos (USA)
		Kirigane (FR)

SAXON WARRIOR (JPN)

There were many memorable aspects of the 2018 flat season, and the rivalry between Saxon Warrior and Roaring Lion was one of them. It started on their final outing of 2017 when a neck separated the pair of previously undefeated colts at the end of the Group 1 Racing Post Trophy, and Saxon Warrior made it two-nil when taking the Group 1 Qipco 2000 Guineas in style at Newmarket on his seasonal reappearance in May. He landed the classic by a length and a half from Tip Two Win, with Masar a head back in third, Elarqam another half-length away in fourth and a neck in front of Roaring Lion.

At this point, any predictions that the pair might develop a rivalry would have seemed fanciful as their careers appeared to be going in different directions. One was an unbeaten classic star with a pedigree that shouted Epsom and of whom there was talk of a Triple Crown bid, while the other had disappointed in his first two starts of the year, leading to the inevitable speculation as to whether or not he had trained on. The Group 1 Investec Derby changed all of that.

Masar, who had shown a touch of brilliance with a nine-length demolition job in the Group 3 Craven Stakes in April, stormed home to a length-and-a-half victory at Epsom, chased home by Dee Ex Bee, who outstayed Roaring Lion for third, the grey losing second place near the line. Odds-on favourite Saxon Warrior, however, never looked like winning, and although he kept going to the end, he had to settle for fourth, two and a half lengths behind the grey. Young Rascal (seventh), Kew Gardens (ninth) and Knight To Behold (11th) would later become significant players in the middle-distance division, but on the day the impression was that only the first two truly stayed the mile and a half.

The Triple Crown dream was over, but connections gave Saxon Warrior another try at the distance, and he was favourite for the Group 1 Dubai Duty Free Irish Derby at the Curragh. He was only beaten by half a length and a neck, but with all due respect to Latrobe and Rostropovich, nothing they had done before or achieved since indicated that this was anything other than an unremarkable edition of the classic. It was no surprise, therefore, to see him drop in trip for his next start.

The combination of fast ground and a good pace set by the 2016's winner Hawkbill helped to produce a fast time for the Group 1 Coral-Eclipse at Sandown in July, and the race provided viewers with an exciting finish as Roaring Lion and Saxon Warrior did battle. It was clear from around two furlongs from home that it was the three-year-olds who would fight it out, the bay went to the front, the grey caught him and inched ahead, but his rival fought back all the way. There was only a neck separating them at the post, then a gap of two and a half-lengths to the staying-on Cliffs Of Moher in third.

The pair met again six and a half weeks later, although this time Saxon Warrior disappointed. Roaring Lion won York's Group 1 Juddmonte International Stakes impressively by three and a quarter lengths from Poet's Word, with Thundering Blue – the only non Group 1 winner in the line-up – staying on into third, a length and a quarter ahead of the Guineas star. His Irish Derby conqueror finished a never-dangerous seventh of the eight. The Group 1 Qipco Irish Champion Stakes was an obvious next target and, as at Sandown, the pair put on quite a show for the crowds. Saxon Warrior went to the front with under a quarter-mile to go and briefly looked like he might be about to even the score, but Roaring Lion caught him near the post and won by a neck. There was a gap of two and three-quarter lengths back to Deauville in third, and another length and a quarter gap to US Grade 1 scorer Athena.

The score was now four-two to Roaring Lion, with three of the six meetings having been settled by just a neck, and both colts held entries at the British Champions Weekend in late October. Sadly, a seventh encounter did not come about. It quickly emerged that Saxon Warrior picked up a career-ending injury at Leopardstown – what might have happened that day had this not occurred? – and he was immediately retired. He is now about to embark on a stallion career at Coolmore Stud.

Saxon Warrior's juvenile Group 1 win and classic victory were important from a pedigree point of view as they further advertised the potential of outstanding Japanese sire Deep Impact (by Sunday Silence) to have a significant influence in this part of the world. That 2000 Guineas win was not, as some said on the day, a first European classic success for the stallion because the Elie Lellouche-trained Beauty Parlour carried the famous Wildenstein colours to victory in the Group 1 Poule d'Essai des Pouliches (French 1000 Guineas) in 2012. She was then runner-up to the ill-fated Valyra in the Group 1 Prix de Diane (French Oaks). But with the number of regally bred mares who have been sent to Deep Impact recently, especially by Coolmore, it's a fair bet that there are more to come.

Indeed, Saxon Warrior was not his only classic star of 2018, in Europe or elsewhere. Study Of Man won the Group 1 Prix du Jockey Club (French Derby), Wagnerian took the Grade 1 Tokyo Yushun (Japanese Derby), and Fierement landed the Grade 1 Kikuka Sho (Japanese St Leger).

Deep Impact, who is out of Group 1 winner Wind In Her Hair (by Alzao), has the influential Highclere (by Queen's Hussar) as his third dam. He was one of the most brilliant racehorses ever to be trained in Japan and the Timeform 134-rated, seven-time Group 1 ace, who stands at Shadai Stallion Station, has followed in the hoofprints of his dynasty-making sire by becoming one of the greatest stallions of the modern era.

His triple-digit tally of stakes winners consists mostly of horses who have won at Grade 3 level or above, 39 of them have won at the highest level and, in addition to standouts such as Gentildonna, Kizuna, Real Steel, Tosen Stardom and Vivlos – to name just a few – they also include Prix d'Ispahan scorer A Shin Hikari, making it four Group 1 stars for him in Europe, so far.

Saxon Warrior, who was Timeform-rated 120p at two and 124 at three, is yet another top-level winner bred by Orpendale, Chelston & Wynatt, he is a full-brother to the stakes-placed filly Pavlenko and he is the second foal of Maybe (by Galileo), a filly who finished a three-and-three-quarter-length fifth to Was in the Group 1 Oaks at Epsom on her only attempt beyond a mile. She had been a 10-length third to Homecoming Queen in the Group 1 1000 Guineas on her previous start – her first defeat – and won both the Group 1 Moyglare Stud Stakes and Group 2 Debutante Stakes over seven furlongs at the Curragh as a juvenile.

Maybe has the potential to produce both high-class milers and middle-distance horses, and given that he's a son of Deep Impact, there was every chance that Saxon Warrior would be the latter or both. His relationship to two Epsom classic stars boosted his prospects of staying 12 furlongs, but it was over eight and 10 that he showed his best form.

Promise To Be True, a full-sister to Maybe, was never asked to try beyond a mile, but then she only ran once as a three-year-old. At two she won the Group 3 Silver Flash Stakes over seven furlongs at Leopardstown, chased home Wuheida in the Group 1 Prix Marcel Boussac over a mile at Chantilly, and then took third behind Thunder Snow in the Group 1 Criterium International at Saint-Cloud, over seven furlongs on soft ground. There was no guarantee that she or Maybe would stay the Oaks distance, despite being Galileo and out of a stakes-winning three-parts sister to Oaks heroine Dancing Rain (by Danehill Dancer), and that's because their dam, Sumora (by Danehill), was a sprinter whose blacktype success came over five furlongs and as a two-year-old. The odds were very good, of course, but likely to be dependant on which attribute Sumora had passed on to them. Maybe's Oaks fifth suggests that she may have got the stamina assist, and that would boost her prospects of producing offspring who can stay that trip.

Sumora and Dancing Rain are out of the unraced Indian Ridge (by Ahonoora) mare Rain Flower and, in addition to her three-quarter-length defeat of Wonder Of Wonders at Epsom in 2011, Dancing Rain also took the Group 1 Preis der Diana (German Oaks) over a furlong less on soft ground at Dusseldorf before adding victory in the Group 2 British Champions Fillies and Mares Stakes at Ascot. Originally a

€200,000 Goffs Orby Sale graduate, Dancing Rain made 4,000,000gns when sold at the Tattersalls December Mare Sale in Newmarket four years later, and her second foal is Magic Lily (by New Approach). That eight-length Newmarket debut winner was only beaten by three-quarters of a length when third to Laurens and September in the Group 1 bet365 Fillies' Mile at Newmarket but has not run since.

It may seem surprising that a pair of three-part sisters could show such different aptitudes – one a five-furlong filly and the other an Oaks star – but it is not really so when you consider the mixed potential of their pedigrees.

Their dam is by a leading source of sprinter and miler speed, and she is a half-sister to two horses of particular note, one of whom is the high-class sprinter Archway (by Thatching). He won the Group 3 Greenlands Stakes and Listed Waterford Testimonial Stakes when trained by Vincent O'Brien, and the brightest stars among his offspring are Roman Arch, Grand Archway, Rose Archway, and Group 1 Melbourne Cup runner-up She's Archie – the latter trio all Group 1 winners over 12 furlongs. Roman Arch got his top-level wins at eight and 10 furlongs. Strange? No, not when you consider that Archway was a half-brother to Group 1 Derby and Group 1 Irish Champion Stakes star Dr Devious (by Ahonoora) – a three-parts brother to Rain Flower – and that their dam, Rose Of Jericho, was a daughter of dual Arc hero and noted stamina influence Alleged (by Hoist The Flag).

Former Peter Chapple-Hyam-trained ace Dr Devious died in 2017, at the age of 29, and although his overall record as a stallion was disappointing for a horse of his calibre and pedigree, he did leave us the Group 1 winners Kinnaird (Prix de l'Opera) and Collier Hill (Irish St Leger, Canadian International, Hong Kong Vase). With the support that Saxon Warrior is likely to receive at stud, there is every reason to hope that he will become a much more successful sire than Dr Devious was. His better two-year-olds are likely to be effective from mid-summer onwards and, also depending on the mares, his best representatives are likely to be successful within the broad seven-to-14-furlong range. His fee for 2019 is €30,000.

SUMMARY DETAILS

Bred: Orpendale, Chelston & Wynatt
Owned: Derrick Smith, Mrs John Magnier & Michael Tabor
Trained: Aidan O'Brien
Country: Ireland
Race record: 111-143242-
Career highlights: 4 wins inc Qipco 2000 Guineas (Gr1),
Racing Post Trophy (Gr1), Juddmonte Beresford Stakes (Gr2),
2nd Qipco Irish Champion Stakes (Gr1), Coral-Eclipse Stakes
(Gr1), 3rd Dubai Duty Free Irish Derby (Gr1)

SAXON WARRIOR (JPN) - 2015 bay colt

Deep Impact (JPN)	Sunday Silence (USA)	Halo (USA)
		Wishing Well (USA)
	Wind In Her Hair (IRE)	Alzao (USA)
		Burghclere
Maybe (GB)	Galileo (IRE)	Sadler's Wells (USA)
		Urban Sea (USA)
	Sumora (IRE)	Danehill (USA)
		Rain Flower (IRE)

SEA OF CLASS (IRE)

There is such an obsession with precocity and early-season two-year-old speed that a relative newcomer to the racing and bloodstock world could be forgiven for thinking that this must important if a horse is to become a future Group 1 star. But many of those brief shining lights blink out before the serious Group 1 candidates begin to show their worth, or prove unable to compete at a comparable or stronger level at three or older. There are others who soon show that what they did on the track at two was a long way behind their true talent – they needed time to hit their peak – and many Group 1 stars run only once or twice at two – sometimes quite late in the year and/or in minor company – with some not getting to the racetrack at all until they turn three.

There are many reasons why a horse may have a light to non-existent juvenile career before going on to become a Group 1 winner, and date of birth is just one. Those born after about May 20th are seen as being late foals. Those horses will still be short of their physical third birthday by the time most of the mile classics have been run, and those going for a Derby or Oaks will have a slight physical disadvantage against rivals who are even a month or two older. By late autumn, however, most have caught up completely. The late foal (or late maturer) who shows talent at three could have more improvement in them than their slightly older cohorts, enabling them to move even farther up the rankings at the age of four.

So, imagine what Sea Of Class might achieve in 2019.

The William Haggas-trained chestnut was born on May 23rd, 2015, is a 170,000gns graduate of the yearling section of the Tattersalls December Sale, and she was runner-up in a mile maiden at Newmarket on her debut on April 18th of this year, beaten a neck. And the answer to the trivia question 'aside from Enable, who is the only horse to have beaten Sea Of Class?' is Ceilidhs Dream. That rival, herself a May 8th foal, had the benefit of a previous run, but she was unplaced in each of her subsequent outings.

Sea Of Class beat Athena by two lengths in a 10-furlong listed contest at Newbury in mid-May, earning an 8/1 quote from one firm for the Group 1 Investec Oaks, but she bypassed Epsom and picked up a second listed prize at that Berkshire venue. However, it was her next start that suggested she could be a real standout in the making. Under a hands-and-heels ride from regular partner James Doyle, she caught Forever Together near the line to take the Group 1 Darley Irish Oaks by a neck. Remarkably, that rival, who had won the Group 1 Investec Oaks the previous month, is even younger than her, by two days, whereas third-placed Mary Tudor was a May 14th foal.

She earned a Timeform rating of 119p for her classic victory and that figure was raised to 123p after she beat the talented four-year-old Coronet by two and a quarter lengths in the Group 1 Darley Yorkshire Oaks a month later. Lah Ti Dar, a March 22nd foal who had also been unraced at two, put up a Timeform 122p performance when running away with a listed race on that same card, and both were suddenly to the fore of discussions about the major players for the Group 1 Prix de l'Arc de Triomphe. The latter bypassed ParisLongchamp, was runner-up in the Group 1 St Leger, third in the Group 1 Qipco British Champions Fillies & Mares Stakes, and could be a middle-distance star of 2019.

Sea Of Class, on the other hand, was supplemented for the Arc, she met with traffic problems and had to switched a furlong and a half out, then stormed home, failing by only a short-neck to catch Enable. The now dual winner, who went on to a historic victory in the Grade 1 Breeders' Cup Turf, was having just her second outing in a year, so was not quite at her peak. But she also stays in training for another season, in a bid to become the first triple Arc winner. If she retains her considerable talent at five, and Sea Of Class does manage to find a bit more improvement, and if Magical really is the newfound 12-furlong star she looked at Churchill Downs, and if Japanese champion Almond Eye shows up in October with her rising superstar status still intact, then we could be set for a race for the ages.

And who knows what Group 1 standout(s) could be as yet unveiled from among the unraced or lightly raced juveniles of 2018?

Sea Of Class finished her first season on the track as Timeform's champion three-year-old filly, her mark of 129 putting her 1lb ahead of the joint title runners-up Alpha Centauri and Magical. She is one of nine Group 1 winners for her Timeform 140-rated sire Sea The Stars (by Cape Cross) – who raced in the same colours – and the 49 blacktype scorers for Gilltown Stud's half-brother to Galileo (by Sadler's Wells) also include 2018's standout stayer Stradivarius, Arc third Cloth Of Stars, and Group 2 winners Crystal Ocean, Knight To Behold, and Listen In. He will be 13 years old in January and is already well established as being one of the very best sires in Europe.

Holy Moon, the dam of Sea Of Class, was an 11-furlong listed scorer in Italy and the daughter of Hernando (by Niniski) has been an outstanding broodmare. Her best son, Back On Board (by Nathaniel), was runner-up in the Group 2 Derby Italiano, but her daughters Cherry Collect (by Oratorio), Charity Line (by Manduro) and Final Score (by Dylan Thomas) have all won the Group 2 Oaks d'Italia. The latter pair have also both won the Group 1 Premio Lydia Tesio, and it was in another edition of that race that Cherry Collect got her Group 1 placing. Their half-sister Wordless (by Rock Of Gibraltar) got her best win in a 10-furlong Group 3 at San Siro. Holy Moon was an interesting one to send to Sea The Stars as, with all of her offspring already inbred 4x4 to Nijinsky (by Northern Dancer), Sea Of Class has an added duplication on her chart, one of 3x4 to Miswaki (by Mr Prospector).

The mare was the best of several winners out of Centinela (by Caerleon) who, although a half-sister to Group 1 Oaks d'Italia scorer and Group 1 Moyglare Stud Stakes runner-up Bright Generation (by Rainbow Quest), showed little aptitude in a half-dozen starts. That talented filly went on to become the dam of a juvenile Group 3 scorer in Italy, but more notable is that she is the grandam of Dabirsim (by Hat Trick). He won the Group 1 Prix Morny and Group 1 Prix Jean-Luc Lagardere, he stands at Haras De Grandcamp in France, and his first crop – three-year-olds of 2018 – includes the Group 1-placed pattern-winning fillies Coeur De Beaute and Different League.

It is to be hoped that Sea Of Class will be at least as good at four as she was at three. She is a top-class middle-distance filly by a major sire, and out of a prolific dam, and she will make a fascinating broodmare prospect whenever her racing days come to an end. And the fact that she was unraced at two does not mean that at least some of her offspring won't be winners at that age, or that one or more of them could even be stakes or pattern horses then. As for Holy Moon – her 2017 Oasis Dream (by Green Desert) colt was a vendor buy-back at Book 1 of the Tattersalls October Yearling Sale, and her 2018 foal is a son of Golden Horn (by Cape Cross).

SUMMARY DETAILS

Bred: Razza Del Velino Srl
Owned: Sunderland Holdings Inc
Trained: William Haggas
Country: England
Race record: -211112-
Career highlights: 4 wins inc Darley Irish Oaks (Gr1), Darley Yorkshire Oaks (Gr1), Johnny Lewis Memorial British EBF (Abingdon) Stakes (L), Haras de Bouquetot Fillies' Trial Stakes (L), 2nd Qatar Prix de l'Arc de Triomphe (Gr1)

SEA OF CLASS (IRE) - 2015 chestnut filly

Sea The Stars (IRE)	Cape Cross (IRE)	Green Desert (USA)
		Park Appeal
	Urban Sea (USA)	Miswaki (USA)
		Allegretta
Holy Moon (IRE)	Hernando (FR)	Niniski (USA)
		Whakilyric (USA)
	Centinela (GB)	Caerleon (USA)
		New Generation

SHEIKHA REIKA (FR)

Timing can make a massive difference in the bloodstock business.

Darley's draft consigned to the Tattersalls December Mare Sale in 2013 included an eight-year-old grey mare who had run just once but won that seven-furlong Redcar event by 11 lengths, earning a Timeform rating of 110, a big figure for a two-year-old and a massive one for such a minor event. The daughter of unfashionable stallion Tobougg (by Barathea) was out of a stakes-placed mare called Actoris (by Diesis), her grandam was a dual winner called Avice Caro (by Caro), and those were the highlights of the top half of her page. Her third dam was US juvenile filly champion Outstandingly (by Exclusive Native), which made her grandam a half-sister to Group 2 Falmouth Stakes winner Sensation (by Soviet Star), but it was beginning to look as though she was from a weak branch of a good family.

At the time of her appearance in the auction ring, Screen Star's first foal – Silent Movie (by Cape Cross) – had made a winning debut at Wolverhampton but been beaten since, and her second one – Nabeel (by Invincible Spirit) – had been well-beaten on his debut at Newcastle and then gelded. She had a yearling Iffraaj (by Zafonic) colt and a Shamardal (by Giant's Causeway) filly foal, and she was now due to Exceed And Excel (by Danehill). Mark Johnston had trained her for that sole two-year-old appearance and it was he who bought her for 52,000gns that day in Newmarket.

The mare's value soared two years later when that last Darley-bred foal, now named Lumiere, became one of the stars of the juvenile division in England. Johnston trained her too, she ran away with a Newmarket maiden in July, chased home Besharah in the Group 2 Lowther Stakes at York, and then beat Illuminate by half a length to take the Group 1 Cheveley Park Stakes at Newmarket. She was unplaced in the Group 1 1000 Guineas on her reappearance at three, but then ran away with a one-mile listed contest on the July course at Newmarket, finished third in the Group 3 Sceptre Stakes over seven at Doncaster, and then chased home Aclaim in the Group 2 Challenge Stakes over the same trip at Newmarket.

Mark Johnston put the mare back in the ring and, now in foal to Golden Horn (by Cape Cross), she was sold to Ballylinch Stud for 675,000gns. At that point, Screen Star had produced the Exceed And Excel colt she'd been carrying in utero – now Wolverhampton juvenile winner X Rated – she had a yearling full-sister to Lumiere and an Authorized (by Montjeu) colt foal. That Golden Horn covering resulted in a grey colt that her new owners sold for 210,000gns in Newmarket in October, and she had a Lope De Vega (by Shamardal) filly in late April of this year, before being bred back to that stallion.

Roger Varian bought the Golden Horn colt, which was hardly a surprise given that the Shamardal half-sister he'd bought for 550,000gns two years before had just won a listed race at Yarmouth by four and a half lengths. And in another example of how that timing thing can work, the colt went through the ring on October 9th, four days before the filly won the Grade 1 E.P. Taylor Stakes at Woodbine. His price would likely have been higher had those dates been reversed.

The filly is, of course, Sheikha Reika. She was runner-up in all three of her starts at two and got off the mark in promising fashion first time out in 2018, when dropping back a furlong to take a Newmarket maiden by three lengths. But then she was a beaten favourite in a conditions race at Leicester – also over seven furlongs – and finished only fourth in a mile handicap at Ascot on her next run, three months later. Her final two starts of the year represented vastly improved form, and they were both over 10 furlongs. It will be interesting to see how she might fare if kept in training as four-year-old for a campaign at that trip.

Of course, Sheikha Reika is also now a very valuable broodmare prospect who is by the dam-sire of 2018's Group 1 Irish Derby winner Latrobe (by Camelot) and Group 1 Prix Morny heroine Pretty Pollyanna (by Oasis Dream). Should any of her future offspring appear in an auction then Outstandingly and the various talented horses that descend from her – and that appear under branches of the next generation of the family – will no longer appear on the page. It is debatable if they added much interest to Screen Star and her offspring anyway, as their connection ranges from distant to remote, but with Group/Grade 1 stars Lumiere and Sheikha Reika to the fore it is clear that was had become a weakened branch of the family has found strength again.

SUMMARY DETAILS

Bred: Mark Johnston Racing Ltd
Owned: Sheikh Mohammed Obaid Al Maktoum
Trained: Roger Varian
Country: England
Race record: 222-12411-
Career highlights: 3 wins inc E.P. Taylor Stakes (Gr1), EBF Stallions John Musker Fillies' Stakes (L)

SHEIKHA REIKA (FR) - 2015 bay filly

Shamardal (USA)	Giant's Causeway (USA)	Storm Cat (USA)
		Mariah's Storm (USA)
	Helsinki (GB)	Machiavellian (USA)
		Helen Street
Screen Star (IRE)	Tobougg (IRE)	Barathea (IRE)
		Lacovia (USA)
	Actoris (USA)	Diesis
		Avice Caro (USA)

SKITTER SCATTER (USA)

"Another talented member of the Fanghorn family" is a phrase that I have used many times in pedigree reviews over the past two decades, and although her connection to Skitter Scatter is now remote, she is a direct ancestor of 2018's Group 1 Moyglare Stud Stakes heroine.

The chestnut was born in 1966, was trained in France by Etienne Pollet, and won two of her 10 starts. She finished third in the Poule d'Essai des Pouliches (French 1000 Guineas), and her initial fame at stud came through the success of her brilliant son Double Form (by Habitat). He was a high-class performer at three but hit his peak at four when he landed the Group 1 King's Stand Stakes and Group 1 Prix de l'Abbaye de Longchamp, and he retired to Airlie Stud with a rating of 130 from Timeform. Sadly, misfortune beset him as he died during his fourth season.

His outstanding sire turned out to be a poor sire of stallions, but what Double Form left behind in those four crops – all very small by today's standards, of course – showed that he could have been the one among the Habitat sons to make it in their second career. Double Form gave us Group 1 sprint star Double Schwartz, dual pattern-winning juvenile sprinter Bermuda Classic, Norfolk Stakes scorer and Group 2-winning sprinter Marouble, Group 1 Dewhurst Stakes winner Huntingdale, US stakes winner Nasib, and Cambridgeshire scorer Tremblant.

It is, however, Fanghorn's daughters who have kept her name alive in pedigrees.

Her Lupe Stakes winner Scimitarra (by Kris) looked set for possible victory in the Group 1 Oaks at Epsom in 1987 but broke down in the straight, and although none of her offspring was of note on the track, her grandson Captain Gerrard (by Oasis Dream) is the Mickley Stud-based dual sprint pattern winner whose son Alpha Delphini won the Group 1 Nunthorpe Stakes at York in August. Scimitarra is also the third dam of Group 2 Park Stakes winner Ansgar (by Celtic Swing).

Her half-sister Smaoineamh (by Tap On Wood) was a dual listed winner in Ireland and third in the Group 3 Royal Whip Stakes, and although she did get a couple of stakes-placed daughters, it is her descendants who excelled on the track. They include Group 1 National Stakes winner Verbal Dexterity (by Vocalised), classic-placed dual Group 3 sprint winner Cuis Ghaire (by Galileo), Group 1-placed, Group 3 Meld Stakes winner Scintillula (by Galileo), and Group 1-placed, Group 3 Brownstown Stakes scorer Tobann (by Teofilo).

Fanghorn's daughter Galka (by Deep Diver) managed third place in the Group 3 Molecomb Stakes at two before going on become the grandam of Group 1 Phoenix Stakes heroine and Irish juvenile filly champion Eva Luna (by Double Schwartz) and that one's pattern-winning full-brother Cois Na Tine, and her descendants include Group 1 Criterium International scorer Loch Garman (by Lawman), Group 2 Flying Childers Stakes winner Beacon (by Paco Boy), and classic-placed Group 3 winner Rehn's Nest (by Authorized).

Angor (by Lorenzaccio) was the dam of pattern-placed stakes winner Nordic Soprano (by Nordico), who became the grandam of Group 3 Noblesse Stakes scorer Midnight Soprano (by Celtic Swing), whereas Double Form's full-sister Belle Epoque came up with Aminata (by Glenstal) – the Group 3-winning dam of Group 3 Desmond Stakes scorer Swift Gulliver (by Gulch) – and is a direct ancestor of Grade 1 Queen Elizabeth II Challenge Cup Stakes star Kitten's Dumplings (by Kitten's Joy).

The other notable daughter of Fanghorn is also her most influential one: Gradiva (by Lorenzaccio).

Classic-placed Group 1 winner Sholokhov (by Sadler's Wells), runaway Group 1 Irish Derby hero Soldier Of Fortune (by Galileo), and Group 1 Dewhurst Stakes scorer Intense Focus (by Giant's Causeway), head the roll of honour of her descendants, and each of that trio has had success at stud. The first pair are now National Hunt stallions, and in addition to

German classic heroine and champion Night Magic from his earlier flat-bred stock, Sholokhov is arguably best known as being the sire of Grade 1 Cheltenham Gold Cup star Don Cossack. Soldier Of Fortune's early success has made him the busiest stallion in service, whereas Intense Focus gave us the ill-fated Group 1 Middle Park Stakes scorer Astaire.

Soldier Of Fortune's Group 3 Meld Stakes-winning full-brother Heliostatic has sired a dual Grade 1 winner on the flat in Argentina, their winning half-brother and young National Hunt stallion Affinisea (by Sea The Stars) caught the eye with his first foals this year, and the many other notable descendants of Gradiva also include pattern winners Flight Risk (by Teofilo), Marionnaud (by Spectrum), and Danelissima (by Danehill) – the latter a talented middle-distance performer who won the Group 3 Noblesse Stakes and finished third in the Group 2 Lancashire Oaks. There are also many who were listed winners or 'merely' blacktype placed.

It is Danelissima's Group 3-placed full-sister Daneleta who gave us Intense Focus, and the speedy daughter of tough multiple listed scorer Zavaleta (by Kahyasi; half-sister to Sholokhov and to the dam of Soldier Of Fortune) is also responsible Dane Street (by Street Cry). That filly began her career in the Jessica Harrington stable, won a 10-furlong Fairyhouse maiden on her third start, failed miserably in a pair of 12-furlong listed contests, and then returned to 10 furlongs and won a handicap at Leopardstown. She left Ireland shortly after that, was covered by leading sire More Than Ready (by Southern Halo) the following spring, and that first foal, a $145,000 Fasig-Tipton yearling now named Data Dependent, was runner-up in a one-mile Grade 3 event on turf on her final start as a two-year-old. The mare's third foal is a yearling full-brother to that filly, but her second foal is Skitter Scatter.

Fanghorn is the seventh dam of that Patrick Prendergast-trained rising star, the top juvenile filly in Ireland in 2018 and a leading contender for the mile fillies' classics of 2019.

She began her career with a third-place finish over five furlongs at Dundalk in late March and caused a minor shock at the venue a fortnight later when short-heading a 4/9 colt from the Ballydoyle stable. What a maiden that turned out to be, one of exceptional strength for so early in the season, as Skitter Scatter pipped Sergei Prokofiev (by Scat Daddy) that day, with The Irish Rover (by No Nay Never) a length and a quarter back in third, and the rest nowhere. She was third in a listed contest over six furlongs at Naas on her turf debut in May, then chased home So Perfect in the Group 3 Grangecon Stud Stakes at the Curragh.

This was all useful early-season form, but she then stepped up seven furlongs and has not been beaten since. First, she won the Group 3 Silver Flash Stakes by a length and a half at Leopardstown, then came home a two-and-a-quarter-length winner of the Group 2 Debutante Stakes at the Curragh, and finally, she justified favouritism with a two-length victory in the Group 1 Moyglare Stud Stakes, beating Lady Kaya, who was a length and a quarter in front of Hermosa. That third-placed filly won a Group 3 contest next time out and then chased home Iridessa in the Group 1 bet365 Fillies' Mile at Newmarket.

Skitter Scatter holds an entry in the Group 1 Tattersalls Irish 1000 Guineas, and victory there would be a hugely popular result. We won't know for certain if she stays a mile until she tries it, but with what her half-sister and many talented relations have achieved, there is every reason to believe that the distance will not prove a problem for her.

What about her sire?

There is a perception among many that her late and much-lamented sire Scat Daddy (by Johannesburg) is all about precocity and sprinting speed – and standouts such as Caravaggio, Acapulco, Lady Aurelia, and No Nay Never support that – but that is just one of his angles. Before his brilliant son Justify swept through 2018's US Triple Crown series undefeated, there seemed to be many in this part of the world unaware that most of the good US Scat Daddys are mile to 10-furlong horses, and that in South America he was an outstanding classic sire, and yes, of 12 furlong ones. What the dam brings to the table is of great importance in his offspring. Aside from Justify, of course, the Aidan O'Brien-trained

Mendelssohn is a fine example; he is a half-brother to the outstanding mile to 10-furlong mare Beholder (by Henny Hughes) and to eight-and-a-half-furlong Grade 1 scorer and leading sire Into Mischief (by Harlan's Holiday).

At the time of writing, Timeform has Skitter Scatter on a rating of 113p – joint-second among the year's juvenile fillies and on the same mark as potential Oaks candidate Iridessa – 3lbs below Group 1 Prix Morny heroine Pretty Pollyanna, who looks a sprinter. It is possible that, like many of her relations, she will prove better at a mile than she has been over seven, and it would be no surprise to see her become one of the stars of the year in Ireland.

SUMMARY DETAILS

Bred: Three Chimneys Farm Llc & Airlie Stud
Owned: Anthony Rogers & Mrs Sonia Rogers
Trained: Patrick Prendergast
Country: Ireland
Race record: 3132111-
Career highlights: 4 wins inc Moyglare Stud Stakes (Gr1), Debutante Stakes (Gr2), Jockey Club of Turkey Silver Flash Stakes (Gr3), 2nd Grangecon Stud Stakes (Gr3), 3rd Coolmore Stud Irish EBF Fillies' Sprint Stakes (L)

SKITTER SCATTER (USA) - 2016 bay filly

Scat Daddy (USA)	Johannesburg (USA)	Hennessy (USA)
		Myth (USA)
	Love Style (USA)	Mr Prospector (USA)
		Likeable Style (USA)
Dane Street (USA)	Street Cry (IRE)	Machiavellian (USA)
		Helen Street
	Daneleta (IRE)	Danehill (USA)
		Zavaleta (IRE)

STRADIVARIUS (IRE)

There have been a number of positive changes made to the industry in recent years and the strengthening of the stayers' programme is one of those. The rush for early two-year-old speed appears to be doing little to enhance the breed in the long term, more stamina is needed, and to hear some say that 'Derby winner equals National Hunt stallion' is disturbing.

The advent of genetic testing for the speed and stamina genes has provided some scientific back-up for points that some of we traditional analysts have been making for decades when using our reading of a horse's pedigree to make predictions about future prospects on the track, or to explain distance preferences, but these tests have also shown the need for stamina. A possessor of two 'speed genes' can only pass on the speed gene – potential ability from five to 10 furlongs – and if all we breed is horses with two copies of that gene, then what happens to the Derby, St Leger, King George, and Arc, never mind the Cup races?

Should a stallion be shunned because he has two copies of the stamina gene instead? From the choices that many make each year in choosing mares, choosing stallions, and making sales selections, it would appear that for some the answer is yes. And yet prolific champion sire Galileo (by Sadler's Wells), one of the greatest progenitors of all time, is such a horse. You breed a mare to him and your foal will get a stamina gene. It is what your mare contributes to the mix that will influence the distance preference of that foal.

So why not give elite stayers a chance as flat sires? Not every elite stayer would be a potential candidate, of course – indeed, most would not be suitable prospects – but those with high Timeform figures, whose pedigree gave them a chance for success in the eight-to-12-furlong range while excelling at two miles and above, and a distaff line that gives them a shot at being a good flat sire, deserve the chance. Of course, they won't be 'commercial' because they are not going to have any appeal with the Royal Ascot-juvenile-speed-hungry, and potentially limited appeal for the breeze-up markets, but, who knows, there could be another Sadler's Wells or Galileo among them.

Order Of St George is an elite stayer who was bred to excel over a shorter range and who was placed in the Arc, and it is to be hoped that he gets some chances with decent flat mares in addition to the no doubt huge numbers of National Hunt types he will cover. Stradivarius is another.

He is by Galileo's brilliant half-brother Sea The Stars (by Cape Cross), who has been getting his top-level winners from a mile and upwards, and he comes from a branch of the famous family of Pawneese (by Carvin II) and Peintre Celebre (by Nureyev). The latter's offspring included the triple Group 1-winning Australian sprinter Bentley Biscuit.

Stradivarius won over a mile at two, was a runaway winner over 10 furlongs first time out at three, then stepped up in trip, narrowly beat Count Octave in the Group 2 Queen's Vase over 14 furlongs at Royal Ascot and then sealing his future with a one-and-three-quarter-length defeat of Group 1 Gold Cup hero Big Orange in the Group 1 Qatar Goodwood Cup over two miles. It was an outstanding performance for a three-year-old.

He finished a half-length and short-head third to Capri and Crystal Ocean in a vintage edition of the Group 1 William Hill St Leger Stakes next time out – in which Rekindling was fourth, Coronet fifth, and Count Octave sixth and a long way clear of the rest – and then took on his elders again in the Group 2 Qipco British Champions Long Distance Cup at Ascot, finishing third Order Of St George and Torcedor, beaten just half a length and the same.

Timeform rated him 123 for that campaign – just shy of true Group 1 level (Timeform-rated 125) – but having swept through his four-year-old campaign undefeated in five starts, he is now on 127.

He kicked off the season with an easy three-length defeat of Desert Skyline in the Group 2 Mansionbet Yorkshire Cup over 14 furlongs, beat Vazirabad by three-parts of a length in the Group 1 Gold Cup, beat Torcedor by half a length in the Group 1 Qatar Goodwood Cup, and then beat Count Octave by a length and a half to take the Group 2 Weatherbys Hamilton Lonsdale Cup Stakes and the £1 million Weatherbys Hamilton Stayers' Million bonus for sweeping for sweeping those four races. He rounded off the year with victory in the Group 2 Qipco British Champions Long Distance Cup over two miles at Ascot in late October, beating Thomas Hobson by a length and a quarter on ground softer that is ideal for him.

Stradivarius is a half-brother to the dual German 10-furlong Group 3 scorer Persian Storm (by Monsun) and out of Private Life (by Bering), a stakes-placed half-sister to the 15-furlong listed race winner Pretty Tough (by Desert King) and also to Parisienne (by Distant Relative), a juvenile stakes winner with a famous grandson: Protectionist (by Monsun), the Group 1 Melbourne Cup hero of 2014. He was a pattern-winning stayer before making the trip to Flemington, but an extended stay in Australia did not work out for him so he returned to Germany, added Group 1 success in the Grosser Preis von Berlin over 12 furlongs at Hoppegarten, and took up stallion duties at Gestut Rottgen in 2017.

His third dam, Poughkeepsie (by Sadler's Wells), is the grandam of Stradivarius and that one-time winner is among five successful runners from the dozen foals produced from Pawneese, the Group 1 Oaks, Group 1 Prix de Diane (French Oaks) and Group 1 King George VI and Queen Elizabeth Stakes heroine whom Timeform rated 131 in her championship season – 1976.

Pawneese's half-sister Petroleuse (by Habitat), who won the Group 3 Princess Elizabeth Stakes, is the grandam of Peintre Celebre, the Timeform 137-rated star who took the Group 1 Prix de l'Arc de Triomphe, Group 1 Grand Prix de Paris and Group 1 Prix du Jockey-Club (French Derby) in 1997. Although he has not achieved the sort of fame at stud as he did on the track, the brilliant chestnut supplied 65 stakes winners, 12 of whom won at the highest level, including the Group 1 standouts Pride, Vallee Enchantee, and the aforementioned Bentley Biscuit.

Bjorn Nielsen's homebred star is trained by John Gosden and his return to action as a five-year-old is eagerly anticipated. A place at stud surely awaits him whenever his racing days come to an end, and hopefully it will not be solely National Hunt mares in his books.

SUMMARY DETAILS

Bred: Bjorn Nielsen
Owned: Bjorn Nielsen
Trained: John Gosden
Country: England
Race record: 041-121133-11111-
Career highlights: 9 wins inc Gold Cup (Gr1), Qatar Goodwood Cup Stakes (Gr1-twice), Qipco British Champions Long Distance Cup (Gr2), Weatherbys Hamilton Lonsdale Cup Stakes (Gr2), Mansionbet Yorkshire Cup (Gr2), Queen's Vase (Gr2), 3rd William Hill St Leger Stakes (Gr1), Qipco British Champions Long Distance Cup (Gr2)

STRADIVARIUS (IRE) - 2014 chestnut colt

Sea The Stars (IRE)	Cape Cross (IRE)	Green Desert (USA)
		Park Appeal
	Urban Sea (USA)	Miswaki (USA)
		Allegretta
Private Life (FR)	Bering	Arctic Tern (USA)
		Beaune (FR)
	Poughkeepsie (IRE)	Sadler's Wells (USA)
		Pawneese

STUDY OF MAN (IRE)

There was some understandable disappointment when 1989's US champion three-year-old and Horse of the Year was exported to take up stallion duties at Shadai Stallion Station in Japan, after a career where won the Grade 1 Kentucky Derby, Grade 1 Preakness Stakes, Grade 1 Santa Anita Derby, Grade 1 Super Derby and Grade 1 Breeders' Cup Classic, and earned close to $5 million.

We can only speculate as to how a US stallion career may have turned out for him, but as a big fish in the comparatively smaller pond in Japan, the black son of Halo (by Hail To Reason) transformed that nation's racing and bloodstock industry and forged one of the world's most powerful dynasties. Sunday Silence's influence as a sire of sires and as a broodmare sire has also ensured that his name will live on for a long time to come, and although he has many excellent stallion sons among a total of 171 stakes winners, one is building up a profile that may some day rival that of his father.

Deep Impact was arguably his most brilliant son and the Timeform 134-rated star, who came from his penultimate crop, quickly took over the mantle as both the chief flag bearer for Shadai Stallion Station and that of the most dominant stallion in the region.

He will be 17 years old in January, is currently on a total of 124 stakes winners, with 39 of those having won at least once at the highest level, and awareness of his might has been raised in Europe in the past year and a half, with the Coolmore team making greater use of him for their star mares, and classic star Saxon Warrior doing them proud.

That colt gave Deep Impact a second European Group 1 classic winner when taking the 2000 Guineas in style at Newmarket, and it was second-crop daughter Beauty Parlour who was his first. She took the Group 1 Poule d'Essai des Pouliches (French 1000 Guineas) in 2012 and lost her unbeaten record when chasing home the ill-fated Valyra in the

Group 1 Prix de Diane (French Oaks) the following month. Just weeks after the Newmarket race, Deep Impact got his third European classic star.

The Pascal Bary-trained Study Of Man, a homebred for the Niarchos's Flaxman Stables Ireland Ltd who put up a visually impressive performance when beating runaway German stakes winner Alounak easily in the Group 2 Prix Greffulhe at Saint-Cloud in May, landed the Group 1 Qipco Prix du Jockey Club (French Derby) by half a length from Patascoy, with Louis D'Or a head back in third and another head back to subsequent Group 1 scorer Intellogent in fourth.

This 10-and-a-half-furlong victory came on soft ground, his Greffulhe success was over the same trip on good ground, and his two prior outings came on heavy. Conditions should have been in his favour in at least two of his final three starts of the year, but he proved disappointing each time. He was odds-on when finishing a six-length third to Knight To Behold in the Group 2 Prix Guillaume d'Ornano at Deauville, beaten by the same amount when unplaced behind Roaring Lion in the Group 1 Qipco Irish Champion Stakes on fast ground at Leopardstown in September, and then, on his first attempt at the mile and a half, was beaten a total of four and a half lengths (ninth) by Enable in the Group 1 Qatar Prix de l'Arc de Triomphe.

It would be no surprise to see the Irish-born Study Of Man show improvement as an older horse, which could make him a leading candidate for some of the best 10 and 12-furlong events of 2019. Looking farther ahead, his pedigree and classic success will surely make him a popular member of the stallion ranks when his current career comes to an end.

Study Of Man is the best of a few winners out of Second Happiness (by Storm Cat), a placed mare whose siblings feature classic stars East Of The Moon (by Private Account) and Kingmambo (by Mr Prospector) and whose dam is, of course, the brilliant Miesque (by Nureyev). Also a Niarchos homebred, she was a top filly at two, a Timeform 131-rated classic heroine at three, and retired at the end of her four-year-old season with a Timeform figure of 133 and career total of

10 Group/Grade 1 wins, including two editions of the Breeders' Cup Mile. Her triple Group 1-winning son Kingmambo, of course, became a leading international sire, with 24 top-level winners among a total of 85 blacktype scorers, and although his sons have met with mixed success at stud – leading sires King Kamehameha and Lemon Drop Kid stand out – his broodmare daughters have excelled.

Kingmambo's Group 3-winning full-brother Miesque's Son has sired the Group/Grade 1 winners Miesque's Approval and Whipper, and his full-sister Monavassia is the dam of juvenile Group 1 star Rumplestiltskin (by Danehill) and so grandam of that filly's classic-placed, Group 1 Yorkshire Oaks-winning daughter Tapestry (by Galileo). She is also the grandam of dual classic-placed Group 1 Dubai Turf winner Real Steel (by Deep Impact), who will stand his first season at Shadai Stallion Station in 2019.

Their stakes-winning three-parts sister Moon Is Up (by Woodman) is the dam of South African mile Grade 1 winner Amanee (by Pivotal) and grandam of Group 1 Poule d'Essai des Poulains (French 2000 Guineas) and Grade 1 Breeders' Cup Mile ace Karakontie (by Bernstein), who stands at Gainesway Farm in Kentucky, will have his first runners in 2019, and had first-crop yearlings fetch up to $220,000.

East Of The Moon, of course, completed the Group 1 Poule d'Essai des Pouliches and Group 1 Prix de Diane double in 1994, and she is the grandam of this year's Timeform 128-rated, four-time Group 1 star Alpha Centauri (by Mastercraftsman), who is covered elsewhere in this volume.

Miesque was out of the dual French listed scorer Pasadoble (by Prove Out) and her siblings included seven-furlong Saint-Cloud blacktype winner Massaraat (by Nureyev), a mare who produced only four winners from 11 foals but whose descendants include Group 2 Ribblesdale Stakes winner Silkwood (by Singspiel), Group 2 Cherry Hinton Stakes scorer Silent Honor (by Sunday Silence), and also Permian (by Teofilo). That tragically ill-fated colt was a notable middle-distance three-year-old in 2017 – Timeform-rated 117 – when he won the Group 2 Dante Stakes and Group 2 King Edward

VII Stakes and failed by just a nose to take the Group 1 Grand Prix de Paris.

Pasadoble was also the dam of Yogya (by Riverman), the unraced mare who gave us the classic-placed Group 1 Prix Marcel Boussac, Group 1 Prix Jacques le Marois and Grade 1 Breeders' Cup Mile heroine Six Perfections (by Celtic Swing). That Timeform 124-rated champion is, in turn, the dam of Group 2 Prix du Gros-Chene scorer Planet Five (by Storm Cat), US Grade 3 winner Faufiler (by Galileo), and the Aidan O'Brien-trained Yucatan (by Galileo), a Group 1-placed pattern winner in Ireland who impressed when taking a 12-furlong Group 2 contest at Caulfield in October.

With pedigree connections like these, Study Of Man is clearly bred to achieve anything on the track and to make an impact at stud. He was not absolutely guaranteed to stay 12 furlongs, given that his dam is a Storm Cat (by Storm Bird) mare out of Miesque, but his Arc performance suggests that this could be an option for him in 2019.

SUMMARY DETAILS

Bred: Flaxman Stables Ireland Ltd
Owned: Flaxman Stables Ireland Ltd
Trained: Pascal Bary
Country: France
Race record: 1-211300-
Career highlights: 3 wins inc Qipco Prix du Jockey Club (Gr1), Prix Greffulhe (Gr2), 2nd Prix La Force (Gr3), 3rd Prix Guillaume d'Ornano Haras du Logis Saint-Germain (Gr2)

STUDY OF MAN (IRE) - 2015 bay colt

Deep Impact (JPN)	Sunday Silence (USA)	Halo (USA)
		Wishing Well (USA)
	Wind In Her Hair (IRE)	Alzao (USA)
		Burghclere
Second Happiness (USA)	Storm Cat (USA)	Storm Bird (CAN)
		Terlingua (USA)
	Miesque (USA)	Nureyev (USA)
		Pasadoble (USA)

TEN SOVEREIGNS (IRE)

Countless now-forgotten horses have received ante-post classic odds, heaped praise, potential stallion advert quotes, and predictions of stardom following their maiden success, but every now and then you get one whose successful debut genuinely does measure up as being out of the ordinary. Those horses, some of whom score by double-digit margins (e.g Galileo won his only juvenile start by 14 lengths), are few and often far between. Ten Sovereigns won a six-furlong maiden at the Curragh in late August by seven lengths on good ground, utterly outclassing opposition of questionable merit, but in a time and manner that earned a Timeform rating of 106P and made him look the likely winner of the following month's Group 1 Juddmonte Middle Park Stakes at Newmarket.

That's a large P and not a small one, indicating that the horse both looks capable of improvement and may be considerably better than what he's been given. And he earned that symbol after his second run too.

He was an easy three-and-three-quarter-length winner of the Group 3 John Silk & Son Round Tower Stakes over the same course and distance just seven days. The colt who chased him home had finished a well-beaten sixth behind him on their debut – and has not been seen out since – and the third has been well-beaten in each of her three subsequent starts, but the clock again indicated that the winner's effort was as good on paper as it looked to the eye, and Timeform raised him to 114P.

He duly headed to England four weeks later. This time, however, he was made to work, and perhaps to learn for the first time how to race. It was, however, an effort worthy of a 120p end-of-year Timeform figure, and the colt who made him fight was the Simon Crisford-trained Jash, a Kodiac colt who had won his only two races by a combined margin of 13 and a half lengths. There was a three-and-a-half-length gap back to third-placed Rumble Inthejungle (Group 3 Molecomb

Stakes winner), with Group 3 Anglesey Stakes winner Marie's Diamond another half-length behind in fourth, and followed home by Emaraaty Ana and Legends Of War – who were the one-two in the previous month's Group 2 Gimcrack Stakes – and Sergei Prokofiev.

Some of those likely did not run up to their best, or had issues with the trip – the last-named, for example, won a five-furlong Group 3 in style next time out – but this was a highly promising from both the winner and runner-up. Those two colts hold an entry in the Group 1 Tattersalls Irish 2000 Guineas, and there are elements of Jash's pedigree that suggest he could stay the mile (and even a bit farther), but what about Ten Sovereigns? Is he a potential Guineas colt or would the Group 1 Commonwealth Cup be a more suitable target?

His sire is the first noticeable thing about his pedigree and he represents the first crop of Coolmore Stud's highly regarded No Nay Never. That horse was a high-class sprinter at two and three, he is from a family of mostly sprinters and milers, with some who stay a bit farther, and he is a son of the late and much lamented Scat Daddy (by Johannesburg). There is a perception in Ireland and the UK that Scat Daddy is all about precocity and sprinting speed – and when his European runners have featured Acapulco, Caravaggio, Lady Aurelia, No Nay Never, and Sioux Nation, it's easy to understand why.

There is no doubt that he can be an influence for both of those traits. However, Scat Daddy was a Grade 1 winner at eight and nine furlongs, and he was bred to excel at around that distance. In North America he has been primarily a source of milers and 10-furlong horses – before 2018's undefeated US Triple Crown hero Justify emerged – whereas in South America he was also a leading sire of 12-furlong classic horses. In short, Scat Daddy could get his best winners in the broad five to 12-furlong range, with input from the mare being important. And this means that No Nay Never, a horse who was never asked to go beyond sprints after a disappointing second-place finish in the Grade 2 Swale Stakes over seven furlongs, is a stallion who is bred to sire sprinters, milers and, with the right mares, some who could be 10-furlong horses.

With a lot of speed-bred mares among his earliest books, it is likely that most of his early stakes winners will be sprinters, but with his fee catapulted to €100,000 from 2019, which will likely see classic-type mares go his way, his profile will broaden over time.

What about Ten Sovereigns? Does the distaff side of his family give him the potential to stay a mile? Yes, it does. And it may depend on whether his dam, Seeking Solace, passed on speed from her sire, Exceed And Excel (by Danehill), or the stamina of her broodmare sire, Theatrical (by Nureyev). She won over 10 furlongs in heavy ground and was a one-length runner-up in an 11-furlong listed contest on good, so she likely had some of his middle-distance stamina in her. But that does not necessarily mean that her son has it too.

Seeking Solace is also the dam of Learza (by High Chaparral), who has won over a mile, and she is out of Flamelet. That former John Oxx trainee ran only three times, all within the space of six weeks in the spring of her three-year-old season, and she was runner-up by a head in a mile Group 3 at Leopardstown on her second start. That mare's son My Boy Lewis (by Dandy Man) won a six-furlong Doncaster nursery in November, his half-sister Trevanna (by Requinto) won twice over seven furlongs for the Kevin Prendergast stable, whereas half-brother Arc Lighter (by Street Cry) came within a head of scoring over 11 and a half furlongs at Windsor a few years ago. And then there's the Timeform 116-rated Flash Fire (by Shamardal), a four-time winner over seven furlongs who has been Group 2-placed over that trip at Meydan and also placed at a mile.

The first two generations of a pedigree will usually be most influential, as those ancestors are making the largest contribution, and if you look only at these two levels then you could say with confidence that Ten Sovereigns will likely stay a mile. If you look at the third generation then you will find mixed support, but the fourth generation strengthens the case for his prospects of staying the distance.

Darling Flame (by Capote), his third dam, was runner-up in the Group 3 Cherry Hinton Stakes over six furlongs as a juvenile, her son Bezrin (by Danzig) was a seven-furlong stakes winner who stayed a mile, and her granddaughter Al Thakhira (by Dubawi) won the Group 2 Rockfel Stakes and a listed contest over seven but was well-beaten each time she tried a mile. But she is also the grandam of the Robert Smerdon-trained Shamal Wind (by Dubawi). That one is the first foal out of seven-furlong winner Firemaid (by Machiavellian), she has raced exclusively over five and six furlongs and took the Group 1 Oakleigh Plate over five and a half furlongs at Caulfield almost four years ago.

The fourth dam is the flashy chestnut My Darling One (by Exclusive Native), and in addition to being the dam of Heart Lake (by Nureyev) – a seven-furlong Group 3 scorer in Ireland who won at the highest level over a mile in Japan – she still holds the race record time in the Fantasy Stakes at Oaklawn Park. That eight-and-a-half-furlong contest carried Grade 1 status that day in 1984. She also won the Grade 3 Fair Ground Oaks over the same trip, she was third in the Grade 1 Kentucky Oaks, and she was a granddaughter of Marshua (by Nashua), who won the Coaching Club American Oaks over 10 furlongs in 1965.

Ten Sovereigns finished his first season as joint third best, on Timeform ratings, with Calyx, and behind only Too Darn Hot (127p) and Quorto (122p), and it is quite remarkable that all four of those colts are, as yet, undefeated. His pedigree gives him every chance of not just staying a mile but excelling at it, but the impression he created with those juvenile runs suggests that he could be as good, if not better, as a sprinter. He is an exciting prospect, and it will be fascinating to see how his career turns out.

SUMMARY DETAILS
Bred: Camas Park, Lynch Bages & Summerhill
Owned: Derrick Smith, Mrs John Magnier & Michael Tabor
Trained: Aidan O'Brien
Country: Ireland
Race record: 111-

Career highlights: 3 wins inc Juddmonte Middle Park Stakes (Gr1), John Sisk & Son Round Tower Stakes (Gr3)

TEN SOVEREIGNS (IRE) - 2016 bay colt

No Nay Never (USA)	Scat Daddy (USA)	Johannesburg (USA)
		Love Style (USA)
	Cat's Eye Witness (USA)	Elusive Quality (USA)
		Comical Cat (USA)
Seeking Solace (GB)	Exceed And Excel (AUS)	Danehill (USA)
		Patrona (USA)
	Flamelet (USA)	Theatrical
		Darling Flame (USA)

TEPPAL (FR)

Coolmore Stud's late Danehill (by Danzig), the prolific champion sire whose early success served as the catalyst for the enduring might of the business of shuttling stallions, holds the world record for the number of stakes (348) and Group/Grade 1-winning (83) offspring and he forged a dynasty that will ensure his name lives on in pedigrees for a long time to come. His long list of sons who have at least one top-level winner to their name at stud gained an extra name in mid-May 2018 when Teppal scored a narrow victory in the Group 1 Poule d'Essai des Pouliches (French 1000 Guineas).

The David Simcock-trained bay is the first to win at the highest grade for her sire, Camacho. Apart from a single season spent at Mickley Stud in England, the Yeomanstown Stud stallion – a stakes-winning half-brother to the notably successful and increasingly popular Showcasing (by Oasis Dream) – is now about to start his 13th year with the O'Callaghans in Co Kildare. His 14 stakes winners include Group 2 Flying Childers Stakes scorer Green Door, Group 3 Prix de Cabourg winner My Catch, Group 3 Fred Darling Stakes heroine Puff, and nine listed scorers – plus his classic star and one of the leading juveniles of 2018.

The latter is, of course, the John Quinn-trained Signora Cabello. She is a 20,000gns graduate of Book 3 of the Tattersalls October Yearling Sale in Newmarket, won the Listed Marygate Stakes at York just a few days after Teppal's classic victory, and followed-up with a short-head success in the Group 2 Queen Mary Stakes at Royal Ascot. A month later she added the Group 2 Prix Robert Papin at Maisons-Laffitte before stepping up to six furlongs for the Group 1 Darley Prix Morny at Deauville, in which she chased home three-quarter-length winner Pretty Pollyanna. She was unplaced in the Group 1 Juddmonte Cheveley Park Stakes on her final start, made 900,000gns at the Tattersalls December Mare Sale and is now owned outright by her former part-owner Phoenix Thoroughbreds.

Camacho's stock are typically sprinters but, like his half-brother, it was always on the cards that he could get some milers too. It would depend on the mares.

It may seem, at first glance, that a Camacho out of a daughter of Cadeaux Genereux (by Young Generation) would surely be a sprinter, but Teppal began her career with a couple of seven-furlong wins – her only starts at two. The second of those was a four-length score on the Polytrack at Kempton, making her yet another Group 1 star who got one of their earliest wins on an artificial track. Cross Counter and Enable are just two other examples from among the Class of 2018.

The 14 runners in the Poule d'Essai des Pouliches were covered by just six lengths at the line, which suggested that the form of the race be treated with caution. She had hit the front about half a furlong from home and kept on well to hold off Coeur De Beaute, Wind Chimes, and Capla Temptress by a short-neck, head and head. It remains a career-best effort for her, however, as she was beaten by over 14 lengths when unplaced behind Alpha Centauri in the Group 1 Coronation Stakes at Royal Ascot in June and was then off the track until finishing out of the frame in the Group 1 Qatar Prix de la Foret at ParisLongchamp, won by One Master. She was ninth in both of those races, but in the latter was only beaten by a total of four lengths.

Teppal was bred in France by Gestut Zur Kuste Ag and was snapped up for €60,000 by noted judge Con Marnane from Book 2 of the Arqana August Sale. Marnane then sold her on for €105,000 at the Arqana May Breeze-Up Sale. Her siblings include the ill-fated prolific blacktype-placed colt Another Party (by Pomellato), who was effective from five to seven furlongs, and her dam, Jummana, is a full-sister to Listed Radley Stakes scorer Party. That stakes-winning filly has also done her part for the family at stud as she is the dam of Observational (by Galileo), a multiple blacktype scorer from eight to 10 and a half-furlongs – including a Group 3 contest at Caulfield – and stakes-placed at a few metres short of the mile and a half.

Forty Belles (by Forty Niner), who is the grandam of Teppal, was placed a few times but a half-sister to a string of successful runners, several of whom were blacktype horses. Those include pattern-placed French listed scorer Bellona (by Bering) – who is the grandam of Group 1 Hong Kong Vase winner Dominant (by Cacique) and Group 2 Lennox Stakes winner Es Que Love (by Clodovil) – and In Clover (by Inchinor), the Group 3 Prix de Flore-winning heroine who would be a leading candidate for European Broodmare of the Year, if such an accolade was awarded.

At the time of the Pouliches, in May, we could describe In Clover as being the dam of three stakes winners, headed by Group 1 Prix de l'Opera star We Are (by Dansili). But then her three-year-old daughter With You (by Dansili) won the Group 1 Prix Rothschild over a mile at Deauville in July, and her four-year-old son Call The Wind (by Frankel) landed the Group 1 Prix du Cadran over two and a half miles at ParisLongchamp in October. In Clover is on the verge of earning 'blue hen' status, and having such a celebrity broodmare in her family provides an eye-catching boost to Teppal's prospects.

The middle-distance and even staying stamina that appears in the pedigree may have something to do with Teppal's third dam, Bellarida (by Bellypha), being inbred 3x3 to the stallion Le Fabuleux (by Wild Risk). That mare won the Group 3 Prix de Royaumont over 12 furlongs and was a granddaughter of Group 1 Prix Saint-Alary winner Lalika (by Le Fabuleux). The speed being contributed by Camacho always made it unlikely that her young descendant would be asked to try such distances, let alone have the stamina for them, but excellence over a mile was always possible, and in the case of this filly, more likely than her becoming a sprinter.

SUMMARY DETAILS

Bred: Gestut Zur Kuste Ag
Owned: H H Sheikh Mohammed Bin Khalifa Al Thani

Trained: David Simcock
Country: England
Race record: 11-100-
Career highlights: 3 wins inc The Emirates Poule d'Essai des Pouliches (Gr1)

TEPPAL (FR) - 2015 bay filly

Camacho (GB)	Danehill (USA)	Danzig (USA)
		Razyana (USA)
	Arabesque (GB)	Zafonic (USA)
		Prophecy (IRE)
Jummana (FR)	Cadeaux Genereux	Young Generation
		Smarten Up
	Forty Belles (USA)	Forty Niner (USA)
		Bellarida (FR)

THE TIN MAN (GB)

Acclamation (by Royal Applause) has been something of a surprise as a sire of stallions as he has given us both leading sire Dark Angel and Group 1-producer Equiano. The latter stands at Newsells Park Stud, his Group 1-placed, pattern-winning son Strath Burn had foals of his own in 2018, and his celebrity representative is the James Fanshawe-trained The Tin Man, now a triple Group 1 star.

Timeform-rated 126 in 2016, and 125 in both 2017 and 2018, he added a half-length defeat of Brando in the Group 1 32Red Sprint Cup Stakes on heavy ground at Haydock to prior wins in the Group 1 Qipco British Champions Sprint Stakes and Group 1 Diamond Jubilee Stakes. His five starts this year included a listed race success on fast ground at Windsor in May, he was fourth to Merchant Navy in the blanket finish to the Group 1 Diamond Jubilee Stakes at Ascot in June, and a three-length third to Polydream in the Group 1 Prix Maurice de Gheest at Deauville in August.

The six-year-old's overall record stands at nine wins and three placings from 21 starts, he has earned over £1.18 million in prize money, and there is every reason to hope that he can do well at the top level again in 2019, at the age of seven.

The Tin Man is a member of his sire's first crop, he was bred by Elizabeth Grundy and is an 80,000gns graduate of Book 1 of the Tattersalls October Yearling Sale. His half-sister Holley Shiftwell (by Bahamian Bounty), who won four times over the minimum trip, was second in listed races at Ayr and Bath, had an Equiano colt in 2017, a filly by that sire in 2018, and was the bred to Muhaarar (by Oasis Dream).

The best of his string of successful siblings, however, is his half-brother Deacon Blues (by Compton Place). He won on the second of his two starts as a juvenile and picked up a Yarmouth handicap at three, but at the age of four, and following a seasonal reappearance when a neck runner-up over six furlongs at Ascot, the gelding went unbeaten for the rest of that campaign, culminating in an impressive length and a half defeat of Wizz Kid in the Group 2 Qipco British Champions Sprint Stakes.

Deacon Blues's tally in 2011 also included the Wokingham at Royal Ascot, the Group 3 Hackwood Stakes at Newbury and the Group 3 Phoenix Sprint Stakes at the Curragh – all over six furlongs – plus the Group 3 Dubai International World Trophy over the minimum trip at Newbury. His official rating was 120, but Timeform placed him on a figure of 130, putting him high among the best European sprinters of recent years.

Getting two top-class sprint sons, both of whom won the Qipco British Champions Sprint at Ascot, is a notable achievement for their dam, Persario (by Bishop Of Cashel), a seven-furlong maiden winner at three who got her second win with a six-furlong handicap success at Kempton at the age of five. She was also trained by Fanshawe, as was Deacon Blues.

Persario is one of four winners from six foals out of dual scorer Barford Lady (by Stanford), and they also include two performers of note. Her full-brother Heretic did not earn any blacktype, but this capable miler won at two, three, four, five and six years of age, reaching a peak handicap mark of 110. Their half-brother Warningford (by Warning) – who could be described as being their three-parts brother – notched up 10 wins from three to eight years of age. Those included three editions of the Group 3 Leicestershire Stakes, two renewals of the Listed John of Gaunt Stakes, plus one running of the Listed Dubai Duty Free Cup.

Warningford was only beaten a neck by Medicean in the Group 1 Lockinge Stakes, he was third to Mount Abu in the Group 1 Prix de la Foret, and fourth (no blacktype) to Slickly in the Group 1 Prix du Moulin de Longchamp, he achieved a peak handicap mark of 116 and, at the age of seven, was rated 119 by Timeform.

Barford Lady was among six winners from 10 foals out of the stakes-placed triple scorer Grace Poole (by Sallust) and the best of those was Ansellman (by Absalom), who won the Listed Doncaster Stakes over five furlongs as a juvenile and got the final of his 11 wins, from 128 starts, at the age of 10. Winning is something that this family does.

SUMMARY DETAILS

Bred: Mrs Elizabeth Grundy
Owned: Fred Archer Racing - Ormonde
Trained: James Fanshawe
Country: England
Race record: 011014-10121-01030-14310-
Career highlights: 9 wins inc Qipco British Champions Sprint (Gr1), Diamond Jubilee Stakes (Gr1), 32Red Sprint Cup Stakes (Gr1), bet365 Hackwood Stakes (Gr3), Weatherbys Hamilton Leisure Stakes (L-twice), 2nd 32Red Sprint Cup Stakes (Gr1), 3rd LARC Prix Maurice de Gheest (Gr1), 32Red Sprint Cup Stakes (Gr1)

THE TIN MAN (GB) - 2012 bay gelding

Equiano (FR)	Acclamation (GB)	Royal Applause (GB)
		Princess Athena
	Entente Cordiale (IRE)	Ela-Mana-Mou
		Mirmande (GB)
Persario (GB)	Bishop Of Cashel (GB)	Warning
		Ballet Classique (USA)
	Barford Lady	Stanford
		Grace Poole

THUNDER SNOW (IRE)

What an admirable colt Thunder Snow is. The racing and
bloodstock industry has transformed in the near four decades
since it became part of my life, and the many changes include
the extent to which the best horses compete on the
international circuit. In the mid-1980s, Triptych was known as
"The Iron Lady" for the unusual amount of travel that she did
and the number of top races in which she took on, and often
beat, the colts. Nowadays many of the leading horses have a
schedule that makes hers pale in little in comparison, and
Thunder Snow is among them.

He is an epitome of the modern racehorse, yet with a twist
– he's as good on dirt as he is on turf. A mile or 10 furlongs,
dirt or turf – it matters not to him. He'll turn up and, more
often than not, put up a top-class effort. When he finished
third to Accelerate and Gunnevera in the Grade 1 Breeders'
Cup Classic at Churchill Downs in November he pushed his
earnings past the £6.8 million mark, and it seems that he's not
done yet.

Godolphin's homebred son of reverse-shuttle stallion
Helmet (by Exceed And Excel) is trained by Saeed bin Suroor
and he began his career in late May of his juvenile season,
winning a six-furlong Leicester maiden. He disappointed
behind Caravaggio in the Group 2 Coventry Stakes at Royal
Ascot a fortnight later but bounced back to put up four good
efforts in a row and to earn an end-of-year Timeform rating of
119.

First he chased home War Decree in the Group 2 Vintage
Stakes at Goodwood, then failed by just a head to beat Rivet in
the Group 2 Champagne Stakes at Doncaster, was a two-
length fourth to Churchill in the Group 1 Dewhurst Stakes at
Newmarket, and then ran away with the Group 1 Criterium
International over seven furlongs on soft ground at Saint-
Cloud, taking the prize by five lengths.

His three-year-old campaign began with a classic double in Dubai – a five-and-three-quarter-length score in the Group 3 UAE 2000 Guineas followed by a short-head success in the Group 2 UAE Derby – and then came that unforgettable first trip to the United States.

Only the Dermot Weld-trained Go And Go has travelled from Europe to win a leg of the US Triple Crown – the Belmont Stakes in 1990 – but Clive Brittain went close four years before when he sent over Bold Arrangement to chase home Ferdinand in the Kentucky Derby. Thunder Snow looked to have a shot of making the frame in the Churchill Downs feature but, instead, he did a good impersonation of a bucking bronco shortly after the start and was pulled up. It's an odd blip on his record, and aside from that, the Coventry Stakes, and two last-place finishes at Ascot and York, he has been a model of consistency throughout his career. Every horse has the occasional off day.

His first start after the rodeo was the Group 1 Irish 2000 Guineas at the Curragh and he redeemed himself by chasing home Churchill. He was then third to Barney Roy in the Group 1 St James's Palace Stakes at Ascot before making all to take the Group 1 Prix Jean Prat at Chantilly, by a length and a quarter from Trais Fluors. He had that rival the same margin behind at Deauville several weeks later, but this time had to settle for third in the Group 1 Prix du Haras de Fresnay-le-Buffard Jacques le Marois, beaten a short-head and short-neck by Al Wukair and Inns Of Court. Then came the Ascot blip, trailing home last of 15 in the Group 1 Queen Elizabeth II Stakes – the one time he wore a visor.

Thunder Snow finished that campaign on a Timeform rating of 122 and raised that figure to 126 in 2018. A surprise defeat by Heavy Metal in a mile Group 2 on dirt at Meydan in mid-January preceded a neck win over North America in a similar contest over a furlong and a half farther a month later. He was odds-on when surprisingly beaten easily by that same rival in the Group 1 Al Maktoum Challenge R3 a month after that, but then posted an outstanding performance when thrashing US star West Coast by five and three-quarter lengths in the Group 1 Dubai World Cup. This time North America finished in the rear.

He was next seen in action in August when he lined up for the Group 1 Juddmonte International Stakes at York, but having set out in a bid to make all, he dropped away and finished last. It later emerged that he had lost two shoes during the race. He didn't rest for long as five and a half weeks later he was at Belmont Park for the Grade 1 Jockey Club Gold Cup Stakes over 10 furlongs on dirt – his final start before the aforementioned Breeders' Cup Classic bid. He hit the front a furlong from home but was caught near the line by longshot Discreet Lover, who won by a neck. The much-travelled Aidan O'Brien-trained colt Mendelssohn was one and three-quarter lengths back in third.

Thunder Snow is the standout runner for his sire, Helmet, but having spent two seasons at Kildangan Stud and four at Dalham Hall Stud, the reverse-shuttler and grandson of Danehill (by Danzig) has left the Darley roster for 2019 to join the team at Gestut Fahrhof in Germany. He has had two Group 3 winners in Australia, three listed race winners in Europe, and also Anda Muchacho, an Irish-bred dual Group 2 scorer in Italy. That's a surprisingly poor record for a triple Group 1 star from a prolific international blacktype family, one whose branches also yielded 2018's shock Group 1 1000 Guineas heroine Billesdon Brook (by Champs Elysees).

Thunder Snow is the fourth foal and one of five blacktype winners out of Eastern Joy (by Dubai Destination) and he is a half-brother to four fillies of note, headed by Ihtimal (by Shamardal), who won the Group 2 May Hill Stakes at two, added both the Listed UAE 1000 Guineas and a runaway victory in the Group 3 UAE Oaks at three, and was then third in the Group 1 1000 Guineas at Newmarket. Her final start was when finishing fifth behind Taghrooda in the Group 1 Oaks at Epsom.

The lightly raced First Victory (by Teofilo) won the Group 3 Oh So Sharp Stakes, and listed scorer Always Smile (by Cape Cross) finished third in the Group 1 Falmouth Stakes and runner-up in the Group 1 Sun Chariot Stakes in 2016, both races won by Alice Springs. Sadly, Always Smile died this year. White Lightning (by Shamardal) is the youngest of the talented siblings and that Saeed bin Suroor-trained bay won the Listed UAE 1000 Guineas at Meydan in February, finished third in the Group 3 UAE Oaks and then third to Veracious in the Group 3 188Bet Casino Atalanta Stakes over a mile at Sandown in early September.

It is no surprise that Eastern Joy has become such a successful broodmare. Not only is she by a stallion who has proved to be an excellent broodmare sire, but she is a half-sister to the Group 1 Prix de Diane (French Oaks) winner West Wind (by Machiavellian) and out of a high-class sibling to two classic performers.

Her dam is the Group 2 Sun Chariot Stakes winner Red Slippers (by Nureyev), and that mare is both a full-sister to Romanov and half-sister to Balanchine (by Storm Bird). Romanov won the Group 2 Jockey Club Stakes and Group 3 Rose of Lancaster Stakes, he was runner-up in the Group 1 Grand Prix de Saint-Cloud and finished third in both the Group 1 Derby at Epsom and the Group 1 Irish 2000 Guineas at the Curragh.

Balanchine was Europe's champion three-year-old filly in 1994 when, after being short-headed by Las Meninas in the Group 1 1000 Guineas at Newmarket, she won the Group 1 Oaks at Epsom and beat the colts to take the Group 1 Irish Derby at the Curragh, joining Salsabil (1990) and Gallinaria (1900) as the most recent fillies to achieve that latter classic feat. Sadly, she disappointed at stud, but her placed half-sister Subtle Breeze (by Storm Cat) is the dam of the Australian seven- and eight-furlong Group 1 scorer Trust In A Gust (by Keep The Faith), unraced Alleged Devotion (by Alleged) is the dam, grandam and third dam of several talented performers, and stakes-placed First Night (by Sadler's Wells) is the grandam of the Group 1-placed Australian Group 3 winner Havana Cooler (by Hurricane Run).

Thunder Snow is, therefore, a triple Group 1 winner from a family that has a strong recent tradition of producing Group 1 performers and, despite his own sire's record, there is every reason to hope that he will have a successful stallion career whenever his racing days come to an end.

SUMMARY DETAILS

Bred: Darley
Owned: Godolphin
Trained: Saeed bin Suroor
Country: England
Form: 102241-11P23130-2121023-
Career highlights: 7 wins inc Dubai World Cup sponsored by Emirates Airline (Gr1), Prix Jean Prat (Gr1), Criterium International (Gr1), Al Maktoum Challenge R2 sponsored by Gulf News (Gr2), UAE Derby sponsored by The Saeed & Mohammed Al Naboodah Group (Gr2), UAE 2000 Guineas sponsored by District One Mohammed Bin Rashid Al Maktoum City (Gr3), 2nd Jockey Club Gold Cup Stakes (Gr1), Tattersalls Irish 2000 Guineas (Gr1), Al Maktoum Challenge R3 sponsored by Emirates Airline (Gr1), Al Maktoum Challenge R1 presented by Longines Gents Master Collection (Gr2), At The Races Champagne Stakes (Gr2), Qatar Vintage Stakes (Gr2), 3rd Breeders' Cup Classic (Gr1), Prix du Haras de Fresney-le-Buffard Jacques le Marois (Gr1), St James's Palace Stakes (Gr1)

THUNDER SNOW (IRE) - 2014 bay colt

Helmet (AUS)	Exceed And Excel (AUS)	Danehill (USA)
		Patrona (USA)
	Accessories (GB)	Singspiel (IRE)
		Anna Matrushka
Eastern Joy (GB)	Dubai Destination (USA)	Kingmambo (USA)
		Mysterial (USA)
	Red Slippers (USA)	Nureyev (USA)
		Morning Devotion (USA)

TOO DARN HOT (GB)

Everything about the distaff side of Too Darn Hot's pedigree says that he is a guaranteed middle-distance performer, one who could excel at 10 furlongs and who is quite likely to stay the Derby distance. He is a full-brother to this year's Group 1 St Leger runner-up, his dam was a Group 1 star over 12 furlongs, as was his grandam, and the latter's half-brother not only won a classic over that trip but went on to become an influential stallion, one associated with stamina.

There is, however, another dimension to the colt, something that seems different from his celebrity relations, and that is his rapid stride frequency or cadence. The visual is more akin to that of a sprinter than of a middle-distance horse, and in watching and rewatching his races again, I have been reminded of another undefeated Group 1 Dewhurst Stakes champion of many years ago, one who had an even higher Timeform rating – and I have rewatched those replays too.

That horse was Ajdal, and even though he earned a Timeform rating of 130 that year it was not enough to see him top that organisation's rankings for the season. Reference Point earned 132p after running away with the Futurity at Doncaster. The latter looked every inch a potential Derby and St Leger hero, which is what he turned out to be, but he and Ajdal were to meet in the 2000 Guineas first. Sadly, illness prevented Reference Point from taking his place in the line-up at Newmarket, whereas Ajdal suffered the first defeat of his career there, finishing third to Don't Forget Me. He was beaten in the Irish 2000 Guineas too, still looked in with a chance coming into the straight at Epsom, and only really seemed to falter about a quarter of a mile from home, but just five weeks after being unplaced in the Derby, he scraped home in the Group 1 July Cup at Newmarket. He then dropped down to five furlongs and was an easy winner of the Group 1 William Hill Sprint Championship at York (previously and since the Nunthorpe Stakes). He remained on a 130 Timeform rating that year.

That Northern Dancer (by Nearctic) colt was related to talented horses at 10 furlongs and upwards, and to the speedy Formidable (by Forli). There were no cadence calculations in those days, but it would be fascinating to know how Ajdal compares to Too Darn Hot in that respect. Much of what his pedigree told us was that a mile would be no problem, 10 furlongs was likely, and the Derby distance possible. There was that speed angle in there too and, ultimately, that was what was expressed on the track. And the image that has always stuck in my mind about his career was the speed at which he appeared to be striding in the Dewhurst, up to the point where he almost seemed to be not quite lasting home.

I am not trying to make a case for Too Darn Hot becoming the next Ajdal – there is no speed angle evident in the distaff side of his family – but his cadence suggests that he may not stay as far as his pedigree predicts. And that adds to his intrigue.

An April 12th article by Simon Rowlands, published on the At The Races website, discussed the analysis of Total Performance Data (TPD) from a particular week's racing and noted that "it is possible to suggest that a horse with a cadence of 2.43 or higher is likely to be a sprinter, that in order to stay beyond a mile a horse's peak cadence ideally needs to be below 2.40, and that peak cadence ideally needs to be 2.35 or less for a horse to be fully effective at 12f or further." The piece noted that there are still things we do not know, for example "the degree to which cadence changes (or doesn't) as a horse matures", and quoted a figure for then potential classic candidate Saxon Warrior that looks even more interesting now. By my understanding of the article and its included graph, that figure of 2.36 is one that could be associated with a horse who might be effective at seven to 10 furlongs but struggle at the Derby distance, which is how he turned out despite being related to two Epsom classic stars.

The TPD figures for Too Darn Hot's performance at Doncaster, where he won the Group 2 Champagne Stakes in style, recorded him as having demonstrated a 24.7ft stride length and a cadence of 2.4. He preceded that win with a four-length defeat of Arthur Kitt in the Group 3 Solario Stakes at Sandown and rounded off his season with an impressive two-and-three-quarter-length victory in the Group 1 Darley Dewhurst Stakes at Newmarket, chased home by Advertise. There are no TPD figures for those two races.

Although a reading of his pedigree would say he'd be a mile to 10-furlong horse who'd have good prospects of staying farther, especially given the exploits of his full-sister Lah Ti Dar, his cadence would appear to pull back that outer margin. He has already won over a mile, albeit a maiden first time out and while looking a bit green, and his other three races have all been over seven. He has earned a Timeform rating of 127p, putting him 5lbs ahead of Quorto, who is by the same sire – Dubawi (by Dubai Millennium) – and he could be the most fascinating member of the three-year-old class of 2019.

So what is that pedigree?

In addition to being a full-brother to Lah Ti Dar, who stormed home by 10 lengths in the 12-furlong Galtres Stakes at York before chasing home Kew Gardens at Doncaster and then taking third to Magical in the Group 1 Qipco British Champions Fillies & Mares Stakes at Ascot, he is also a full-brother to So Mi Dar. She won over a mile on her only start at two, took the 10-furlong Investec Derby Trial at Epsom on her seasonal reappearance, and followed that with an impressive four-length victory in the Group 3 Tattersalls Musidora Stakes at York. Unfortunately, she missed the Oaks, and although a potential Arc bid was spoken of after her defeat of Nezwaah in a 10-furlong listed contest at Yarmouth in September, she never ran over 12 furlongs.

They are all trained by John Gosden and are homebred by Lord Lloyd-Webber's Watership Down Stud, as was their Timeform 124-rated dam, Dar Re Mi. As a daughter of Singspiel (by In The Wings) and Darara (by Top Ville), she was always odds-on to stay a mile and a half, and it was no surprise to see her prove good enough to take the Group 1 Yorkshire Oaks and Group 1 Dubai Sheema Classic over that trip. She also won the Group 1 Pretty Polly Stakes over 10, and the Group 3 Prix Minerve over 12 and a half, and aside from the maiden in which she was a neck runner-up in her only start at two, she never ran over anything shorter than the mile and a quarter.

Her ill-fated half-brother Rewilding (by Tiger Hill) also won the Group 1 Dubai Sheema Classic, was third in the Derby and won the Group 1 Prince of Wales's Stakes, and her siblings also featured Hong Kong 12-furlong Group 1 scorer Diaghilev (aka River Dancer) and his full-brother Darazari (by Sadler's Wells), who won the Group 1 Ranvet Stakes over 10 furlongs at Rosehill in Sydney. Another half-brother – multiple listed scorer Dariyoun (by Shahrastani) – was third in the Group 1 Prix du Cadran, as was Darasim (by Kahyasi), the Group 2 Goodwood Cup-winning son of their half-sister Dararita (by Halo).

Darara, who was bought by Lloyd-Webber at Goffs in 1994, was an Aga Khan homebred and a Timeform 129-rated star who won the Group 1 Prix Vermeille. Her half-sister Dalara (by Doyoun) won the Group 2 Prix de Royallieu and took third in the Group 1 Prix Royal-Oak before going on to become the dam of Derby-placed Group 1 Coronation Cup winner Daliapour (by Sadler's Wells) and his Group 3 Queen's Vase-winning half-brother Dalampour (by Shernazar), whereas her half-brother Darshaan (by Shirley Heights) won the then 12-furlong Group 1 Prix du Jockey Club (French Derby) before going on to such a high-profile career and legacy at stud.

Given that he's a Group 1-winning juvenile from the immediate family of such an important stallion, it is no surprise that a future place at stud has already been secured for Too Darn Hot. It was announced in November that he will join his sire and the rest of the roster at Dalham Hall Stud in Newmarket whenever his racing career is complete.

There is another notable son of Dubawi in the family, and he will be a freshman sire of 2019. The Haras du Logis resident had 65 registered foals in his first crop, although a top price of only 52,000gns for a yearling in Newmarket. Hunter's

Light was well-beaten on two of the three times that he tried 12 furlongs, but won the Group 1 Premio Roma over 10 furlongs on heavy ground, the Group 1 Al Maktoum Challenge R3 over 10 furlongs on Tapeta at Meydan, and was a six-and-a-half-length winner of the Group 1 Jebel Hatta over nine furlongs on good ground at that same venue, after which he was Timeform-rated 126. His winning dam, Portmanteau (by Barathea), is out of a full-sister to Darshaan.

With even just part of all this talent on the page, one would still rate Too Darn Hot as all but guaranteed to stay 10 furlongs and probably a bit farther. But that stride frequency. Availability and application of such data is still a developing field, there is so much more of it to be collected and analysed, and much to learn. Might this colt be a mile star of 2019? Effective at up to the Juddmonte International Stakes distance? Or, with that cadence of 2.4, could he even be a Group 1 Prix de la Foret or Group 1 Prix Maurice de Gheest horse – from that family? It is going to be fascinating to see how he turns out.

SUMMARY DETAILS

Bred: Watership Down Stud
Owned: Lord Lloyd-Webber
Trained: John Gosden
Country: England
Race record: 1111-
Career highlights: 4 wins inc Darley Dewhurst Stakes (Gr1), Howcroft Industrial Supplies Champagne Stakes (Gr2), 188Bet Solario Stakes (Gr3)

TOO DARN HOT (GB) - 2016 bay colt

Dubawi (IRE)	Dubai Millennium (GB)	Seeking The Gold (USA)
		Colorado Dancer
	Zomaradah (GB)	Deploy
		Jawaher (IRE)
Dar Re Mi (GB)	Singspiel (IRE)	In The Wings
		Glorious Song (CAN)
	Darara	Top Ville
		Delsy (FR)

U S NAVY FLAG (USA)

If asked, in mid-August 2017, to name the colt likely to end up champion two-year-old, many shortlists would have included Expert Eye, Unfortunately, or Sioux Nation. But the one who topped the final rankings would surely not have been on anyone's list. By that time, U S Navy Flag had run seven times, beaten in his first four starts, then a Curragh maiden winner in first-time blinkers before chasing home Cardsharp in the Group 2 Arqana July Stakes at Newmarket and then taking fourth to Sioux Nation in the Group 1 Keeneland Phoenix Stakes.

Then came a transformation. Just a fortnight after his Phoenix Stakes run, the Aidan O'Brien-trained colt put up a surprisingly good performance to win the Group 3 Plusvital Round Tower Stakes by six lengths from Landshark, on ground described as yielding. It is fair to say that it was not a particularly strong race for the grade, but he could hardly have been more impressive. Even so, he was not the stable's first string in the following month's Group 1 Juddmonte Middle Park Stakes. But Sioux Nation disappointed in sixth there, just ahead of another Ballydoyle runner, Declarationofpeace, while U S Navy Flag stayed on well to beat the other Aidan O'Brien-trained runner, Fleet Review, by half a length.

This was still not enough to put the colt at the top of the rankings, but then he beat his stable companions Mendelssohn, Seahenge, and Threeandfourpence – by two and a half lengths, two and a half lengths, and a head – in the Group 1 Darley Dewhurst Stakes at Newmarket, with old rival Cardsharp another length and a half back in fifth. He set a new juvenile course record for the distance, and Timeform raised his rating to 123, the highest figure awarded to any two-year-old that year. The runner-up advertised the form with victory in the Grade 1 Breeders' Cup Juvenile Turf over a mile at Del Mar.

With 11 races already behind him, there were grounds to doubt that there would be much, if any, improvement still to come from U S Navy Flag – which did not rule out his chance of winning a Guineas – but the pattern of his three-year-old form was somewhat like what he did at two, with a few standout efforts punctuated by below-par performances. Indeed, it is somewhat remarkable that this classic-placed, triple Group 1 star goes to stud with a record of having made the frame in fewer than 50% of his races.

Distance preference at three promised to be interesting as his pedigree gave him a chance of staying 10 furlongs, while his best juvenile form suggested that six to eight furlongs would be ideal. He was not asked to try beyond the mile.

His distant last of four in a seven-furlong listed race on heavy ground at Leopardstown in April was forgettable, especially after he followed that with a three-length fifth to Olmedo in the Group 1 Poule d'Essai des Poulains (French 2000 Guineas) on good ground at ParisLongchamp and then ran well in the Group 1 Tattersalls Irish 2000 Guineas on fast ground at the Curragh. He set a strong pace in the latter and although he kept on when headed, he had to give best to Romanised, who won by two and a quarter lengths. Gustav Klimt was another length and a quarter back in third, with Threeandfourpence fourth.

That quartet met again in the Group 1 St James's Palace Stakes at Royal Ascot, but this time only Gustav Klimt ran up to form, finishing a half-length runner-up to Without Parole, while his old rivals filled three of the last four placings. It was almost inevitable that U S Navy Flag would now drop back in trip for the Group 1 Darley July Cup, and he won that in style, beating Brando by a length and three-quarters.

Rather than stay in Europe to contest the season's other major sprints, he travelled to Australia for a crack at the massive prize on offer for The TAB Everest over six furlongs at Randwick. With the winner to earn over £3,785 million, and more than £1.2 million going to the runner-up, and generous prize money back through the field, it was a hard one to pass up for a team that is no stranger to travelling horses for major pots around the world, but this colt's trip 'down under' did not work out.

He was slowly away in The Everest, which was run on heavy ground, and whatever chance he might have of pulling back a top European sprint in those circumstances, he had little chance against the Australian horses and finished only ninth. He was also slowly away when finishing last of 14 in the Group 1 Ladbrokes Manikato Stakes over the same trip on good ground at Moonee Valley a fortnight later and then trailed home behind Santa Ana Lane in the Group 1 VRC Sprint Classic at Flemington, also over six on good ground. A stewards' report noted that he finished lame.

U S Navy Flag has now been retired and looks sure to be very popular in his new role as a stallion at Coolmore Stud, where he is being introduced at a fee of €25,000. Not only is he a son of War Front – the top-class Danzig (by Northern Dancer) sire whose early stallion sons include the Group 1 sires Declaration Of War and The Factor – but he is out of a Group 1-winning daughter of prolific champion sire Galileo (by Sadler's Wells).

That mare is Coolmore's top-class runner Misty For Me, the Group 1 Moyglare Stud Stakes, Group 1 Prix Marcel Boussac and Group 1 Irish 1000 Guineas heroine who trounced Midday by six lengths in the Group 1 Pretty Polly Stakes over 10 furlongs at the Curragh. He is her third foal, is a half-brother to the US mile Grade 3 winner Cover Song (by Fastnet Rock) and a full-brother to his Timeform 121-rated fellow former Ballydoyle resident Roly Poly.

Her Group 1 wins came in the Kingdom of Bahrain Sun Chariot Stakes – in which she beat subsequent Group 1 scorer Persuasive by a length and a quarter – the Falmouth Stakes on the July Course at Newmarket – in which she beat Wuheida by one and a quarter lengths – and in the Prix Rothschild at Deauville, where she beat the sadly ill-fated Via Ravenna by a short-neck. Roly Poly was also a tough and talented juvenile who won the Group 3 Grangecon Stakes and Group 2 Duchess of Cambridge Stakes before being short-headed by Brave Anna in the Group 1 Cheveley Park Stakes.

These credentials gave U S Navy Flag a chance, on pedigree, to a high-class miler or 10-furlong horse, but these star relations are just the tip of the iceberg, so to speak, and there are also some promising signs on his page concerning his stallion potential.

One of the things that we look at when assessing a stallion's prospects is the presence or absence of previously or currently successful stallions in the distaff side of his family. Absence could indicate that it's a racing family only for its colts, yet does not mean he cannot succeed. Similarly, presence shows precedent and can give us an indication of what we might hope for, yet it does not guarantee success. The sires of those horses can be very influential, and of course breeder, support can be crucial.

Misty For Me is a full-sister to the Group 1 Prix Marcel Boussac winner Ballydoyle, who chased home Minding in both the Group 1 1000 Guineas and Group 1 Irish 1000 Guineas of 2016, and she is out of Butterfly Cove (by Storm Cat), who is an unraced half-sister to the unbeaten juvenile Group 1 sprint star Fasliyev (by Nureyev). He compiled a respectable record at stud, getting stakes and pattern winners among a long list of successful runners, and the same can be said of his dam's half-brothers Desert Wine (by Damascus) and Menifee (by Harlan).

Each of those stallions got at least one winner at the highest level, each represents a different sire line, and two of them got a Group 1 scorer in Europe. They were successful without becoming notable. U S Navy Flag, of course, represents another different sire line and is by one who could be on the verge of developing long-term significance, and he looks sure to receive strong support.

He was a champion and Group 1 star at two, and in being classic-placed over a mile before taking a Group 1 over six furlongs, he shares something in common with both major sire-sons of Danzig, albeit something that has no meaning beyond mere coincidence. Green Desert, who was a pattern winner at two, chased home Dancing Brave in the 2000 Guineas at Newmarket before dropping to sprints and retiring a Group 1 star over six furlongs, whereas Danehill was third to

Nashwan in the 2000 Guineas before doing the same. With strong and plentiful support likely, there is every reason to hope that U S Navy Flag can become a sire of note. Some of his offspring may do well at two, but it is as a sire of sprinters, milers, and potentially some 10-furlong horses – even the occasional mile-and-a-half one – that he seems likely to make his name at stud.

SUMMARY DETAILS

Bred: Misty For Me Syndicate
Owned: Coolmore, Tabor & Wynaus
Trained: Aidan O'Brien
Country: Ireland
Race record: 43301241110-40201000-
Career highlights: 5 wins inc Darley July Cup Stakes (Gr1), Darley Dewhurst Stakes (Gr1), Juddmonte Middle Park Stakes (Gr1), Plusvital Round Tower Stakes (Gr3), 2nd Tattersalls Irish 2000 Guineas (Gr1), Arqana July Stakes (Gr2), 3rd Cold Move Irish EBF Marble Hill Stakes (L)

U S NAVY FLAG (IRE) - 2015 bay/brown colt

War Front (USA)	Danzig (USA)	Northern Dancer (CAN)
		Pas De Nom (USA)
	Starry Dreamer (USA)	Rubiano (USA)
		Lara's Star (USA)
Misty For Me (IRE)	Galileo (IRE)	Sadler's Wells (USA)
		Urban Sea (USA)
	Butterfly Cove (USA)	Storm Cat (USA)
		Mr P's Princess (USA)

URBAN FOX (GB)

Group 1-winning Australian sprinter Foxwedge (by Fastnet Rock) was a reverse-shuttle stallion to Whitsbury Manor Stud, in England, for four seasons, and although he has not yet set the world alight here, he has come up with three Group 1 winners from his global first crop. Foxplay has won at the top level over a mile in Australia, Volpe Veloce achieved the feat over six furlongs in New Zealand in January, and Urban Fox put up the performance of her life to take the Group 1 Juddmonte Pretty Polly Stakes at the Curragh in early July. The stallion is based at Newgate Stud in New South Wales, Australia.

Urban Fox was a talented two-year-old who was third in each of the Group 1 Fillies' Mile, Group 2 May Hill Stakes and Group 3 Prestige Stakes, but she was disappointing at three, was sold for 425,000gns at the Tattersalls December Mare Sale in Newmarket and left the James Tate yard to join William Haggas. She won a mile handicap on the straight course at Ascot on her seasonal reappearance in May, finished fourth to Aljazzi in the Group 2 Duke of Cambridge Stakes over the same course and distance in June, and then sprang something of a surprise with her Irish success, beating Oaks heroine Forever Together by three and a quarter lengths on her first attempt at 10 furlongs.

She was raised to 118 by Timeform after this, and although she met with defeat on each of her subsequent starts, two of those placed efforts were in Group 1 company. She chased home two-length winner Wild Illusion in the Group 1 Qatar Nassau Stakes at Goodwood just 17 days before failing by just a neck to beat Nonza in the Group 1 Darley Prix Jean Romanet. Each of her top-level runs has been over 10 furlongs – all her prior form was over shorter trips – and her final outing of the year was in the Group 1 Prix de l'Opera Longines, in which she finished only ninth.

Urban Fox was bred by Mascalls Stud, who sold her for 10,000gns from Book 2 of the Tattersalls October Yearling Sale. A half-sister to the blacktype-placed chaser Hollow Penny (by Beat Hollow), and to several flat winners, she is a daughter of the winning Nashwan (by Blushing Groom) mare Lomapamar and is not the first member of her family to surprise at the Curragh.

The best of her dam's eight winning siblings was Mons (by Deploy), the impressive Group 2 Royal Lodge Stakes winner who went on to be placed in the Group 1 Racing Post Trophy, Group 1 Gran Premio del Jockey Club, Group 2 Great Voltigeur Stakes and Group 2 Yorkshire Cup, but they also include Inforapenny (by Deploy) who finished third, at 100/1, to Petrushka in the Group 1 Irish Oaks back in 2000.

Their dam, Morina (by Lyphard), won once in France as a three-year-old and was a half-sister to 10 winners out of Arewehavingfunyet (by Sham), who got the best of her blacktype wins in the Grade 1 Oak Leaf Stakes, Grade 2 Del Mar Debutante Stakes and Grade 3 Landaluce Stakes, all as a two-year-old. That star is the dam of listed scorer Have Fun (by Topsider) and ancestor of a host of blacktype-placed horses, and this daughter of listed race winner Just Jazz (by Exclusive Native) is a half-sister to a stakes-winning filly called Northern Jazz (by Northern Jove) and from a branch of an Argentine family.

Urban Fox clearly has plenty of ability, and her Group 1 win will look attractive on the catalogue page of any of her future offspring who may go through the ring. It will be interesting to see how she fares as a broodmare.

SUMMARY DETAILS

Bred: Mascalls Stud
Owned: Barnane Stud Ltd
Trained: William Haggas
Country: England
Race record: 11443313-2004044-141220-
Career highlights: 5 wins inc Juddmonte Pretty Polly Stakes (Gr1), 2nd Darley Prix Jean Romanet (Gr1), Qatar Nassau

Stakes (Gr1), Dubai Duty Free Stakes (Gr3), 3rd Dubai Fillies'
Mile (Gr1), Clugston Construction May Hill Stakes (Gr2),
Prestige Stakes (Gr3)

URBAN FOX (GB) - 2014 bay filly

Foxwedge (AUS)	Fastnet Rock (AUS)	Danehill (USA)
		Piccadilly Circus (AUS)
	Forest Native (USA)	Forest Wildcat (USA)
		Miss Timebank (USA)
Lomapamar (GB)	Nashwan (USA)	Blushing Groom (FR)
		Height Of Fashion (FR)
	Morina (USA)	Lyphard (USA)
		Arewehavingfunyet (USA)

WALDGEIST (GB)

Such has been the emphasis on producing speed that, in recent years, it has often been hard to identify serious Derby candidates among the leading juveniles, colts about whom you could say with confidence 'he will definitely stay the mile and a half.' The French juvenile crop of 2016 did include one who looked sure to stay, and he went into those winter quarters with a major win to his name. His connections are no strangers to classic success, and there was every reason to hope that they had another emerging star.

He almost won the Group 1 Prix du Jockey Club (French Derby) over 10 and a half furlongs at Chantilly – beaten a nose by the previous month's Group 1 Poule d'Essai des Poulains (French 2000 Guineas) scorer Brametot – and ran quite well when fourth to Capri, Cracksman and Wings Of Eagles in the Group 1 Dubai Duty Free Irish Derby, but had to wait until 2018 to get his top-level victory over 12 furlongs.

Given the talent and promise that Waldgeist showed as a juvenile when a Timeform 111p-rated winner of the Group 1 Criterium de Saint-Cloud over 10 furlongs – by a length from Best Solution – it was something of a surprise that he failed to win as a three-year-old. His three seconds and two fourths were good enough for an end-of-year rating of 122 in "racing's bible", but left an impression of promise unfulfilled. His four-year-old campaign would be crucial if he was going to earn recognition as a top-class performer and perhaps secure a good berth at stud whenever his track career comes to an end.

The season did not begin well – he was only fifth to Air Pilot in a Group 2 over 10 furlongs on heavy ground at ParisLongchamp in early April – but when the better ground arrived, we saw the real Waldgeist. He justified favouritism with a length-and-a-half success in the Group 3 Prix d'Hedouville over 12 furlongs at that same venue, followed that with a three-length defeat of Dschingis Secret in the Group 2 Grand Prix de Chantilly, and then beat Coronet by a nose in the Group 1 Grand Prix de Saint-Cloud at the start of July.

He made it four-in-a-row when beating Talismanic by two and a half lengths in the Group 2 Qatar Prix Foy at ParisLongchamp in mid-September and then finished an honourable fourth in the Group 1 Qatar Prix de l'Arc de Triomphe, beaten just a short-neck, three-parts of a length, and the same – by Enable, Sea Of Class and Cloth Of Stars – with old rival Capri another length and a half back in fifth. He was only fifth in the Grade 1 Longines Breeders' Cup Turf at Churchill Downs on his final start – which was dominated by star fillies Enable and Magical – but that took away none of the shine of his earlier achievements, nor dented his Timeform 127 rating. His final run of the year was in the Grade 1 Longines Hong Kong Vase over 12 furlongs at Sha Tin in December, but although sent off the favourite, he met with trouble in running in the straight, and by the time he finally had a clear run, it was too late. He stayed on into fifth as the Teofilo gelding Exultant, who was classic-placed in Ireland in 2017 under the name Irishcorrespondent, landed the spoils.

The chestnut was bred by The Waldlerche Partnership, he is the first foal out of the Group 3 Prix Penelope winner Walderche (by Monsun), and he has a notable sibling in Waldlied (by New Approach) and a promising one in Waldstern (by Sea The Stars). Indeed, he could be described as being a three-parts brother to the first-named, a fellow Fabre-trained runner. She finished out of the frame in a mile maiden on heavy on her only start at two, stepped up to 12 furlongs for her first outing of 2018 and won that Saint-Cloud maiden a month before chasing home Pollara in the Group 3 Prix de Royaumont at Chantilly. Both of those races were on soft ground, but it was good-to-soft at Saint-Cloud in early July when she took the Group 2 Prix de Mallaret by two and a half lengths. This was the same day that Waldgeist got his Group 1 win at the venue – a notable double for the mare's first two offspring!

Waldlied was entered in the Group 1 Qipco British Champions Fillies & Mares Stakes at Ascot but was not seen out again after her pattern success. Her juvenile half-brother, on the other hand, ran three times in the second half of the season. The John Gosden-trained colt won a mile maiden on the July Course at Newmarket on his debut in mid-August, was odds-on when runner-up to Kadar in a novice race at Haydock three weeks later, and then finished fourth to Norway in the Listed Godolphin Flying Start Zetland Stakes over 10 furlongs. Waldstern holds an entry in the Group 1 Investec Derby, and although he has a lot of improvement to make to be up to that standard, he is a promising middle-distance and/or staying prospect for 2019.

Waldlerche is a half-sister to the middle-distance listed race winner Waldnah (by New Approach) and, more notably, also to 2011's Group 1 St Leger hero Masked Marvel (by Montjeu). Europe's champion three-year-old stayer of that season, he also won the Group 3 Bahrain Trophy and Listed Cocked Hat Stakes, he stands at Haras d'Etreham, in France, has had just one runner so far, and his first crop will be three-year-olds in 2019.

Their dam, Waldmark (by Mark Of Esteem), was runner-up in the Group 2 Falmouth Stakes at Newmarket and in a 10-furlong listed contest at Newbury, and she is a half-sister to the Group 1 Deutsches Derby star Waldpark (by Dubawi), who stands at Haras du Thenney and also has three-year-olds of next season. His handful of juvenile runners include the Henri-Alex Pantell-trained filly Arum who won on the first of her four starts. Waldmark's siblings also include the pattern-placed middle-distance pair Waldvogel (by Polish Precedent) and Waldjagd (by Observatory), and her dam is the twice joint-champion German runner Wurfaube (by Acatenango). Her string of blacktype successes featured the Group 2 Gerling Preis over 12 furlongs and the 14-furlong Group 2 Deutsches St Leger, in which she beat Night Petticoat by 11 lengths.

In addition to being a half-sister to the dual Group 3 scorer Wurfscheibe (by Tiger Hill), Wurftaube is also a half-sister to Wurfspiel (by Lomitas), who is the stakes-placed dam of Wake Forest (by Sir Percy) and grandam of Wonderment (by Camelot). The latter won the Group 1 Criterium de Saint-

Cloud over 10 furlongs in late October, beating Sydney Opera House by a neck, and her only defeat in three starts, so far, is her third-place finish to subsequent Grade 1 star Line of Duty in the Group 3 Prix de Conde.

Wake Forest, on the other hand, was a multiple Group 3 scorer in Germany before crossing the Atlantic, he won the Grade 1 Man O'War Stakes over 11 furlongs at Belmont Park in 2016, was only beaten a neck when runner-up to The Pizza Man in the Grade 1 Northern Dancer Stakes over 12 furlongs at Woodbine that September, and added the Grade 2 Mac Diarmida Stakes over 11 on firm turf at Gulfstream Park in early 2017. He was back in the news again in November, but due to unfortunate circumstances that, thankfully, have ended well. He had been sold as a horse in training earlier in the year but failed to do well on the track and was put in a claimer for just $8,000. Michael Dubb, one of his former owners, bought him back, and unable to find interest in him as a prospective stallion, reported that the entire would retire to Old Friends Farm in Georgetown, Kentucky. Wake Forest, who arrived at his new home in early December, won a total of eight of his 28 starts and earned over $950,000.

Waldgeist, who is trained by Andre Fabre, is a classic-placed dual Group 1 star by prolific champion sire Galileo (by Sadler's Wells), and that will make him an eye-catching new addition to the stallion ranks, whenever that time comes. His racing and pedigree profiles suggest that he will be able to get milers, middle-distance horses and stayers and that any two-year-olds of his who do well will do so in the latter part of the season. And being a top-class 12-furlong horse bred on a Galileo-Monsun (by Konigsstuhl) cross, he is also likely to attract National Hunt breeders too.

SUMMARY DETAILS

Bred: The Waldlerche Partnership
Owned: Gestut Ammerland & Newsells Park
Trained: Andre Fabre (France)
Country: France
Race record: 131-22424-01111400-

Career highlights: 6 wins inc Grand Prix de Saint-Cloud (Gr1), Criterium de Saint-Cloud (Gr1), Qatar Prix Foy (Gr2), Grand Prix de Chantilly (Gr2), Prix d'Hedouville (Gr3), 2nd Qatar Prix du Jockey Club (Gr1), Prix Greffulhe (Gr2), Gigaset Cumberland Lodge Stakes (Gr3), 3rd Prix de Conde (Gr3)

WALDGEIST (GB) - 2014 chestnut colt

Galileo (IRE)	Sadler's Wells (USA)	Northern Dancer (CAN)
		Fairy Bridge (USA)
	Urban Sea (USA)	Miswaki (USA)
		Allegretta
Waldlerche (GB)	Monsun (GER)	Konigsstuhl (GER)
		Mosella (GER)
	Waldmark (GER)	Mark Of Esteem (IRE)
		Wurftaube (GER)

WELL TIMED (GER)

It was a notable year for Castlehyde Stud stallion Holy Roman Emperor (by Danehill) as the Coolmore horse added two new Group 1 classic stars to his tally. In past years, Homecoming Queen ran away with the 1000 Guineas at Newmarket, Mongolian Khan took both the New Zealand Derby and BMW Australian Derby, and Rollout The Carpet landed the New Zealand 1000 Guineas, and to that list you can now add 2018's Irish 2000 Guineas scorer Romanised and Preis der Diana (German Oaks) heroine Well Timed. They are among 13 top-level winners for their sire – two more and his name earns a spot on the protected list – and the tally also includes Glorious Empire, who won the Grade 1 Sword Dancer Stakes at Saratoga in August.

His success is no surprise, and for a horse with his race record, pedigree and early support it was always a question of how many Group 1 winners he would sire rather than if he would get any at all. Indeed, "a stallion with the potential to sire classic winners" was my assessment of him in the *Irish Racing Yearbook 2010*, which was published several months before the juvenile star had his first runners.

Stall Ullmann's homebred Well Timed is trained by Jean-Pierre Carvalho and began her career with a fourth-place finish over just short of nine furlongs at Dortmund in early October of her juvenile year. She got off the mark over 10 and a half furlongs at Dusseldorf in late April, followed that with listed success over the same course and distance, and then landed the Group 2 Soldier Hollow - Diana Trial over 10 furlongs on good ground at Hoppegarten in June, taking it up a furlong from home and keeping on well to beat Taraja by a length and a quarter. Two months later she was sent off favourite for the Group 1 Henkel-Preis der Diana - German Oaks over 11 furlongs at Dusseldorf, and having hit the front with a furlong and a half to go, stayed on strongly for an authoritative one-and-three-quarter-length victory from Night Of England.

She was clearly the best three-year-old filly in Germany, and although her three subsequent runs resulted in unplaced finished abroad, the second of those was quite a good effort. She had finished down the field behind Kitesurf in the Group 1 Qatar Prix Vermeille – her only attempt so far at a mile and a half – and was a disappointing favourite behind God Given in the Group 1 Premio Lydia Tesio Sisal Matchpoint over 10 furlongs at Capannelle in early November – that could have been due to the heavy ground – but she was only beaten a total of three and a half lengths when fifth to Wild Illusion in the Group 1 Prix de l'Opera Longines at ParisLongchamp on Arc Day, on good ground. This was a third Group 1 success for the winner, Group 2 Ribblesdale Stakes winner Magic Wand was the runner-up, classic-placed Homerique was third, Group 1 scorer With You fourth, and My Sister Nat, Athena, Urban Fox, and Lady Frankel were among those behind.

Well Timed is the best of several winners for the pattern-placed German stakes winner Wells Present (by Cadeaux Genereux), who stayed 11 furlongs, and her dam, in turn, has three blacktype siblings. They include Grade 3-winning chaser Whispered Secret (by Selkirk) who was also a Group 3-placed listed scorer on the flat. The mare's siblings also include a minor winner and an unraced filly who have gone on to become blacktype producers at stud, and it is the latter who is more notable. Wonder Why (by Tiger Hill) has had five winners to date and they include the talented full-brothers Akeed Mofeed (by Dubawi) and Jordan Sport. The latter won a Group 3 contest at Meydan, whereas his brother won the Group 1 Hong Kong Cup, the Listed Hong Kong Derby, and Listed Centenary Vase - all at Sha Tin – and was also a Group 2-placed stakes winner in Ireland.

Wells Whisper (by Sadler's Wells), the grandam of Well Timed, was out of the Group 1-placed Group 3 Prix du Calvados winner Whakilyric (by Miswaki), she was placed a few times on the track but had six notable siblings, five of them stakes winners and two of them Group 1 stars. Half-sister Apsara (by Darshaan) was only placed but became the dam of Group 2 Beresford Stakes winner Curtain Call (by

Sadler's Wells), whereas half-brothers Adnaan (by Nashwan) and Res Judicata (by Rainbow Quest) were group-placed stakes winners, and full-brother Walter Willy won a couple of listed races in France. Her full-brother Johann Quatz, on the other hand, won the Group 1 Prix Lupin and a Grade 2 race in California and went on to sire the Group 2 scorers Cut Quartz and Geordieland, among others of note. But he was behind his half-brother Hernando (by Niniski) on the track and at stud. The Timeform 127-rated star won the Group 1 Prix du Jockey Club (French Derby) and Group 1 Prix Lupin, was runner-up in the Group 1 Prix de l'Arc de Triomphe and Group 1 Irish Derby, third in the Group 1 Japan Cup, and stood at Lanwades Stud in Newmarket from where he sired Group/Grade 1 standouts such as Casual Conquest, Gitano Hernando, Holding Court, Look Here, and Sulamani, as well as some notable winners under National Hunt rules.

Well Timed is a very valuable broodmare prospect, one with the potential to produce classic horses and, should she have a top-class son, a potentially successful stallion too.

SUMMARY DETAILS

Bred: Stall Ullmann
Owned: Stall Ullmann
Trained: Jean-Pierre Carvalho
Country: Germany
Race record: 4-1111000-
Career highlights: 4 wins inc Henkel-Preis der Diana - German Oaks (Gr1), Soldier Hollow - Diana Trial (Gr2), Preis der BMW Niederlassungen (L)

WELL TIMED (GER) - 2015 bay filly

Holy Roman Emperor (IRE)	Danehill (USA)	Danzig (USA)
		Razyana (USA)
	L'On Vite (USA)	Secretariat (USA)
		Fanfreluche (CAN)
Wells Present (GER)	Cadeaux Genereux	Young Generation
		Smarten Up
	Wells Whisper (FR)	Sadler's Wells (USA)
		Whakilyric (USA)

WELTSTAR (GER)

As at least one Timeform essay from decades ago noted, a major function of the classics is to identify leading candidates for breeding future generations. It's the reason why geldings are excluded from those races in Europe. There are, of course, many classic stars who don't excel at stud, but there have been plenty of times when their sons and daughters have achieved such fame. Australia's victory in the Derby at Epsom is a shining example as he is the son of Derby star Galileo and Oaks heroine Ouija Board.

A filly named Well Proved (by Prince Ippi) won the Group 3 Schwarzgold-Rennen (German 1000 Guineas) in 1983, one of only two blacktype wins for the joint-champion three-year-old filly in a country that, at that time, had a lower racing and breeding profile than it does now. Her victory likely got little attention outside of her native land, but she has been back in the news, to a much wider audience, the past few years.

She became a notably successful broodmare, and although none of her offspring won a classic, Well Minded (by Monsun) finished third in the Group 1 Oaks d'Italia and juvenile champion Well Known (by Konigsstuhl) was runner-up in both the classic her dam won and the Group 2 Preis der Diana (German Oaks). They also included Group 3 Prix de Psyche winner Welluna (by Lagunas) whose granddaughter Well Spoken (by Soldier Hollow) – the juvenile filly champion of 2016 and Group 3 Preis der Winterkonigin winner – was runner-up in the Group 2 Diana Trial before disappointing in the Group 1 Preis der Diana itself.

But back to Well Known as that talented daughter of Well Proved is now the ancestor of three Group 1 stars, two of them classic heroes.

Five of her offspring have earned blacktype and the standout performer among them is Well Made (by Mondrian), a multiple pattern winner whose best success came when beating champion and classic heroine Salve Regina by three-parts of a length in the Group 1 Preis von Europa over 12 furlongs at Cologne. He had only limited success at stud, but his half-sister Wellenspiel (by Sternkonig), who won twice and had no blacktype, has elevated the family's profile as both of her first two foals have won the Group 1 Deutsches Derby.

In 2017, Windstoss (by Shirocco) beat the Nathanial colt Enjoy Vijay to take the classic by a length on soft ground. He added a four-length score in the Group 1 Preis von Europa at Cologne two and a half months later, and although without a win to his name in 2018, he finished third to Cracksman in the Group 1 Investec Coronation Cup at Epsom in June, a performance that came just over a month before his half-brother Weltstar (by Soldier Hollow) beat Destino and Royal Youmzain by a neck and one and a half lengths to take the 149th running of the Group 1 Deutsches Derby.

Weltstar was not seen out again after his classic victory. His previous start resulted in Group 2 success over 11 furlongs at Cologne – also at the immediate expense of the Soldier Hollow colt Destino – and he was fourth to Ancient Spirit in the Group 2 Mehl-Mulhens-Rennen (German 2000 Guineas) the time before that, all on good ground.

He is the latest Group 1 scorer and third Group 1 classic star for leading German stallion Soldier Hollow (by In The Wings), a four-time Group 1-winning grandson of Sadler's Wells (by Northern Dancer). Pastorius won the Deutsches Derby in 2012 and the Group 1 Prix Ganay in 2013, he stood at Haras de la Hetraie this year following four years at Gestut Fahrhof, and has sired winners in his first two crops. Two years ago it was the turn of the Soldier Hollow filly Serienholde and she won the Group 1 Preis der Diana.

The stallion's other two top-level winners are the classic-placed Group 1 Grosser Preis von Berlin scorer Dschingis Secret, who begins his stallion career at Haras de Saint-Arnoult in Normandy in 2019, and top international performer Ivanhowe who, like Weltstar, is out of a daughter of Sternkonig (by Kalaglow). He was a lightly-raced Group 2 winner as a three-year-old, crowned champion older horse in Germany at four when he took both the Group 1 Grosser

Preis von Baden and Group 1 Grosser Preis von Bayern, and then went 'down under' where, as Our Ivanhowe, he added wins in the Group 1 Doomben Cup and Group 1 Ranvet Stakes – both over 10 furlongs – and finished third in a Group 1 Caulfield Cup. He stands at Haras du Thenney, in France, and his first foals will arrive in the coming months.

With a classic victory to his name and a strong classic pedigree, Weltstar looks likely to prove popular whenever the time comes for him to go to stud.

SUMMARY DETAILS

Bred: Gestut Rottgen
Owned: Gestut Rottgen
Trained: Markus Klug
Country: Germany
Race record: 14-2411-
Career highlights: 3 wins inc IDEE 149th Deutsches Derby (Gr1), Oppenheim Union Rennen (Gr2), 2nd Dr Busch Memorial (Gr3)

WELTSTAR (GER) - 2015 bay/brown colt

Soldier Hollow (GB)	In The Wings	Sadler's Wells (USA)
		High Hawk
	Island Race (GB)	Common Grounds
		Lake Isle (IRE)
Wellenspiel (GER)	Sternkonig (IRE)	Kalaglow
		Sternwappen (GER)
	Well Known (GER)	Konigsstuhl (GER)
		Well Proved (GER)

WILD ILLUSION (GB)

Godolphin's homebred Wild Illusion gave her sire a second consecutive winner of the Group 1 Total Prix Marcel Boussac - Criterium des Pouliches when beating Polydream and Mission Impassible by one and a half lengths and a head over a mile at Chantilly last year, a performance that identified her as a potential star in her division for 2018. She did not disappoint.

Twelve months before, the same connections struck in that race with the subsequently classic-placed chestnut Wuheida and, along with South African colt Willow Magic, this trio were the only juvenile top-level winners sired by Dalham Hall Stud's outstanding stallion Dubawi (by Dubai Millennium) until the arrival of the exciting and as yet undefeated pair Quorto and Too Darn Hot in the autumn of 2018. Their sire was slow to get his juvenile Group 1 stars, but is more than making up for lost time now.

Wild Illusion, who was a Group 3-placed winner in her only other starts at two, finished that initial campaign on a Timeform rating of 113p but raised that mark to 120 when failing by just a neck to beat Sistercharlie in the Grade 1 Maker's Mark Breeders' Cup Filly & Mare Turf over 11 furlongs at Churchill Downs in early November. She had been favourite for that event following a pair of Group 1 wins in Europe, both over a mile and a quarter, and had looked set to complete her hat-trick when hitting the front 100 yards from home. It was only close to the line that the year-older US runner caught her. A Raving Beauty was three-parts of a length back in third, the Aidan O'Brien-trained Athena was fifth, and the one that separated that pair was Magic Wand, the only non top-level winner in the first five.

Wild Illusion and Magic Wand have met several times and the score is three to one in favour of the Charlie Appleby-trained filly. First came the Group 1 Investec Oaks when the pair had to settle for second and fourth respectively behind impressive winner Forever Together. That six-and-a-half-length margin of superiority flipped to a four-length deficit at Ascot shortly afterwards when Godolphin's bay could only chase home Coolmore's one in the Group 2 Ribblesdale Stakes, but she showed that form to be but a blip on her record when getting her revenge in the Group 1 Prix de l'Opera Longines at ParisLongchamp in October, staying on well to beat her old rival by a length, with classic-placed pattern winner Homerique a nose away in third, and the Group 1 winners With You and Well Timed filling the next two places.

Between Ascot and Paris, she went to Goodwood where she beat the Group 1 Pretty Polly Stakes winner Urban Fox by two lengths to take the Group 1 Qatar Nassau Stakes. Her only other outing of the year was in early May when she stayed on into fourth place in the Group 1 Qipco 1000 Guineas, won by Billesdon Brook.

It was great news to hear that she will be staying in training as a four-year-old – the middle-distance fillies' division looks like being especially strong in 2019 – and there is no doubt that she also has tremendous future potential as a broodmare, and not just because she's a triple Group 1-winning daughter of one of the world's leading sires.

Wild Illusion is her dam's second foal, and both her older and younger siblings are blacktype fillies too. Really Special (by Shamardal) won the Listed Montrose Fillies' Stakes over a mile at Newmarket on the second of two starts at two, added a valuable conditions race over seven at Meydan three months later, and finished third in a seven-furlong listed contest at that venue a few weeks later. She is trained by Saeed bin Suroor but, like Wild Illusion, their juvenile half-sister is with Charlie Appleby. Ceratonia (by Oasis Dream) disappointed on her final two starts, both in October, but was a debut winner over seven furlongs at Ascot in late July and only beaten three-parts of a length when runner-up to Rocques in the Group 3 Prix d'Aumale over a mile at ParisLongchamp.

They are the first three foals out of the Listed Ballymacoll Stud Stakes winner Rumh (by Monsun), whose Andreas

Wohler-trained half-sister (could be called a three-parts sister) Realeza (by Maxios) won a 10-furlong listed contest at Mulheim in July. Their dam, Royal Dubai (by Dashing Blade), won the Group 3 Preis der Winterkonigin, was the joint-champion German juvenile filly of 2002 and is a half-sister to Grade 1 Beverly D Stakes heroine Royal Highness (by Monsun), who could be described as being a three-parts sister to Rumh.

That German-bred star began her career in Europe, where she won the Group 2 Prix de Mallaret and was placed in both the Group 1 Prix Ganay and two editions of the Group 1 Prix Vermeille, and her successful offspring include Free Port Lux (by Oasis Dream), the Group 2 Prix Dollar and Group 2 Prix Hocquart scorer who stands at Haras de Cercy and had his first foals in 2018.

Reem Dubai (by Nashwan), the third dam of Wild Illusion, was only placed but is a half-sister to Elbaaha (by Arazi), the mare who gave us the pattern-placed stakes winner Grigorieva (by Woodman) and the top-class but tragically ill-fated Electrocutionist (by Red Ransom). He won the Group 1 Dubai World Cup, Group 1 Juddmonte International Stakes and Group 1 Gran Premio di Milano, he was runner-up in each of the Group 1 King George VI and Queen Elizabeth Stakes, Group 1 Prince of Wales's Stakes and Group 1 Gran Premio del Jockey Club, and he took third place in the Grade 1 Canadian International Stakes, but died due to a heart attack in early September of his five-year-old season.

Electrocutionist was rated 125 by Timeform at the age of three and 127 at both four and five, but he is not the most highly rated member of the family. Reem Dubai was out of Group 3 Prix de Flore scorer Gesedeh (by Ela-Mana-Mou), and that chestnut was, in turn, out of Le Melody (by Arctic Slave), which made her a half-sister to the Arc-placed dual Group 1 Gold Cup star Ardross (by Run The Gantlet), one of the greatest stayers of all time. Timeform rated him 134.

There are many other notable horses in this famous family, including all of those descended from Le Melody's Group 1 Irish 1000 Guineas-winning half-sister Arctique Royale (by

Royal And Regal), but their connection to Wild Illusion is remote. Even so, there is more than enough close up on her page to suggest that her glittering racing career may be just the first chapter in the book of her life.

SUMMARY DETAILS

Bred: Godolphin
Owned: Godolphin
Trained: Charlie Appleby
Country: England
Race record: 131-422112-
Career highlights: 4 wins inc Prix de l'Opera Longines (Gr1), Qatar Nassau Stakes (Gr1), Total Prix Marcel Boussac - Criterium des Pouliches (Gr1), 2nd Investec Oaks (Gr1), Maker's Mark Breeders' Cup Filly & Mare Turf (Gr1), Ribblesdale Stakes (Gr2), 3rd Prix d'Aumale (Gr3)

WILD ILLUSION (GB) - 2015 bay filly

Dubawi (IRE)	Dubai Millennium (GB)	Seeking The Gold (USA)
		Colorado Dancer
	Zomaradah (GB)	Deploy
		Jawaher (IRE)
Rumh (GER)	Monsun (GER)	Konigsstuhl (GER)
		Mosella (GER)
	Royal Dubai (GER)	Dashing Blade
		Reem Dubai (IRE)

WITH YOU (GB)

George Strawbridge's homebred filly In Clover was a talented racehorse and the Freddy Head-trained bay notched up four wins and seven places from 18 starts in France. She won the Group 3 Prix de Flore over 10 and a half furlongs on very soft ground at Saint-Cloud and was runner-up in the Group 3 Prix Fille de l'Air over the same trip at Toulouse, and she was also a winner and placed in blacktype company over a mile. Her wins came on good, soft, very soft, and heavy ground, and her blacktype record would have looked even more eye-catching if fourth place still counted then. She filled that position behind Mandesha in the Group 1 Prix d'Astarte and to Satwa Queen in the Group 2 Prix Jean Romanet.

The Timeform 114-rated bay was a promising prospect when she went to stud, a potential dam of stakes and pattern horses, because not only did she have this good racing career to her name but she's a daughter of the speedy and well-bred Ahonoora (by Lorenzaccio) stallion Inchinor – who died young – and she was out of Group 3 Prix de Royaumont scorer Bellarida (by Bellypha). But whatever hopes there were for her back then, surely not even the most optimistic of dreamers could have foreseen just how she would excel in that new role. Her tally of stakes-winning offspring stands at five, and thanks to the exploits of two of them in 2018, three of the quintet have won at the highest level.

Mares who produce at least three Group/Grade 1 winners plus at least one other pattern winner are often referred to as 'blue hen' mares. Her juvenile daughter Featuring (by Dansili) finished third in a one-mile Chantilly maiden in September on her only start, that one's full-brother will be a two-year-old of 2019, she had a chestnut son of Dubawi (by Dubai Millennium) in 2018, and was then bred to Invincible Spirit (by Green Desert), so it is entirely possible that she will achieve that status. It's not inconceivable that she could even add to her Group 1 tally.

The first of her progeny to hit that target was We Are (by Dansili), the Group 1 Prix de l'Opera heroine of 2014 who had been first past the post in the earlier Group 1 Prix Saint-Alary only to lose it subsequently due to an issue with her hormones – an ovarian tumour produced elevated testosterone levels – which was rectified. That Freddy Head-trained bay was also placed in a couple of Group 1s, and she chased home the mighty Treve – at a respectable four-length distance – in the Group 2 Prix de Corrida at Saint-Cloud. She was Timeform-rated 117 at three and four, and her first foal is a Galileo (by Sadler's Wells) filly born in April 2017.

In Clover is also responsible for the stakes-winning full-sisters Dream Clover (by Oasis Dream) and Incahoots, and, in late July, With You (by Dansili) was a three-length winner of the Group 1 Prix Rothschild over a mile at Deauville. She had been a half-length fifth to Laurens in the Group 1 Prix de Diane (French Oaks) at Chantilly the previous month, and short-headed by that same rival in the Group 1 Prix Saint-Alary at ParisLongchamp the time before. She was beaten by a total of six lengths when third to Alpha Centauri and Recoletos in the Group 1 Prix du Haras de Fresney-le-Buffard Jacques le Marois at Deauville in mid-August – the margins were two and a half lengths and three and a half lengths – and was fourth to Wild Illusion in the Group 1 Prix de l'Opera Longines at ParisLongchamp on her final start of the year.

That performance came the day after her lightly-raced, year-older half-brother Call The Wind (by Frankel) won the Group 1 Qatar Prix du Cadran over two and a half miles at the same venue.

Her only other runs have been two easy scores as a two-year-old. She was a wide-margin winner of a mile newcomers' race on heavy ground and then made most of the running to take the Group 3 Prix des Reservoirs - Etalon Kendargent by two and a half lengths on very soft ground at Deauville a month later.

With You is clearly a very valuable prospect as a broodmare, and not just because of the exploits of her dam. She is a daughter of the now-retired leading international stallion Dansili (by Danehill) – for years a flag bearer at Banstead Manor Stud – and his influence is being carried on through some of his sons and daughters. In 2018, for example, he was the broodmare sire of Grade 1-winning miler Expert Eye (by Acclamation), who has now joined the roster at that famous Newmarket farm.

Also important is that she is out of a half-sister to five mares who have produced stakes-winning offspring. Noyelles (by Docksider) is the dam of Group 1-placed pattern scorer Lily's Angel (by Dark Angel) and of Group 2-placed stakes winner Zurigha (by Cape Cross), whereas Belesta (by Xaar) has given us the Australian Group 2 winner Adjusted (by Montjeu) and Scandinavian champion and multiple pattern race star Giuseppe Piazzi (by Galileo). Bayourida (by Slew O' Gold) is the stakes-winning dam of middle-distance Group 2-placed stakes winner Telluride (by Montjeu), and Forty Belles (by Forty Niner) is the grandam of 2018's Group 1 Poule d'Essai des Pouliches heroine Teppal (by Camacho).

The fifth of the sisters is Bellona (by Bering), who won the Listed Prix Rose de Mai and took third in the Group 3 Prix Penelope. She is the dam of listed scorer Glorious Sinndar (by Sinndar) and grandam of 2018 Italian mile listed race winner Domagnano (by Planteur), but more notable is the record of her daughter Es Que (by Inchinor). That one-time scorer is closely related to In Clover, her first foal is Group 1 Hong Kong Vase winner Dominant (by Cacique), her second is Group 2 Lennox Stakes scorer and successful 2018 freshman sire Es Que Love (by Clodovil), her stakes-winning son Zhui Feng (by Invincible Spirit) beat Blair House by half a length to take 2017's Royal Hunt Cup, and in 2018 their half-sister Listen in (by Sea The Stars) landed the Group 2 Prix du Conseil de Paris.

With the combination of pedigree, race record, and connections that With You possesses, it will be quite a surprise if she fails to become the dam of stakes and pattern horses some day. Indeed, she is one with serious prospects of producing a Group 1 or classic performer, or two.

SUMMARY DETAILS

Bred: George Strawbridge
Owned: George Strawbridge
Trained: Freddy Head
Country: France
Race record: 11-20134-
Career highlights: 3 wins inc Prix Rothschild (Gr1), Prix des Reservoirs - Etalon Kendargent (Gr3), 2nd The Gurkha Coolmore Prix Saint-Alary (Gr1), 3rd Prix du Haras de Fresnay-le-Buffard Jacques le Marois (Gr1)

WITH YOU (GB) - 2015 bay filly

Dansili (GB)	Danehill (USA)	Danzig (USA)
		Razyana (USA)
	Hasili (IRE)	Kahyasi
		Kerali
In Clover (GB)	Inchinor (GB)	Ahonoora
		Inchmurrin (IRE)
	Bellarida (FR)	Bellypha
		Lerida (FR)

WITHOUT PAROLE (GB)

In 2012, John Gunther was at Royal Ascot on the day that Frankel (by Galileo) produced that incredible 147 Timeform rating with an 11-length victory in the Group 1 Queen Anne Stakes. Two years later he sent his unraced but well-related mare Without You Babe (by Lemon Drop Kid) to visit the champion at Banstead Manor Stud, and in June 2018 the result of that mating gave his owner-breeder one of what he called his favourite moments in racing.

Without Parole extended his unbeaten record to four with a half-length defeat of Group 1 Irish 2000 Guineas third Gustav Klimt in the Group 1 St James's Palace Stakes, the pair finishing three and a quarter lengths clear of the third, French pattern scorer and Group 1 Poule d'Essai des Poulains (French 2000 Guineas) fourth Wootton. In post-race interviews, trainer John Gosden pointed out that the colt was still green and learning. It was his fourth start, but his first two races had been very easy. A six-length debut winner on the Tapeta at Newcastle in mid-December of his juvenile year, the March-born bay thrashed Ostilio by the same margin at Yarmouth in April, and with a setback making him miss a crack at the Group 1 2000 Guineas at Newmarket, he took a mile listed contest at Sandown in late May instead, beating Gabr by three-parts of a length. Improvement would surely follow.

He had been Timeform-rated 117p before Ascot, moved to 125p after that win, and looked set for a good season at the top level. Unfortunately, he disappointed in each of his three subsequent starts. He was sent off favourite to take the Group 1 Qatar Sussex Stakes at Goodwood but beat only one home, he was only sixth to Roaring Lion in the Group 1 Juddmonte International Stakes at York, and then filled that same position in the Group 1 Prix du Moulin de Longchamp in early September, finishing two and three-quarter lengths behind the winner, Recoletos. Timeform dropped his rating to 122. It is to be hoped that he can come back at four, stronger and wiser, and fulfil his potential then.

Without Parole is one of five Group 1 winners to have emerged from among 33 stakes winners from the first two crops by Frankel, which is a highly promising start. The stallion's third crop, who will be the classic generation of 2019, features the Kevin Ryan-trained East, who topped the Goresbridge Breeze-Up Sale at €315,000 in May, made a winning debut over six furlongs at Hamilton in late September and followed that with a Group 3 success over seven at Saint-Cloud before chasing home the brilliant Newspaperofrecord in the Grade 1 Breeders' Cup Juvenile Fillies Turf over a mile at Churchill Downs in November.

For his owner-breeder, the Ascot Group 1 success completed a remarkable international double as Gunther is, of course, also the breeder of the undefeated US Triple Crown hero Justify (by Scat Daddy).

When Without You Babe met Frankel it was just a few months after her first foal had taken his record to three wins from five starts for the Saeed bin Suroor Stable. His 2014 campaign was short and disappointing, but a month before his star sibling arrived he notched up a first blacktype success with a four-length score in the Group 3 Firebreak Stakes over a mile on the dirt at Meydan. He followed-up in the Group 3 Burj Nahaar a few weeks later and made it a hat-trick when short-heading Sloane Avenue in the Group 2 Godolphin Mile, eight days after Without Parole was born. Those wins were for trainer Musabbeh Al Mheiri, but then he crossed the Atlantic to join the Kiaran McLaughlin stable, running seven times and rounding off his career with a three and a half-length defeat of Gun Runner in the Grade 1 Breeders' Cup Dirt Mile at Santa Anita. That top performer is Tamarkuz (by Speightstown) and he stands at Shadwell Farm in Kentucky. His first foals arrived this year.

Without You Babe has also produced the multiple US winners Tempietto (by Bernardini) and Always On My Mind (by Congrats), and her two-year-old is a first-crop Kingman (by Invincible Spirit) filly named She's Got You. She had an Oasis Dream (by Green Desert) filly in 2017 and a son of Dubawi (by Dubai Millennium) in 2018.

The mare is out of one-time scorer Marozia (by Storm Bird) and that makes her a half-sister to three Grade 1 performers, most notably Grade 1 Travers Stakes and Grade 1 Cigar Mile Handicap star Stay Thirsty (by Bernardini). That classic-placed horse has stood six seasons at Ashford Stud in Kentucky and his offspring include 2018's Grade 1 Hopeful Stakes winner Mind Control, plus the Grade 2-winning sprinter Coal Front and Peruvian classic star Golden Leaf. The other pair are Grade 1-placed stakes winner Superfly (by Fusaichi Pegasus) and his classic-placed, nine-furlong Grade 3-winning full-brother Andromeda's Hero, who has sired stakes winners.

Make Change (by Roberto), the third dam of Without Parole, had a listed race success among five wins from two to four years of age but far more notable is the string of top races in which she was placed: Alabama Stakes, Monmouth Oaks, Coaching Club American Oaks, Acorn Stakes, Ladies Handicap, Ruffian Handicap, and Shuvee Handicap – all Grade 1s. Time Changes (by Danzig), who won a listed contest in France, was the best of her offspring and produced the Group 1 Gran Premio di Milano runner-up Age Of Reason (by Halling).

The next dam is the Grade 1 Coaching Club American Oaks runner-up Equal Change (by Arts And Letters) and her descendants – all remotely connected to Without Parole – include Grade 1 scorers Crisp (by Elusive Quality) and Whywhywhy (by Mr Greeley), Group 1-placed Group 2 Lennox Stakes winner Nayyir (by Indian Ridge), and classic-placed pattern winners Sky Hunter (by Motivator) and Highest (by Selkirk).

It is to be hoped that Without Parole can return to form as a four-year-old and fulfil the considerable potential he showed at Ascot. Further enhancements to his record would dull the memory of those disappointing runs and boost his prospects of getting a good berth at stud when his racing days end.

SUMMARY DETAILS

Bred: John Gunther
Owned: John Gunther & Tanya Gunther
Trained: John Gosden
Country: England
Race record: 1-111000-
Career highlights: 4 wins inc St James's Palace Stakes (Gr1), Matchbook Is Commission Free Heron Stakes (L)

WITHOUT PAROLE (GB) - 2015 bay colt

Frankel (GB)	Galileo (IRE)	Sadler's Wells (USA)
		Urban Sea (USA)
	Kind (IRE)	Danehill (USA)
		Rainbow Lake (GB)
Without You Babe (USA)	Lemon Drop Kid (USA)	Kingmambo (USA)
		Charming Lassie (USA)
	Marozia (USA)	Storm Bird (CAN)
		Make Change (USA)

WONDERMENT (IRE)

Coolmore Stud's triple classic star Camelot (by Montjeu) has made a promising start to his second career, and the 13 stakes winners who have emerged so far from his first two crops include three that have won at the highest level. Latrobe won the Group 1 Dubai Duty Free Irish Derby at the Curragh at the end of June, Athena took the Grade 1 Belmont Oaks Invitational Stakes in New York a week later, and then the stallion's second-crop daughter Wonderment landed the Group 1 Criterium de Saint-Cloud in France in late October.

The latter, a Nicolas Clement-trained bay, beat Group 2 Royal Lodge Stakes runner-up Sydney Opera House by a neck in the 10-furlong contest, with Fox Tal third and a gap back to Listed Zetland Stakes winner Norway in fourth. It was her second win from just three starts and came almost four weeks after she had finished third to Line of Duty in the Group 3 Prix de Conde over nine furlongs at Chantilly. That colt went on to take the Grade 1 Breeders' Cup Juvenile Turf on his next start.

Wonderment was bred by Manfred Wurtenherger and Reinhard Stockil and she is a €60,000 graduate of the Arqana Deauville October Yearling Sale. She is the second foal of Wiwilia (by Konigstiger), her Dawn Approach (by New Approach) half-sister made €87,000 at the 2018 edition of the same auction, and her older sibling is the five-furlong Goodwood maiden scorer Short Call (by Kodiac). Her dam won twice in Switzerland as a two-year-old and comes from a prolific blacktype family whose many stars include another of 2018's Group 1 winners.

Wiwilia has eight winning siblings, and although the three blacktype horses among them include the pattern-placed multiple blacktype producer Wildfahrte (by Mark Of Esteem), the most notable of them is Wake Forest (by Sir Percy). He was a Group 3 winner in Germany before crossing the Atlantic and went on to become a leading middle-distance turf horse, winning the Grade 1 Man O'War Stakes and Grade 2 Mac Diarmida Stakes and taking the runners-up spot in the Grade 1 Northern Dancer Turf Stakes. He was back in the news in late November due to unfortunate circumstances that have worked out well in the end. He had been sold as a horse in training but failed to shine for his new connections and was found, by one of his former owners, Michael Dubb, to be running for an $8,000 tag in a claimer. Dubb was unable to find a stallion position for the horse, so he retired the horse to Old Friends Farm in Georgetown, Kentucky instead.

Their dam, Wurfspiel (by Lomitas), is a stakes-placed half-sister to nine winners, including the multiple pattern scorers Wurfscheibe (by Tiger Hill) and Wurtfaube (by Acatenango). Both of those horses became the dams of pattern-winning offspring, the former is very closely related to Wonderment's dam, but it is the latter who is of particular note and who provides the connection to the other 2018 Group 1 star.

Wurftaube's seven wins featured the Group 2 Gerling Preis, Group 2 Deutsches St Leger, and two Group 3 contests, she was runner-up in the Group 1 Deutschland-Preis, and the best of her representatives on the track has been her Group 1 Deutsches Derby-winning son Waldpark (by Dubawi). He stands at Haras du Thenney, in France, and his first crop will be three-year-olds in 2019. His unraced half-sister Waldbeere (by Mark Of Esteem) is the dam of multiple pattern scorer Wiesenpfad (by Waky Nao) and classic-placed stakes winner Waldtraut (by Oasis Dream), but that record pales in comparison to that of Waldpark's Group 2 Falmouth Stakes-placed half-sister Waldmark (by Mark Of Esteem).

Her best son, Masked Marvel (by Montjeu), is somewhat closely related to Wonderment and he won the Group 1 St Leger, Group 3 Bahrain Trophy and Listed Cocked Hat Stakes in 2011 before eventually taking up stallion duties at Haras d'Etreham. He also has his first three-year-olds in 2019. The mare's daughters include middle-distance listed scorer Waldnah (by New Approach) and Group 3 Prix Penelope winner Waldlerche (by Monsun), and that latter is the mare who gave us Waldgeist (by Galileo) and his high-class half-sister Waldlied (by New Approach).

Like his young relation, Waldgeist won the Group 1 Criterium de Saint-Cloud as a juvenile, which made him a leading classic contender for 2017. He was runner-up in the Group 1 Prix du Jockey Club (French Derby) and fourth in the Group 1 Irish Derby in a winless campaign at three but bounced back at four to score four times, notably in the Group 1 Grand Prix de Saint-Cloud, Group 2 Qatar Prix Foy and Group 2 Grand Prix de Chantilly. The Andre Fabre-trained chestnut achieved a Timeform rating of 127 this year.

Waldlied is a year younger than him, and on the day that he got his Group 1 win at Saint-Cloud in July, she landed the Group 2 Prix de Mallaret by two and a half lengths at the same venue. It's not often that you see siblings win major races on the same day.

With a pedigree like this, there is clearly every reason to hope that Wonderment could become a leading middle-distance three-year-old, one who could be seen in action in the Group 1 Prix de Diane and Group 1 Prix Vermeille, and maybe even the Group 1 Prix de l'Arc de Triomphe. The success of Wake Forest and Waldgeist shows that stars in this family can excel as older horses too, which could make her an interesting prospect in 2020 if she stays in training that long. Of course, her pedigree also makes her a very valuable prospective broodmare, especially with that Group 1 win to her name, and so hers is a name that we could be writing about for years to come.

SUMMARY DETAILS

Bred: Manfred Wurtenberger & Reinhard Stockil
Owned: Mme Stella Thayer
Trained: Nicolas Clement
Country: France
Race record: 131-
Career highlights: 2 wins inc Criterium de Saint-Cloud (Gr1), 3rd Prix de Conde (Gr3)

WONDERMENT (IRE) - 2016 bay filly

Camelot (GB)	Montjeu (IRE)	Sadler's Wells (USA)
		Floripedes (FR)
	Tarfah (USA)	Kingmambo (USA)
		Fickle (GB)
Wiwilia (GER)	Konigstiger (GER)	Tiger Hill (IRE)
		Kittiwake (GB)
	Wurfspiel (GER)	Lomitas (GB)
		Wurfbahn (GER)

GROUP 1 WINNERS OF 2018
BY SIRE

Acclamation (GB) – Expert Eye (GB)

Adlerflug (GER) – Iquitos (GER)

Camacho (GB) – Teppal (FR)

Camelot (GB) – Athena (IRE)
Camelot (GB) – Latrobe (IRE)
Camelot (GB) – Wonderment (IRE)

Captain Gerrard (IRE) – Alpha Delphini (GB)

Champs Elysees (GB) – Billesdon Brook (GB)

Dandy Man (IRE) - La Pelosa (IRE)

Dansili (GB) – With You (GB)

Declaration Of War (USA) – Olmedo (FR)

Deep Impact (JPN) – Saxon Warrior (JPN)
Deep Impact (JPN) – Study Of Man (IRE)

Delegator (GB) – Accidental Agent (GB)

Dubawi (IRE) – Benbatl (GB)
Dubawi (IRE) – Kitesurf (GB)
Dubawi (IRE) – Quorto (IRE)
Dubawi (IRE) – Too Darn Hot (GB)
Dubawi (IRE) – Wild Illusion (GB)

Dutch Art (GB) – Mabs Cross (GB)

Equiano (FR) – The Tin Man (GB)

Fastnet Rock (AUS) – Merchant Navy (AUS)
Fastnet Rock (AUS) – One Master (GB)

Foxwedge (AUS) – Urban Fox (GB)

Frankel (GB) – Call The Wind (GB)
Frankel (GB) – Cracksman (GB)
Frankel (GB) – Without Parole (GB)

Galileo (IRE) – Flag Of Honour (IRE)
Galileo (IRE) – Forever Together (IRE)
Galileo (IRE) – Kew Gardens (IRE)
Galileo (IRE) – Line of Duty (IRE)
Galileo (IRE) - Magical (IRE)
Galileo (IRE) – Rhododendron (IRE)
Galileo (IRE) – Waldgeist (GB)

Halling (USA) – Desert Encounter (IRE)

Havana Gold (IRE) – Havana Grey (GB)

Helmet (AUS) – Thunder Snow (IRE)

Hold That Tiger (USA) – Holdthasigreen (FR)

Holy Roman Emperor (IRE) – Romanised (IRE)
Holy Roman Emperor (IRE) – Well Timed (GER)

Iffraaj (GB) – Jungle Cat (IRE)

Intello (GER) – Intellogent (IRE)

Invincible Spirit (IRE) – Eqtidaar (IRE)
Invincible Spirit (IRE) – Magna Grecia (IRE)
Invincible Spirit (IRE) – Royal Meeting (IRE)

Kitten's Joy (USA) – Hawkbill (USA)
Kitten's Joy (USA) – Roaring Lion (USA)

Kodiac (GB) – Best Solution (IRE)
Kodiac (GB) – Fairyland (IRE)

Mastercraftsman (IRE) – Alpha Centauri (IRE)

Nathaniel (IRE) – Enable (GB)
Nathaniel (IRE) – God Given (GB)

New Approach (IRE) – Masar (IRE)

No Nay Never (USA) – Ten Sovereigns (IRE)

Oasis Dream (GB) – Polydream (IRE)
Oasis Dream (GB) – Pretty Pollyanna (GB)

Panis (USA) - Sands Of Mali (FR)

Pivotal (GB) – Blair House (IRE)
Pivotal (GB) – Lightning Spear (GB)

Poet's Voice (GB) – Poet's Word (IRE)

Raven's Pass (USA) – Royal Marine (IRE)

Ruler Of The World (IRE) – Iridessa (IRE)

Santiago (GER) – Khan (GER)

Scat Daddy (USA) – Skitter Scatter (USA)

Sea The Stars (IRE) – Sea Of Class (IRE)
Sea The Stars (IRE) – Stadivarius (IRE)

Shamardal (USA) – Blue Point (IRE)
Shamardal (USA) – Sheikha Reika (FR)

Showcasing (GB) – Advertise (GB)

Siyouni (FR) – Laurens (FR)

Soldier Hollow (GB) – Weltstar (GER)

Style Vendome (FR) – Lily's Candle (FR)

Teofilo (IRE) - Cross Counter (GB)

War Front (USA) – Lancaster Bomber (USA)
War Front (USA) – U S Navy Flag (USA)

Whipper (USA) – Recoletos (FR)

Zanzibari (USA) – Nonza (FR)

Acclamation (GB) – The Tin Man (GB), by Equiano (FR)

Anabaa (USA) – Lily's Candle (FR), by Style Vendome (FR)

Cape Cross (IRE) – Sea Of Class (IRE), by Sea The Stars (IRE)
Cape Cross (IRE) – Stadivarius (IRE), by Sea The Stars (IRE)

Danehill (USA) – Best Solution (IRE), by Kodiac (GB)
Danehill (USA) – Billesdon Brook (GB), by Champs Elysees
    (GB)
Danehill (USA) – Fairyland (IRE), by Kodiac (GB)
Danehill (USA) – Merchant Navy (AUS), by Fastnet Rock (AUS)
Danehill (USA) – One Master (GB), by Fastnet Rock (AUS)
Danehill (USA) – Romanised (IRE), by Holy Roman Emperor
    (IRE)
Danehill (USA) – Teppal (FR), by Camacho (GB)
Danehill (USA) – Well Timed (GER), by Holy Roman Emperor
    (IRE)
Danehill (USA) – With You (GB), by Dansili (GB)

Danehill Dancer (IRE) – Alpha Centauri (IRE), by
    Mastercraftsman (IRE)

Dansili (GB) – Accidental Agent (GB), by Delegator (GB)

Danzig (USA) – Lancaster Bomber (USA), by War Front (USA)
Danzig – U S Navy Flag (USA), by War Front (USA)

Diesis – Desert Encounter (IRE), by Halling (USA)

Dubai Millennium (GB) – Benbatl (GB), by Dubawi (IRE)
Dubai Millennium (GB) – Kitesurf (GB), by Dubawi (IRE)
Dubai Millennium (GB) – Quorto (IRE), by Dubawi (IRE)
Dubai Millennium (GB)– Too Darn Hot (GB), by Dubawi (IRE)
Dubai Millennium (GB) – Wild Illusion (GB), by Dubawi (IRE)

Dubawi (IRE) – Poet's Word (IRE), by Poet's Voice (GB)

El Prado (IRE) – Hawkbill (USA), by Kitten's Joy (USA)
El Prado (IRE) – Roaring Lion (USA), by Kitten's Joy (USA)

Elusive Quality (USA) – Royal Marine (IRE), by Raven's Pass (USA)

Exceed And Excel (AUS) – Thunder Snow (IRE), by Helmet (AUS)

Fastnet Rock (AUS) – Urban Fox (GB), by Foxwedge (AUS)

Galileo (IRE) – Call The Wind (GB), by Frankel (GB)
Galileo (IRE) – Cracksman (GB), by Frankel (GB)
Galileo (IRE) – Cross Counter (GB), by Teofilo (IRE)
Galileo (IRE) – Enable (GB), by Nathaniel (IRE)
Galileo (IRE) – God Given (GB), by Nathaniel (IRE)
Galileo (IRE) – Intellogent (IRE), by Intello (GER)
Galileo (IRE) – Iridessa (IRE), by Ruler Of The World (IRE)
Galileo (IRE) – Masar (IRE), by New Approach (IRE)
Galileo (IRE) – Without Parole (GB), by Frankel (GB)

Giant's Causeway (USA) – Blue Point (IRE), by Shamardal (USA)

Green Desert (USA) – Eqtidaar (IRE), by Invincible Spirit (IRE)
Green Desert (USA) – Magna Grecia (IRE), by Invincible Spirit (IRE)
Green Desert (USA) – Polydream (IRE), by Oasis Dream (GB)
Green Desert (USA) – Pretty Pollyanna (GB), by Oasis Dream (GB)
Green Desert (USA) – Royal Meeting (IRE) by Invincible Spirit (IRE)

Highest Honor (FR) – Khan (GER), by Santiago (GER)

In The Wings – Iquitos (GER), by Adlerflug (GER)
In The Wings – Weltstar (GER), by Soldier Hollow (GB)

Johannesburg (USA) – Skitter Scatter (USA), by Scat Daddy (USA)

BY GRANDSIRE

Medicean (GB) – Mabs Cross (GB), by Dutch Art (GB)

Miesque's Son (USA) – Recoletos (FR), by Whipper (USA)

Miswaki (USA) - Sands Of Mali (FR), by Panis (USA)

Montjeu (IRE) – Athena (IRE), by Camelot (GB)
Montjeu (IRE) – Latrobe (IRE), by Camelot (GB)
Montjeu (IRE) – Wonderment (IRE), by Camelot (GB)

Mozart (IRE) – La Pelosa (IRE), by Dandy Man (IRE)

Oasis Dream (GB) – Advertise (GB), by Showcasing (GB)
Oasis Dream (GB) – Alpha Delphini (GB), by Captain Gerrard
    (IRE)

Pivotal (GB) – Laurens (FR), by Siyouni (FR)

Polar Falcon (USA) – Blair House (IRE), by Pivotal (GB)
Polar Falcon (USA) – Lightning Spear (GB), by Pivotal (GB)

Royal Applause (GB) – Expert Eye (GB), by Acclamation (GB)

Sadler's Wells (USA) – Flag Of Honour (IRE), by Galileo (IRE)
Sadler's Wells (USA) – Forever Together (IRE), by Galileo (IRE)
Sadler's Wells (USA) – Kew Gardens (IRE), by Galileo (IRE)
Sadler's Wells (USA) – Line of Duty (IRE), by Galileo (IRE)
Sadler's Wells (USA) - Magical (IRE), by Galileo (IRE)
Sadler's Wells (USA) – Rhododendron (IRE), by Galileo (IRE)
Sadler's Wells (USA) – Waldgeist (GB), by Galileo (IRE)

Scat Daddy (USA) – Ten Sovereigns (IRE), by No Nay Never
    (USA)

Smart Strike (CAN) – Nonza (FR), by Zanzibari (USA)

Storm Cat (USA) – Holdthasigreen (FR), by Hold That Tiger
    (USA)

Sunday Silence (USA) – Saxon Warrior (JPN), by Deep Impact (JPN)

Sunday Silence (USA) – Study Of Man (IRE), by Deep Impact (JPN)

Teofilo (IRE) – Havana Grey (GB), by Havana Gold (IRE)

War Front (USA) – Olmedo (FR), by Declaration Of War (USA)

Zafonic (USA) – Jungle Cat (IRE), by Iffraaj (GB)

GROUP 1 WINNERS OF 2018
BY GREAT-GRANDSIRE

Danehill (USA) – Alpha Centauri (IRE), by Mastercraftsman
(IRE), by Danehill Dancer (IRE)

Danehill (USA) – Accidental Agent (GB), by Delegator (GB), by
Dansili GB)

Danehill (USA) – La Pelosa (IRE), by Dandy Man (IRE), by
Mozart (IRE)

Danehill (USA) – Thunder Snow (IRE), by Helmet (AUS), by
Exceed And Excel (AUS)

Danehill (USA) – Urban Fox (GB), by Foxwedge (AUS), by
Fastnet Rock (AUS)

Danzig (USA) – Best Solution (IRE), by Kodiac (GB), by
Danehill (USA)

Danzig (USA) – Billesdon Brook (GB), by Champs Elysees (GB),
by Danehill (USA)

Danzig (USA) – Eqtidaar (IRE), by Invincible Spirit (IRE), by
Green Desert (USA)

Danzig (USA) – Fairyland (IRE), by Kodiac (GB), by Danehill
(USA)

Danzig (USA) – Lily's Candle (FR), by Style Vendome (FR), by
Anabaa (USA)

Danzig (USA) – Magna Grecia (IRE), by Invincible Spirit (IRE),
by Green Desert (USA)

Danzig (USA) – Merchant Navy (AUS), by Fastnet Rock (AUS),
by Danehill (USA)

Danzig (USA) – Olmedo (FR), by Declaration Of War (USA), by
War Front (USA)

Danzig (USA) – One Master (GB), by Fastnet Rock (AUS), by
Danehill (USA)

Danzig (USA) – Polydream (IRE), by Oasis Dream (GB), by
Green Desert (USA)

Danzig (USA) – Pretty Pollyanna (GB), by Oasis Dream (GB), by
Green Desert (USA)

Danzig (USA) – Romanised (IRE), by Holy Roman Emperor
(IRE), by Danehill (USA)

Danzig (USA) – Royal Meeting (IRE), by Invincible Spirit (IRE),
by Green Desert (USA)

Danzig (USA) – Teppal (FR), by Camacho (GB), by Danehill (USA)

Danzig (USA) – Well Timed (GER), by Holy Roman Emperor (IRE), by Danehill (USA)

Danzig (USA) – With You (GB), by Dansili (GB), by Danehill (USA)

Dubai Millennium (GB) – Poet's Word (IRE), by Poet's Voice (GB), by Dubawi (IRE)

Galileo (IRE) – Havana Grey (GB), by Havana Gold (GB), by Teofilo (IRE)

Gone West (USA) – Jungle Cat (IRE), by Iffraaj (GB), by Zafonic USA)

Gone West (USA) – Royal Marine (IRE), by Raven's Pass (USA), by Elusive Quality (USA)

Green Desert (USA) – Advertise (GB), by Showcasing (GB), by Oasis Dream (GB)

Green Desert (USA) – Alpha Delphini (GB), by Captain Gerrard (IRE), by Oasis Dream (GB)

Green Desert (USA) – Sea Of Class (IRE), by Sea The Stars (IRE), by Cape Cross (IRE)

Green Desert (USA) – Stradivarius (IRE), by Sea The Stars (IRE), by Cape Cross (IRE)

Halo (USA) – Saxon Warrior (JPN), by Deep Impact (JPN), by Sunday Silence (USA)

Halo (USA) – Study Of Man (IRE), by Deep Impact (JPN), by Sunday Silence (USA)

Hennessy (USA) – Skitter Scatter (USA), by Scat Daddy (USA), by Johannesburg (USA)

Johannesburg (USA) – Ten Sovereigns (IRE), by No Nay Never (USA), by Scat Daddy (USA)

Kenmare (FR) – Khan (GER), by Santiago (GER), by Highest Honor (FR)

Machiavellian (USA) – Mabs Cross (GB), by Dutch Art (GB), by
    Medicean (GB)

Mr Prospector (USA) – Nonza (FR), by Zanzibari (USA) by
    Smart Strike (CAN)
Mr Prospector (USA) – Recoletos (FR), by Whipper (USA), by
    Miesque's Son (USA)
Mr Prospector (USA) – Sands Of Mali (FR), by Panis (USA), by
    Miswaki (USA)

Northern Dancer (CAN) – Flag Of Honour (IRE), by Galileo
    (IRE), by Sadler's Wells (USA)
Northern Dancer (CAN) – Forever Together (IRE), by Galileo
    (IRE), by Sadler's Wells (USA)
Northern Dancer (CAN) – Kew Gardens (IRE), by Galileo
    (IRE), by Sadler's Wells (USA)
Northern Dancer (CAN) – Lancaster Bomber (USA), by War
    Front (USA), by Danzig (USA)
Northern Dancer (CAN) (CAN) – Line of Duty (IRE), by Galileo
    (IRE), by Sadler's Wells (USA)
Northern Dancer (CAN) (CAN) - Magical (IRE), by Galileo
    (IRE), by Sadler's Wells (USA)
Northern Dancer (CAN) – Rhododendron (IRE), by Galileo, by
    Sadler's Wells (USA)
Northern Dancer (CAN) – U S Navy Flag (USA), by War Front,
    by Danzig (USA)
Northern Dancer (CAN) – Waldgeist (GB), by Galileo (IRE), by
    Sadler's Wells (USA)

Nureyev (USA) – Blair House (IRE), by Pivotal (GB), by Polar
    Falcon (USA)
Nureyev (USA) – Lightning Spear (GB), by Pivotal (GB), by Polar
    Falcon (USA)

Polar Falcon (USA) – Laurens (FR), by Siyouni (FR), by Pivotal
    (GB)

Royal Applause (GB) – The Tin Man (GB), by Equiano (FR), by
    Acclamation (GB)

Sadler's Wells (USA) – Athena (IRE), by Camelot (GB), by Montjeu (IRE)

Sadler's Wells (USA) – Call The Wind (GB), by Frankel (GB), by Galileo (IRE)

Sadler's Wells (USA) – Cracksman (GB), by Frankel (GB), by Galileo (IRE)

Sadler's Wells (USA) – Cross Counter (GB), by Teofilo (IRE), by Galileo (IRE)

Sadler's Wells (USA) – Enable (GB), by Nathaniel (IRE), by Galileo (IRE)

Sadler's Wells (USA) – God Given (GB), by Nathaniel (IRE), by Galileo (IRE)

Sadler's Wells (USA) – Hawkbill (USA), by Kitten's Joy (USA), by El Prado (IRE)

Sadler's Wells (USA) – Intellogent (IRE), by Intello (GER), by Galileo (IRE)

Sadler's Wells (USA) – Iquitos (GER), by Adlerflug (GER), by In The Wings

Sadler's Wells (USA) – Iridessa (IRE), by Ruler Of The World (IRE), by Galileo (IRE)

Sadler's Wells (USA) – Latrobe (IRE), by Camelot (GB), by Montjeu (IRE)

Sadler's Wells (USA) – Masar (IRE), by New Approach (IRE), by Galileo (IRE)

Sadler's Wells (USA) – Roaring Lion (USA), by Kitten's Joy (USA), by El Prado (IRE)

Sadler's Wells (USA) – Weltstar (GER), by Soldier Hollow (GB), by In The Wings)

Sadler's Wells (USA) – Without Parole (GB), by Frankel (GB), by Galileo (IRE)

Sadler's Wells (USA) – Wonderment (IRE), by Camelot (GB), by Montjeu (IRE)

Seeking The Gold (USA) – Benbatl (GB), by Dubawi (IRE), by Dubai Millennium (GB)

Seeking The Gold (USA) – Kitesurf (GB), by Dubawi (IRE), by Dubai Millennium (GB)

Seeking The Gold (USA) – Quorto (IRE), by Dubawi (IRE), by Dubai Millennium (GB)

Seeking The Gold (USA) – Too Darn Hot (GB), by Dubawi (IRE), by Dubai Millennium (GB)

Seeking The Gold (USA) – Wild Illusion (GB), by Dubawi (IRE), by Dubai Millennium (GB)

Sharpen Up – Desert Encounter (IRE), by Halling (USA), by Diesis

Storm Bird (CAN) – Holdthasigreen (FR), by Hold That Tiger (USA), by Storm Cat (USA)

Storm Cat (USA) – Blue Point (IRE), by Shamardal (USA), by Giant's Causeway (USA)

Storm Cat (USA) – Sheikha Reika (FR), by Shamardal (USA), by Giant's Causeway (USA)

Waajib – Expert Eye (GB), by Acclamation (GB), by Royal Applause (GB)

GROUP 1 WINNERS OF 2018
BY DAM

Al Andalyya (USA) - Best Solution (IRE), by Kodiac (GB)

Alpha Lupi (IRE) - Alpha Centauri (IRE), by Mastercraftsman (IRE)

Atlantic Destiny (IRE) - Lightning Spear (GB), by Pivotal (GB)

Blanc De Chine (IRE) - Havana Grey (GB), by Havana Gold (IRE)

Cabaret (IRE) - Magna Grecia (IRE), by Invincible Spirit (IRE)

Chelsea Rose (IRE) - Kew Gardens (IRE), by Galileo (IRE)

Cherry Hinton (GB) - Athena (IRE), by Camelot (GB)

Concentric (GB) - Enable (GB), by Nathaniel (IRE)

Coplow (GB) - Billesdon Brook (GB), by Champs Elysees (GB)

Dane Street (USA) - Skitter Scatter (USA), by Scat Daddy (USA)

Dar Re Mi (GB) - Too Darn Hot (GB), by Dubawi (IRE)

Eastern Joy (GB) - Thunder Snow (IRE), by Helmet (AUS)

Easy To Imagine (USA) - Alpha Delphini (GB), by Captain Gerrard (IRE)

Enticing (IRE) - One Master (GB), by Fastnet Rock (AUS)

Ever Rigg (GB) - God Given (GB), by Nathaniel (IRE)

Exemplify (GB) - Expert Eye (GB), by Acclamation (GB)

Furbelow (GB) - Advertise (GB), by Showcasing (GB)

Golden Lily (FR) - Lily's Candle (FR), by Style Vendome (FR)

Green Room (USA) - Forever Together (IRE), by Galileo (IRE)

Greentathir (FR) - Holdthasigreen (FR), by Hold That Tiger
(USA)

Halfway To Heaven (IRE) - Magical (IRE), by Galileo (IRE)
Halfway To Heaven (IRE) - Rhododendron (IRE), by Galileo
(IRE)

Hawala (IRE) - Flag Of Honour (IRE), by Galileo (IRE)

Highphar (FR) - Recoletos (FR), by Whipper (USA)

Holy Moon (IRE) - Sea Of Class (IRE), by Sea The Stars (IRE)

In Clover (GB) - Call The Wind (GB), by Frankel (GB)
In Clover (GB) - With You (GB), by Dansili (GB)

Inner Secret (USA) - Royal Marine (IRE), by Raven's Pass (USA)

Irika (GER) - Iquitos (GER), by Adlerflug (GER)

Jacqueline Quest (IRE) - Line of Duty (IRE), by Galileo (IRE)

Jummana (FR) - Teppal (FR), by Camacho (GB)

Kadiania (FR) - Sands Of Mali (FR), by Panis (USA)

Kapitol (GER) - Khan (GER), by Santiago (GER)

Khawlah (IRE) - Masar (IRE), by New Approach (IRE)

La Chicana (IRE) - Desert Encounter (IRE), by Halling (USA)

Lauren's Girl (IRE) - La Pelosa (IRE), by Dandy Man (IRE)

Legally Bay (AUS) - Merchant Navy (AUS), by Fastnet Rock
(AUS)

Lomapamar (GB) - Urban Fox (GB), by Foxwedge (AUS)

Madany (IRE) - Eqtidaar (IRE), by Invincible Spirit (IRE)

Maybe (IRE) - Saxon Warrior (JPN), by Deep Impact (JPN)

Mike's Wildcat (USA) - Jungle Cat (IRE), by Iffraaj (GB)

Miss Meggy (GB) - Mabs Cross (GB), by Dutch Art (GB)

Misty For Me (IRE) - U S Navy Flag (USA), by War Front (USA)

Nahrain (GB) - Benbatl (GB), by Dubawi (IRE)

Nuit Polaire (IRE) - Intellogent (IRE), by Intello (GER)

Patroness (GB) - Blair House (IRE), by Pivotal (GB)

Persario (GB) - The Tin Man (GB), by Equiano (FR)

Polygreen (FR) - Polydream (IRE), by Oasis Dream (GB)

Private Life (FR) - Stradivarius (IRE), by Sea The Stars (IRE)

Queenofthefairies (GB) - Fairyland (IRE), by Kodiac (GB)

Question Times (GB) - Latrobe (IRE), by Camelot (GB)

Recambe (IRE) - Laurens (FR), by Siyouni (FR)

Rhadegunda (GB) - Cracksman (GB), by Frankel (GB)

Rock Opera (SAF) - Royal Meeting (IRE), by Invincible Spirit (IRE)

Romantic Venture (IRE) - Romanised (IRE), by Holy Roman Emperor (IRE)

Roodle (GB) - Accidental Agent (GB), by Delegator (GB)

Rumh (GER) - Wild Illusion (GB), by Dubawi (IRE)

Scarlett Rose (GB) - Blue Point (IRE), by Shamardal (USA)

Screen Star (IRE) - Sheikha Reika (FR), by Shamardal (USA)

Second Happiness (USA) - Study Of Man (IRE), by Deep Impact (JPN)

Seeking Solace (GB) - Ten Sovereigns (IRE), by No Nay Never (USA)

Senta's Dream (GB) - Iridessa (IRE), by Ruler Of The World (IRE)

Shimmering Surf (IRE) - Kitesurf (GB), by Dubawi (IRE)

Sun Shower (IRE) - Lancaster Bomber (USA), by War Front (USA)

Super Pie (USA) - Olmedo (FR), by Declaration Of War (USA)

Terra Alta (FR) - Nonza (FR), by Zanzibari (USA)

Trensa (USA) - Hawkbill (USA), by Kitten's Joy (USA)

Unex Mona Lisa (GB) - Pretty Pollyanna (GB), by Oasis Dream (GB)

Vionnet (USA) - Roaring Lion (USA), by Kitten's Joy (USA)

Volume (GB) - Quorto (IRE), by Dubawi (IRE)

Waitress (USA) - Cross Counter (GB), by Teofilo (IRE)

Waldlerche (GB) - Waldgeist (GB), by Galileo (IRE)

Wellenspiel (GER) - Weltstar (GER), by Soldier Hollow (GB)

Wells Present (GB) - Well Timed (GER), by Holy Roman Emperor (IRE)

Whirly Bird (GB) - Poet's Word (IRE), by Poet's Voice (GB)

Wiwilia (GB) - Wonderment (IRE), by Camelot (GB)

Without You Babe (USA) - Without Parole (GB), by Frankel (GB)

GROUP 1 WINNERS OF 2018
BY BROODMARE SIRE

Acclamation (GB) - Eqtidaar (IRE), by Invincible Spirit (IRE)

Areion (GER) - Iquitos (GER), by Adlerflug (GER)

Bering - Stradivarius (IRE), by Sea The Stars (IRE)

Bishop Of Cashel (GB) - The Tin Man (GB), by Equiano (FR)

Bushranger (IRE) - La Pelosa (IRE), by Dandy Man (IRE)

Cadeaux Genereux - Teppal (FR), by Camacho (GB)
Cadeaux Genereux - Well Timed (GER), by Holy Roman
    Emperor (IRE)

Cape Cross (IRE) - Laurens (FR), by Siyouni (FR)
Cape Cross (IRE) - Masar (IRE), by New Approach (IRE)

Cozzene (USA) - Alpha Delphini (GB), by Captain Gerrard (IRE)

Danehill (USA) - Iridessa (IRE), by Ruler Of The World (IRE)

Danehill Dancer (IRE) - Kitesurf (GB), by Dubawi (IRE)

Dansili (GB) - Expert Eye (GB), by Acclamation (GB)

Dark Angel (IRE) - Havana Grey (GB), by Havana Gold (IRE)

Desert King (IRE) - Kew Gardens (IRE), by Galileo (IRE)

Dolphin Street (IRE) - Lily's Candle (FR), by Style Vendome (FR)

Dubai Destination (USA) - God Given (GB), by Nathaniel (IRE)
Dubai Destination (USA) - Thunder Snow (IRE), by Helmet
    (AUS)

Dubawi (IRE) - Blair House (IRE), by Pivotal (GB)

Exceed And Excel (AUS) - Ten Sovereigns (IRE), by No Nay
    Never (USA)

Forest Wildcat (USA) - Jungle Cat (IRE), by Iffraaj (GB)

Galileo (IRE) - Magna Grecia (IRE), by Invincible Spirit (IRE)
Galileo (IRE) - Saxon Warrior (JPN), by Deep Impact (JPN)
Galileo (IRE) - U S Navy Flag (USA), by War Front (USA)

Giant's Causeway (USA) - Hawkbill (USA), by Kitten's Joy (USA)

Green Desert (USA) - Athena (IRE), by Camelot (GB)

Green Tune (USA) - Polydream (IRE), by Oasis Dream (GB)

Hernando (FR) - Sea Of Class (IRE), by Sea The Stars (IRE)

Highest Honor (FR) - Recoletos (FR), by Whipper (USA)

Inchinor (GB) - Call The Wind (GB), by Frankel (GB)
Inchinor (GB) - With You (GB), by Dansili (GB)

Indian Ridge - Lancaster Bomber (USA), by War Front (USA)
Indian Ridge - Romanised (IRE), by Holy Roman Emperor (IRE)

Indian Rocket (GB) - Sands Of Mali (FR), by Panis (USA)

Invincible Spirit (IRE) - Desert Encounter (IRE), by Halling
    (USA)

Kaldounevees (FR) - Nonza (FR), by Zanzibari (USA)

Kheleyf (USA) - Intellogent (IRE), by Intello (GER)

Kingmambo (USA) - Best Solution (IRE), by Kodiac (GB)
Kingmambo (USA) - Cross Counter (GB), by Teofilo (IRE)

Konigstiger (GER) - Wonderment (IRE), by Camelot (GB)

Lecture (USA) - Royal Meeting (IRE), by Invincible Spirit (IRE)

334

Lemon Drop Kid (USA) - Without Parole (GB), by Frankel (GB)

Manduro (GER) - Billesdon Brook (GB), by Champs Elysees (GB)

Monsun (GER) - Waldgeist (GB), by Galileo (IRE)
Monsun (GER) - Wild Illusion (GB), by Dubawi (IRE)

Mount Nelson (GB) - Quorto (IRE), by Dubawi (IRE)

Muhtathir (GB) - Holdthasigreen (FR), by Hold That Tiger (USA)

Nashwan (USA) - Poet's Word (IRE), by Poet's Voice (GB)
Nashwan (USA) - Urban Fox (GB), by Foxwedge (AUS)

Pivotal (GB) - Advertise (GB), by Showcasing (GB)
Pivotal (GB) - Cracksman (GB), by Frankel (GB)
Pivotal (GB) - Fairyland (IRE), by Kodiac (GB)
Pivotal (GB) - Mabs Cross (GB), by Dutch Art (GB)
Pivotal (GB) - Magical (IRE), by Galileo (IRE)
Pivotal (GB) - Olmedo (FR), by Declaration Of War (USA)
Pivotal (GB) - One Master (GB), by Fastnet Rock (AUS)
Pivotal (GB) - Rhododendron (IRE), by Galileo (IRE)

Rahy (USA) - Alpha Centauri (IRE), by Mastercraftsman (IRE)

Rock Of Gibraltar (IRE) - Line of Duty (IRE), by Galileo (IRE)

Royal Academy (USA) - Lightning Spear (GB), by Pivotal (GB)

Royal Applause (GB) - Blue Point (IRE), by Shamardal (USA)

Sadler's Wells (USA) - Enable (GB), by Nathaniel (IRE)

Selkirk (USA) - Benbatl (GB), by Dubawi (IRE)

Shamardal (USA) - Latrobe (IRE), by Camelot (GB)
Shamardal (USA) - Pretty Pollyanna (GB), by Oasis Dream (GB)

Singspiel (IRE) - Royal Marine (IRE), by Raven's Pass (USA)
Singspiel (IRE) - Too Darn Hot (GB), by Dubawi (IRE)

Snippets (AUS) - Merchant Navy (AUS), by Fastnet Rock (AUS)

Sternkonig (IRE) - Weltstar (GER), by Soldier Hollow (GB)

Storm Cat (USA) - Study Of Man (IRE), by Deep Impact (JPN)

Street Cry (IRE) - Skitter Scatter (USA), by Scat Daddy (USA)

Street Sense (USA) - Roaring Lion (USA), by Kitten's Joy (USA)

Theatrical - Forever Together (IRE), by Galileo (IRE)

Tobougg (IRE) - Sheikha Reika (FR), by Shamardal (USA)

Warning - Flag Of Honour (IRE), by Galileo (IRE)

Winged Love (IRE) - Khan (GER), by Santiago (GER)

Xaar (GB) - Accidental Agent (GB), by Delegator (GB)

GROUP 1 WINNERS OF 2018
BY BREEDER

Aherne, Monica - Romanised (IRE)

Barhan, C - Merchant Navy (AUS)

Barronstown Stud - Flag Of Honour (IRE)
Barronstown Stud - Kew Gardens (IRE)

Bloodstock Agency Ltd - Laurens (FR)

Buhmann, Dr Erika - Iquitos (GER)

Camas Park, Lynch Bages & Summerhill - Ten Sovereigns (IRE)

Cheveley Park Stud Ltd - Advertise (GB)

Darley - Benbatl (GB)
Darley - Blair House (IRE)
Darley - Jungle Cat (IRE)
Darley - Thunder Snow (IRE)

Devin, Mme H - Nonza (FR)

Dream With Me Stable Inc - Olmedo (FR)

Ecurie Des Monceaux - Intellogent (IRE)

Elton Lodge Stud - La Pelosa (IRE)

Flaxman Stables Ireland Ltd - Study Of Man (IRE)

Gestut Karlshof - Khan (GER)

Gestut Rottgen - Weltstar (GER)

Gestut Zur Kuste Ag - Teppal (FR)

Gilbert, Jean & Le Fay, Claude - Holdthasigreen (FR)

337

Godolphin - Cross Counter (GB)
Godolphin - Masar (IRE)
Godolphin - Quorto (IRE)
Godolphin - Royal Marine (IRE)
Godolphin - Royal Meeting (IRE)
Godolphin - Wild Illusion (GB)

Grundy, Mrs Elizabeth - The Tin Man (GB)

Gunther, John - Without Parole (GB)

Hascombe and Valiant Studs - Cracksman (GB)

Helen K Groves Revokable Trust - Hawkbill (USA)

Highfield Farm Llp - Mabs Cross (GB)

Johnson Houghton, Mrs R F - Accidental Agent (GB)

Juddmonte Farms Ltd - Enable (GB)
Juddmonte Farms Ltd - Expert Eye (GB)

Khosla, Vilam and Gillian - Forever Together (IRE)

Lael Stables - One Master (GB)

Lepeudry, Mme P - Lily's Candle (FR)

Mark Johnston Racing Ltd - Sheikha Reika (FR)

Mascalls Stud - Urban Fox (GB)

Matthews, Mrs B A - Alpha Delphini (GB)

McCracken, Cecil and Martin - Best Solution (IRE)

Mickley Stud & Lady Lonsdale - Havana Grey (GB)

Misty For Me Syndicate - U S Navy Flag (USA)

Newsells Park Stud - Lightning Spear (GB)

Niarchos Family - Alpha Centauri (IRE)

Nielsen, Bjorn - Stradivarius (IRE)

Oak Lodge Bloodstock - Blue Point (IRE)

Orpendale, Chelston & Wynatt - Magical (IRE)
Orpendale, Chelston & Wynatt - Rhododendron (IRE)
Orpendale, Chelston & Wynatt - Saxon Warrior (JPN)

Ranjan Racing Inc - Roaring Lion (USA)

Razza Del Velino Srl - Sea Of Class (IRE)

Roncon & Chelston - Athena (IRE)

Sarl Darpat France - Recoletos (FR)

Shadwell Estate Company Limited - Eqtidaar (IRE)

St Albans Bloodstock Llp - God Given (GB)

Stall Ullmann - Well Timed (GER)

Stetchworth & Middle Park Studs Ltd - Pretty Pollyanna (GB)

Stowell Hill Partners - Billesdon Brook (GB)

Strawbridge, George - Call The Wind (GB)
Strawbridge, George - With You (GB)

Sun Shower Syndicate - Lancaster Bomber (USA)

Sweetmans Bloodstock - Latrobe (IRE)

Tally-Ho Stud - Desert Encounter (IRE)
Tally-Ho Stud - Fairyland (IRE)

The Waldlerche Partnership - Waldgeist (GB)

Three Chimneys Farm Llc & Airlie Stud - Skitter Scatter (USA)

Triermore Stud - Line of Duty (IRE)

Urizzi, Simon - Sands Of Mali (FR)

Watership Down Stud - Too Darn Hot (GB)

Wertheimer et Frere - Polydream (IRE)

Whisperview Trading Ltd - Iridessa (IRE)

Winkworth, Peter - Kitesurf (GB)

Woodcote Stud Ltd - Poet's Word (IRE)

Woodnook Farm Pty Ltd - Magna Grecia (IRE)

Wurtenberger, Manfred & Stockil, Reinhard - Wonderment (IRE)

GROUP 1 WINNERS OF 2018
BY OWNER

Abdullah, Khalid - Enable (GB)
Abdullah, Khalid - Expert Eye (GB)

Al Maktoum, Hamdan - Eqtidaar (IRE)

Al Maktoum, Sheikh Mohammed Obaid - Sheikha Reika (FR)

Al Mansoori, Abdulla - Desert Encounter (IRE)

Armstrong, David W - Mabs Cross (GB)

Barnane Stud Ltd - Urban Fox (GB)

Bin Khalifa Al Thani, H H Sheikh Mohammed - Teppal (FR)

Carmichael, Fiona - Intellogent (IRE)

Coolmore, Tabor & Wynaus - U S Navy Flag (USA)

Dance, John - Laurens (FR)

Darius Racing - Khan (GER)

Devin, Mme H - Nonza (FR)

Ecurie Antonio Caro & Gerard Augustin-Normand - Olmedo
    (FR)

Flaxman Stables Ireland Ltd - Study Of Man (IRE)

Fred Archer Racing-Ormonde - The Tin Man (GB)

Gestut Ammerland & Newsells Park - Waldgeist (GB)

Gestut Rottgen - Weltstar (GER)

Gilbert, Jean & Le Lay, Claude - Holdthasigreen (FR)

Global Racing Club & Mrs E Burke - Havana Grey (GB)

Godolphin - Benbatl (GB)
Godolphin - Best Solution (IRE)
Godolphin - Blair House (IRE)
Godolphin - Blue Point (IRE)
Godolphin - Cross Counter (GB)
Godolphin - Hawkbill (USA)
Godolphin - Jungle Cat (IRE)
Godolphin - Kitesurf (GB)
Godolphin - La Pelosa (IRE)
Godolphin - Line of Duty (IRE)
Godolphin - Masar (IRE)
Godolphin - Quorto (IRE)
Godolphin - Royal Marine (IRE)
Godolphin - Royal Meeting (IRE)
Godolphin - Thunder Snow (IRE)
Godolphin - Wild Illusion (GB)

Gredley, W J & T C O - Pretty Pollyanna (GB)

Gunther, John & Gunther, Tanya - Without Parole (GB)

Johnson Houghton, Mrs R F - Accidental Agent (GB)

Lael Stables - One Master (GB)

Lloyd-Webber, Lord - Too Darn Hot (GB)

Magnier, Mrs John; Tabor, Michael; & Smith, Derrick - Flag Of
    Honour (IRE)
Magnier, Mrs John; Tabor, Michael; & Smith, Derrick -
    Rhododendron (IRE)

Martin S Schwartz Racing - Lily's Candle (FR)

Merchant Navy Syndicate / Smith / Magnier / Tabor - Merchant
    Navy (AUS)

Ng, Robert - Romanised (IRE)

Niarchos Family - Alpha Centauri (IRE)

Nielsen, Bjorn - Stradivarius (IRE)

Oppenheimer, A E - Cracksman (GB)

Pall Mall Partners & Mrs R J McCreery - Billesdon Brook (GB)

Phoenix Thoroughbreds Limited 1 - Advertise (GB)

Qatar Racing Ltd - Lightning Spear (GB)
Qatar Racing Ltd - Roaring Lion (USA)

Regalado-Gonzalez, Mrs C C - Iridessa (IRE)

Rogers, Anthony & Rogers, Mrs Sonia - Skitter Scatter (USA)

Sarl Darpat France - Recoletos (FR)

Smith, Derrick; Magnier, Mrs John; & Tabor, Michael - Athena
    (IRE)
Smith, Derrick; Magnier, Mrs John; & Tabor, Michael - Kew
    Gardens (IRE)
Smith, Derrick; Magnier, Mrs John; & Tabor, Michael - Magical
    (IRE)
Smith, Derrick; Magnier, Mrs John; & Tabor, Michael - Saxon
    Warrior (JPN)
Smith, Derrick; Magnier, Mrs John; & Tabor, Michael - Ten
    Sovereigns (IRE)

Smith, Derrick; Magnier, Mrs John; Tabor, Michael; & Flaxman
    Stables Ireland - Magna Grecia (IRE)

St Albans Bloodstock Limited - God Given (GB)

Stall Mulligan - Iquitos (GER)

Stall Ullmann - Well Timed (GER)

Stockwell, Mrs E M; Tabor, Michael; & Smith, Derrick - Fairyland (IRE)

Strawbridge, George - Call The Wind (GB)
Strawbridge, George - With You (GB)

Suhail, Saeed - Poet's Word (IRE)

Sunderland Holdings Inc - Sea Of Class (IRE)

Tabor, Michael; Smith, Derrick; & Magnier, Mrs John - Forever Together (IRE)
Tabor, Michael; Smith, Derrick; & Magnier, Mrs John - Lancaster Bomber (USA)

Thayer, Mme Stella - Wonderment (IRE)

The Alpha Delphini Partnership - Alpha Delphini (GB)

The Cool Silk Partnership - Sands Of Mali (FR)

Wertheimer et Frere - Polydream (IRE)

Williams, N C & Williams, Mr & Mrs Lloyd J - Latrobe (IRE)

GROUP 1 WINNERS OF 2018
BY TRAINER

Trained in Ireland

Condon, Ken - Romanised (IRE)

Harrington, Jessica - Alpha Centauri (IRE)

O'Brien, Aidan - Athena (IRE)
O'Brien, Aidan - Fairyland (IRE)
O'Brien, Aidan - Flag Of Honour (IRE)
O'Brien, Aidan - Forever Together (IRE)
O'Brien, Aidan - Kew Gardens (IRE)
O'Brien, Aidan - Lancaster Bomber (USA)
O'Brien, Aidan - Magical (IRE)
O'Brien, Aidan - Magna Grecia (IRE)
O'Brien, Aidan - Merchant Navy (AUS)
O'Brien, Aidan - Rhododendron (IRE)
O'Brien, Aidan - Saxon Warrior (JPN)
O'Brien, Aidan - Ten Sovereigns (IRE)
O'Brien, Aidan - U S Navy Flag (USA)

O'Brien, Joseph - Iridessa (IRE)
O'Brien, Joseph - Latrobe (IRE)

Prendergast, Patrick - Skitter Scatter (USA)

Trained in the United Kingdom

Appleby, Charlie - Blair House (IRE)
Appleby, Charlie - Blue Point (IRE)
Appleby, Charlie - Cross Counter (GB)
Appleby, Charlie - Hawkbill (USA)
Appleby, Charlie - Jungle Cat (IRE)
Appleby, Charlie - La Pelosa (IRE)
Appleby, Charlie - Line of Duty (IRE)
Appleby, Charlie - Masar (IRE)
Appleby, Charlie - Quorto (IRE)
Appleby, Charlie - Wild Illusion (GB)

Bell, Michael - Pretty Pollyanna (GB)

Bin Suroor, Saeed - Benbatl (GB)
Bin Suroor, Saeed - Best Solution (IRE)
Bin Suroor, Saeed - Royal Marine (IRE)
Bin Suroor, Saeed - Royal Meeting (IRE)
Bin Suroor, Saeed - Thunder Snow (IRE)

Burke, Karl - Havana Grey (GB)
Burke, Karl - Laurens (FR)

Cumani, Luca - God Given (GB)

Dods, Michael - Mabs Cross (GB)

Fahey, Richard - Sands Of Mali (FR)

Fanshawe, James - The Tin Man (GB)

Gosden, John - Cracksman (GB)
Gosden, John - Enable (GB)
Gosden, John - Roaring Lion (USA)
Gosden, John - Stradivarius (IRE)
Gosden, John - Too Darn Hot (GB)
Gosden, John - Without Parole (GB)

Haggas, William - One Master (GB)
Haggas, William - Sea Of Class (IRE)
Haggas, William - Urban Fox (GB)

Hannon, Richard - Billesdon Brook (GB)

Johnson Houghton, Eve - Accidental Agent (GB)

Meade, Martyn - Advertise (GB)

Simcock, David - Desert Encounter (IRE)
Simcock, David - Lightning Spear (GB)
Simcock, David - Teppal (FR)

Smart, Bryan - Alpha Delphini (GB)

Stoute, Sir Michael - Eqtidaar (IRE)
Stoute, Sir Michael - Expert Eye (GB)
Stoute, Sir Michael - Poet's Word (IRE)

Varian, Roger - Sheikha Reika (FR)

Trained in France
Audouin, Bruno - Holdthasigreen (FR)

Bary, Pascal - Study Of Man (IRE)

Chappet, Fabrice - Intellogent (IRE)

Clement, Nicolas - Wonderment (IRE)

Devin, Henri-François - Nonza (FR)

Fabre, Andre - Kitesurf (GB)
Fabre, Andre - Waldgeist (GB)

Head, Freddy - Call The Wind (GB)
Head, Freddy - Polydream (IRE)
Head, Freddy - With You (GB)

Laffon-Parias, Carlos - Recoletos (FR)

Rouget, Jean-Claude - Olmedo (FR)

Vermeulen, Fabrice - Lily's Candle (FR)

Trained in Germany
Carvalho, Jean-Pierre - Well Timed (GER)

Grewe, Henk - Khan (GER)

Groschel, Hans-Jurgen - Iquitos (GER)

Klug, Markus - Weltstar (GER)

EUROPEAN GROUP 1 RACES OF 2018
BY COUNTRY

Ireland

Tattersalls Irish 2000 Guineas (1m, Curragh, 3yo, no geldings) - Romanised (IRE)

Tattersalls Irish 1000 Guineas (1m, Curragh, 3yo fillies) - Alpha Centauri (IRE)

Tattersalls Gold Cup (1m 2.5f, Curragh, 4yo+) - Lancaster Bomber (USA)

Dubai Duty Free Irish Derby (1m 4f, Curragh, 3yo, no geldings) - Latrobe (IRE)

Juddmonte Pretty Polly Stakes (1m 2f, Curragh, 3yo+ fillies) - Urban Fox (GB)

Darley Irish Oaks (1m 4f, Curragh, 3yo fillies) - Sea Of Class (IRE)

Keeneland Phoenix Stakes (6f, Curragh, 2yo, no geldings) - Advertise (GB)

Coolmore Fastnet Rock Matron Stakes (1m, Leopardstown, 3yo+ fillies) - Laurens (FR)

Qipco Irish Champion Stakes (1m 2f Leopardstown, 3yo+) - Roaring Lion (USA)

Derrinstown Stud Flying Five Stakes (5f, Curragh, 3yo+) - Havana Grey (GB)

Moyglare Stud Stakes (7f, Curragh, 2yo fillies) - Skitter Scatter (USA)

Goffs Vincent O'Brien National Stakes (7f, Curragh, 2yo, no geldings) - Quorto (IRE)

Comer Group International Irish St Leger (1m 6f, Curragh, 3yo+) - Flag Of Honour (IRE)

United Kingdom

Qipco 2000 Guineas (1m, Newmarket, 3yo, no geldings) - Saxon Warrior (JPN)

Qipco 1000 Guineas (1m, Newmarket, 3yo fillies) - Billesdon Brook (GB)

Juddmonte Lockinge Stakes (1m, Newbury, 3yo+) - Rhododendron (IRE)

Investec Derby (1m 4f, Epsom, 3yo, no geldings) - Masar (IRE)

Investec Oaks (1m 4f, Epsom, 3yo fillies) - Forever Together (IRE)

Investec Coronation Cup (1m 4f, Epsom, 4yo+) - Cracksman (GB)

Queen Anne Stakes (1m, Ascot, 4yo+) - Accidental Agent (GB)

King's Stand Stakes (5f, Ascot, 3yo+) - Blue Point (IRE)

St James's Palace Stakes (1m, Ascot, 3yo colts) - Without Parole (GB)

Prince of Wales's Stakes (1m 2f, Ascot, 4yo+) - Poet's Word (IRE)

Gold Cup (2m 4f, Ascot, 4yo+) - Stradivarius (IRE)

Commonwealth Cup (6f, Ascot, 3yo) - Eqtidaar (IRE)

Coronation Stakes (1m, Ascot, 3yo fillies) - Alpha Centauri (IRE)

Diamond Jubilee Stakes (6f, Ascot, 4yo+) - Merchant Navy (AUS)

Coral-Eclipse (1m 2f, Sandown, 3yo+) - Roaring Lion (USA)

Tattersalls Falmouth Stakes (1m, Newmarket, 3yo+ fillies & mares) - Alpha Centauri (IRE)

Darley July Cup Stakes (6f, Newmarket, 3yo+) - U S Navy Flag (USA)

King George VI and Queen Elizabeth Stakes (sponsored by Qipco) (1m 4f, Ascot, 3yo+) - Poet's Word (IRE)

Qatar Goodwood Cup Stakes (2m, Goodwood, 3yo+) - Stradivarius (IRE)

Qatar Sussex Stakes (1m, Goodwood, 3yo+) - Lightning Spear (GB)

Qatar Nassau Stakes (1m 2f, Goodwood, 3yo+ fillies & mares) - Wild Illusion (GB)

Juddmonte International Stakes (1m 2.5f, York, 3yo+) - Roaring Lion (USA)

Darley Yorkshire Oaks (1m 4f, York, 3yo+ fillies & mares) - Sea Of Class (IRE)

Coolmore Nunthorpe Stakes (5f, York, 2yo+) - Alpha Delphini (GB)

32Red Sprint Cup Stakes (6f, Haydock, 3yo+) - The Tin Man (GB)

William Hill St Leger Stakes (1m 6f 115y, Doncaster, 3yo, no geldings) - Kew Gardens (IRE)

Juddmonte Cheveley Park Stakes (6f, Newmarket, 2yo fillies) - Fairyland (IRE)

Juddmonte Middle Park Stakes (6f, Newmarket, 2yo colts) - Ten Sovereigns (IRE)

Kingdom of Bahrain Sun Chariot Stakes (1m, Newmarket, 3yo+ fillies & mares) - Laurens (FR)

Bet365 Fillies' Mile (1m, Newmarket, 2yo fillies) - Iridessa (IRE)

Darley Dewhurst Stakes (7f, Newmarket, 2yo, no geldings) - Too Darn Hot (GB)

Qipco British Champions Sprint Stakes (6f, Ascot, 3yo+) - Sands Of Mali (FR)

Qipco British Champions Fillies & Mares Stakes (1m 4f, Ascot, 3yo+ fillies & mares) - Magical (IRE)

Queen Elizabeth II Stakes (sponsored by Qipco) (1m, Ascot, 3yo+) - Roaring Lion (USA)

Qipco Champion Stakes (1m 2f, Ascot, 3yo+) - Cracksman (GB)

Vertem Futurity Trophy Stakes (1m, Doncaster, 2yo, no geldings) - Magna Grecia (IRE)

France (distances in metres)

Prix Ganay - Prix de l'Inauguration de ParisLongchamp (2100m, ParisLongchamp, 4yo+) - Cracksman (GB)

The Emirates Poule d'Essai des Poulains (1600m, ParisLongchamp, 3yo colts) - Olmedo (FR)

The Emirates Poule d'Essai des Pouliches (1600m, ParisLongchamp, 3yo fillies) - Teppal (FR)

The Gurkha Coolmore Prix Saint-Alary (2000m, ParisLongchamp, 3yo fillies) - Laurens (FR)

Churchill Coolmore Prix d'Ispahan (1800m, ParisLongchamp, 4yo+) - Recoletos (FR)

Qipco Prix du Jockey Club (2100m, Chantilly, 3yo, no geldings) - Study Of Man (IRE)

Prix de Diane Longines (2100m, Chantilly, 3yo fillies) - Laurens (FR)

Grand Prix de Saint-Cloud (2400m, Saint-Cloud, 4yo+) - Waldgeist (GB)

Qatar Prix Jean Prat (1600m, Deauville, 3yo, no geldings) - Intellogent (IRE)

Juddmonte Grand Prix de Paris (2400m, ParisLongchamp, 3yo, no geldings) - Kew Gardens (IRE)

Prix Rothschild (1600m, Deauville, 3yo+ fillies & mares) - With You (GB)

Larc Prix Maurice de Gheest (1300m, Deauville, 3yo+) -
Polydream (IRE)

Prix du Haras de Fresnay-le-Buffard Jacques le Marois (1m,
Deauville, 3yo+, no geldings) - Alpha Centauri (IRE)

Darley Prix Morny (1200m, Deauville, 2yo, no geldings) - Pretty
Pollyanna (GB)

Darley Prix Jean Romaet (2000m, Deauville, 4yo+ fillies & mares)
- Nonza (FR)

Prix du Moulin de Longchamp (1600m, ParisLongchamp, 3yo+,
no geldings) - Recoletos (FR)

Qatar Prix Vermeille (2400m, ParisLongchamp, 3yo+ fillies &
mares) - Kitesurf (GB)

Qatar Prix du Cadran (4000m, ParisLongchamp, 4yo+) - Call The
Wind (GB)

Qatar Prix Marcel Boussac - Criterium des Pouliches (1600m,
ParisLongchamp, 2yo fillies) - Lily's Candle (FR)

Qatar Prix Jean-Luc Lagardere sponsorise par Manateq (1600m,
ParisLongchamp, 2yo, no geldings) - Royal Marine (IRE)

Qatar Prix de l'Arc de Triomphe (2400m, ParisLongchamp, 3yo+,
no geldings) - Enable (GB)

Prix de l'Opera Longines (2000m, ParisLongchamp, 3yo+ fillies
& mares) - Wild Illusion (GB)

Prix de l'Abbaye de Longchamp Longines (1000m,
ParisLongchamp, 2yo+) - Mabs Cross (GB)

Qatar Prix de le Foret (1400m, ParisLongchamp, 3yo+) - One
Master (GB)

Criterium de Saint-Cloud (2000m, Saint-Cloud, 2yo, no geldings) -
Wonderment (IRE)

Prix Royal-Oak (3000m, Chantilly, 3yo+) - Holdthasigreen (FR)

Criterium International (1400m, Chantilly, 2yo, no geldings) -
Royal Meeting (IRE)

Germany

IDEE 149th Deutsches Derby (1m 4f, Hamburg, 3yo, no
geldings) - Weltstar (GER)

Grosser Dallmayr Preis - Bayerisches Zuchtrennen (1m 2f,
Munich, 3yo+) - Benbatl (GB)

Henkel-Preis der Diana - German Oaks (1m 3f, Dusseldorf, 3yo
fillies) - Well Timed (GER)

128th Longines Grosser Preis von Berlin (1m 4f, Hoppegarten, 1m 4f, 3yo+) - Best Solution (IRE)

146th Longines Grosser Preis von Baden (1m 4f, Baden-Baden, 3yo+) - Best Solution (IRE)

56th Preis von Europa (1m 4f, Cologne, 3yo+) - Khan (GER)

Italy

Premio Lydia Tesio Sisal Matchpoint (1m 2f, Capannelle, 3yo+ fillies & mares) - God Given (GB)

GROUP/GRADE 1 RACES OUTSIDE OF EUROPE
BUT WON BY EUROPEAN-TRAINED HORSES
IN 2018

Australia

Ladbrokes Sir Rupert Clarke Stakes (7f, Caulfield, 2yo+) - Jungle
Cat (IRE)

Ladbrokes Stakes (1m 2f, Caulfield, 3yo+) - Benbatl (GB)

Stella Artois Caulfield Cup (1m 4f, Caulfield, 3yo+) - Best
Solution (IRE)

Lexus Melbourne Cup (2m, Flemington, 3yo+) - Cross Counter
(GB)

Canada

Natalma Stakes (1m, Woodbine, 2yo fillies) - La Pelosa (IRE)

Pattison Canadian International Stakes (1m 4f, Woodbine, 3yo+)
- Desert Encounter (IRE)

E.P. Taylor Stakes (1m 2f, Woodbine, 3yo+ fillies & mares) -
Sheikha Reika (FR)

United Arab Emirates

Jebel Hatta sponsored by Emirates Airline (1m1f, Meydan, 3yo+)
- Blair House (IRE)

Al Quoz Sprint sponsored by Azizi Developments (6f, Meydan,
3yo+) - Jungle Cat (IRE)

Dubai Turf sponsored by DP World (1m 1f, Meydan, 3yo+) -
Benbatl (GB)

Longines Dubai Sheema Classic (1m 4f, Meydan, 3yo+) -
Hawkbill (USA)

Dubai World Cup sponsored by Emirates Airline (1m 2f,
Meydan, 3yo+) - Thunder Snow (IRE)

United States of America

Belmont Oaks Invitational Stakes (1m 2f, Belmont Park, 3yo
fillies) - Athena (IRE)

Breeders' Cup Juvenile Turf (1m, Churchill Downs, 2yo colts &
geldings) - Line of Duty (IRE)

Breeders' Cup Mile (1m, Churchill Downs, 3yo+) - Expert Eye
(GB)

Longines Breeders' Cup Turf (1m 4f, Churchill Downs, 3yo+) -
  Enable (GB)

INDEX
Group 1 winners and sires mentioned

INDEX

Free Drop Billy, 102
French Fifteen, 137
Frenchpark, 168
Fusaichi Pegasus, 309
Galileo, 2, 13, 20-1, 36, 46-9, 53, 56-8, 67, 69, 81-2, 84-6, 88, 90-2,
   94-98, 108, 110-112, 114-116, 120, 122, 128, 130, 155-7, 161,
   164-7, 169-70, 172-3, 184, 186, 191, 208-10, 212-13, 235, 237,
   240, 246, 250-1, 256-8, 264, 282, 284, 291-2, 296, 304-5, 307,
   310, 313, 316, 320-1, 324-6, 328-9, 331, 333-6
Galileo Gold, 71
Gallinaria, 273
Ganges, 151
Garswood, 158
General Assembly, 40, 136, 186
Generous, 27-8, 89, 96
Gentildonna, 234
George Vancouver, 40
George Washington, 84
Ghanaati, 64
Ghostzapper, 216
Giant Treasure, 89
Giant's Causeway, 21-2, 42, 44-5, 89, 97, 101, 104, 140-1, 172,
   186, 200-1, 242, 244, 246, 320, 327, 334
Gitano Hernando, 295
Gladiatorus, 89, 97
Gleneagles, 144
Glenstal, 157, 246
Glorious Empire, 218, 293
Go And Go, 148, 271
God Given, 1, 67, 91-94, 223, 294, 317, 320, 326, 328, 333, 339,
   343, 346, 352
Golan, 109, 156
Gold Fever, 40
Golden Fleece, 135, 147
Golden Horn, 29-30, 52, 62, 99, 241, 243
Goldhill, 156
Gone West, 119, 224, 324
Gordon Lord Byron, 75
Grand Archway, 236
Great Commotion, 121